Newspaper Power

WITHDRAWN

Newspaper Power

THE NEW NATIONAL PRESS IN BRITAIN

JEREMY TUNSTALL

CLARENDON PRESS · OXFORD

Oxford University Press, Great Clarendon Street, Oxford OX2 6DP

Oxford New York
Athens Auckland Bangkok Bogota Bombay
Buenos Aires Calcutta Cape Town Dar es Salaam
Delhi Florence Hong Kong Istanbul Karachi
Kuala Lumpur Madras Madrid Melbourne
Mexico City Nairobi Paris Singapore
Taipei Tokyo Toronto
and associated companies in
Berlin Ibadan

Oxford is a trade mark of Oxford University Press

Published in the United States by
Oxford University Press Inc., New York

British Library Cataloguing in Publication Data
Data available

Library of Congress Cataloging in Publication Data
Tunstall, Jeremy.
Newspaper power: the new national press in Britain/Jeremy Tunstall.
Includes bibliographical references.
1. English newspapers—Great Britain—History.
2. Government and the press—Great Britain.
3. Press and politics—Great Britain.   I. Title.
PN5117.T86   1995   072'.09048—dc20   95-50042

ISBN 0-19-871132-8
ISBN 0-19-871133-6 (pbk)

10 9 8 7 6 5 4 3 2

Printed in Great Britain on acid-free paper by
Bookcraft Ltd., Midsomer Norton, Avon

Acknowledgements

My thanks to 217 senior journalists and executives (including six-teen editors) of British national newspapers who agreed to be inter-viewed during 1990–4. Thanks also to David Wood who conducted sixty-four of these interviews.

This study was supported by a generous grant from the Econ-omic and Social Research Council (ESRC). The study was orig-inally intended as a comparison between television producers and senior people in newspapers, but the TV part became a separate book: *Televison Producers* (Routledge, 1993).

While the present book relies primarily on 1990s material, some baseline use is made of previous studies. I remain grateful, there-fore, to some 340 journalists interviewed in 1965–8. In addition 207 journalists completed lengthy questionnaires. Oliver Boyd-Barrett worked as research assistant on that study, and he conducted about a hundred interviews. The study was reported in *The Westminster Lobby Correspondents* (1970) and *Journalists at Work* (1971).

Some further reference is made here to research carried out for the Royal Commission on the Press in 1974–7. I undertook 31 interviews with editors of national newspapers, provincial dailies, and weeklies. About half of these interviews were carried out jointly with Colin Seymour-Ure.

Special words of thanks to the following people for draft reading, advice, and other help over the last few years: Oliver Boyd-Barrett, Mark Dunford, Colin Seymour-Ure, Hugh Stephenson, David Walker, David Wood, Helena Tunstall and Sylvia Tunstall. Thanks also to Maggie Brough, who transcribed interviews, and Frances Bruce, who twice typed the manuscript.

Finally, love and thanks to my family and apologies to my wife Sylvia for the heaps of newspapers around the house which, as I write, add up to a pile over 30 feet high.

J. T.

v

Contents

Contents

List of Figures

List of Tables

Introduction

NEWSPAPERS remain powerful in the video age. The arrival of television greatly increased the significance of the mass media around the world. But in terms of broad political and societal power, television was added to—not subtracted from—the press in general and the newspapers in particular.

In Western democracies much of the potential political and partisan power of television has been deliberately neutered in line with consensual public interest. Newspapers, however, exercise a continuing prerogative both to bias the news and to slant the comment. It is the newspapers, not television, which go for the politician's jugular. Typically it is a newspaper which first spills the politician's blood; only then does television swoop in for the action replay.

Certainly newspapers constitute a 'mature' industry, but so also do the conventional 'terrestrial' television networks. Fewer people may now read a daily newspaper each day; many people may only read their 'regular' daily perhaps three or four days a week. But each newspaper is much fatter than the newspaper of a few decades ago. We are now in an age of semi-regular newspaper reading, just as we are in an age of the semi-regular viewing of every second episode of a favoured television series. Both press and video have fragmented with the arrival of many small publications and many small video services. The somewhat reduced TV networks and the somewhat arthritic daily newspapers still tower and stoop over the fragmented new media, most of whose market shares are measured in fractions of 1 per cent.

In big cities across the world, the leading people in politics, commerce, and other major fields all read the same few leading newspapers. Many senior people start to read these newspapers at home each morning or as they are chauffeured to work; when they arrive at the office most top politicians and administrators are presented with press cuttings culled from a wider range of that morning's publications. The top person scanning the morning's newspapers, and reading the quickie press cuttings service, is aware that across the city most of the other top people are similarly engaged.

The press in general and key newspaper agendas in particular overlap with agendas at the top levels of government, politics, and business. Amongst the papers for committee, board, and Cabinet meetings there will often be cuttings from the financial daily, a press report on a political speech, the text of a press statement about to be released.

Most larger population democracies have a nationally important press of perhaps ten or twelve publications; in most countries some of these are capital city newspapers, some are newspapers from other cities, and some are magazines. These are the publications which are cut and extracted for top people to scan each morning. While these top publications can draw people's attention to many stories about the same topic, the press also has the opposite power to ignore, to exclude, to reject. For every one political speech reported, a hundred political speeches are excluded from any coverage; the ever-eager politician crafts an enticing sentence or two for television and an enticing paragraph or two for the press, but sentences, paragraphs, and entire speeches are typically rejected.

Newspapers and their owners and editors tend to understate the extent of their power for two sound, and potentially embarrassing, reasons. First, there is the issue of whether it is compatible with, or healthy for, democracy to have so much power residing in so few unregulated hands. Secondly most daily newspapers—including some capital city ones, such as the *Washington Post*—have local monopolies or semi-monopolies; here is the embarrassing question of whether a democratic press and the market-place of ideas are compatible with unregulated local private press monopoly.

This book is about British newspapers and their power. Like other national presses the British press is highly idiosyncratic. The British press is an extreme case within Europe in the extent to which it is dominated by national newspapers published in one city. The leading publications are all London daily newspapers (and their even more idiosyncratic Sunday stable companions). Because they are so competitive, these newspapers have none of those inhibitions which semi-monopoly generates elsewhere. The London newspapers are less restrained than the leading newspapers of most other countries; they are all public companies, open to public and financial scrutiny. Their senior people are willing to be interviewed. As an extreme example of a press which is *national*, which is *competitive*, and which is a *newspaper* press, the British national press provides a case-study of newspaper power which may be of some wider significance.

There is no attempt in this book to present a definitive analysis of newspaper power. Clearly that power has to do with including in, and excluding from, the public agenda; it involves ranking individuals, organizations, and issues as worthy or unworthy of coverage; it also involves a moral dimension by which the players in various public arenas are presented as heroes and/or villains. This power stretches even beyond the grave, when the obituaries editor makes decisions as to which few of today's deaths deserve to be recorded.

Part I contains a description of Britain's unusually dominant and unusually competitive national newspapers. Although the main focus is upon these national newspapers in the 1990s, the late 1960s are used as a convenient baseline for comparison. 1968 was just before Rupert Murdoch arrived in London and newspaper competition became more bruising; it was also the year in which I was concluding a study about national newspaper journalists in Fleet Street.

Part II focuses on power at the top end of the national newspaper business. It argues that editors as well as owners and managers have all become more powerful, especially since the printing trade unions lost their industrial muscle in 1986.

Part III looks at changes in the practice of journalism—including the sectionalization revolution and the proliferation of new journalist stars, such as columnists.

Part IV, the longest in the book, focuses on politics and newspapers. It looks at the big changes in British political journalism since my *The Westminster Lobby Correspondents* was published in 1970. One key power of newspapers is to impose a 'political crisis' definition on current events, a definition to which the incumbent government then has to respond.

Subsequent chapters look beyond narrowly defined politics. The tabloid press has taken the lead in a redefinition of the British monarchy. The popular papers have also largely given up the reporting of foreign news, although they have retained their interest in tabloid foreign policy comment. Financial journalism, it is

3

argued here, is taking over from political journalism as the senior field.

Part V focuses on the potency of the press in British policy-making for the mass media. In practice the Prime Minister agrees with selected newspaper allies as to which media policies will prevail. Press monopoly legislation has effectively been redeployed as a Newspaper Preservation policy; token 'self-regulation' of newspapers prevails because the newspapers refuse to accept legislation or state regulation. And the newspapers are allowed what amounts to a veto over policy for television and radio.

The 217 senior newspaper people interviewed for this study during 1990–4 included sixteen editors (out of a total twenty-one) and the same number of political editors. Also interviewed were a majority of the news editors, features editors, foreign editors, sports editors, women's editors, picture editors, financial (business or city) editors, and royal correspondents. These and others (such as editors of sections, columnists, advertising and circulation executives, and some chief executives) are referred to in the text. Nearly all interviews took place in the newspaper building and averaged about 70 minutes of taped talk.

The approach involved interviewing at least half of the most senior and powerful people in British national newspapers. To a considerable extent this results in a view of newspaper power as seen through the eyes of the newspaper élite. Although it is not intended as a straight portrait of the newspaper élite, it does contain a fair amount of information about them. There have been many changes between the mid-1960s, when women constituted about 2 per cent of the journalism élite, and the mid-1990s, when women made up about 20 per cent.

Between the 1960s and the 1990s the journalism hierarchy has been stretched both upwards and downwards. Those at the bottom now do more work for less pay and with less security. But at the top end of national newspapers there is now a greater sense of an élite which, despite the arrival of some women, still has a fairly macho view of itself and is more aware than previously of its own power and position. Where there was deference (to politicians, royals, and business people) there is deference no more.

Part I
NATIONAL COMPETITION

1 National Tabloids and Broadsheets

LONDON is the home of the biggest national newspaper press in Western Europe. London produces seven out of every ten daily papers sold in Britain in the 1990s. This national daily press includes not only Western Europe's premier collection of large-sale tabloid newspapers, but also its largest collection of capital city upmarket newspapers; the newspaper market is sharply segmented on social class lines. Britain also differs from the rest of Western Europe in having big sales of Sunday newspapers; and it differs from the American pattern in that the London Sundays traditionally have been quite separate publications from the dailies. Why, then, has London become the base of such a national and such a social class segmented press?

I

Geography and history explain much. Britain is a geographically small country with most of the population living close to the London–Birmingham–Manchester–Glasgow road and rail routes. Moreover, London has long been an unusually dominant capital, the largest population city in Western Europe. The provincial daily press had its best years in the late Victorian period, and in 1920 non-London dailies still had half the sales. But from 1920 London dominance strengthened.

London dominance is also partly the result of long historical continuity; in France and Germany, for instance, the press was reborn in 1944–5. In many other countries the press moved with the frontier or contracted with military seizure. But in Britain there was relative continuity; this is a collection of newspapers which mostly have lengthy histories. The *Daily Mirror*, for example, which began life in 1903, is one of the newer national dailies; only four were launched later than 1903, while six national dailies were launched in 1900 or before. The *News of the World*, the Sunday tabloid circulation leader, has been engaged in Sunday sex and sensationalism since 1843; while the *Observer*, like *The Times*, has passed its two hundredth birthday.

Within the tradition of London dominance are the facts of London as capital of British commerce, politics, and news (and in the past of empire). In addition there has long been a strong element of prestige, of motivations which were not entirely commercial. For example, during the twentieth century there has been an increased tendency for national newspaper companies also to own provincial chains of daily newspapers. Today three companies whose national flagships are the *Financial Times*, *Daily Mail* and *Daily Express* also own major chains of provincial dailies and weeklies; these companies see their provincial papers mainly in terms of profit, while they see their national flagships in terms of prestige as well as profit. When times are bad, when advertising dips with the trade cycle, such companies give preference to investing in their national dailies, not their provincial papers. From time to time profitable provincial papers have been used to subsidize national dailies.

II

In Britain the newspapers split very much along social class lines. Table 1.1 shows that about 87 per cent of the readers of upmarket papers are indeed middle class, against only about 31 per cent for the downmarket dailies. This is based on the standard market research definition and the dividing line between middle and working class is fairly fuzzy. In some cases, for example, one partner in a marriage will have a 'white-collar' job while the other partner has a manual job; this common situation then leads to one 'middle-class' spouse and one 'working-class' spouse both reading the identical copy of the same newspaper. In view of this and other kinds of fuzziness at the dividing line, the degree of class segregation in Table 1.1, and in the readership of the national press, is very sharp indeed.

What is unusual about this readership class segregation in Britain is not that it occurs at all, but that it is so heavily focused into national daily newspapers. In most comparable countries the

Table 1.1. British national dailies split by social class
(Percentage of middle-class (ABC1) readers)

Upmarket dailies	
Financial Times	90
The Times	89
Independent	87
Daily Telegraph	87
Guardian	83
Midmarket dailies	
Daily Mail	65
Daily Express	64
Today	46
Downmarket dailies	
Daily Mirror	34
Sun	31
Daily Star	27
All UK adults	50

Source: National Readership Survey, Jan.–June 1995.

newspapers are much more middle class in one of two possible ways. Some countries (such as Japan) have big newspapers which are more or less uniformly middle class. Also common is the pattern (found in the USA and Southern Europe) of daily newspaper readership being mainly a middle-class habit; here the bottom half or one-third of the population (in class/education/income terms) do not read daily newspapers, but read instead, for example, sports dailies or various kinds of weekly magazines, including the American supermarket-sold scandal publications.

The British press today is internationally known for its tabloid national newspapers. The term 'tabloid' was borrowed from medicine in tablet form; it originally meant simply mini-newspaper and usually also picture newspaper. Britain had picture papers from the start of the twentieth century; the *Daily Mirror* began life as a small-size picture paper in 1903, but it did not become what we would now think of as a tabloid until the 1940s. The full 'tabloidization' of both downmarket and midmarket British national newspapers was not completed until the 1980s.

Segregation into the three social class levels thus pre-dates the present divide between upmarket broadsheets and the other half-size, or 'tabloid', newspapers. Table 1.2 shows that right up to 1945

Table 1.2. British national newspapers: percentages of total sales achieved by upmarket, midmarket, and downmarket dailies, 1930–1995

(a) National daily newspapers (Jan.)

	1930	1937	1945	1955	1965	1975	1985	1995
Upmarket e.g. *The Times*	6	8	8	8	13	15	16	20
Midmarket e.g. *Daily Mail*	71	72	68	57	49	32	25	27
Downmarket e.g. *Daily Mirror*	23	20	23	35	38	53	58	53
TOTAL	100	100	100	100	100	100	100	100

(b) National Sunday newspapers (Jan.)

	1930	1937	1945	1955	1965	1975	1985	1995
Upmarket e.g. *Sunday Times*	2	3	4	4	12	14	15	17
Midmarket e.g. *Sunday Express*	35	36	26	24	18	18	23	22
Downmarket e.g. *News of the World*	63	61	70	72	70	68	62	61
TOTAL	100	100	100	100	100	100	100	100

Sources: Colin Seymour-Ure, *The British Press and Broadcasting since 1945* (Oxford: Blackwell, 1991); *Royal Commission on the Press 1947–49 Report* (London: HMSO, 1949); Audit Bureau of Circulations (ABC).

it was the midmarket dailies which predominated. This midmarket group (especially the *Daily Mail* and *Daily Express*) were the circulation leaders for the first fifty years of the twentieth century; but then they were badly hit by television, which in Britain was especially strongly committed to a consensual and midmarket approach. Meanwhile the other two categories prospered; the upmarket papers continued to offer something more demanding than television, while the downmarket papers also prospered by locating themselves 'below' television and increasingly as complementary to, and dependent on, television. But Table 1.2 also shows that the separate Sunday newspaper market had already been dominated by downmarket publications, well before the main impact of television was felt in the 1950s. The separate sensational Sunday newspaper was a product of the 1840s; a century later these sensational Sundays were sticking to much the same formula—sex and crime culled from the law courts—and from the 1930s to the 1970s continued to account for about two-thirds of all Sunday sales.

For at least a century before 1969 (the year in which Rupert Murdoch bought the *News of the World* and the *Sun*) the British newspaper market was characterized by much bigger sales of sensational and downmarket newspapers on Sundays than on weekdays. This points to another long-term characteristic of Britain's class-segmented national press. There was a strong element of newspaper companies pitching their daily products somewhat above what Sunday sales indicated about the true level of popular taste; there was also an element of daily deference, of working-class people being willing—every day except Sunday—to read mid-market newspapers.

III

The *Sun*, *Daily Mirror*, and *Daily Star*, the super-popular 'lower' tabloids, share some key characteristics. These daily papers focus on light news, the entertaining touch, and human interest; this in practice means focusing on crime, sex, sport, television, showbusiness, and sensational human interest stories. There is an overwhelming emphasis on personalities; such 'serious' news as is covered is often presented via one personality attacking another personality. Much material in these papers is 'look-at' material—there are many pictures, big headlines, and the advertising also is mainly display, which again involves pictures and big headlines. The remainder of the tabloid is 'quick read' material with most stories running to less than 400 words. The most densely written part of the downmarket tabloid tends to deal with entertainment—such as the television schedule, the racing card, and sporting statistics. The tabloid is designed to draw the reader through the entire paper, looking at all pages; an alternative route is provided (mainly for male readers), which starts on the back sports page.

The entire approach of the haughty national broadsheets, however, is different. The *Daily Telegraph*, *The Times*, *Guardian*, *Independent*, and *Financial Times* present themselves as providing predominantly serious news (garnished with sport and some entertainment as well). While the *Sun* and *Daily Mirror* use political and other heavy stories on their front pages very sparingly, the haughty broadsheets assume that their readers are more interested in serious news. The broadsheet typically carries at least three times as many words in a week as does the tabloid; for example if the *Sun* is carrying 40,000 or 50,000 words a day, *The Times* (also published by News International and printed in the same building) will be carrying 120,000 or 150,000 words per day. The haughty broadsheets carry longer stories, including many pieces of over 800 words; the assumption is of a serious but selective reader who will want to choose some (but not all) serious financial news, or serious arts, or serious domestic political and foreign coverage. The broadsheet is thus demarcated, in clearly signposted, specialized sections.

Behind this polarization lies reliance on two contrasted sources of finance. The broadsheets rely primarily on *advertising* revenue, while the tabloids rely primarily on *sales* or circulation revenue. The finances of the haughty broadsheets are advertising driven because they are able to charge advertisers high rates per thousand affluent readers. The broadsheets are attractive to display advertisers who are selling expensive consumer products, such as expensive cars or clothes. In order to remain as vehicles suitable for advertising higher-salaried jobs and upmarket consumer products—and to gain high rates from advertisers—the broadsheet paper must retain a high proportion of educated and affluent readers. British broadsheet dailies do indeed seek prestige of a general and a political kind, but this prestige-seeking is not out of line with its commercial goals. Certainly the upmarket newspaper wants more readers (and the sales revenue involved), but it only wants more affluent (and preferably young) readers, whom the upmarket advertisers want to reach.

Tabloids in general, and the *Sun–Mirror–Star* tabloids in particular, operate within completely different financial guidelines. The lower tabloid is primarily dependent on sales revenue, and hence upon a continuing sales war with its competitors. Certainly the tabloid does carry advertising and does benefit financially from this.

But the *Sun*, the market leader, was only obtaining 30 per cent of its revenue from advertising when (in 1993) it was selling at 25 pence; after the wholesale and retail margins, the *Sun* was receiving about 16 pence in sales revenue and 7 pence in advertising revenue. But a sizeable slice of that 7 pence from advertising was needed to

---

BOX 1.1. THE DOWNMARKET LEADERS

The Sunday leader is the *News of the World*, which was first published on 1 October 1843; the 'taxes on knowledge' were still in place and the sale price was three pence. The *News of the World* always focused on sex and murder as revealed in the previous week's court cases. By 1930 it was the British circulation leader, selling 3.4 million copies each Sunday. In the 1930s its standard diet of sex, crime, sport, and serial fiction was spiced with the memoirs of British and Hollywood entertainment stars and several series of articles by the out-of-office Winston Churchill. Its sale peaked in June 1950 at 8.44 million. In early 1969 the *News of the World* became Rupert Murdoch's first British paper. Appointed in 1994, Piers Morgan was the twelfth editor in twenty-five years of Murdoch ownership. But the editorial formula has not greatly altered, since the emphasis still remains on sex, sport, crime, and celebrities garnished with small amounts of mainly right-wing politics.

The daily downmarket leader is the *Sun*, which, when Rupert Murdoch acquired it in 1969, was a money-losing and midmarket broadsheet paper. It was Murdoch's first British daily and he quickly turned it into virtually a new paper—a highly profitable downmarket tabloid. The *Sun* soon overwhelmed the *Daily Mirror* (passing it in 1977). Murdoch introduced the expensive promotional device of 'sale or return'; the *Sun* really invented or reinvented contemporary British tabloid journalism. It was nevertheless careful not to go too far or too fast for its working-class readership; for example, female nudes on page 3 only became a regular feature when it became apparent that this did not repel either readers or advertisers. While the *Sun* has been more anti-Labour than pro-Conservative it was devoted to Mr Murdoch's political friend, Mrs Thatcher. Two long-serving editors, Larry Lamb and Kelvin MacKenzie, largely shaped the *Sun* and developed its unique, jocular, venomous style.

pay for the paper and ink (and other linked expenses), leaving even this successful tabloid with only 2 or 3 pence net advertising income per copy. By contrast the upmarket daily leader, the *Daily Telegraph*, was selling in 1993 at 48 pence, about 32 pence of which would return to the paper; the *Telegraph* would have been earning perhaps an additional 60 pence from advertising, of which about 40 pence would be net income. Thus after paying the costs of printing the advertising, it would be earning per copy from advertising about ten times as much as the downmarket *Sun*. The details of the calculations are complex, and newspapers engage in discounting which is both massive and varies from week to week. Non-market leaders discount more deeply; some downmarket tabloid advertising is so heavily discounted that it scarcely covers its own printing costs. Undoubtedly some single copies of an upmarket paper generate more than twenty times the advertising income of some single copies of a downmarket paper.

In terms of commercial income, upmarket papers are primarily in the advertising business, while downmarket papers are primarily in the sales business. Upmarket papers must sell to upmarket people, for whom they can charge high advertising rates per thousand readers. These contrasted forms of revenue, it can be said, exaggerate the real differences between their two sets of readers. But there is also a further element of polarization or exaggeration; while downmarket papers simply focus on selling more copies (thus maximizing sales revenue), the upmarket papers tend to focus upon the more affluent (and more attractive to advertisers) readers even within their middle-class audience.

IV

The newspaper business has distinctive characteristics which make the struggle for market leadership especially fierce; the strong tend to get stronger and the weak tend to get weaker. Newspapers as a species tend either to generate big losses or big profits. Mass media industries tend to be extreme examples of the economies of scale. A newspaper selling one million copies is at a huge disadvantage in competing directly against a paper selling three million copies. The smaller circulation paper needs to produce a similar number of pages, and to employ similar numbers of personnel to produce the first copy of the paper; but the paper with three times the sale is likely to have three or four times the revenue of the weaker paper.

In practice the market leader tends to be managed on a more lavish basis; it usually has more pages, employs more journalists, advertising people, and others, and spends more money on promotion, television advertising, book serialization, and so on.

The overall market leader tends also to be the sales price leader within its particular market. The number two paper tends to raise its sales price only when the market leader has already announced

---

BOX 1.2. THE MIDMARKET LEADERS

The *Daily Mail* was launched by Alfred Harmsworth (later Lord Northcliffe) on 4 May 1896; it was an immediate success and quickly became the leader of a new type of midmarket national daily; selling at a halfpenny it appealed to white-collar workers. It was the midmarket leader for thirty-five years; in relative decline for the next forty years, the *Daily Mail* had an especially turbulent time in the 1960s. It was transformed in 1971 by merging with its stable companion the *Daily Sketch*, by going tabloid, and by the appointment of David English as editor. English was editor for two decades, during which he won back the midmarket sales lead (in 1987) and was the main architect of a new style of midmarket tabloid journalism. The *Daily Mail* depends heavily on star columnists and interviewers and on lengthy human interest features; the paper was no less uncritical of Mrs Thatcher and hypercritical of Labour than the *Sun*. The *Daily Mail* has largely given up foreign reporting to become the voice of affluent middle-class, middle-aged middle (or Southern) England.

The *Mail on Sunday* is a relatively late arrival on the London newspaper scene; its launch on 2 May 1982 coincided with the Falklands War but was unsuccessful. David English performed the rescue act and from 1983 sales rose steadily; by 1989 the seven-year-old *Mail on Sunday* was the Sunday midmarket leader. Like the daily paper, the Sunday depended heavily on features and it also developed an extremely successful glossy magazine (*You*). The *Mail on Sunday* resembled the daily in being the creation of a dominant editor, his personality and interests. This editor was Stewart Steven; his *Mail on Sunday* reflected his slightly more liberal views and his fertile range of interests. After a brilliantly successful decade at the *Mail on Sunday*, Stewart Steven took over the London *Evening Standard* with excellent results.

BOX 1.3. UPMARKET LEADERS

The *Daily Telegraph* was launched in 1855 and quickly outsold its main competitor, *The Times*. Providing a more readable version of *The Times*, the *Telegraph* specialized not only in sport and politics, but also in sexy court cases and in providing an unrivalled news service. From nearly 300,000 in the early 1890s the *Telegraph*'s sales sank to 84,000 in 1927; it was then acquired by William Berry (Lord Camrose). After a 1930 price cut (from twopence to one penny) the circulation took off like a rocket,[a] reaching 637,000 by 1937. Since 1930 the *Daily Telegraph*, then, has been the upmarket leader; it was especially dominant in the 1960s, when it had much the strongest reporting of both British and foreign news. Under Lord Hartwell (from 1954) it gradually got into trouble, with inadequate business management and an inflexible editorial formula. The Canadian, Conrad Black, rescued the *Daily Telegraph* and turned around its business position in the late 1980s; he failed, however, to alter another result of the previous regime, the *Telegraph*'s ageing readership.

The *Sunday Times* has been the Sunday upmarket leader since the 1930s. It was launched on 20 October 1822, but had no connection with *The Times* (daily). The British Sunday newspaper took a long time to establish itself as a fully respectable activity. Although in the 1930s both the *Sunday Times* and its rival the *Observer* were over a hundred years old, both papers were small circulation slim journals of reviews and opinion rather than major newspapers. In 1930 the *Sunday Times* was selling only 153,000 copies; its editor W. Hadley became a leading appeaser of Hitler and political ally of Neville Chamberlain. It was in the 1950s that the *Sunday Times* became a major influence in British journalism; during 1945–65 its sales nearly trebled. It was acquired by Roy Thomson (in 1959) and by Rupert Murdoch (in 1981); it had continued to be Britain's fattest newspaper, with ten separate sections by the 1990s. It also became much the most profitable-per-issue title in British newspaper history. The modern *Sunday Times*'s character has been powerfully shaped by Rupert Murdoch's appetite for advertising profits and by the Andrew Neil (editor 1983–94) mixture of a traditional British upmarket approach with a belligerent style which seems to derive more from the New York tabloids than from London.

[a] Lord Hartwell, *William Camrose: Giant of Fleet Street* (London: Weidenfeld and Nicolson, 1992), 153–71.

---

a price change. Sometimes the third paper within a market charges a lower price, but this may mean that the paper is dangerously short of both sales and advertising revenue.

Market leaders in British newspapers have yet another key financial advantage not shared by their competitors. Market leaders can and do charge a premium price for their advertising, and not merely a price which reflects their bigger number of buyers and readers. Market leaders charge a higher advertising rate per thousand readers. This was what the *Daily Telegraph* was doing in 1993, when it had some 42 per cent of the total sales of the five upmarket national dailies; this figure meant that many advertisers who wanted to reach people with high incomes had little alternative but to include the *Daily Telegraph* in their advertising schedule. It was this situation which allowed the *Telegraph* to charge premium rates and to be so enormously profitable in the early 1990s. It was also this market leadership ability to charge premium rates which its management believed was threatened by *The Times*'s 1993 price cut, and which led the *Telegraph* to cut its own price from 48 pence to 30 pence in 1994. The sale price war was a price war about market leadership and advertising rates.

2 Murdoch's Wapping Power Shift

Sunday January 26 (1986) was the day on which Fleet Street, as we have known it for all our working lives, ceased to exist. That was the day on which Rupert Murdoch proved that it was possible to produce two mass circulation Sunday newspapers without a single member of his existing print workforce, without using the railways, and with roughly one fifth of the numbers that he had been employing before.

THUS commented another newspaper executive (Frank Barlow of the *Financial Times*) speaking one year later. This move to Wapping by two national dailies and two Sundays was much the most dramatic single event in the 1986 'Newspaper Revolution' and 'Death of Fleet Street'. The event had all the necessary news value ingredients; there was a sudden event, bitter conflict, and a central personality, a hero/villain, in the shape of Rupert Murdoch.

The conflict was about Power and Money. The result was a major shift in power and money away from the trade unionized labour force and in favour of owners, managers, and editors. The trade unions had largely forbidden for two decades the introduction of the newspaper computer systems. They had vetoed most kinds of labour-saving equipment and had insisted that all material must be keyboarded twice, first by a journalist and secondly by a compositor (typesetter). The printing unions were in rapid retreat after January 1986; massive staff cuts, of 50 per cent and more, were imposed or negotiated. There was a series of quick moves to new printing plants, several of which were already completed or under construction by January 1986. Some newspapers moved their office and editorial workers to one location and their printing operations to a separate new location on a cheaper site in the East

London docklands. The companies financed these moves partly through the inflated (property boom) 1986 value of their old all-in-one inner London, Fleet Street, buildings. They benefited too from the Stock Market flotation of the buoyant Reuters news agency, of which each national press group owned a slice.

Distribution practices were also transformed. There was a rapid switch from the Victorian pattern of national distribution by rail to distribution at night on the national road network. Wholesaling arrangements also altered. At their new plants the newspaper groups could now print larger numbers of pages and additional sections. Increasingly also the managements planned and introduced run-of-the-paper high-quality colour printing.

This revolution was obviously most traumatic for that majority of previous Fleet Street employees who lost their jobs, which in some cases had been remarkably highly paid. All of this had already happened in the USA, in much of Western Europe, and in some of Asia. Britain was unusual only in that the exceptional power of the trade unions had delayed the changes for so long.

Although the January 1986 events in the Murdoch/News plant at Wapping dramatized and encapsulated the essentials of the revolution, other events and other managements had, of course, played their parts in the story. Even in the 1930s the extraordinary power of the London newspaper unions was documented.[1] Other major reports twenty years[2] and ten years[3] before Wapping documented the massive overmanning in damning detail. The outside authors of these reports were astonished at the way in which union 'chapels' (branches) within each company were the effective employers of labour; union officials made up a warring caste of middle managers.

The *Daily Courant*, the first British daily, began publication in 1702 at Fleet Bridge; for the next 284 years daily newspapers were both written and printed in the Saint Paul's–Fleet Street area. In January 1986 all of Britain's national newspapers were still both written and printed within one mile of Fleet Street; but three years later, in 1989, the last newspapers had left Fleet Street.

---

[1] Political and Economic Planning, *The British Press* (London: PEP, 1938).
[2] Economist Intelligence Unit, *The National Newspaper Industry* (London: EIU, 1966)
[3] Royal Commission on the Press, *Interim Report: The National Newspaper Industry* (London: HMSO, 1976).

I

The British Newspaper Revolution and the Death of Fleet Street would have happened even if Rupert Murdoch had not ordered the dramatic January 1986 move to Wapping. A sequence of events in 1984 and 1985, but also stretching back into the 1970s, was making a major power shift more and more inevitable.

The 1930s power of the unions had been deep frozen during the era of newsprint rationing and thin newspapers which persisted for a decade after 1945. When this frozen era eventually ended in the 1950s, the old Fleet Street abuses appeared in extra-virulent form. But by the early 1980s the main trade union leaders knew that major change was inevitable; however, union members in general, and in particular the highly paid typesetting members of the National Graphical Association (NGA), preferred to enjoy the high pay and low hours for as long as possible.

Rupert Murdoch as an entrepreneur had long had an excellent sense of timing, of not getting into new situations or new technologies too quickly. By 1985 there were several major indications that Fleet Street's days were numbered. A new breed of local freesheet publishers had already challenged the NGA outside London. Eddie Shah, three years before he launched *Today* as a new national daily, had become famous for both printing and distributing local papers in the greater Manchester area without union labour. Major publishers of daily newspapers outside London—for example in Nottingham and Wolverhampton—had also broken through into single keyboarding.

Reuters, the world news agency, 'went public' in 1983, meaning that the national newspapers (which together owned 37.5 per cent of Reuters) received a major financial bonus. This cash windfall did indeed encourage Fleet Street publishers to consider investing in new plant and new technology systems. Reuters were important in other ways; several national newspaper directors had sat on the Reuters board and were well aware that Reuters had for two decades been a computerization pioneer.

The first national newspaper owner to attack the Fleet Street unions head on was not Murdoch, but Robert Maxwell. The larger-than-life Maxwell acquired control of Mirror Group Newspapers in July 1984; recognizing the massive overmanning problem, he devoted much of his enormous energy to threatening, bullying, and frightening the *Mirror* trade unions into submission. In summer 1985 Maxwell sacked 240 NGA members working on the MGN horse-racing daily, the *Sporting Life*. He also threatened to print the *Daily Mirror* and the two Sundays outside London.[4] After high-energy and high-temperature negotiations through the autumn, on 1 November 1985 Robert Maxwell demanded 2,000 redundancies from a remaining work-force of 6,500. By 10 December 2,100 redundancies were finally accepted by the unions;[5] this one-third cut in the MGN work-force was agreed seven weeks before the Murdoch move to Wapping.

Also in 1985 decisions were made to go ahead with the launch of two new national dailies: both the *Independent* and *Today* were to be printed away from Fleet Street. The *Independent*'s founders were planning the paper and raising finance through the second half of 1985.[6] Eddie Shah had decided by March 1984 on what eventually became the launch of *Today*, just six weeks after the Wapping move. Shah received massive publicity for his over-ambitious launch plans; he intended to instal new colour printing plants outside London; to use state-of-the-art editorial computer systems; to make *Today* the first British national with colour through the paper; and to launch as well as the daily, a *Sunday Today*. The Murdoch papers gave especially enthusiastic coverage to Eddie Shah; this publicity was a deliberate Murdoch management decision, intended to frighten the trade unions, because Shah was going to produce his paper without any printing union members.

Finally, nearly all of the Fleet Street managements were making plans and commencing investments for new plant and new equipment, well before January 1986.[7] In early 1983 the *Telegraph* management was committed to expenditure of £105 million for new printing plants in both east London and in Manchester and for an Atex computer system.[8] Their docklands plant began operations in September 1986.

[4] Helen Hague and John Lloyd, 'Mirror papers "to be printed outside city"', *Financial Times*, 31 Aug. 1985.

[5] Tom Bower, *Maxwell, The Outsider* (London: Mandarin, 1991 edition), 397–400.

[6] Stephen Glover, *Paper Dreams* (Harmondsworth: Penguin, 1994).

[7] 'Exodus from Fleet Street: Maggie Brown reports on the inexorable move eastwards', *Guardian*, 26 Apr. 1985.

[8] Duff Hart-Davis, *The House the Berrys Built: Inside The Telegraph* (London: Coronet, 1991), 344–8.

II

The Thatcher government was strongly supportive of newspaper managements in general and of Rupert Murdoch in particular. Several Thatcher policies were helpful to the Fleet Street owners. Government deregulation of financial services helped fund the boom in Reuters's services and the subsequent Reuters cash windfall; the Murdoch/News windfall was worth £125 million. The City boom also boosted the value of Fleet Street properties; and the Thatcher policy of supporting the London docklands as a development area enabled the Fleet Street papers to obtain cheap sites for their new East London plants.

It was also Mrs Thatcher's personal intervention which had allowed Rupert Murdoch in 1981 to acquire *The Times* and *Sunday Times* without a reference to the Monopolies Commission. But two other Thatcher government policies had an even more immediate impact on the Wapping events. Determined to reform the trade unions and to reduce their power, the Thatcher government put through Parliament three separate pieces of trade union reform legislation—in 1980, 1982, and 1984. These new laws applied to all trade unions and were first implemented on a big scale during the year-long coalminers' strike (26 million working days lost) which began in March 1984. But after the National Union of Mineworkers, the printing unions were high on the list of trade unions whose powers the Thatcher government was determined to reduce.

This meant that when the mass picketing began in early February 1986 and continued for many months, there was a massive deployment of police in the Wapping area. According to one (trade union) estimate there was an average presence of 1,000 police at Wapping for the first 300 days of the dispute. Certainly many hundreds of police and demonstrators were injured as the demonstrators attempted to stop trucks leaving the plant each evening. On the first anniversary—24 January 1987—mounted police carried out what union demonstrators described as a 'cavalry charge'.[9]

Perhaps the severest blows for the trade unions were court actions flowing from the Thatcher legislation. The largest union, SOGAT, was fined and suffered sequestration (seizure) of its entire assets as early as February 1986.

[9] The chronology of the dispute is recounted at great length by the American author Suellen Littleton, in *The Wapping Dispute* (Aldershot: Avebury, 1992), 57–125.

BOX 2.1. THE END OF FLEET STREET

24–6 January 1986	News Group papers (*The Times, Sunday Times, Sun, News of the World*) move to Wapping.
4 March 1986	Eddie Shah's *Today* launches, printed outside London.
31 March 1986	Express Newspapers' Unions agree to 2,500 'voluntary' redundancies (a 37 per cent cut).
29 September 1986	*Telegraph* papers start printing in docklands.
7 October 1986	The *Independent* launches, printed outside London.
1986	Eddie Shah sells *Today* to Lonrho.
1986–8	Strong growth in press advertising.
June 1987	*Financial Times* building (Bracken House) sold for £143 million.
August 1988	Mirror Group Newspapers commence on-the-run colour.
November 1989	*Daily Express* and *Sunday Express* are the last newspapers to leave Fleet Street; by December only 1700 of 6,804 workers remain in the company—a 75 per cent cut.
Late 1989	Advertising decline begins in 1989's last quarter.
28 January 1990	*Independent on Sunday* launches, printed outside London.

III

Up until 1986 the trade unions not only did much of the effective general and personnel management and insisted on the preservation of Victorian technology and working practices; they also had time and energy in reserve for fighting between themselves. This feuding, especially during 1983–5, had the fatal effect of distracting the unions' attention from what was happening to the industry in general and what was going on at Wapping in particular.

First there was conflict between and within the two big printing unions. The NGA was the smaller union, covering typesetting and other skills close to the editorial operation; the NGA was a craft, male,[10] highly paid union. SOGAT (Society of Graphical and Allied Trades) had more Fleet Street members—it was a predominantly clerical and white-collar union with a high proportion of female, less well-paid, members. Secondly, the rogues in the union pack (as seen by SOGAT and NGA) were the Electricians (EEPTU). The EEPTU General Secretary, Eric Hammond, was prepared to do special deals with newspaper owners. The electricians were the only union accepted by Eddie Shah for *Today* and by the Murdoch/News management for Wapping. Eric Hammond, a self-admitted maverick,[11] seemed prepared to accept very high levels of animosity within the trade union movement, in return for a few hundred extra members. Thirdly, there was the National Union of Journalists (NUJ). The NUJ had been involved in merger discussions with the NGA, but these talks had broken down in 1983. The computerized technology, still waiting in the wings, promised the virtual abolition of the NGA and its typesetters in newspapers; in future the journalists, using computer terminals, would do the single keyboarding. There were NGA–NUJ disputes at several provincial newspaper locations over these issues, and by 1985 there was considerable bitterness between the two leaderships.

In addition the NUJ itself was split along several dimensions. The NUJ's leaders were—as usual—at each others' throats. There was also a big gap between the NUJ headquarters near King's Cross and the national newspaper members a mile or two to the south around Fleet Street.

At the two Murdoch/News sites (*The Times/Sunday Times* and *Sun/News of the World*) there were some 6,700 employees of whom only 750—or about 12 per cent—were journalists. They were the key to the dispute. If the majority of these journalists did not move to Wapping, the newspapers could not appear, or could not appear at an acceptable level of editorial quality. In order to prevail—and to justify its potential as the most powerful occupational/union force in Fleet Street—the NUJ needed to convince its Murdoch/News members not to go to Wapping. The NUJ's claim to have 650 of the 750 journalists in membership was probably highly

---

[10] Cynthia Cockburn, *Brothers* (London: Pluto Press, 1983).
[11] Eric Hammond, *Maverick* (London: Weidenfeld and Nicolson, 1992).

Table 2.1. Ten[a] newspaper births and five funerals, 1986–1990

	Launch date	Editorial approach	Date of death	Causes of death
Today	4 March 1986	Midmarket tabloid		
Sunday Today	9 March 1986	Midmarket tabloid	31 May 1987	Cash starvation
Sunday Sport	14 September 1986	Soft porn and sport		
Independent	7 October 1986	Upmarket broadsheet		
London Daily News	24 February 1987	Midmarket London 24-hour daily	24 July 1987	Bad business plan (Robert Maxwell); adroit defence by *Evening Standard*
News on Sunday	26 April 1987	Left-wing midmarket tabloid Sunday	20 November 1987	Management and editorial chaos
Sport (Wednesday)	17 August 1988	Midweek soft porn and sport		
Post	10 November 1988	Downmarket daily tabloid	17 December 1988	Half-hearted second national daily effort by Eddie Shah
Sport (Friday)	31 March 1989	More soft porn		
Sunday Correspondent	17 September 1989	Upmarket Sunday	25 November 1990	*Independent on Sunday* and advertising starvation
Independent on Sunday	28 January 1990	Upmarket companion for the daily		
Sport (Thursday)[a]	23 August 1990	More soft porn		

[a] The *Sport's* daily versions counted here as one newspaper.

optimistic. In any case, the NUJ failed. About 90 per cent of the 750 journalists went to Wapping; the strike was broken there and then.

A fourth element of trade union weakness was the Trade Union Congress. This umbrella union body became involved in the negotiations in late 1985; but it remained ineffectual. A fifth weakness was the inability of the newspaper unions' London membership to earn the support of their fellow members outside London. SOGAT especially completely failed to persuade its members in newspaper wholesalers not to handle the Murdoch papers.

IV

Rupert Murdoch and his team of Australian, American, and British managers exhibited an impressive combination of planning, management opportunism, and adroit timing. They were also extremely lucky. The plant at Wapping was no secret. Indeed, when the construction of the plant was beginning, all News Group employees were given a four-page *Sun*-style tabloid publicity sheet about the new plant. *UK Press Gazette* gave it page 1 and 2 treatment on 7 July 1980. When the plant was completed in 1983 the unions refused to work there.

Nevertheless during 1985 the Murdoch management succeeded in getting the 'biggest newspaper printing plant in Europe' ready for action; even by Christmas 1985—a month before the plant would be printing some 20 million newspapers a week—the union leadership still did not realize that the plant was already fully equipped and ready to operate without any of the existing printing work-force.

Murdoch management thinking followed its usual preference for well-established technology, not the state-of-the-art but unreliable technology favoured by Eddie Shah. The Wapping plant was equipped with already quite old-fashioned Goss Headliner rotary presses. The large capacity computer system was purchased from Atex, (an American company which had already installed newspaper computer systems at some 500 locations in the USA and around the world). Along with this reliable and easy-to-learn technology, Murdoch also got the benefit of a massive backlog of management experience. The Wapping operation was to be a replay of a drama enacted literally hundreds of times before by Atex and

Fig. 2.1 Rupert Murdoch displays the first Wapping-printed issues of the *Sun* and *The Times* published on 27 January 1986

others: first acquire new site, new plant, new equipment; then secretly train up a fresh, cheaper, and smaller printing work-force; finally switch on the new plant, leaving behind the old plant and the old work-force. This familiar American plot was also well known in Britain,[12] but the Murdoch management correctly calculated that they could maintain a high degree of secrecy, while the unions did not realize what had happened until it was too late.

The new Wapping plant was—and is—huge; it was generously stocked not only with printing presses and computer equipment but with huge supplies of paper and ink. The Murdoch management had also decided to switch to road transport; a contract was agreed with the (part-Murdoch-owned) TNT company, which

[12] See for example Rex Winsbury, *New Technology and the Press: A Study of Experience in the United States* (London: HMSO for Royal Commission on the Press, 1975).

undertook to purchase an extra 900 vehicles for the job. The management was well supplied with expensive legal advice. New subsidiary—but legally separate—companies were brought into existence, so as to push the trade unions into illegal 'secondary picketing'. The management was well apprised also of the need to make demands which the unions would reject; by striking—as they did in January 1986—union members lost both their jobs and all rights to compensation.

The management also adroitly shuffled the possible matching of plants and publications in a manner which did indeed confuse the unions. They had successfully convinced the unions—even late in 1985—that they might be publishing at Wapping a new evening paper and also only part of the print runs of the national dailies and Sundays.

The Murdoch management was especially adroit at handling the journalists and persuading them to move the two miles to Wapping. This was done by stick-and-carrot methods—the sack if you don't follow the legal request to move to a nearby location, but you get a £2,000 increase and private medical care if you do move. They wisely left each paper's editor to wield the stick and carrot.[13]

Finally, fortune favoured the brave. The Murdoch management was extremely lucky, especially in that the relevant trade union leaders were so remarkably inept. In so far as the trade unions managed the old Fleet Street, they showed themselves in 1985 to be poor managers—with poor planning, bad timing, a weak grasp of the new legislation, and an inability to retain their own members' loyalty.

V

Rupert Murdoch certainly enhanced his reputation as a manager and a newspaper executive. He played a dramatic role in ridding London of some very outdated traditions. To those who saw him as a hero, he enhanced the vigour, or freedom, and independence of the British press. But rather like one of his own newspapers, he focused attention also on the bad news, on four big negatives. First, the Murdoch/News approach was initially to cut off the illegally striking workers without a penny. The other Fleet Street manage-

---

[13] Linda Melvern, *The End of the Street* (London: Methuen, 1986).

ments negotiated their subsequent huge work-force reductions; their workers left with pensions and with sizeable redundancy payments. The management did subsequently relent somewhat, but not much.

A second negative was the dependent connection between a press mogul and a Prime Minister. Rupert Murdoch identified himself closely with a Prime Minister who was soon to enter a phase of terminal unpopularity.

Thirdly, Rupert Murdoch personalized the issue of the foreign ownership of leading newspapers. Was it wise for Britain—unlike most other Western democracies—to have its biggest newspaper group controlled by an owner who was a foreign national and who came to Britain only for brief visits? Was it acceptable that Rupert Murdoch should take the return flight back to New York while his sacked workers and the British police fought pitched battles in the streets of East London? Was he a suitable person to own *The Times* and to publish it in the same plant as the *Sun*? Was there not something deeply insulting in his blunt description of the British papers as 'cash cows' to finance his mid-1980s purchases of the Fox studio and the Metromedia TV stations in the USA?

In further raising his international profile as a media mogul and hero/villain, Rupert Murdoch had antagonized two of the three main political parties in Britain. Rival newspaper executives also had a hero/villain view of Murdoch; while they admired his managerial machismo they criticized his 'methods' as inhumane and they later excluded him from a press owners' lobbying organization significantly named 'The British Media Industry Group'.

VI

Certainly Wapping was about power and money; one reason, perhaps, why Rupert Murdoch succeeded when others had failed was that—from 3,000 miles away—he focused more sharply than either London-based managers or London-based trade unionists on these simple realities of power and money.

Rupert Murdoch's successful press–politician alliance with Mrs Thatcher may have hazarded the long-term legitimacy and viability of News Corporation as a newspaper owner in Britain. Will a subsequent press-politician alliance be directed against News Corporation? Will its ownership of British newspapers survive beyond Rupert Murdoch? Did Murdoch win the industrial battle at Wapping, only to lose the media legitimacy war?

In and around Wapping—and in and around 1986—the national newspaper industry massively cut its costs and boosted its profits. The national press owners, managers, and editors also boosted their own financial and political confidence. Rupert Murdoch's success seemed to indicate that industrial power, political influence, and profitability were consistent goals. All three could be pursued, and put in evidence, at the same time. Wapping extended newspaper power, while also making it more controversial.

3 From the Golden 1960s to 1990s Super-competition

WHEN I started interviewing people in Fleet Street in 1965, nobody claimed that it was a golden age. Indeed 'Newspaper Crisis' was a term commonly used by journalists in conversation and by the authors of reports on Fleet Street.[1] Several newspapers were fighting for their lives. But retrospectively there are some reasons for seeing the 1960s as a golden age. The full plunge into tabloid journalism did not begin until Rupert Murdoch acquired the *Sun* in 1969. Most 'popular' newspapers in the 1960s were still broadsheets employing foreign correspondents and teams of other news specialists. The leading newspaper executives were Lord (Roy) Thomson, owner of the *Sunday Times*, and Cecil King, chief executive of the IPC/Daily Mirror group. Both of these men believed in responsible journalism as propagated by the Press Council, a self-regulatory body which had its most influential decade in the 1960s.

Was the 1960s a golden decade in terms of newspaper sales and did national newspapers decline in the increasingly competitive years between the 1960s and the 1990s? Are newspapers a declining mass medium? In terms of circulation there has been a decline— which is looked at in more detail later in this chapter. But much of this decline was due to very thin 1940s newspapers—for example of only six pages—because of war and post-war paper rationing;[2] some people would each day buy several of these small papers. By

---

[1] e.g. Harford Thomas, *Newspaper Crisis: A Study of Developments in the National Press in Britain, 1966–67.* (Zurich: International Press Institute, 1967); The Economist Intelligence Unit, *National Newspaper Industry* (London: EIU, 1966).

[2] J. Edward Gerald, *The British Press under Government Economic Controls* (Minneapolis: University of Minnesota Press, 1956).

the 1990s the national newspapers had expanded from about six pages to about 40 large pages (or 80 tabloid pages) each weekday (Table 3.1).

This 1940s shrinking down to about six large pages is seen in Table 3.1. But the answer to the 'decline' question does depend upon what you mean. It also depends upon which dates you take. We can draw up one list of reasons why newspapers have declined, followed by a second list of reasons why newspapers have grown since the mid-century.

Newspapers have declined especially in terms of sales figures since the 1940s and 1950s; this drop has been even bigger if you include national Sundays as well as dailies. The drop has been bigger still against population, since the UK population has increased since mid-century. The drop has been yet bigger against the number of households; in the 1940s there were more large households of four, five, or six people buying several daily papers, while in the 1990s there are many more households especially of only one or two people buying perhaps only one daily two or three times a week. The number of readers per copy has declined with the smaller households; home delivery has declined and so also,

Table 3.1. Average (mean) numbers of pages in selected newspapers, 1927–1995, expressed in full page equivalents (tabloids and small size sections counted as half)

	1927	1937	1947	1966	1975	1985	1995
The Times	25	26	10	22	26	33	56
Daily Telegraph	19	25	6	26	28	31	54
Daily Express	17	20	5	15	17	20 (T)	32
Daily Mail	19	19	5	15	17 (T)	20	35
Daily Mirror	23	11 (T)	5	13	14	15	27

Note: (T) indicates that this newspaper has gone tabloid since the previous date.

Sources: (Ross) Royal Commission on the Press 1947–1949 Report (London: HMSO, 1949). National Board for Prices and Incomes, Costs and Revenues of National Newspapers (London: HMSO, 1967), 25. Denis McQuail, Analysis of Newspaper Content (London: HMSO for Royal Commission on the Press, 1977), 15. For 1985 and 1995 (Jan.–July): Express Newspapers.

probably, has loyalty to particular titles. Newspaper readers are also older, on average, than in the 1960s.

After all this gloom, however, there is a contrary list of reasons why, far from declining, British newspapers have expanded. The drop in total sales can be exaggerated. For dailies the sales decline was already levelling out during the 1960s; the total national daily sale remained around 14 million copies from 1969 into the mid-1990s. While the total daily sale has remained fairly constant, the number of pages has more than doubled since 1966 (Table 3.1); on this normal commercial criterion of volume (or weight) the UK national newspaper business roughly doubled between the 1960s and 1990s. Both Saturday and Sunday editions were especially much bigger and offered more sections and choices; many people now buy a daily paper on perhaps three on four days a week but get more to read on those days than on five or six days in the 1960s. There is almost certainly more reading beyond the date of publication; there is also a bigger output of weekly newspapers (both paid for and free).

I

The Wapping move (of 1986) and the 'End of Fleet Street' represented a significant increase in the level of national newspaper competition. But Wapping was only one of four such phases of heightened competition since the golden decade of the 1960s.

Between 1945 and 1995 there was a huge increase in the availability of national media. When BBC television began again in 1946 there were very few TV sets, only two BBC radio channels, and eight national daily newspapers. By 1995 Britons were watching multi-channel TV for three or four hours per day; radio was much more competitive; and there were eleven fat national dailies against eight thin national dailies in 1946.[3]

Previous to the 1960s there were two separate phases. 1945 to 1955 was relatively quiet because paper rationing was only being gradually relaxed and television involved only one channel and few viewers. Both press and television switched quickly into frenetic competition in the years 1955–60. ITV grew rapidly and two-thirds of households had television by 1960. The late 1950s also saw

---

[3] This assumes that the (then) *Manchester Guardian* and *Financial Times* were not yet national dailies in 1946. The closure of *Today* in November 1995 reduced the national dailies to ten.

some national newspapers engaged in a fierce struggle for survival; and in 1960 the liberal *News Chronicle* and its stable companion, the *Star*, a London evening, were closed. There was also especially fierce competition between popular Sundays, three of which also closed around this time—the *Sunday Chronicle* (1955), the *Sunday Graphic* (1960), and *Sunday Dispatch* (1961). Competition led to sensational reporting and this was the last great period of the memoirs of murderers in the Sunday papers; after 1957 capital punishment was limited (before its 1965 abolition).

It was against the frenetic 1955–60 period that the 1960s seemed relatively quiescent. Not only did the Thomson–King–Press Council combination in the 1960s discourage excessive sensationalism; but ITV was now hugely profitable and the Pilkington Committee (1960–2) and subsequent legislation led to a redefining of ITV towards the middle market, plus a second BBC channel in 1964.

After the quieter 1960s there then came no less than four separate quickenings of the competitive pace:

The first competitive increase (1969–71) was opened by Rupert Murdoch's 1969 London arrival. He acquired the leading blood-and-thunder Sunday paper, the *News of the World*, and also the *Sun*. A double change in 1971 was the burial of the *Daily Sketch* in a newly tabloid *Daily Mail*. 1969–71 marked the emergence of a new tabloid middle market and slugging competition for the previously supreme *Daily Mirror* in the daily downmarket.

The second competitive increase (1978–82) also involved Rupert Murdoch, who in 1981 acquired *The Times* and *Sunday Times* from Thomson, and quickly set out to expand the already highly profitable *Sunday Times*. Equally important was the launch of the *Daily Star*, which turned the daily downmarket into a three-sided contest; it was also the *Daily Star* which introduced bingo.

The third competitive increase (1986–8) involved the Wapping move and the end of Fleet Street. This move dramatically cut costs and improved profits; but it also led to fatter newspapers, and to two new dailies (*Today* and the *Independent*) surviving the larger numbers of new launches. This increase in titles, sections, and pages, led to difficulties as advertising and the British economy contracted in 1989–91.

The fourth competitive increase (1993–5) saw the return of severe price cutting, at a time when television and radio were both expanding aggressively in a downmarket direction. The *Sun* cut its price from 25 to 20 pence in 1993. More spectacular was *The Times*'s price cut from 45 to 30 pence in 1993; when the *Daily Telegraph* (mid-1994) cut its price from 48 to 30 pence, *The Times* cut its price to 20 pence. *The Times* continued to pay the wholesalers and retailers the approximately 15 pence which they had together received of the 45 pence selling price. This meant that while *The Times* had been receiving 30 pence per copy, a year later (after the second price cut) it was receiving only 5 pence sales revenue per copy. This massive price cut was challenged by the *Independent* as a clear example of 'predatory pricing' designed to push the opposition out of business. But while 'predatory pricing' is an accepted US legal concept—and might have stopped Rupert Murdoch doing the same thing with an American newspaper—there is no legal prohibition to it in Britain. Meanwhile the *Independent* did lose its previous level of independence, with Mirror Group Newspapers taking over its management and part ownership. Price cutting, which had been used earlier in the century by Lord Northcliffe and others, had raised the competitive stakes in both the daily upmarket and downmarket.

II

Between 1965 and 1995 there was a comprehensive rearrangement of national newspapers into a smaller number of more formidable competing groups. Table 3.2 shows that the number of companies owning national newspapers fell from eleven in 1965 to seven-and-a-half in 1995 (with the two *Independent*[4] papers partly owned by the Mirror Group).

There was an even bigger change in the ownership of particular titles. In fact only one newspaper (*Financial Times*) out of twenty-one dailies and Sundays found itself in exactly the same stable with the same company (the *FT* was a lone horse both times) as in 1965. Only the *FT* and two other 1995 nationals were still owned by the same company as in 1965; these were the *Daily Mail* and the *Guardian*.

Three-quarters of all the 1995 titles had changed owners at least once since 1965; five titles had been launched since 1965; three titles had been launched as well as changed ownership since 1965.

---

[4] The two *Independent*s are each counted below as *half* an acquisition by MGN.

Table 3.2. British national newspaper ownership, 1965 and 1995

1965	Circulation (thousands)	1995	Circulation[a] (thousands)
Associated Newspapers		Associated/Mail	
Daily Mail (M)	2,464	Daily Mail (M)	1,788
Daily Sketch (M)	844	Mail on Sunday (S)	1,959
Evening News (E)	1,238	Evening Standard (E)	456
Beaverbrook Newspapers		United	
Daily Express (M)	3,987	Daily Express (M)	1,279
Sunday Express (M)	4,190	Sunday Express (S)	1,403
Evening Standard (E)	680	Daily Star (M)	738
IPC Newspapers		Mirror Group	
Daily Mirror (M)	5,019	Daily Mirror (M)	2,518
Sun (M)	1,273	Sunday Mirror (S)	2,560
Sunday Mirror (S)	5,082	People (S)	2,066
People (S)	5,538	Newspaper Publishing/ Mirror Group	
Telegraph		Independent (M)	294
Daily Telegraph (M)	1,337	Independent on Sunday (S)	327
Sunday Telegraph (S)	650		
Times Publishing		Telegraph/Hollinger	
The Times (M)	254	Daily Telegraph (M)	1,066
Thomson Organisation		Sunday Telegraph (S)	692
Sunday Times (S)	1,290	News International	
News of the World		The Times (M)	647
News of the World (S)	6,176	Sun (M)	4,086
Manchester Guardian and Evening News		Today (M)[1]	566
Guardian (M)	270	Sunday Times (S)	1,253
		News of the World (S)	4,744
S. Pearson		Guardian Media Group	
Financial Times (M)	146	Guardian (M)	400
The Observer		Observer (S)	464
Observer (S)	824	S. Pearson	
National Co-operative Press		Financial Times (M)	294
Sunday Citizen (S)	233		

[a] Jan.–June 1995.
[1] Today ceased publication in November 1995.

The selling of a national newspaper from one national owner to another was almost an annual event. There were twenty-seven such newspaper sales in the thirty-year period. Table 3.3 shows that three-quarters of all national newspapers were sold at least once; four papers were sold three times; four papers were sold twice; six papers were sold once; the two *Independents* were sold half-a-time.

Table 3.2 makes clear that the main reduction in ownership was of small groups which had owned just one national title. Four groups in 1965 owned just one Sunday—but this British tradition of the separate Sunday was in rapid decline and ceased altogether in 1993 when the *Observer* was acquired. The separate national daily tradition also ceased at the same time, with the exception of the *Financial Times*.

The 1965 average was 1.7 titles per owner, but by 1995 the average was 2.8 titles per owner. By latter-day standards all of the 1965 titles and companies had been run in a fairly lackadaisical way by short-sighted trade unions and equally short-sighted managements. Going through the list:

The Associated Group in 1965 was in a state of near terminal decline presided over by Lord Rothermere, who had none of his uncle's (Lord Northcliffe) talent. Both the *Daily Sketch* and *Evening News* were heading towards their deathbeds.

Beaverbrook Newspapers were in even worse disarray. Lord Beaverbrook, who had dominated the company for forty-eight years, died in 1964 leaving behind management chaos, dated editorial formulas for both the *Daily Express* and *Sunday Express*, and overmanning on a grand scale even by Fleet Street standards.

IPC Newspapers was the biggest ownership with 200 magazines also in the company. IPC and Cecil King prided themselves on modern management; the company was a success only because the *Daily Mirror* had a monopoly (of the daily downmarket) as had many of the magazines.

The *Telegraph* looked to be in better health. Presiding there was Lord Hartwell, whose father Lord Camrose was the real maker of the mid-century *Daily Telegraph*. Hartwell in 1965 was aged 51 and the editor-in-chief who presided over the *Daily Telegraph*'s uniquely comprehensive news operation. But the *Sunday Telegraph* (launched 1961) was a relative failure, indicative of inadequate long-term business management.

The Times newspaper had still not really recovered from its

Table 3.3. Ownership history of 1995 titles over 1965–1995 period

Associated/Mail	
Daily Mail (M)	No change
Mail on Sunday (S)	Launched 1982
Evening Standard (E)	Acquired 1980
United News	
Daily Express (M)	Acquired by Trafalgar House 1977 and United 1985
Sunday Express (S)	Acquired by Trafalgar House 1977 and United 1985
Daily Star (M)	Launched by Trafalgar House 1978, acquired by United 1985
Mirror Group Newspapers	
Daily Mirror (M)	Acquired by Reed 1970, Maxwell 1984, and banks 1992
Sunday Mirror (S)	Acquired by Reed 1970, Maxwell 1984, and banks 1992
The People (S)	Acquired by Reed 1970, Maxwell 1984, and banks 1992
Newspaper Publishing	
Independent (M)	Launched 1986; Mirror Group acquisition-in-part 1994
Independent on Sunday (S)	Launched 1990; Mirror Group acquisition-in-part 1994
Telegraph/Hollinger	
Daily Telegraph (M)	Acquired by (Hollinger) Black 1987
Sunday Telegraph (S)	Acquired by (Hollinger) Black 1987
News International	
The Times (M)	Acquired by Thomson 1967 and News/Murdoch 1981
Sunday Times (S)	Acquired by News/Murdoch 1981
Sun (M)	Acquired by News/Murdoch 1969
Today (M)	Launched (Shah) 1986. Acquired by Lonrho 1986 and News/Murdoch 1987. Closed 1995
News of the World (S)	Acquired by News/Murdoch 1969
Guardian Media Group	
Guardian (M)	No change
Observer (S)	Acquired by Atlantic-Richfield 1976, by Lonrho 1980, and by *Guardian* 1993
S. Pearson	
Financial Times (M)	No change

disastrous record of appeasing Hitler in the 1930s. In 1965 *The Times* still had classified advertising on its front page; this changed in 1966, when, however, the paper was making increased losses and was sold to Thomson.

The Thomson organisation had recently bought the Kemsley chain of provincial dailies as well as the *Sunday Times*, which was the most admired and most heavily promoted editorial product of this period.

The *News of the World* in 1965 was owned by the Carr family and was sticking to its knitting in the traditional mould of Sunday sex, sensation, and sport. It was to be sold four years later to Rupert Murdoch, who recognized the absurdity of using the presses only once a week for a massive Sunday print run.

The *Guardian* was also committing plenty of management howlers around 1965. For a smallish daily it was still awkwardly split between London and Manchester; advertising revenue was grossly inadequate; and there was a deep conflict between on the one hand the editor and senior journalists, who wanted to soldier on with a left-of-centre national daily, and on the other hand the chairman, who wanted to merge with *The Times*.

The *Financial Times* was doing better than most; but it was still only coming to regard itself as a national daily and its old Etonian gentlemen were being taken to the cleaners by the in-house trade union players.

The *Observer's* management set-up was one of the most eccentric; David Astor was the benign owner-editor, who was a lot more interested in editing than in money.

The *Sunday Citizen* supported the Labour and Co-operative Movement, and was closed down in 1967.

Thirty years later the ownership pattern, management approach, and editorial style had all considerably changed. The competitive atmosphere had greatly altered not least because trade union constraints—which had made, for example, additional pages or sections prohibitively (overtime) expensive—had now been removed. But also there was now a leading group of four companies—the Mail, Express, Mirror, and News groups—managing, between them no less than sixteen national newspapers.

Each of these four groups—by 1995—was thus deploying a typical stable of two national dailies and two Sundays; on average each group was selling some 20 million newspapers per week.

National Competition

These companies were using their large total sales and their several titles for a more concentrated and more belligerent style of competition than prevailed in the 1960s. Now the struggle was not against the trade unions; the struggle was against advertisers to maintain advertising margins and to limit rate discounting; it was a battle for market share, market leadership, and market dominance which in 1995 the News and Mail groups seemed to be winning against the Express and Mirror groups; it was a struggle in which editors and their journalists were required to seek out appropriate readers more aggressively than in the sleepy, golden sixties.

III

There was very little change in total downmarket sales between 1965 and 1995. As Table 3.4 shows over 50 million copies of downmarket national newspapers were sold each week in both years; there was a big drop in Sunday downmarket sales, which was balanced out by an increase in daily sales. There was also a big switch in the dominant company; during these thirty years Mirror Group sales declined by half while the Murdoch/News company

Table 3.4. Total downmarket sales (millions)

(*a*) Daily and Sunday

	1965	1995
Dailies	35.18	44.02
Sundays	16.80	9.37
WEEKLY TOTAL	52.00	53.39

(*b*) Mirror Group and News Group

	1965	1995[a]
IPC/Mirror Group	40.73	19.73
(Murdoch) News International	—	29.22
Others	11.27	4.43
WEEKLY TOTAL	52.00	53.38

Table 3.5. The downmarket, 1955–1995

(a) Daily sales (in thousands)

	1955	1965	1975	1985	1995[a]
Daily Mirror (1903)	4,725	5,019	3,968	3,033	2,518
Daily Sketch (1908)	950	844	—	—	—
Sun (1969)	—	—	3,446	4,125	4,080
Daily Star (1978)	—	—	—	1,455	738
TOTAL	5,675	5,863	7,414	8,613	7,336

[a]First six months.

(b) Sunday sales (in thousands)

	1955	1965	1975	1985	1995
Empire News (1884)	2,049	—	—	—	—
News of the World (1843)	7,971	6,176	5,479	5,103	4,744
People (1881)	5,075	5,538	4,188	2,962	2,066
Sunday Graphic (1915)	1,220	—	—	—	—
Sunday Mirror (1915)	5,539	5,082	4,251	3,009	2,560
TOTAL	21,854	16,796	13,918	11,074	9,370

Source: ABC and Colin Seymour-Ure, *The British Press and Broadcasting since 1945.*

took over dominance of the downmarket—primarily, of course, through the success of the *Sun*.

The *Sun* was reborn on 17 November 1969 as a Murdoch-owned tabloid, and its explosive sales growth in the early 1970s was the dominant single fact of downmarket British journalism over these thirty years. Inheriting sales of about one million from the old IPC *Sun*, the Murdoch *Sun* had its most spectacular growth—and already nearly caught up the *Daily Mirror*—between 1970 and 1975 (see Table 3.5). It was not the publishing of a female nude photograph per day which accounted for the *Sun*'s rocketing sales; the most rapid sales growth occurred in the first year, before the regular nude pictures began.[5]

[5] The then editor, Larry Lamb, devotes a chapter of his book ('Page Three or Bust?') to this issue of nude pictures: Larry Lamb, *Sunrise* (London: Macmillan, 1989), 110–17.

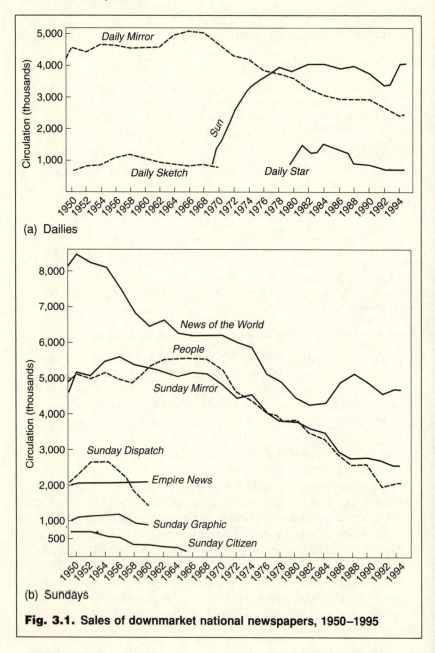

(a) Dailies

(b) Sundays

Fig. 3.1. Sales of downmarket national newspapers, 1950–1995

There were several more important reasons for the *Sun*'s success in eventually passing the *Daily Mirror* sales during winter 1977–8.[6] The *Sun* under its editor, Larry Lamb, adopted much from Murdoch's recent Sunday acquisition, the *News of the World*; Lamb abolished all of the specialist news jobs (except the political journalists) and focused instead on human interest, entertainment, sex, and sport. The *Sun* was promoted more vigorously and expensively than any other paper in British newspaper history; it was lavishly advertised on television, while promotional contests and other marketing gimmickry were heavily used. Perhaps most important of all Murdoch's innovations was 'sale or return'—the newsagents were deluged with copies, but only had to pay for the ones they sold.

However, the biggest single reason for the *Sun*'s success was the *Daily Mirror*. In 1965 and immediately thereafter the *Daily Mirror* outsold its only downmarket tabloid competitor the *Daily Sketch* by six to one. The Mail group were embarrassed to own a popular tabloid and the *Daily Sketch* paper was half-hearted, shabby-genteel. The *Daily Mirror* had been fashioned into a brilliantly successful formula in the 1940s—it was initially targeted at wartime servicemen and women; it also adapted well to television in the 1950s. In 1967 sales reached their peak; by this time the editorial formula was becoming fixed and over-cautious. The *Daily Mirror* was also becoming more serious; it was gaining some new readers from the then declining midmarket *Express* and *Mail*. But it was also losing touch with younger working people. The caution and self-satisfaction of the *Daily Mirror* is illustrated in Box 3.1. The *Daily Mirror* was 'responsibly' playing down the then current Moors Murder case, which was receiving much more sensational coverage in the midmarket *Daily Express*, which *Mirror* journalists regarded as their main competitor. Compared with the torrid Sundays of the day the *Daily Mirror* also played down sex and preferred pictures of cuddly animals. All of this provided great opportunities for Rupert Murdoch when he acquired the *Sun* three years later.

The *Sun*'s sales rose steadily for nine years; the first dip was caused by the *Daily Star*'s November 1978 launch. The *Star* was initially intended to use spare capacity on the Manchester presses of the *Daily Express* (acquired the year before by Trafalgar House).

---

[6] Ken Viney, 'ABC figures confirm Sun leads Mirror', *Campaign*, 12 May 1978.

BOX 3.1. A SMUG AND GENTLE GIANT: THE FIVE MILLION SALE *DAILY MIRROR* IN 1966

Daily Mirror sales peaked in 1967 at 5.25 million copies; during April of the previous year I spent twelve hours at the *Mirror*.

On the *Daily Mirror* everything goes through the News Desk except features, television, women's and sport . . . There are Mirror staff correspondents in Bonn, Paris, Rome, New York, and Washington. There's a roving man currently in Rhodesia and another (Donald Wise) in Saigon.

They pride themselves on the thoroughness with which stories are checked before a reporter is sent out or before copy is released to the sub-editors' table . . . A daily digest of readers' letters is circulated in the newsroom each day for information and to keep desk staff in touch with readers . . .

Three reporters say that the *Mirror* never sacks staff journalists. You are extremely carefully vetted beforehand; they only want people who will not get the paper into disrepute . . .

The *Mirror* has mainly three types of home specialist—three industrial correspondents, four political, and three television specialists. Others include a Pet's Club correspondent and City Editor Robert Head . . .

At the main editorial conference (5.30 p.m.) the editor sits at his desk and everyone else sits around him, one or two sitting on tables . . . Marjorie Proops, and just one other woman—2 women, 12 men . . . the average age of these 14 senior journalists is about 45.

The Night Desk has 16 pages to fill including the two centre pages . . . The Night Editor does a rough layout for each of these 16 pages; he picks the page lead story and the main picture . . . He carries on a continual dialogue with desk assistants to left and right. The height of his effort is at about 8.30 p.m. He quickly looks through the pictures on offer from the picture editor and in five minutes has chosen the five main pictures.

This is a day with no obvious main story. The afternoon conference had a Commons row on Vietnam as the probable main story. But at 8 p.m. an 'exclusive' Rhodesia story arrives and becomes the front-page splash. This story concerns a secret visit by Prime Minister Wilson's private secretary to Rhodesia . . . They discuss whether this 'exclusive' should be held out of the first edition, in order to sabotage the chance of late night follow-ups by competitors: they decide to run the Rhodesia story in the first edition.

The Cassandra column is going on the front page . . . Also, unusually, Hugh Cudlipp has vetoed the Jon cartoon. The Comp Room phone to check whether there is a cartoon tonight.

Continued

There's a good picture of a rabbit on a girl's shoulder but the Night Editor worries: is the girl as attractive as the rabbit? They also want one girl picture alongside a full column length . . . They choose three pictures of the same dog for the centre spread and then argue a Moscow panda against a good picture of some birds . . .

This was a day on which the Moors murder case made the lead in both London evening papers. But the *Mirror* had it down as the sixth story; there was clearly a strong directive from on high not to sensationalize the Moors murders. Two journalists commented that the *Daily Express* was dragging the last ounce of sadism out of the story.

I was shown a column inches count of what all the nationals have given the Moors case so far. The *Express* to date is far out ahead and the *Mirror* and *Telegraph* are about second equal in amount of space given . . .

The Moors case in the *Mirror* is the lead story on page 7. The tape-recording used direct by the *Evening Standard* and *Evening News* makes the headline wording, but the most horrific part of the tape-recording—the murdered children's screams—is firmly left out of the *Mirror* story.

The atmosphere is predominantly ex-provincial, with a good supply of Scottish and Manchester accents; 23 sub-editors (all 23 are men) sit along two tables at right angles to the back-bench . . . The subs eat sandwiches where they sit; two read books some of the time. Shirt-sleeves and tie are standard, while a few favour corduroys and open-necked shirts.

From 9.20 p.m. for twenty minutes the three back-benchers discuss the heading for the front-page splash . . . Between them they write down and discount 30 or 40 different wordings before producing the final heading.

The last material misses the 10.10 p.m. first edition deadline by five minutes, which is normal . . . At 10.30 p.m. to the 'Stab-in-the-Back' pub across the street. The editor is already there, also other senior people; the Night Editor eats a beef sandwich. The number three night desk man says he will be working on the later editions until 2 a.m. then a drink at the Press Club in Fleet Street before he drives home. When he arrives home around 4 a.m. his wife usually wakes up and reads the Perishers cartoon strip in his *Daily Mirror*.

The *Daily Star* was planned to compete with the *Sun*; the *Daily Star*'s sale rose to 1.42 million for 1981, but it had been pumped up with the help of bingo. Rupert Murdoch fought back in 1981 with bigger bingo prizes and a price cut; the *Sun* registered a 1980–2 sales increase of 9 per cent.

1981 marked a new phase in daily downmarket competition as the *Sun*'s new editor, Kelvin MacKenzie, increasingly targeted the *Daily Star* as well as the *Daily Mirror*. As the *Daily Star* lost sales, the new owners of the Express Newspapers (United) decided to go further downmarket by merging with the soft porn *Sunday Sport* (launched September 1986). For a few disastrous weeks in 1987 the *Daily Star* moved into soft pornography: the loss of both sales and respectability was too much for the Express management and Lord Stevens (United Newspapers chairman). Between 1986 and 1988 the *Daily Star* lost 27 per cent of its sales; this was a serious lapse in judgement. It also indicated that the *Sun*'s editors did indeed understand their ten million daily readers—at least well enough not to feed them soft pornography at breakfast.

In both the daily and Sunday downmarket fields the Murdoch/News management was more astute than the Mirror management; three different Mirror Group managements—IPC, Reed, and Maxwell—were about equally unsuccessful. IPC committed the fundamental error of virtually giving the *Sun* to Rupert Murdoch in 1969 and then failing adequately to respond to the competition. The Reed management (1970–84) presided over steady decline and seemed happy to sell the Mirror newspapers (and the trade unions) at a semi-nominal price to Robert Maxwell in 1984. Robert Maxwell initially used the *Daily Mirror* as a personal publicity sheet and his eventual descent into fraud and suicide did not help. During 1984–93 the *Daily Mirror* lost 23 per cent of its circulation, the *Sunday Mirror* lost 25 per cent, and the *People* lost a mammoth 39 per cent.

The *News of the World* continued with the same ownership, and the same old formula (although with different editors). By 1994 it was outselling the two Mirror Group Sundays combined.

IV

The upmarket British national press during 1945–95 grew very substantially in terms of straight sales and grew many times in terms of total pages sold; this growth was also accompanied by a growth in the number of titles. As the upmarket papers have become both more numerous and heavier in weight, they have also become lighter in approach, with huge increases in consumer features, personality interviews, columns, and entertainment.

The *Manchester Guardian* of 1955 might be counted as half-a-national newspaper, while the *Financial Times* was still a daily trade paper. On this reckoning the number of national upmarkets exactly doubled from four-and-a-half in 1955 to nine dailies and Sundays in the 1990s.

How and why has Britain developed so many upmarket national newspapers? One reason is that these publications do not compete head-on with television and can charge high advertising rates for their affluent readers. They exert political and cultural influence, which brings prestige. The motivations here are less commercial than in the other two market sectors. Several of these publications have been close to death; for example *The Times* and the *Guardian* came very close to merging in 1966. The *Observer* had its best days before 1965 and has sunk since then, needing to be rescued three times. The *Independent* and its Sunday companion, despite remarkably successful launches, needed rescuing in 1994.

Table 3.6.

(*a*) Upmarket daily sales, 1955–1995 (in thousands)

	1955	1965	1975	1985	1995[a]
Daily Telegraph (1855)	1,055	1,337	1,331	1,202	1,060
The Times (1785)	222	254	319	478	647
Financial Times (1888)	80	146	181	234	294
Guardian (1821)	156	270	319	487	400
Independent (1986)	—	—	—		294
TOTAL	1,513	2,007	2,150	2,401	2,701

[a] First six months.

(*b*) Upmarket Sunday sales, 1955–1995 (in thousands)

	1955	1965	1975	1985	1995[a]
Observer (1791)	564	824	730	736	464
Sunday Times (1822)	606	1,290	1,380	1,251	1,253
Sunday Telegraph (1961)	—	650	752	686	692
Independent on Sunday (1990)	—	—	—	—	327
TOTAL	1,170	2,764	2,862	2,673	2,736

[a] First six months.

In the upmarket the Sunday papers are extremely important; British newspaper managers over recent decades have looked towards the *Sunday Times* as the most commercially successful title in the upmarket. The *Sunday Times* was unusual in growing rapidly in just one decade (1957–67). Contrary to popular belief this was not mainly due to the glossy colour magazine launched in February 1962.[7] The *Sunday Times* first passed the one million sale in 1960.

From 1945 to 1956 it was the *Observer* which set the pace, under its young owner-editor, David Astor. Well behind its sole upmarket rival the *Sunday Times* in 1947, by early 1956 the *Observer* finally (and briefly) took the circulation lead. Readers found its youthful flair more readable, and stimulating than the stodgy, predictable, and faithfully Conservative *Sunday Times*.

Denis Hamilton, who presided over the editorial revival of the *Sunday Times*, attributes this success to three things. First, David Astor and the *Observer* opposed the British-French invasion of Suez in October 1956 and consequently lost sales. Secondly, the *Sunday Times* discovered the 'Big Read'; this was a revival of the old Victorian device of serializing books. The General Allenbrooke diaries in 1957 were followed in 1958 by no less than fourteen weeks of Field Marshal Montgomery memoirs. The 1962 launch of a 'colour magazine' as part of the *Sunday Times* package only helped to extend further an already big circulation lead over the *Observer*.[8]

In many respects in 1966 the *Sunday Times* (just before Harold Evans became editor) was very similar to the *Observer*.[9] Both Sunday papers were fairly centrist in their political stance; the *Observer* was a shade left of centre, the *Sunday Times* a shade right of centre—but neither paper had a firm political commitment. Our impression was that most journalists on both papers would vote either Labour or Liberal.

In both papers there was something of a clash of generations. There were some extremely experienced senior journalists, although the foreign correspondents and political journalists were

---

[7] Harry Henry, 'Thirty Three Years of Colour Supplements', *Admap* (Sept. 1994), 58–61.

[8] Denis Hamilton, *Editor-in-Chief* (London: Hamish Hamilton, 1989), 82–90.

[9] I spent nearly two weeks at the *Sunday Times* in spring 1966; Oliver Boyd-Barrett, my research assistant, spent a week at the *Observer* in 1967. In total we interviewed over 40 senior people at the two papers combined including David Astor, Denis Hamilton, Harold Evans, and circulation and advertising managers.

Golden 1960s to 1990s Super-competition

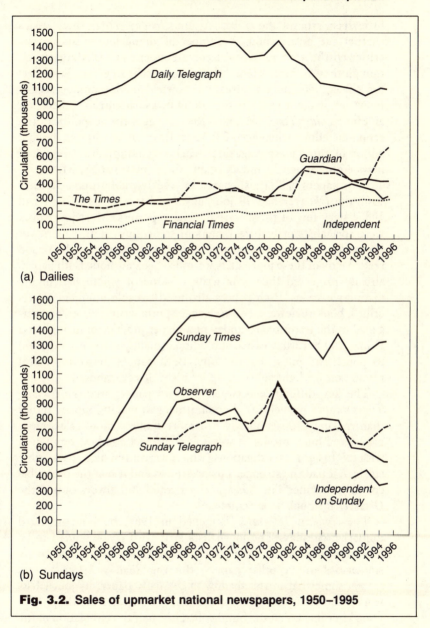

(a) Dailies

(b) Sundays

Fig. 3.2. Sales of upmarket national newspapers, 1950–1995

49

little seen around the office. At the *Sunday Times* there was a sharper age polarization. A number of young journalists heavily criticized the veteran political correspondent James Margach, although they admired Henry Brandon, who had been in Washington since 1950 and was already renowned for his unique access. However, in some respects the young turks had already taken over at the *Sunday Times*. William Rees-Mogg became political and economic editor when aged 33; Mark Boxer at age 30 was the first editor of the colour magazine; Michael Cudlipp was appointed news editor at age 23 and assistant editor (news) at age 31.

Both papers had largish staffs for weekly publications. In early 1969 the *Observer* had 79 journalists and the *Sunday Times* had 108.[10] Very few of these were general reporters. Most journalists were specialists or feature-writers of some kind. Both papers put tremendous emphasis on writing—the big read must also be a good read. Many of these journalists were also book authors. Both papers already projected their star writers, some of whom had highly distinctive styles. Both papers also used sizeable numbers of arts critics, book reviewers, and freelance sports writers. Both also engaged in the traditional Sunday newspaper practice of hiring in on Friday and Saturday casual sub-editors (mainly from other dailies) to polish the piles of staff copy. Both papers, however, had a reputation for light sub-editing by Fleet Street standards.

The key difference between the two papers was the *Sunday Times*'s more wholehearted commitment to making money rather than making propaganda. It had more money, more sales, more pages, and more profits. It was able to project a radical reputation with its 'Insight' investigations (which were often high-class crime stories); it had the stronger business news and it had the profitable colour magazine. The *Sunday Times* could still always outbid the *Observer* for book serializations.

The *Sunday Telegraph*, launched in 1961, became the third upmarket Sunday. The journalists at its two rivals tended to be contemptuous of the new paper, although in fact it had many similarities to the other papers. But the *Sunday Telegraph* was always somewhat in the shadow of the daily paper; its journalists worked on an upper floor of the *Daily Telegraph* building. Five years after its launch the Sunday had just half the circulation of the daily. A second oddity was that the *Sunday Telegraph* failed to

---

[10] National Board for Prices and Incomes, *Journalists' Pay* (London: HMSO, 1969), 16.

adopt the tactic usually pursued by new publications of going after a young readership.

All three Sundays continued over the next two decades broadly along the trajectories already established in the 1960s. The *Sunday Times* gradually increased its circulation lead over the other two papers. In 1983 its new owner Rupert Murdoch played some part in the paper's publication of the 'Hitler Diaries', thus becoming a victim of one of the great press hoaxes of all time. Also in 1983 Murdoch appointed a new young editor, Andrew Neil. There followed a distinct changing of the generations. Both now and after the 1986 Wapping events many of the 1960s recruits left the paper. There was a distinct move back to the Conservative slant of the 1950s, but in many other respects the *Sunday Times* was merely continuing down its established path. Under Murdoch, as under Lord Thomson, it continued to be immensely profitable, in sharp contrast to its daily stable companion, *The Times*, which was acquired by Thomson in 1966.

In many of the years between 1955 and 1995 both *The Times* and the *Guardian* made a loss. The story of the daily upmarket was a much more gradual growth; the daily field also had in the *Daily Telegraph* a market leader whose massive two-thirds market share in both 1955 and 1965 had sunk to 39 per cent of sales by 1995.

The Times in the early 1960s was a stuffy and somewhat lethargic newspaper; until 2 May 1966 it still carried only classified advertising on its front page. *The Times* had continued with other Victorian customs such as the anonymity of all journalists. The editor, Sir William Haley, was aware that change was needed. In 1966 the owning Astor family sanctioned some changes, whose cost led to the paper's being sold. News on the front page and related changes led to an increase in sales without any increase in advertising revenue. Lord (Roy) Thomson, the jolly, common man mogul from Ontario, was the one person to whom the Astors (an American family which had acquired *The Times* after Northcliffe's death) did not wish to sell. Sales of *The Times* which would have led to a merging of titles were separately discussed with the owners of the *Observer*, the *Guardian*, the *Daily Telegraph*, and the *Financial Times*.[11]

Denis Hamilton, who was Thomson's negotiator and later editor-in-chief of the two *Times* papers, wrote in retrospect: 'Again

[11] Monopolies Commission, *The Times Newspaper and the Sunday Times Newspaper* (London: HMSO, Dec. 1966).

and again I warned Gavin Astor, Colonel Astor's son and representative in London, that the *Times* would sink unless it did something; but each time I was rebuffed. By 1967, I now realise, it was too late.'[12]

In the 1960s the *Daily Telegraph* was overwhelmingly the leader in classified and job advertising. In 1964 it added a colour magazine to its Friday issue; in April 1967 it expanded its City coverage to compete with the Thomson changes at *The Times*. In the late 1960s the *Daily Telegraph* exemplified an era of still gentlemanly competition. Reporters actually said that they were treated 'like gentlemen'. The *Telegraph* staff were somewhat in awe of their largely unseen owner, Michael Berry (Lord Hartwell), who was located on an upper floor and known to examine the news columns in minute detail. Reporters received memos from on high with some trepidation, but Michael Berry was generally respected as a man with good news judgement who was his own editor-in-chief. In the 1960s, Berry was in his fifties and both he and the *Daily Telegraph* were at the height of their success.

In contrast to the serenely successful and Conservative *Daily Telegraph*, the *Guardian* was having a much more turbulent and difficult time but it was, nevertheless consolidating its switch from being a Liberal Manchester daily to being a non-Tory London daily. The London printing began in September 1960, but the editor (Alastair Hetherington) did not move to London until 1963. The company had very modest resources compared with some of the long-established London titles. There were many kinds of teething problems. In the winter of 1965–6 the *Guardian* made severe cutbacks in staff in order that the overall company (including the *Manchester Evening News*) should make profits and allow for new investment in the paper. In November 1965 I interviewed the deputy editor (Harford Thomas) and London news editor (John Cole). Soon afterwards I met them together again in a pub off Gray's Inn Road; they were going through a list of *Guardian* journalists, deciding which ones to sack. Gradually the *Guardian* got its act together. One of the last areas to be heavily revamped was the advertising department; the leap forward here after 1967 was quite dramatic. By the early 1970s the paper was relishing the results of the turbulent 1960s; the paper had developed a strong niche market as the only left-of-centre broadsheet daily

---

[12] Denis Hamilton, *Editor-in-Chief* (London: Hamish Hamilton, 1989), 132.

and was blessed with the youngest readership of the upmarket dailies.

During this period the *Financial Times* was also consolidating its hold on a quite different niche within the newspaper upmarket. Both the *Financial Times* and the *Guardian* were successfully established as new important daily titles. The *Guardian* had cornered the young and left-of-centre readers; the *Financial Times* had established its corner in financial news and high-priced financial advertising. It was the two more general upmarket dailies, *The Times* and *Daily Telegraph*, which still were not quite sure where to go.

In 1986 both *The Times* and the *Telegraph* papers were in turmoil. *The Times* moved to the new Wapping plant in January 1986. The *Telegraph* papers were involved in a forced sale to a new owner. While these two upmarket dailies were in turmoil, a new daily, the *Independent*, appeared with perfect timing and an excellent editorial product. During 1990 the *Independent*, *The Times*, and the *Guardian* all had almost identical ABC sales figures at around 420,000.

The *Independent* seemed to have proved that there was room for a fifth upmarket daily; there seemed to be a niche between *The Times* and *Daily Telegraph* on the political right and the *Guardian* on the left. Some of the *Independent*'s senior journalists, interviewed in 1990, saw themselves as taking over from *The Times* as Britain's politically unattached newspaper-of-record. Journalist self-confidence and antagonism towards Rupert Murdoch were both at high levels:

... most people are here because they don't want to work for Murdoch, and we despise *The Times*.

It certainly was the case before I left *The Times* that I put stories in which agreed with the leader line of the paper; it's never been the case here, no pressure whatsoever. . . . I think the leader line here is somewhat to the right of where I would stand, but it's no pressure on me politically.

I was at *The Times* during the Wapping dispute and, like a lot of people, was unhappy about it . . . We didn't like the way *The Times* was going downmarket and that it didn't have much room for serious foreign and other specialist journalism; also the way journalists were treated in the dispute, like cogs in a factory.

But 1990 was the year when the *Independent*'s luck—and perhaps also its good judgement—ran out. In 1989–90 the British economy and thus advertising expenditure turned downwards; the *Independent*'s advertising (especially classified) was already its least effective business area, and—as in other recessions—the weakest paper in the market suffered most. Trouble was compounded by the launch of the *Independent on Sunday* in the inauspicious month of January 1990. Another excellent editorial product—with a hugely admired and copied Review section—the Sunday paper achieved its initial objective by dispatching the *Sunday Correspondent* (aged 14 months) to an early grave. But the Sunday launch nearly killed the *Independent* as well.

After peaking in 1990 the *Independent*'s sales began a relentless fall. The three immediate competitors—*The Times*, *Daily Telegraph*, and *Guardian*—all improved their editorial acts; all

Table 3.7.

(a) Midmarket daily sales, 1955–1995 (in thousands)

	1955	1965	1975	1985	1995
Daily Express (1900)	4,036	3,987	2,822	1,902 (T)	1,279
Daily Mail (1896)	2,068	2,464	1,726 (T)	1,815	1,788
Daily Herald/Sun (1912)	1,759	1,273	—	—	—
News Chronicle (1930)	1,253	—	—	—	—
Today (1986)	—	—	—	—	566[1]
TOTAL	9,116	7,724	4,548	3,717	3,633

(b) Midmarket Sunday sales, 1955–1995 (in thousands)

	1955	1965	1975	1985	1995
Sunday Citizen (1850)	579	233	—	—	—
Sunday Chronicle (1885)	830	—	—	—	—
Sunday Dispatch (1801)	2,549	—	—	—	—
Sunday Express (1918)	3,235	4,190	3,715	2,449	1,403 (T)
Mail on Sunday (1982)	—	—	—	1,631	1,959
TOTAL	7,193	4,423	3,715	4,080	3,362

Source: ABC and Colin Seymour-Ure, *The British Press and Broadcasting since 1945*.
[1] *Today* was closed in November 1995.

three had by 1990 digested their post-1986 reforms and economies; all three drew upon their greater resources of finance and experience.

In 1993–4 competitive conditions in the upmarket grew still more severe. The *Guardian* absorbed the *Observer*; the *Independent* papers became partly owned (and fully managed) by the Mirror Group; a savage price-cutting war was launched by *The Times* to which the *Daily Telegraph* and the *Independent* replied by cutting their prices. The upmarket—both daily and Sunday—had become

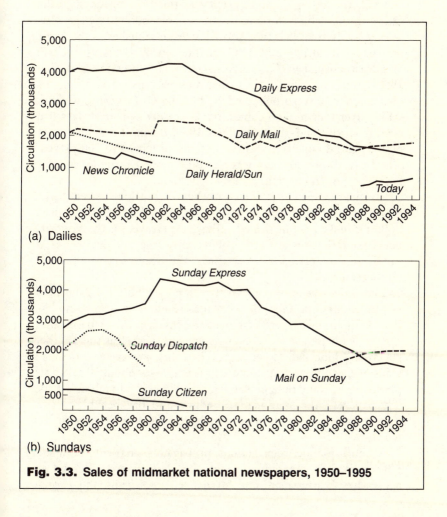

Fig. 3.3. Sales of midmarket national newspapers, 1950–1995

super-competitive. At issue were prestige, flagship publications, and political influence. Like most newspaper wars, it was about both power and money.

V

In 1955 the two *Express* newspapers dominated the midmarket, which was then hit especially severely by midmarket British television. While the sales of both *Express* papers have continued to fall and fall, the key midmarket event was the 1971 relaunch of the *Daily Mail* in tabloid format; its success was followed by the *Mail on Sunday*. In the 1980s the *Daily Mail* was established as the single newspaper most admired, read, and feared by British print and broadcast journalists. *Daily Express* journalists interviewed during 1965–8 recognized that the paper was past its peak. When its owner, Lord Beaverbrook, died in 1964 the *Daily Express* was still selling over four million copies, but the paper's greatest days had been from the mid-1930s to about 1950; during this fifteen-year period sales doubled, as did the number of journalists employed. The Beaverbrook formula was a middle market formula, suitable for the age of cinema and radio.

Like its newspapers, the Express building in Fleet Street had a glossy appearance. From across the street the black glass art deco building looked sophisticated, glitzy, expensive. In the editorial department the impression was of overcrowding, and discomfort; if the outside suggested an ocean liner, the inside suggested third-class accommodation.

The *Daily Express* was a lavishly run publication. It was printed in Manchester and Glasgow as well as London; in 1968–9 no less than 415 journalists were employed to provide a 16–18-page *Daily Express*; with about ten full non-advertising pages this was a rather generous 40 journalists per page. The *Daily Express* tried to avoid using agency pictures; its picture desk employed about 50 full-time photographers and desk personnel, including six retouching artists. The paper was the creation of sub-editors and 'backbench' processing executives. Sub-editors routinely cut 800-word stories to 200 words.

A confusion between serious propaganda and entertainment glitz seemed to run right through the *Daily Express*. Behind an aggressive 'Expressman' and 'exclusive' news front, the *Express* regime was often gently paternalistic rather than despotic. Sub-editors only had to work seven hours a day. *Express* journalists were as deeply involved as any in the pub culture of Fleet Street; they seemed to favour the next door Red Lion pub and the Press Club bar (across the street) and many played golf together on their days off.

There was a family element in the Beaverbrook paternalism. One sub-editor, Donald Farthing, told me that his father had worked on the *Daily Express* from its 1900 foundation into the 1930s; he himself had started in 1932 in the *Express* library and had then become a reporter and sub-editor. Both father and son had also written the paper's gardening column (mainly in the spring) and both had done so under the name of 'Mr Blossom'.

But the journalists—especially young reporters and sub-editors—knew that the *Express* formula was not working and several said the *Daily Mail* was the paper to watch. The readers recruited in the growth years of the 1930s and 1940s were ageing. By 1968 the *Daily Express* had already lost 10 per cent of its peak circulation and the journalists accurately predicted a further steep decline. After 1970 its management failed to steer a consistent course. A series of crisis management decisions included the closure of the Glasgow operation and finally the sale of Beaverbrook Newspapers in 1977.[13]

Sunday Express sales held up better than those of the daily through the 1960s and it was the Sunday profits which then subsidized the daily. The *Sunday Express* had no real competition in the middle market and it did especially well with fashion and other glossy advertising; it projected an expensive and gracious life-style. By 1982 the *Sunday Express* readership was quite affluent but also older than the readership of any other national Sunday; 53 per cent of readers were aged 45 and over;[14] and not surprisingly its sales continued to fall. In 1982 the Mail management launched their Sunday competitor.

In the 1960s the *Daily Mail* was clearly undergoing severe traumas. Its sales drop was, however, exaggerated by its taking on, and later losing, many readers from the *News Chronicle* (which folded in 1960). Apart from this upward blip in the early 1960s, the *Daily Mail*'s circulation hovered around 1.8 to 2 million from 1930 right into the 1990s.

---

[13] Lewis Chester and Jonathan Fenby, *The Fall of the House of Beaverbrook* (London: Andre Deutsch, 1979).

[14] Jeremy Tunstall, *The Media in Britain* (London: Constable, 1983), 98.

In 1971 the Mail group was in financial difficulty with two sick national dailies—the *Sketch* as well as the *Mail*. The old Lord Rothermere (the second) died—after nearly four decades in charge—and his son agreed to drastic changes. The *Daily Sketch* was closed and its editor (David English) put in charge of a new tabloid version of the *Daily Mail*. During the 1970s the *Daily Mail* developed a successful new formula for the midmarket national newspaper.

The *Mail on Sunday*'s 1982 launch illustrated the ruthlessness and good judgement of the management. Like many launches, this one was not a success and the launch editor, Bernard Shrimsley, quickly became a sacrificial victim. As part of their reputation for ruthlessness the Mail management were known as the kings of the 'spoiler'. When a competing newspaper is about to publish a big exclusive story, a 'spoiler' is rapidly rushed forward on the same subject and proclaimed as the real 'exclusive'. The Associated/ Mail management deployed this old competitive tactic on a larger scale when in February 1987 Robert Maxwell launched the *London Daily News* to compete with Associated's *Evening Standard*. The Associated management still owned the old 'Evening News' title and they used this old title to launch a spoiler newspaper on the same day as Maxwell's new publication. Faced by an escalation from one to three London evenings and unable to distinguish between the *London Daily News* and the *Evening News*, most purchasers stuck with the familiar *Evening Standard*. Maxwell's (editorially excellent) paper lasted only five months.

As the leaders of the midmarket, the two *Mails* have emerged as the papers which all newspaper managements—as well as almost all journalists—follow. They have become leaders in the midmarket human interest news story (complete with plot, villain, and hero or heroine), in feature coverage, and in fatter papers. Through the twentieth century the *Mail* managers have avoided the once successful *Daily Express* urge to appeal to three-quarters of the entire population. Although its readership is predominantly middle-aged the *Daily Mail* is especially strong in appealing to middle-class women aged 25–44 in Southern England.

VI

This chapter has tried to focus primarily upon how British national newspapers became more commercially competitive between the 1960s and 1990s. There were, of course, also big editorial changes—some of which are the focus of subsequent chapters. The biggest single editorial change can be summarized as three overlapping trends towards features, towards sections, and towards tabloid size and approach. The national newspapers introduced many more non-news items—features, women's pages, life-style, travel, and entertainment; the removal of trade union restraints led to an expansion of separate sections of many kinds.

The latter changes overlapped with a strong trend towards the tabloid size. In the 1950s most of the big sale papers (including the *Daily Express*, *Mail*, and *Herald* and the *News Chronicle*) were still large size. When the *Sunday Express* went tabloid (in 1992) all the midmarket as well as all of the downmarket dailies and Sundays had gone tabloid. But the key moves to tabloid size were made by the *Sun* in 1969 and the *Daily Mail* in 1971. There are other senses in which the bulk of the British press has 'gone tabloid', including the use of tabloid sections within large-size papers, and the adoption of colour.

British national newspapers have moved since the 1960s towards much larger doses of entertainment. The downmarket papers located themselves decisively 'below' television and now focus on telling readers about the gossip and scandals behind the screen. The general trend towards leisure coverage is also reflected in the larger Saturday editions; Saturday now outsells all other weekdays, with Saturday and Sunday now carrying nearly as many pages as the other five days.

There have also been major commercial changes since the 1960s; there is now much more marketing of the newspapers as products as well as marketing by the newspaper of clothing, gardening tools, cheap flights, restaurant meals, and much else. The newspaper has partly been redefined as a leisure and consumption aid rather than a vehicle reporting yesterday's events.

4 Local Press Meltdown: Freesheet and Tabloid Triumph

THE British local press in recent decades has grown ever more local; it has also increasingly become a vehicle whose prime purpose is to deliver classified and retail advertising. The free local weekly has been the prime cause of both these trends. Virtually unknown in Britain in the 1960s, in the 1970s and especially the 1980s these freesheets were the most dynamic force in the British non-national press. They were financed entirely by advertising and their impact on all aspects of the local press was revolutionary. By providing 90–100 per cent household coverage at the local level they seized ever-increasing shares of advertising; they also pushed the editorial output towards the super-local.

The local press in Britain—as in almost every other country— carries more advertising than does the national press; the split in Britain is about 42 per cent for the nationals with non-nationals getting 58 per cent of newspaper advertising. To retain this advertising the local press has largely dropped all but extremely local news.

Advertising in general and classified advertising for jobs and houses in particular are subject to the trade cycle. Most local dailies and weeklies—being highly dependent on advertising—make profits in years of economic downturn; but in good economic years—as the job, house, and car markets boom—local papers are extremely profitable. In good years an operating profit of 35 per cent on revenue is not unusual, especially if the local newspaper group is a monopoly, or near monopoly, which many are. The local press is about the parish pump, the job and property ads, as well as the power to charge monopoly prices for advertising.

Table 4.1. Provincial newspaper circulation, 1983–1993 (in millions)

	1983	1993
Mornings	1.27	1.17
Evenings	5.39	4.54
Sundays	0.42	1.03
Weekly paid	9.10	7.00
Weekly free	29.90	33.10
Daily free	—	0.06
Total per week	79.38	75.45

Source: Zenith.

I

The scale of the local press meltdown depends upon which year you take as a baseline. The provincial dailies melted down twice; they declined steeply in the 1920s and 1930s, then grew again and peaked during 1953–5, only to decline again.

Britain had a big provincial press before 1914. But during 1918–39 the national newspapers killed off much of the provincial morning press; after 1955 television sharply cut back the provincial evening press. In 1960 Manchester still had two large evening newspapers with a combined evening sale of over 600,000 copies. By 1995 the lone *Manchester Evening News* sold only a little above 200,000 copies (and a little below on Saturday). By 1965 even cities as big as Manchester, Liverpool, Birmingham, and Leeds only had a single evening; thirty years later these four big city evenings had lost more than half their combined 1965 sale.

The paid-for weekly was the most pervasive type of local newspaper until the 1970s; after that the local freesheet took over. After 1975—while the freesheet grew—the rest of the local press melted down in several ways. The local evenings continued to decline in sales; the huge declines in the big cities were partly counterbalanced by growth in smaller urban centres. But from 1955 to 1995 evening newspapers overall lost sales at around 1 per cent per year. The local evenings also melted down in another sense—they increasingly went tabloid; at a glance many of them looked more and more like a local version of the *Sun* or *Daily Mirror*.

National Competition

The local evening papers 'melted down' also in the sense of focusing on very local news. When I interviewed provincial evening editors in 1966–7 and again in 1976–7 they were still carrying the major national and international news from the Press Association agency; and most editors were also writing editorials on both national and world, as well as local, topics. Evening editors, interviewed in 1994, said that their concerns were now overwhelmingly local.

There has been a modest increase in the success of provincial Sundays; but this is mainly a Scottish phenomenon and English provincial Sundays are really sports papers. Also surviving quite well in a small way are a few provincial morning papers; but the largest English ones, accounting for two-thirds of the sales of English provincial mornings, are located in the five cities of Norwich, Leeds, Darlington, Liverpool, and Bristol—cities which are an average 173 miles from London.

II

Scotland is the main exception in Britain to the dominance of the London newspapers. Table 4.2 shows that the highest readership

Table 4.2. Percentage of adult population reading a regional daily (a.m. or p.m.) newspaper, 1995

North Scotland	66
North-East	51
South-West	41
Central Scotland	37
Yorkshire	37
Midlands	35
Wales/West	34
NW/Lancashire	31
East of England	30
Border	24
South	20
London	14
All UK	30

Source: National Readership Survey Jan.–June 1995.

of non-London morning papers is in North Scotland. Being distant from London, Scotland developed its own strong daily press in the horse era and maintained it in the rail era. After the *Daily Mail* began printing in Manchester in 1900 it sent copies on by train to Scotland. Then in 1927–8 Lord Beaverbrook began printing both *Express* papers in both Manchester and Glasgow.

Scotland thus acquired a unique competitive situation. In 1995 as in 1965 there were strong morning and evening newspaper operations in Aberdeen and Dundee as well as in Glasgow and Edinburgh. Glasgow became an exceptionally competitive regional centre. The *Express* was the pace-setter with a lavish printing and editorial operation producing a *Scottish Daily Express*, which was one of Beaverbrook's and Fleet Street's biggest extravagances. Another Glasgow group, which included the *Daily Record* and *Sunday Mail*, was acquired by the Mirror Group in 1955.

The *Daily Record*—half Scottish *Daily Mirror*, half a genuinely separate Glasgow paper—set out in pursuit of the *Scottish Daily Express*. The *Record* v. *Express* circulation war was eventually won by the *Record*; the *Scottish Daily Express* was closed in 1974 as the Beaverbrook management closed the Glasgow operation. The *Daily Record* went on to being read each day by half of all Scottish adults.

The editor of the *Daily Record*, Alex Little, told me in June 1966 that the London bosses of the Mirror Group (Cecil King and Hugh Cudlipp) had lost touch with genuine competitive popular journalism. The London papers had become dull and grey; Cecil King and the *Daily Mirror* were too keen to be respectable and to avoid libel actions. Scotland, Alex Little pointed out, had in 1966 Britain's fiercest circulation war, which was generating very high sales figures from the *Scottish Daily Express* (still ahead at this time), *Daily Record*, and *Daily Mail*. But later in 1966 the *Daily Mail* closed its oddly located Edinburgh operation and withdrew to Manchester.

This 1966 move by the *Daily Mail* was the beginning of a great national newspaper retreat from Scotland. In 1974 the Express group closed its massive Glasgow operation and retreated to Manchester; *Daily Express* sales in Scotland dropped steeply and the *Daily Record* commenced two decades of morning sales dominance in Scotland with sales figures of up to 800,000. As the London papers retreated south the Scottish morning market was dominated by the downmarket *Daily Record* and the mid-to-upmarket

Scotsman (Edinburgh), *Herald* (Glasgow), *Courier and Advertiser* (Dundee), and *Press and Journal* (Aberdeen). Scotland also had and has two huge popular Sundays, and now also has the upmarket *Scotland on Sunday*.

The 1986 Wapping saga had its repercussions in Scotland, because the subsequent economies encouraged further retreats back to London. However, the Murdoch/News management were an exception here; their Wapping drama also had a Glasgow sub-plot in the form of a new printing plant there. The *Sun*, which initially had most of its sales in Southern England, now began to attack the Scottish market. Its Glasgow editions also adopted the cause of Scottish independence and Scottish sales crept up behind those of the *Daily Record*.

Scotland, then, continues to be the only major British region which has a significant morning and Sunday, as well as evening, newspaper press of its own. Very obviously also Scotland's different press parallels Scotland's different and distant geography, its separate culture and history, its separate governmental system and—especially important in news terms—its separate systems of courts and sports. Obviously also the Scottish newspaper press parallels Scottish politics, with the *Daily Record* versus the *Sun* contest paralleling the Labour Party versus Scottish National Party contest.

III

Until 1970 the typical provincial situation was as follows. The monopoly evening would sell the bulk of the copies within an urban radius of a few miles; each mile you went away from the city, the weaker the evening became, and the stronger the local (paid-for) weeklies became. Some of these weeklies were owned by competitors, while other weeklies were under the same ownership as the evening, acting as a sort of defensive flotilla. In some cases the evening and the weeklies would share a network of small local offices; a weekly would supposedly be based on one of these satellite offices (also a focus for selling advertising), but the weekly would in fact be edited back in the main office and printed on the central presses when these were not busy with printing the evening. David Murphy's *The Silent Watchdog*[1] describes the quiescent

---

[1] David Murphy, *The Silent Watchdog* (London: Constable, 1976).

journalism practised on such newspapers. The printing trade unions helped to ensure that these were high-cost local operations, but the evenings and weeklies shared the lush classified and other local advertising.

The free weeklies began quietly about 1970, often the creation of local journalists or advertising sales people who knew how profitable the paid-for weeklies had become. When I was interviewing regional editors in 1976 the freesheets were a new topic for anxious discussion. The freesheet offered the advertiser 100 per cent of some specified target audience—for example one suburb, or every house within three miles of a specific shopping centre.

By 1979 some 14 million freesheets were being printed per week. By 1989 it had trebled to a peak of 42 million copies per week. This was almost two freesheets per household per week. The number of freesheets then fell back towards one-and-a-half per household per week, but their share of weekly advertising continued to grow, reaching 66 per cent in 1992.

This freesheet movement had a more profound impact on the provincial press than the Wapping events did on the national press. The freesheets revolutionized ownership, trade unions, production, advertising, editorial, and profits. Many of the new freesheet owners were—like Eddie Shah in Warrington—general printers; they typically operated out of very modest local premises. These new entrepreneurs increasingly challenged the printing trade unions and thus ultimately hugely reduced labour costs for all provincial newspapers. They also focused on 'new technology'— including offset printing, colour, and computerized advertising systems. The freesheet entrepreneurs focused on advertising, especially on classified advertising, which was the 'highest yield' (or most over-priced) part of the traditional operation. The freesheet entrepreneur was offering higher market coverage at a much lower cost per household reached. The freesheeters also revolutionized editorial by running 'newspapers' whose editorial content (and costs) were only a small fraction of traditional paid-for weekly standards. Finally, they revolutionized profits; dozens of these entrepreneurs became millionaires and more within a very few years.

In the late 1970s the major provincial newspapers began the fightback to recover control of local classified and retail advertising. This trend continued:

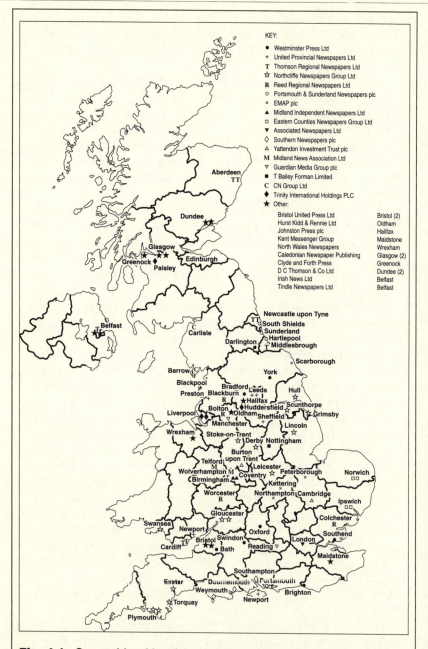

KEY:

- ● Westminster Press Ltd
- + United Provincial Newspapers Ltd
- T Thomson Regional Newspapers Ltd
- ☆ Northcliffe Newspapers Group Ltd
- R Reed Regional Newspapers Ltd
- ○ Portsmouth & Sunderland Newspapers plc
- × EMAP plc
- ▲ Midland Independent Newspapers Ltd
- □ Eastern Counties Newspapers Group Ltd
- ▼ Associated Newspapers Ltd
- ◇ Southern Newspapers plc
- △ Yattendon Investment Trust plc
- M Midland News Association Ltd
- ▽ Guardian Media Group plc
- ■ T Bailey Forman Limited
- C CN Group Ltd
- ◆ Trinity International Holdings PLC
- ★ Other:

Bristol United Press Ltd	Bristol (2)
Hurst Kidd & Rennie Ltd	Oldham
Johnston Press plc	Halifax
Kent Messenger Group	Maidstone
North Wales Newspapers	Wrexham
Caledonian Newspaper Publishing	Glasgow (2)
Clyde and Forth Press	Greenock
D C Thomson & Co Ltd	Dundee (2)
Irish News Ltd	Belfast
Tindle Newspapers Ltd	Belfast

Fig. 4.1. Ownership of local and regional daily newspapers, 1993

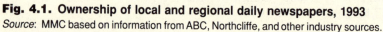

Source: MMC based on information from ABC, Northcliffe, and other industry sources.

The second half of the 1980s was really the story of how the older, more established, regional Press groups reasserted themselves. The larger groups responded in two ways—they either started their own 'defensive' frees, or simply bought out the opposition. This latter development can be seen very clearly in the concentration of ownership figures. In 1989 the top 20 regional publishers controlled 81 per cent of the industry, whereas in 1979 they only controlled 61 per cent . In other words, not only were the 1980s a time of great change in the number of free titles, but also in the nature of ownership. As all the major publishing groups now have a mixture of paid and free titles, it is more difficult to isolate the free newspaper industry as a result.[2]

The Big Five regional newspaper publishers—Thomson, Reed, Northcliffe, United, Westminster Press—were by 1994 also the five biggest freesheet publishers, producing 36 per cent of all freesheets. By now the provincial newspaper business had been redefined as involving primarily dailies and free weeklies; paid-for weeklies were in third place with only about one-fifth of local press advertising.

IV

The response of the major national groups of provincial newspapers involved more than simply acquiring successful local freesheet publishers. The intention increasingly was to adopt the freesheet publishers' commercial formulas as well. The big groups succeeded in adopting two key lessons of the freesheets, while they failed with a third. They cut costs drastically, by gradually in the late 1980s and early 1990s undermining printing and journalism trade unionism and by introducing expensive new plants with much lower associated labour costs. Secondly, the big groups increasingly focused on advertising and trying to win it back from still independent freesheet companies; in many cases big publishers launched freesheets which they called 'defensive' but which were really subsidized predators intended to undercut the advertising prices of (and hence to kill) rival freesheets.

The big groups in general failed to learn a third freesheeter lesson—to hold down management, office, and related costs. These biggest regional groups are themselves the regional newspaper subsidiaries of still bigger companies. A regional subsidiary then has

---

[2] Roy Jeans (of Zenith), *UK Press Gazette*, 3 Dec. 1990.

perhaps a dozen printing and publishing centres in its various daily and weekly localities. Each of these centres may be printing twenty of its own titles plus contract printing of others. A common pattern is of a printing centre which operates numerous shifts and prints an evening paper whose biggest print runs are on Thursday and Friday; on Tuesday and Wednesday most of the weekly news-papers (free and paid) are printed. Contract printing of internal house magazines, local government and property publications, and weeklies owned by other companies in the area, takes place on Monday and at other spare times in the week. With all of this goes an elaborate management structure of accountants, cost con-trol, budgets, consultants' reports, detailed acquisition planning, and so on. The freesheeters' low overheads lesson is not learned.

But the key regional groups have instead focused on another strategy, more appropriate to their larger size. This is the strategy of owning Adjacent Local Dailies. Box 4.1 shows the leading exam-ples of such Adjacencies. This is a bigger-scale version of the single evening paper with its flotilla of associated weeklies. Publishers have deliberately sold one lone evening title, while buying another evening paper printed 30 miles from an existing property. Groups have also engaged in swaps.

An example of an established adjacent publisher was Southern Newspapers, which at the time of a 1991 report[3] was the thirteenth largest UK provincial newspaper publisher. It owned three evening papers (Southampton, Bournemouth, Weymouth) and twenty-seven weeklies. Its evenings sold 155,000 copies, its paid-for week-lies 143,000, while its free weekly copies totalled 919,000. This meant that Southern Newspapers dominated not only some 75 miles of affluent south of England coastline but its weeklies also held a commanding position thirty and forty miles inland. These adjacent groups focus heavily on modern colour-printing presses. In some cases a bigger publisher may acquire a smaller company primarily for its printing press. The Guardian group admitted that its motivation in buying the Reading-based Thames Valley News-papers in 1993–4 was to acquire TVN's 'modern printing and production facilities'; these would be able also to print the Guard-ian group's *Surrey Advertiser* weekly titles as well.[4]

[3] Monopolies and Mergers Commission, *Southern Newspapers PLC, and EMAP PLC, Reed International PLC and Trinity International Holdings PLC* (London: HMSO, 1991).
[4] Monopolies and Mergers Commission, *The Guardian and Manchester Evening News plc and Thames Valley Newspapers* (London: HMSO, 1993), 1.

BOX 4.1. REGIONAL PRESS POWER: GROUP OWNER-
SHIP OF ADJACENT LOCAL DAILIES, 1995
(Daily newspapers in all cases: (2) indicates a morning-and-evening
combination)

Northcliffe Newspapers (Daily Mail)
Hull–Scunthorpe–Grimsby–Lincoln–Nottingham–Derby–Stoke–
Leicester. Exeter–Torquay–Plymouth (2) Gloucester–Cheltenham

United Provincial Newspapers (United)
Blackpool–Preston
Leeds (2)–Sheffied

Westminster Press (Pearson)
Bradford–York–Darlington
Oxford–Swindon–Bath

Thomson Regional Newspapers
Newcastle (2)–Edinburgh (2)

Portsmouth and Sunderland
South Shields–Sunderland–Hartlepool

EMAP
Northampton–Kettering–Peterborough

Eastern Counties Newspapers
Norwich (2)–Ipswich (2)

Southern Newspapers
Southampton–Bournemouth–Weymouth

Midland Independent Newspapers
Birmingham (2)–Coventry

Larger groups in the 1990s were starting also to print two adjacent evenings on a single press. There is a tendency to operate more
intensively a smaller number of higher-technology, higher-cost
printing presses which are 'written down' more quickly. The group
thus retains flexibility and is ready for the next twists in technology
and market. The biggest British adjacent company, the Daily
Mail/Northcliffe group was in 1994 allowed to buy the *Nottingham
Evening Post*; this gave the Daily Mail company eight adjacent
dailies between Hull, Stoke, and Leicester. In arguing against this
purchase the Monopolies and Mergers Commission suggested that
one company would become too dominant over too big an area of
the East Midlands and Eastern England. Having literally absorbed
the freesheet revolution, the major regional groups now faced the

new commercial threat in the early 1990s of the *Loot*-style publications, which combine a high cover price with free insertion of personal classified advertisements. This type of publication, if it sells 100,000 copies a week at £1, generates £5.2 million annually in retail sales. The big newspaper publishers responded with three types of incorporation—either buying the free ad paper, or launching their own free ad weekly, or offering free ads for items below £100 in their conventional newspapers.

Once more the focus was on local classified advertising. Local newspaper publishers, thus, now incorporate evenings and weekly frees as their main output, while they also offer contract printing, weekly paid-for papers, and free-ad papers. Some publishers are also building up databases of their local customers in the hope of using them to offer electronic services. In offering local electronic services they will seek to present themselves as the super-local heroes as opposed to distant and alien telephone and cable suppliers.

V

Local newspapers in Britain have melted down to the most local of local levels in their news coverage. The most national media are obviously the national newspapers and television; since the 1950s and 1960s regional television news based especially on ITV's fourteen regions (and some subregions) also offers a 'regional' coverage, perhaps as regional as the regional morning papers. But the local evenings and weeklies have defined themselves as offering a very much more local definition of 'local'. The great bulk of both evening and weekly circulation is within ten miles or less of the publication centre.

Even in the 1970s local evenings devoted only about a quarter of their space to national and international news, and much of this was sport.[5] But by the 1990s these papers appeared to have still lower amounts of national or international news; faced with what they saw as fierce early evening competition from national press, regional TV, and local radio, the provincial evenings had settled down into a relentless pursuit of the local. Four evening papers visited in the East Midlands in autumn 1994 averaged 52 tabloid

[5] Denis McQuail, *Analysis of Newspaper Content* (London: HMSO, 1977), 63–71.

pages per weekday with 25 editorial pages. On some days it is difficult to find even one story, let alone a page of stories, which would satisfy a strict definition of either 'national' or 'international'. 'National stories' tend to be local follow-ups on stories already in the national media. Almost all 'international' stories are TV, entertainment, or sports related; there is quite a lot of nationally originated 'service' material such as horoscopes, crosswords, puzzles, TV schedules, and stock market prices, emphasizing local companies. Both news and feature pages are overwhelmingly local.

Local evening newspaper journalists in 1994 were reaching the office around 7 a.m. There is a succession of editions, each of which is primarily devoted to providing four or so special pages for a particular nearby town or suburb to which that edition goes. Medium-sized evenings with sales between 50,000 and 100,000 employ between 50 and 90 journalists—some of whom are deployed in branch offices collecting the material for the relevant localized edition. The emphasis on local events and personalities, police, and crime, which Denis McQuail found in 1975, is still there, but more so. According to editors, the stories which sell the most copies are local disasters—'The public library burned down' or the 'multiple death minibus crash on the M1'. Editors also say that the classified advertisements are a strong attraction for readers, with more copies sold on the days when the paper carries its main job, house, and car advertising sections.

While the shift in the evening papers has been from very local to even more local, the strategic change since 1965 or 1975 has been from evenings towards local freesheets; such news as the freesheets carry tends to be written by very reduced teams of journalists often producing separate super-local editorial for separate super-local editions.

VI

Within London and the South-East there has also been a trend towards super-localism. Back in 1955 there were three London evening newspapers which together sold two million copies across greater London and beyond; but the *Star* died in 1960 and the *Evening News* in 1980, leaving the lone *Evening Standard* with only one-quarter of the 1955 London evening sale.

Roy Thomson tried launching evening papers beyond the London green belt on the assumption that what flew around London, Ontario, should fly even better around London, England. But new Thomson evenings in places like Reading, Watford, and Luton were failures. Although some London exurban evenings did survive, with small circulations, the publishers of weeklies, both free and paid, reaped much greater success and profits.

Consequently the area up to forty miles away from central London is just an extreme case of the general situation—it has only one major evening paper, the *Evening Standard*, and is otherwise dominated by the nationals and by profitable local weeklies. Across South-East England the few remaining local evenings struggle against this supernational and super-local combination.

The weakness of local daily papers in the South-East of England also has a consequence for the nationals. Although the London nationals aim at the whole of Britain, they sell especially well in the South-East; since this area has the highest number and proportion of affluent AB readers as well as the highest proportion of people who do not see a local daily, it makes good commercial sense for the *Daily Mail*, *Daily Telegraph*, and others to focus heavily on the South-East. The London nationals thus become even more London and South-East oriented than they might otherwise be.

VII

The 1980s saw an increase in polarization between a yet more local local press and a yet more national national press. In terms of national coverage, the provincial groups have closed down what in the 1960s were quite sizeable London offices. A provincial evening editor now may have one day a week of a lobby (political) correspondent with which to cover the locality's Members of Parliament. For such national material as they carry, some provincial dailies rely on the Press Association agency; from 1991 an editor could choose one or more of General, Sport, Racing, Photos, AP/ Reuter Foreign, and Select (a summary version of General). In 1993 two of the national groups (Westminster and Northcliffe) set up a rival national agency targeted at evening papers. But cost-cutting has been a major force behind these changes; these services of tailored material from London to provincial dailies were by 1995 only a trickle compared with the sizeable flows of 1965.

Meanwhile the national newspapers have drastically scaled down their operations outside London. The standard pattern which developed after 1900 was of a London newspaper which also printed in Manchester. In the 1960s Manchester was a major national subcentre, not only for printing but for editorial. In 1977 all the national newspapers (except the *Sun*) had major printing and editorial operations in Manchester; the Thomson Withy Grove plant printed Manchester editions of two dailies (*Mirror* and *Telegraph*) and two Sundays (*Mirror* and *News of the World*). These operations were extremely wasteful; for example, London editorial matter was reset by compositors in Manchester. 19 per cent of the 23,300 national newspaper production (printing) workers[6] and 20 per cent of national newspaper journalists were based in Manchester. With 683 journalists located there (in 1969)[7] a typical national daily newspaper would have fifty journalists in Manchester.

The most lavish Manchester operations—like that of the two *Express* papers—employed around 1,000 people. The London managements recognized that this was needlessly extravagant, and the *Express* papers did withdraw from Glasgow in 1974, but the trade unions were determined to maintain big Manchester operations.

The Wapping events of 1986 led to radical reappraisals of both London and Manchester operations, and the central Manchester offices broadly followed the Fleet Street pattern—they were closed down. Some papers continued to print in Manchester while others did not; but printing outside London fragmented into a bigger number of smaller contract printing operations selected with road—not rail—transport in mind. The *Independent*'s and *Today*'s 1986 printing lead was followed. In many cases regional editions of national dailies were printed at night on presses which earlier in the day printed local evening papers. The common pattern involved one major printing in East London and several smaller printings scattered around the country. By 1995, for example, the *Daily Express* was printed in London, Manchester, Preston, and Dublin,

---

[6] O. R. McGregor (Chairman), *Royal Commission on the Press: Interim Report: The National Newspaper Industry* (London: HMSO, 1976), 56.

[7] National Board for Prices and Incomes, *Journalists' Pay* (London: HMSO, 1969), 19.

while the *Daily Mail* was printed in London, Stoke, Plymouth, Belfast, Newcastle, and Glasgow.

Alongside these printing changes there was a massive cutback by London newspapers of the two main categories of journalists located outside London. In the 1980s and especially after 1986 the big Manchester editorial offices were closed down, including a *Daily Mail* Manchester office which in 1986 employed 100 journalists. Secondly, there was also a reduction in the number of staff correspondents scattered around the whole of Britain. When the Manchester offices were closed after 1986 some of the journalists were offered jobs in London, while the majority became redundant. There was also a tendency to sack staff regional correspondents and to replace them with 'stringers' (part-timers).[8]

From 1988 onwards the national newspapers had rid themselves of most of their staff journalists based outside London. A north of England operation still continued but it was now based on the London news desk and sports desk. In order to report on happenings outside London, the national newspapers now relied on a motley and diminished, mainly part-time, team of journalists. Some full-time correspondents still continued, but these now reported to a London desk and sent their work via modem and telephone line direct into the London editorial computer system; others were part-time correspondents, contracted for example to cover midweek and Saturday sport; increasing reliance was now also placed on local news agencies serving all the London nationals; and finally there was increased use of 'freelances'—many of them either older journalists sacked from staff jobs after 1986 or young aspirants hoping to win regular London employment.

London news editors and sports editors interviewed in 1990–1 were worried that these recent economy measures had 'gone too far'. Later into the 1990s there were signs of some attempt to redress the balance; for example, several national papers in the mid-1990s decided to increase their Scottish editorial effort. But these were minor changes.

There had been a massive redeployment of journalist labour back to central and East London. In the 1960s and 1970s about 30 per cent of all national staff journalists were located outside London (in Manchester and elsewhere). By 1995 probably less than 10 per cent of staff journalists were located outside London. When

[8] Kevin Dowling, 'Mail stands in danger of losing regional grip,' *UK Press Gazette*, 6 Oct. 1986.

the provincial press was becoming more locally oriented the national press was becoming still more London oriented.

VIII

According to MORI opinion polls in the 1990s 'journalists' were the only occupation on a lengthy list of occupations to be more unpopular than politicians. When the British public express such views they are presumably mainly thinking of national tabloids and local weeklies because these are the only two categories of newspaper which reach the majority of British adults each week. (Readers and viewers are further discussed in Chapter 13.)

'Newspaper' has come to mean for most British adults either a super-local freesheet or a supernational London tabloid. While the national press has migrated towards East London, the regional press has melted down towards the parish pump and local classified advertising.

Part II
OWNERS, MANAGERS, AND EDITORS

5 From Press Lords to Moguls and Macho Managers

THIS chapter will argue that, during the 1950s and 1960s, the old style press lords came to an end, although some of their offspring continued as 'crown princes'. There was a new pattern of media moguls and, after 1986 and Wapping, a new wave of macho managers. The following two chapters will argue that in the 1960s and 1970s there was a prevalent myth of the 'sovereign editor'; by the 1980s and 1990s this myth had been replaced by a newly potent reality—the 'entrepreneurial editor'.

Under post-1986 industrial conditions, considerable power resides with mogul owners and chief executives; they are especially important in laying down financial guidelines, in making strategic decisions about the life and death of specific newspapers and in choosing senior managers and editors. But chief executives and owners always were powerful; even the trade unions recognized that and used to insist on dealing direct with the chief executive. The real management change is that entire management teams now manage London newspapers in a much more aggressive, macho manner.

Editors of national newspapers have also become more potent figures, in much the same way as the managers or coaches of major football teams. A new editor is given money and a trial period in charge. If an initial success, the editor—like the football coach— may become a high-profile and enduring figure in the industry. The individual editor will not last for ever, but successful editors tend to last longer than most chief executives.

The latter-day media mogul is active in a range of media and internationally active in other countries. The mogul wants an editor who will last a decade or more. It has become part of the received wisdom of the industry that detailed editorial interference is often the hallmark of the inept and unsuccessful newspaper owner or top executive.

Competitive conditions have led to a star system involving columnists, interviewers, top correspondents, and section heads. Thus it is not only the chief editors, but an echelon of perhaps two or three hundred journalists who have become significantly more powerful. Within an élite of perhaps 400 or 500 senior executives and journalists there is an inner ring of a dozen or so chief executives, moguls, and crown princes. This inner ring has some club-like qualities. The membership of the inner ring changes, as new chief executives, new moguls, and new crown princes replace former inner ring members. But the current membership have between them extraordinary powers. Not only do they control the present ownership and strategic direction of the press; they can also shape its future ownership. They can blackball would-be new members—as Robert Maxwell was blackballed in 1969 (and Rupert Murdoch was let in instead); Maxwell was finally allowed into the club in 1984 after fifteen years on the waiting list. One owner or chief executive may look at some of his publications (such as provincial newspapers) as profit-earners while other publications (such as upmarket national newspapers) are prestige-earning flagships. Motivation can also change over time. Before 1986, said one sports editor, 'Newspaper managers used to sit behind a door, hoping the unions wouldn't come through it.' Each of the four types of ownership to be discussed here has been associated with a characteristic type of goal:

- The old style Press Lord (like Northcliffe or Beaverbrook) successfully accumulates newspapers and then less successfully tries to promote specific political policies through newspaper companies.
- The Crown Prince who inherits the press empire typically tries to imitate his more dynamic father and to maintain the family tradition; this usually means a goal of maintenance rather than growth and a willingness to accept comfortable, rather than dramatic, levels of profit.
- The Media Mogul's driving urge is *acquisition*—to acquire more publications and other media properties and to turn them around from loss into profit. To the mogul it is profits,

growth, and financial performance which come first; but political influence is an amusing extra, not least because it may be turned to commercial advantage.

- The Chief Executive, who is not a major owner, typically has predominantly commercial motivation. Under London conditions he has to think about profits, dividends, and share options; he also has to keep up the share price as a defence against hostile take-over.

I

The British press lord role was first played by Lord Northcliffe at the turn of the century; it lived on into the 1960s in the persons of Lord Beaverbrook (owner of the then midmarket leader, the *Daily Express*) and Lord Camrose (owner of the upmarket leader, the *Daily Telegraph*). Both men came from modest middle-class backgrounds—Beaverbrook from Eastern Canada, Camrose from South Wales. Both built up their own press companies; they controlled the two most dynamic papers of the late 1930s; both were friends of Winston Churchill but were slow to support his anti-appeasement position. Each man had his seventieth birthday in 1949; each handed his leading newspapers on to a son, a crown prince.

Beaverbrook and Camrose handed on some proud traditions—in particular they handed on newspapers which combined serious material with entertainment. Each himself combined editorial with business ability. But they also handed on a *Daily Express* and a *Daily Telegraph* which had changed rather little since the *Daily Telegraph* daringly put news on its front page for the first time in April 1939.

The last of the two men to die was Lord Beaverbrook in 1964. In 1965 journalists who had spoken to Lord Beaverbrook—invariably on the telephone—could still recall every single word he had spoken. There were stories too about how Beaverbrook's rather active interest in young women had continued well past his seventieth birthday. Bob Edwards has described in *Goodbye Fleet Street* what it felt like to be the youthful editor of the *Daily Express* with the menacing voice of Beaverbrook interrupting your breakfast each morning.

But these two grand old press lords contributed substantially to the self-congratulation and lack of change which pervaded Fleet Street through the 1950s and into the 1960s. Lord Beaverbrook and Camrose belonged to an age in which ownership of British newspapers did not seem to lead on logically towards other media. Neither man liked the newfangled gadget of television. These old press lords did not even want to buy more newspapers; the logical way for a press lord to spend his time was in persecuting editors and politicians. Subsequent generations of newspaper owners had other things to occupy their time.

The dynamic William Berry (Lord Camrose) allowed his brother, Gomer (Lord Kemsley) to have the *Sunday Times*. Denis Hamilton, who was Lord Kemsley's personal assistant after 1945, is scathing about this regime:

> Territorial possessiveness and complacency were the hallmark of the *Sunday Times*. . . . Kemsley always dressed formally, even for the office— striped black silk tie and pearl tie pin. Stiff collars were worn by all his sons and I had to conform. . . . The only exception to Kemsley's strict etiquette was Ian Fleming. He always wore blue shirts, black ties and very dark blue suits. . . . In the words of one of our best provincial editors, Alastair Dunnett, it was 'a crumbling and preposterous empire', ruled by a deeply conservative Conservative who had succeeded in life by clinging to his brother's coat-tails and was then saved from real competition within the industry by the war. . . . Kemsley's sons were each given a Rolls Royce, jobs in the organisation, and expense accounts, as well as seats on the board.[1]

When Camrose died in 1954, the *Daily Telegraph* passed into the hands of the second son, a very shy Michael Berry:

> Michael was then forty-two: tall, dark and even in middle age painfully shy, with a habit of muttering very fast out of the right-hand corner of his mouth. . . . when he did laugh, he had a curious way of tucking the laugh back over his shoulder. He was essentially serious and hard-working, and endowed with a formidable sense of duty.[2]

Michael Berry, later Lord Hartwell, was the dominating force behind the *Telegraph* newspapers for three decades (1954–86); his management style involved close monitoring of the editorial, and a relative lack of interest in the business, side. Hartwell controlled,

---

[1] Denis Hamilton, *Editor-in-Chief* (London: Hamish Hamilton, 1989), 55, 59, 70, 72.
[2] Duff Hart-Davis, *The House the Berrys Built: Inside the Telegraph, 1928–1986* (London: Coronet Books, 1991), 187–8.

managed, and shaped his inheritance in an overall strategy which led ultimately to the forced sale to Conrad Black in 1986.

Lord Beaverbrook's control of the *Express* empire passed, on his death in 1964, to his son Max Aitken, who saw his task as continuing with Beaverbrook's policies. Aitken was diffident about his own political expertise (despite having been a Conservative Member of Parliament, 1945–50); he saw a need to have an editor with strong political credentials, an approach which compounded the *Express* newspapers' problems. Aitken may have seen himself as taking a back seat. One *Daily Express* journalist told me in 1967 that the main sign of deference to Aitken was the newspaper's obsessive editorial concern with powerboat racing (Aitken's hobby).

By the 1990s the last remaining example of a crown prince was presiding over the Mail group; this was the third Lord Rothermere, who inherited the Mail/Associated/Northcliffe group in 1971. His father, the second Lord Rothermere presided over the Mail group for nearly four decades (1932–71), a period during which the *Daily Mail* only maintained its circulation while the *Express* and *Mirror* circulations doubled and quadrupled respectively. The early years of the third Rothermere saw the group reverse its fortunes; Rothermere seems to have played a genuine part in this by backing some able executives (such as Mick Shields) and an able editor (David English). Subsequently Rothermere lived abroad for tax reasons and spent most of his time in Paris, Japan, and New York.

This pattern of crown prince ownership certainly shaped the Mail group in distinctive ways. There was an especially strong emphasis on maintaining editorial and commercial strength in the midmarket. The group's commercial status of the 1990s (with the market leading *Daily Mail* and *Mail on Sunday* and the monopoly *Evening Standard*) was greatly improved over the 1971 inheritance of the *Daily Mail*, *Daily Sketch*, and London *Evening News*, all three then in serious decline. The Mail group was also characterized by a willingness to accept only moderate levels of profit and a reluctance to acquire new properties. By the 1990s it had a self-confident management team who were happy to follow slightly unorthodox paths; for example the Flexo printing process was chosen over the more conventional litho printing on web offset presses

The crown prince pattern also involved the *Daily Mail* in

generously chronicling some of the more conventional aspects of Rothermere family life. This included the career of Rothermere's son Jonathan, who followed a common crown prince pattern by going to Glasgow to 'learn the business' at the Mirror Group's *Sunday Mail*.

Although the Lords Rothermere of the Mail group are the only dynasty which goes back a whole century (to the founding of the *Daily Mail* in 1896) there are crown prince and family dynasty elements in other companies, such as the Pearson/Financial Times group.

Even Rupert Murdoch, the grand acquisitor, had a significant crown prince strain in his early career. His father, Keith Murdoch, was a prominent Australian press personality and received a British knighthood. Rupert Murdoch started to 'learn the business' very young; he worked at the *Melbourne Herald* and at the British *Birmingham Gazette* even before entering Oxford University. He also worked on the London *Daily Express* immediately following his final exams. He then returned to Australia—shortly after his father's death—to take up his inheritance, which consisted primarily of the *News*, the then second daily newspaper in Adelaide.

We see here the 'owners' club' phenomenon allowing a crown prince to obtain youthful experience inside another newspaper company. We also see the crown prince obtaining an early breadth of experience which is not available to any other industry entrant. The British newspaper industry—not least because of its craft and union traditions—developed highly segmented career avenues; individuals typically spent their entire careers only in editorial, or only in advertising, or circulation, or production. But a crown prince by age 30 may have spent a year in each of these four areas, as well as having been introduced to highly specialized (but financially important) areas such as newsprint-buying.

At, say, age 30 the crown prince has an enormous advantage over ordinary mortals. A person of exceptional talent such as Rupert Murdoch builds on this. But a crown prince of only average ability has at age 30 an advantage over all of his age equals. It is only later—perhaps after age 40—that under British conditions the leading executives are starting to overtake the crown prince.

This pattern holds obvious dangers. A crown prince taking over in his forties may objectively be equal in competence to the other senior executives. But while their learning curve continues upwards—as they acquire experience of previously unknown areas of the business—the crown prince's competence may peak around age 40 and decline thereafter. Crown princes also seem extremely unwise about knowing when to retire.

II

Since the 1960s the media mogul pattern became one of two dominant ownership patterns in British newspapers. The pattern is exemplified by Rupert Murdoch, Robert Maxwell, and Conrad Black, but it was really pioneered in Britain by the Canadian, Roy Thomson.

The fully fledged media mogul has four characteristics: first, he *owns*; secondly, he *operates* (as chief executive) the media properties. Thirdly, he is a risk-taking *entrepreneur* and media empire builder. Fourthly, he has an idiosyncratic or *eccentric management style*, which may involve political motives.[3]

Thomson, Murdoch, Maxwell, and Black have all exhibited these four mogul characteristics. They have all operated their growing list of media properties through public companies in which they, as individuals, effectively owned (or controlled via family and friends) a majority of the voting shares. In the 1980s especially the march of the media moguls accelerated. The deregulation in Britain of both media and financial services turned newspapers into part of a major stock-market growth area. Moguls who were already specialists at acquiring other companies were able to borrow from banks and to accelerate their acquisition strategies. Murdoch in the late 1980s got into serious trouble in the form of massive bank debt and rising interest rates. Robert Maxwell, having paid too much and borrowed too much, resorted to grand illegality and finally suicide in 1991.

Mogul owners tend to build their acquisitions around their personal management and life-style. Rupert Murdoch only lived in London for about four years (1969–73) before moving to New York, and later to Los Angeles. His world commuter manager style, and his ravenous appetite for acquisitions, led to News Corporation's preference for a small number of big profit-earners in each of the chosen locations (Australia, UK, USA). The *Sun*, the

---

[3] Jeremy Tunstall and Michael Palmer, *Media Moguls* (London: Routledge, 1991).

News of the World, and later the *Sunday Times*, were an extremely profitable trio; the success of these newspapers (and the Australian newspapers) fuelled the profits and boosted the credit rating of News Corporation—and helped Rupert Murdoch to acquire more and more American media properties. This international pattern, which began in 1973, was established partly on the basis of Rupert Murdoch's life-style preference. He deliberately chose not to join the British establishment, not to enter the House of Lords, and to be only a visiting member of the *de facto* London newspaper owners' club. Murdoch's preference for moving his media acquisitions strategy ever westward had implications for both his British titles and the British newspaper industry. Murdoch's company strategy increasingly saw the British newspapers as profit-generators or 'cash cows'. The consequences of this strategy can be seen in the sales-driven belligerence of the *Sun*, and the *News of the World*, the advertising-driven fat of the *Sunday Times*, as well as in the frequent mood and editor changes at *The Times*.

The Telegraph properties in their turn came to reflect the quite different preferences and idiosyncrasies of Conrad Black. While Murdoch moved westward around the world, Conrad Black moved eastward; he first bought the *Telegraph* papers in London before buying the *Jerusalem Post* and becoming a major newspaper player in Australia. Conrad Black's personal style was more intellectual, more interested in politics for its own sake, and more subtle than Murdoch's preference for the frontal assault. Consequently, despite some radical management changes in the late 1980s the *Daily Telegraph* and *Sunday Telegraph* retained much of (perhaps too much of) their previous character. A military history enthusiast, Black chose a military historian journalist (Max Hastings) as his key editor. Conrad Black also made elaborate genuflections towards editorial sovereignty by writing occasional letters to the editor which (when published) indicated his disagreement with details of editorial policy. A more lengthy excursion in this direction was Conrad Black's December 1992 feature article which argued forcefully for short skirts:

> Like many men and almost all women, I have watched the struggle of some fashion houses and many fashion writers to proclaim the impending victory of the long skirt. Fashionable women enjoy change, and couture became so short it had to retreat. The textile and fashion industries obviously wish to avoid stagnation, so some new style must always be coming into vogue.

However, it is bunk to claim that long is in, short is out and anything above the knee, as The Daily Telegraph wrote of the Princess of Wales, is dowdy. The Princess has generally been rather demure and has been a faithful ambassador for the best of British fashion. Anyone visiting Annabel's, any of the more fashionable pre-Christmas parties, or the Pierre Hotel or Mortimer's in New York, or simply watching the general procession of fashion-aware women in London, New York, Paris or almost anywhere except North Korea, Teheran or Algiers, can observe a variety of lengths.[4]

Conrad Black's ponderous preference for short skirts and long sentences perhaps struck just the degree of eccentricity needed both to amuse and to charm the British establishment. It is difficult to imagine Rupert Murdoch engaging in such time-consuming hem-line interventions, with so little relevance to the bottom line.

While the media mogul is above all an individual, we can still list a number of consequences which flow from this individual's personal style and which have implications for newspaper management more generally:

- The media mogul specializes in acquisition; there are phases of stalking, the acquisition itself, and finally the digestion stage. The mogul is always stalking a number of prospects, but is also ready to decide quickly on surprise offers. Cost savings are sought in advance as part of the purchase deal. Digesting the deal involves further cost-cutting and usually putting in new top managers and editors.
- The mogul retains control by using bank finance; credit worthiness with the banks is more important than share price on the stock market. Hostile take-over is not a worry.
- The disparate company requires strong financial controls; while flying the Pacific the mogul can check on the London cash flow.
- The mogul uses the special cachet of newspaper ownership to maintain high-level business contacts; both the main board and the country boards have more illustrious part-time directors than this size of company would normally warrant.
- The mogul's business (and social) connections are used to

---

[4] Conrad Black, 'Hem wars: why the short should have it', *Daily Telegraph*, 31 Dec. 1992, 17.

acquire early business intelligence including early news of possible acquisition targets.

- The mogul also uses his easy access to top politicians, partly for fun, but also on a basis of mutual help-and-interest; the mogul is interested in top political support for future regulatory favours.
- The mogul is not afraid of making mistakes and failing to acquire properties. Shares purchased can be resold (often at a profit). At any one time the mogul is selling, as well as buying, companies.
- Technology is a means not an end; the mogul prefers safe rather than state-of-the-art technology. This leads to subsequent updating investment decisions.
- The mogul believes in the well-timed dramatic intervention—the surprising acquisition, the daring appointment of a very young editor, the huge price cut.
- The mogul keeps in personal contact—mainly on the telephone—with a dozen or so top managers and editors in each major location.

While the mogul style involves the mogul's personal intervention over a range of large and small items, the mogul pattern also depends heavily on a local management team of experienced and capable people. Thomson, Maxwell, Murdoch, and Black all had their teams of managers. Of this group Robert Maxwell was probably the least successful at developing managers. Roy Thomson had a reputation in the 1960s for having developed effective management in certain areas—especially in classified advertising, and in marketing and promotion. In more recent times the Murdoch/News company has generated the largest and most successful team of British media managers. Some of Murdoch's chief executives—like the editors—have not lasted long, but others have. There is a mix of long-stay as well as short-stay managers. The Murdoch management team seems to include a generous ration of Australians, Scots, and non-establishment Britons; but it has included Britons with élite backgrounds as well.

British newspaper management until 1986 was experienced within an internally segmented and largely unchanging industrial scene. Compared with this the Murdoch management was comparatively rich in non-British—mainly Australian and US—experience. The Murdoch/News company in effect was also an international management training school—which offered wider experience and wider career possibilities. 'Murdoch's Rottweilers' was one industry description of these managers. Self-confidence was a Murdoch manager's characteristic, one manager told me, 'because we're used to winning'.

III

The importance of the dominant personality was noted in 1966 in a report on the National Newspaper Industry by the Economist Intelligence Unit:

> When all allowances have been made for variations within the industry, its most striking feature, and possibly its greatest problem, is its dominance by a small number of highly individualistic proprietors with their own personal interests and philosophy of management. We use the term proprietor in this context to indicate the dominant personality in an organisation although some newspaper organisations are public companies or trusts.
>
> . . . In some organisations the essential drive and interest from the top is directed solely towards the editorial function, in others the proprietor has delegated functional responsibilities but has retained the authority which is necessary to let these functions operate efficiently.

This tradition of the 'dominant personality' has both continued and changed since the 1960s. Since the 1960s the central concern of the chief executive has switched from industrial relations to, as one chief executive said, 'marketing, maintaining your market share, promotion, and profitability'.

In the 1960s and 1990s some of the dominant personalities were not chief owners, but nevertheless acted as if they were. Cecil King in the 1960s was not the chief owner of the IPC/Mirror Group, but he acted in a truly king-like manner; he had played a key role in the growth of the *Daily Mirror* and in the creation of IPC—perhaps it was these achievements (plus his membership of the wider Harmsworth/Northcliffe/Rothermere family) which led him to develop such mogul-like behaviour. From his massive office on the top of the Mirror building, he wrote signed pronouncements for the *Daily Mirror* front page and—as a Labour supporter— intrigued ineptly against the Labour Prime Minister, Harold Wilson.

Two and three decades later there were fresh examples of the chief executive who behaved in a lordly mogul manner without being the chief owner; a good example was David (later Lord) Stevens. In a big company there is more than one level of chief executive. For example, the editor of the *Daily Express* has two chief executives above him. One is the managing director of Express Newspapers, which is only about one-quarter of the larger United News and Media. The Mail group has a separate managing director and management team for each of its three national newspapers. Express Newspapers has a single management team for its three dailies. News International also has a single management structure to encompass its five national newspapers; one circulation director, for example, is responsible for selling some 30 million newspapers each week.

The chief executives of the 1990s came from across the range of major newspaper areas; advertising, accountancy, circulation, and editorial backgrounds were common.

Compared with the newspaper managers interviewed in the late 1960s, their successors in 1994 could be described as macho managers. Graham Cleverley, who worked as a manager at the *Daily Mirror* and IPC in the 1960s, gave that management a central place in his subsequent 'study of mismanagement' in Fleet Street. He noted that in Fleet Street the two main industrial forces were the dominant general managers and the trade unions. The numerous and powerful trade unions always insisted on negotiating with the very top of the management hierarchy. Middle management, Cleverley pointed out, scarcely existed in newspapers.[5]

Advertising and circulation directors and managers of national newspapers, when interviewed in the late 1960s, made some lasting impressions on me. They tended to have had extremely narrow careers, often confined to a single department inside a single company. A number of late 1960s heads of advertising or circulation departments had worked in the same department since before 1939. Nearly all of these senior managers seemed less able, less energetic, and less articulate than the senior journalists in the same companies. Several were proud of extremely modest achievements, such as advertisement directors on popular newspapers who had just launched their first ever classified advertising pages.

Whereas the 1960s managers seemed apologetic and passive, the

---

[5] Graham Cleverley, *The Fleet Street Disaster: British National Newspapers as a Case Study in Mismanagement* (London: Constable and Beverly Hills, Calif.: Sage, 1976).

BOX 5.1. DAVID MONTGOMERY

David Montgomery became managing director in October 1992 of Mirror Group Newspapers (MGN), including the *Daily Mirror*, *Sunday Mirror*, *The People*, and the Glasgow *Daily Record*. He was aged 43. He is an example of a journalist becoming the chief executive of a big group.

Montgomery grew up in Northern Ireland and graduated from Queen's University, Belfast, with a degree in history and politics. He joined the Mirror journalism trainee scheme and became a sub-editor in the *Daily Mirror*'s then large Manchester office. He moved to the *News of the World* and was its editor, 1985–7. He was then moved to another Murdoch national, the recently acquired *Today*, which he edited 1987–91. *Today*'s sales rocketed upwards during 1987 and 1988 but then fell back. David Montgomery acquired a reputation as a workaholic dominating editor. He also became managing director of *Today* and after the paper moved into Wapping he was sacked in 1991 by Andrew Knight (another ex-journalist general manager who had just arrived from the Telegraph Group).

David Montgomery (while at the *News of the World*) had helped to persuade Rupert Murdoch to buy *Today* and during his last year as editor/chief executive had attempted a management buyout; he was also 'very interested' in *Today*'s financial coverage, and as editor he began to meet people in the City of London.

Montgomery had already tried (while at *Today*) to buy the *Belfast Newsletter* and also became involved in various television projects. While other journalists thought he was unemployed or doing something in television, Montgomery was pursuing the Mirror Group. This was the time after Robert Maxwell's death when the current *Daily Mirror* editor, Richard Stott, launched a very public (and unsuccessful) management buyout involving other journalists. David Montgomery much more quietly was pursuing his own attempt to buy the group, and he was touring the City banks and institutions, trying to raise the money. But the Maxwell creditors (led by NatWest Bank) wanted to put in their own team to run the Mirror Group, in order to bring it back to profitability and saleability, thus making it possible to recover their money. Montgomery's buyout efforts had been sufficiently convincing for him to be offered the chief executive job.

When Montgomery's name was announced on 22 October 1992 the reaction among *Mirror* journalists was one of shock. Here was a Murdoch-trained reactionary Ulster Unionist being brought in to savage the Mirror Group. Most Mirror Group journalists staged an imme-

Continued

diate sit-down strike. But Montgomery gave written assurances and the strike was called off, without a day's papers being lost. Sitting in Maxwell's chair on the top floor, Montgomery calmly planned the next stage of his coup. He sacked the editors of all three national papers; a hundred freelance journalists were also dispensed with and several stars soon departed—some of them going to the Mirror-in-Exile at *Today*.

Montgomery continued to make huge cuts in all areas of the Mirror organization. The papers moved to Canary Wharf and Montgomery gave a number of senior jobs to people who had worked with him previously at *Today*. Circulations continued to fall, but the Mirror Group came back quite quickly to substantial profit. By 1994 MGN acquired a big minority slice of the *Independent* papers, took over their management, and moved them to Canary Wharf. MGN also started to invest in television.

'David's a bit like a shark; if he smells blood, he just can't help himself', a journalist told me. 'You can't afford to bleed in front of him. . . . once he sees weakness, it's goodbye. He's very Darwinian, it's the survival of the fittest . . . He came from the *Mirror* originally; it was the last to be reformed. He was ruthless.'

1990s managers were confident and saw themselves as aggressive innovators. They were part of newspaper companies which even in poor years were profitable. In 1993—a weak year for the UK economy—the Mirror Group and News International had operating (post tax) profits of 24 per cent and 23 per cent respectively. The Telegraph group had a turnover of £242,600 per employee; chief executives of the six leading groups were apparently earning salaries of £400,000 and upwards,[6] plus bonuses and share options.

The hard bargaining was no longer with trade unions but with newsprint suppliers, with wholesalers, and with advertisers. After 1986, computerization transformed most British newspaper departments, not least circulation. In the 'bad old days' of the 1960s newspapers shipped papers by train to their wholesalers but had relatively little reliable knowledge as to how many were actually purchased by the public; even sales on different days of the week were not accurately known. By the 1990s the entire wholesaling area had been computerized and—with compatible newspaper/wholesaler systems—newspaper circulation directors said they knew how many copies each retailer was selling each and every day.

[6] 'It's a rich man's world', *Newspaper Focus* (June 1994), 16–23.

Wholesaling was reformed after 1986, with News International taking the lead; the main change was greatly to reduce the total number of wholesalers. A smaller number of larger wholesalers received a bigger total amount of money, but a lower percentage of the sale price. While more retail outlets (such as supermarkets and filling stations) carried newspapers, the number of independent wholesalers had sharply reduced.

In advertising, also, there is a struggle between heavyweights. Bigger newspaper groups confront bigger advertising-purchasing units in the form of specialist buying agencies, which claim sizeable bulk discounts. In some cases newspaper companies sign annual contracts in advance to carry a certain large volume at a certain discounted price. All newspaper advertising is heavily discounted from 'rate card', with the sole exception, it says, of the *Financial Times*. Certainly the *Daily Mail*, which has a reputation for being an exceptionally hard bargainer, admits to substantial discounting, but still exercises—it claims—its prerogative as a market leader to charge more per thousand readers than does its rival the *Daily Express*. The latter paper claims to operate a different policy, selling a bigger quantity at a somewhat lower price.

The big ownerships are not the only ones who pride themselves on competitive aggression. The *Guardian*, for example, despite its editorial stance is admired in the newspaper business world for the aggressive manner in which it has developed its left-of-centre,

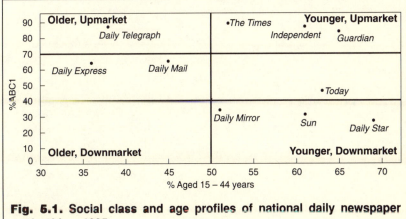

Fig. 5.1. Social class and age profiles of national daily newspaper readerships, 1995

Source: National Readership Survey, Jan.-June 1995.

upmarket, young audience. In 1994 it became the first British newspaper to carry one million column centimetres (or 10 kilometres) of recruitment advertising, three times as much as the *Daily Telegraph*. This classified strength was developed by Caroline Marland, who joined The *Guardian* in 1976. Marland wanted to make the point that advertisers should appeal to The *Guardian*'s readers, who were in the job-seeking age brackets, and should ignore the *Daily Telegraph*, whose readers were too old to be looking for new jobs. The resulting 1983 trade press advertising campaign showed *Daily Telegraph* readers in wheelchairs.

While all of the managements have much more assertive commercial management than in the past, it is the Murdoch/News managers who have been most successful and seem to be most admired in the industry. A number of senior management, as well as editorial, people have moved from the Murdoch/News company to the Mirror Group. But the Murdoch management diaspora spreads still more widely; if the Wapping managers can be described as rottweilers, then the same breed of animal inhabits Canary Wharf, the Isle of Dogs, and the whole of national newspaper management across London.

6 Sovereign Editors and Editor-Managers

THERE have been two major patterns of editorship in British national newspapers in the twentieth century. Up to 1960 an upmarket or élite pattern of sovereign editorship grew less and less common, but still survived, especially at *The Times*. The second, and increasingly the standard, pattern up to 1960 was of the press lord—or other dominant owner or personality—who employed an editor-manager to run the editorial department.

Both of these patterns had changed quite radically by the 1980s and 1990s. A new pattern of the entrepreneurial editor has emerged at all three market levels—an editor who combines creative and business skills and who, subject to successful performance, is allowed a high degree of autonomy. The next chapter focuses on this pattern. This chapter looks at British national newspaper editorship in the 1960s and 1970s, using interviews I conducted with sixteen editors[1] of national daily and Sunday newspapers during 1966–8.

Each national press has its distinctive history and ideology of editorship, managing editorship, directorship—or whatever the precise term may be. In the British history and ideology of editorship *The Times* newspaper has had a special place; *The Times* developed an ideology of sovereign editorship in the decades before 1855 under conditions of effective monopoly. *The Times* editorship was modelled partly on the man of letters, partly on the aristocratic politician, but especially on the lawyer-barrister. John Delane (editor of *The Times*, 1841–77) trained as a barrister and Fleet Street was always a street of lawyers as well as of journalists and writers. There was also an element of the sermon; the anonymous 'leading article' or editorial was the editor's pulpit.

---

[1] Oliver Boyd-Barrett also participated in five of the sixteen.

The Times editor idea was followed by many other British publications, national and local. But the actual editing was anonymous: although John Delane was well known to the leading politicians in London, most readers in the country did not know the name of the editor. There was a strong element of secrecy and mystery. *The Times* editor was indeed sovereign in terms of editorial opinion. John Delane oversaw a thin newspaper, much of which was taken up with classified advertising and reports of political speeches, and with court reports and sport as the main lighter items. He exerted absolute control over opinion and letters (like a present-day 'editorial page editor'); but he also worked long past midnight, reading and editing proofs. Delane was both an opinion editor and what British journalists today would call a hands-on 'back-bench' editor.

What *The Times* editor did not get his hands onto was money—possibly because the London lawyer-barrister model assigned money transactions to a separate occupational category of clerks. It was the manager, not the editor, who employed foreign correspondents whose use of new technology (such as the cable-telegram system) involved sizeable sums of money.

Another key financial aspect—also shrouded in secrecy and mystery—was that *The Times* formula through the Victorian period increasingly became a money-losing formula. *The Times* and its high-minded sovereign editor increasingly required subsidy, in addition to the normal subsidies of the advertising and general printing.[2] This need for subsidy became a continuing theme through the twentieth century. *The Times* continued to need subsidy and was 'rescued' no less than four times—by Lord Northcliffe (1908), by Jacob Astor (1922), by Lord Thomson (1966–7), and by Rupert Murdoch (1981).

The sovereign editorship of the high-minded newspapers required subsidy, and the other examples of such newspapers died out in the early decades of the century. But variations on the sovereign editor theme were subsequently seen in other publications, such as the *Guardian*, *Observer*, and *Independent*.

The second major British editorial tradition is of the editor-manager. This figure was well known in the Victorian period and was standard in, for example, local evening newspapers.

[2] Jeremy Tunstall, '"Editorial Sovereignty" in the British Press', in Oliver Boyd-Barrett, Colin Seymour-Ure, and Jeremy Tunstall, *Studies on the Press* (London: HMSO for Royal Commission on the Press, 1977), 249–341.

Northcliffe's *Daily Mail* (of 1896) and other midmarket papers adopted the editor-manager as part of the commercial newspaper approach. In some respects the editor-manager was the precise opposite of the sovereign editor: he carried out the orders of the presiding owner or press lord. But in another key respect the editor-manager concept copied the sovereign editor concept. The editor-manager exerted absolute control downwards within the editorial department. Editorial discipline was given a military or maritime absoluteness. The editor was the captain on the bridge answerable to the owner-on-shore; but aboard ship—within the editorial department—the editor was accorded extraordinary powers.

Thus within British journalism all newspaper editors had commanding powers. Journalists had no professional defences against editorial power—with the partial exception of the high tide of trade unionism, which happened to fall into the 1960–80 era of transition.

But, broadly speaking, all journalists always accepted that 'the editor's word is law'. A product which is created fresh each day requires quick and firm decisions. Journalists willingly accord editors legitimacy; the legitimacy of owners is accepted more grudgingly. The need for a strong editor is thus recognized by both journalists and owners and is justified both within commercial and non-commercial traditions.

I

The 1960s was a decade of rapid change; television was now a huge phenomenon and the trade press was carrying articles about web-offset printing and editorial computer systems. In 1965 I attended a London meeting of the International Press Institute at which several American newspaper publishers discussed their already installed editorial and advertising computer systems.

The editors whom I interviewed in 1968 felt that their editorial authority was being eroded. There was objective evidence that editorship was insecure; while the self-satisfied *Daily Mirror* had only one editor (Lee Howard) in the 1960s, the *Daily Mail* had three editors in the decade, and the *Daily Express* had four, or five if you count Bob Edwards's two separate spells as editor. Edwards had been fired twice by Beaverbrook—with a spell in exile in

Glasgow in between; he told me (in 1968) that during his four years as *Daily Express* editor he had fired 'only three or four' people, out of a journalist staff of over 400.

Editors in the 1960s recognized a growing trade union strength, which meant that 'you can't sack journalists, you can only move them sideways'. Meanwhile owners, managers, and companies seemed to be getting bigger. Some editors also believed that the Labour government of Harold Wilson was threatening press freedom. Discussions of such issues in the 1960s were somewhat frustrated by the fact that 1939–59 had been two decades of little or no industrial change. For most of these two decades newsprint had been rationed, television had not yet made much impact, and there had been no change in technology. While several of the 1968 editors had distinguished war records from 1939–45, most had no personal experience of 1930s, pre-war, journalism.

Consequently it was difficult for editors to grasp what the key changes were. There was also a strong impression of men (they were all male) who had learned their journalism in the unchanging 1940s and 1950s, and were ill equipped for the rapid changes of the television era, following the newspaper closures around 1960.

The most conspicuous editor-manager of the mid-century was Arthur Christiansen, who edited the *Daily Express* (1933–57) through its most successful period. Christiansen provided the attractive editorial packaging and the entertainment,[3] while Beaverbrook dominated the politics and the heavier news. For the next three decades after Christiansen the *Daily Express* was to have a new editor every three years. I interviewed three of Christiansen's successors and they were very different people with different editorial styles. Lord Beaverbrook chose in Edward Pickering (1957–62) an editor with strong sub-editing and managing editor experience at the *Mail* and *Express*. In sharp contrast, Bob Edwards had previously edited the left-wing weekly *Tribune* and had not served a long sub-editing and back-bench apprenticeship.

After Beaverbrook died, his son (Max Aitken) appointed Derek Marks (editor 1965–71), who did have strong Conservative views and an outstanding political journalism track record, but also lacked sub-editing and production experience. In a 1968 interview Derek Marks[4] spoke enthusiastically about *Express* political report-

---

[3] Arthur Christiansen, *Headlines All My Life* (London: Heinemann, 1961).
[4] Based on author's interviews with Edward Pickering, 1 Feb. 1966, with Robert Edwards, 11 Sept. 1968, and with Derek Marks, 12 Aug. 1968.

ing, but had little to say about sport, crime, showbusiness, or the *Daily Express*'s then still high reputation for pictures and news presentation.

In the *Sunday Express* offices upstairs was the long-stay (1954–86) editor, John Junor, who shared many of Beaverbrook's ideas and his Old Testament writing style. While he favoured an attacking political style, most of the *Sunday Express* reflected John Junor's belief that readers wanted glitzy consumer fantasy mixed with tales of patriotism and bravery at sea. The cramped conditions in Junor's own office, and the slightly threadbare low-slung armchair from which the visitor looked up at the editor, contrasted uncomfortably with the spacious, glossy, and heroic world projected in the newspaper.[5]

The third Beaverbrook paper, the London *Evening Standard*, was edited in the usual cramped and dank Beaverbrook office conditions. Charles Wintour, the upmarket editor (1959–77) of this most upmarket of post-war London evening papers,[6] was clearly the most autonomous and successful editor in the group.[7]

The editorial atmosphere at the *Daily Mirror* and its stable mates was quite different. This was 1968, still one year before Rupert Murdoch's purchase of the *News of the World* and the *Sun* was to shatter the calm satisfaction of the Mirror Group editors. One remarkable feature of the IPC/Mirror group was its willingness to re-employ editors discarded by Beaverbrook—such as Edward Pickering and Bob Edwards—and to employ the mighty Christiansen's son, Michael, as editor of the *Sunday Mirror*.

IPC/Mirror 1960s orthodoxy clearly saw the editor as an editor-manager in a management structure. Above the editors the key figures in the ascending hierarchy were Edward Pickering (editorial director), Hugh Cudlipp, and Cecil King. The *Daily Mirror* editor was Lee Howard, a large relaxed man with red braces and much charm; Howard was the very model of an editor rather pleased with his then still 5 million circulation.[8]

Michael Christiansen at the *Sunday Mirror* and Bob Edwards at the *People* (in 1968) were both equally pleased with their 5 million Sunday sales. Bob Edwards—after his traumatic experiences with Beaverbrook and the *Daily Express*—had found himself a quieter

[5] Author's interview with John Junor, 10 Sept. 1968.
[6] Charles Wintour, *Pressures on the Press* (London: Andre Deutsch, 1972).
[7] Based on author and Oliver Boyd-Barrett interview with Charles Wintour, 7 Aug. 1968.
[8] Author and Oliver Boyd-Barrett interview with Lee Howard, 23 Aug. 1968.

and more comfortable editorship. He was still not interested in sport and not deeply involved in the *People*'s currently very active investigations of corruption. Bob Edwards later edited the *Sunday Mirror* until 1986, when he handed over to Mike Molloy.

Mike Molloy was himself editor of the *Daily Mirror* for a decade, starting in 1975. An interview with him in 1976 indicated that competition from the *Sun* had not greatly changed the Mirror Group style of editorship.[9] The Mirror Group in 1976 had been owned by Reed during most of the *Sun*'s circulation rise under Murdoch ownership. Mike Molloy in May 1976 had been editor of the *Daily Mirror* for six months. He had made no dramatic attempt to repel the *Sun* (which had a 1975 sale of 3.44 million against the *Daily Mirror*'s 4.02 million). Molloy said he believed in gradual change, but he had not introduced any promotable new items nor had he employed any new star names. The Mirror Group was evidently continuing with its conception of the editor located in a hierarchy; a previous *Daily Mirror* editor, Tony Miles, was now Molloy's boss as editorial director. There was an element of collective leadership involving senior journalists such as Terence Lancaster and Geoffrey Goodman, and a close political relationship with the then Labour government. Two years later in 1978, the *Sun* finally passed the *Daily Mirror* circulation.

II

In the late 1960s the sovereign editor concept—self-consciously building on the past practice at *The Times*—was still found in William Rees-Mogg's editorship of *The Times* and David Astor's *Observer*. The Monopolies Commission panel members, whose report of 1966 argued that Lord Thomson should be allowed to buy *The Times*, were well aware of what had happened to *The Times*'s tradition in the interwar period.[10] An awkward fact was that sovereign editors had in the 1930s been leading appeasers of Hitler.[11] Geoffrey Dawson at *The Times*, J. L. Garvin at the *Observer*, and

[9] Author and Colin Seymour-Ure interview with Michael Molloy and Terence Lancaster (political editor), 25 May 1976.

[10] The panel included Lord Francis-Williams, who had edited the *Daily Herald*, and Donald Tyerman, who had been an assistant editor of *The Times*. Monopolies Commission, *The Times Newspaper and The Sunday Times Newspaper* (London: HMSO, 1966).

[11] Richard Cockett, *Twilight of Truth: Chamberlain, Appeasement and the Manipulation of the Press* (London: Weidenfeld and Nicolson, 1989).

W. W. Hadley at the *Sunday Times* were all active appeasers. In each case the relevant owner had granted the editor extraordinary powers. These three individuals served, between them, seventy-six years in their sovereign editorial chairs. Under Geoffrey Dawson sovereign editorship was taken to extremes, partly because (having been sacked previously by Northcliffe) he had a special contract which gave him absolute editorial power over *The Times*; Dawson's case was also extreme because he altered the tradition by being his own foreign editor and he then perverted the tradition by censorship of reports from Germany.[12]

During the 1940s era of newsprint rationing and in the 1950s the sovereign editorship had continued at *The Times* along less controversial lines. Sir William Haley edited the paper for fifteen years (1952–67); he introduced a more collegial version of the sovereign idea, but the tradition of sovereign editorship was followed all too faithfully on the financial dimension, meaning that by Haley's last year (1966) *The Times* needed a new financial saviour.

When William Rees-Mogg took on *The Times* editorship in January 1967 at the age of 38 he defined his role as being mainly a presider over opinion. In a 1968 interview[13] he said that his role was 'to assist, to advise and to encourage'. His focus was on opinion and much of the running of the paper was 'delegated' to the home editor (John Grant) and to other news executives including those in charge of business, foreign, and sports news.

During another interview a decade later in 1976 William Rees-Mogg said that he only directly controlled the leader writers and the letters-to-the-editor operation. He himself was then writing about sixty 'leading articles' per year.[14] He also met the letters editor each day at 3 p.m. to make the final selection of letters for publication. I observed the process in action one day in May 1976; Geoffrey Woolley, the letters editor, had already selected about twenty letters. Rees-Mogg gave each one an extremely quick read, saying simply 'Yes' or 'No'. Most of the Yes letters focused on just two topics. Rees-Mogg indicated which two letters would lead the two topics and across how many columns; the full process involving twenty letters took about thirty minutes.[15]

---

12 Iverach McDonald, *The History of The Times*, v: *Struggles in War and Peace, 1939–1966* (London. Times Books, 1984), 12 19.

13 Author and Oliver Boyd-Barrett interview with William Rees-Mogg, 27 Aug. 1968.

14 Author and Colin Seymour-Ure interview with William Rees-Mogg, 27 May. 1976.

15 'The Times letters: a visit', in Jeremy Tunstall, 'Letters to the Editor', in Boyd-Barrett *et al., Studies on the Press*, 241–8.

Between 1968 and 1976 William Rees-Mogg's editorial style seemed, if anything, to have gone further in the direction of delegation. He was still presiding over a somewhat awkward mix of long-serving *Times* journalists and his fellow interlopers who had arrived from the Thomson *Sunday Times* a mere eleven years ago. Several of the newer senior appointments had Conservative grandee connections—for example, Charles Douglas-Home,[16] who was currently assistant editor (home news); Douglas Hogg[17] was a young lawyer currently providing legal advice in the office.

William Rees-Mogg in 1976 described his working week as being 11 a.m. to 7.30 p.m., Monday to Friday with an earlier departure on Friday. Rees-Mogg also believed in maintaining both lunch-time and dinner-time contact with the political and business worlds. He was out at meetings and dinners about three nights a week and thought that occasional speeches and a certain amount of appearing on television were important. 'There is a need for the public to have some idea of the sort of thoughts that the editor of *The Times* has.' Looking back on his editorship from the vantage-point of 1994, Rees-Mogg told me: 'I was a lazy editor . . . otherwise you miss important people. Also a certain amount of solitude is necessary.'

In 1976 *The Times* had a fixed ration of 17 full editorial pages regardless of the amount of advertising, and Rees-Mogg expressed his satisfaction with this amount. He was not unduly worried that the *Daily Telegraph* had a significantly larger number of journalists. In terms of editorial innovations, Rees-Mogg spoke with some satisfaction of a decision to emphasize the centrality of 'text' in *The Times*; this had involved reducing the number of pictures and using longer headlines in smaller type. He also said that choosing a cartoonist was difficult, because you needed a cartoonist suitable for the distinctive atmosphere of *The Times*; so far he had only found Marc (Mark Boxer), whose mini-size cartoons were acceptable.

This somewhat passive editorial style—outside Rees-Mogg's idiosyncratic Conservative political opinions—was paralleled by the approach of Denis Hamilton, the 'editor-in-chief'. Rees-Mogg was the first *Times* editor ever to serve under an editor-in-chief. Rees-Mogg indicated that Hamilton interfered very little and that

---

[16] Later editor of *The Times*.
[17] Son of Lord Hailsham and later a Conservative Minister.

his main role was as 'chairman' (or general manager of all aspects) of Times Newspapers. Denis Hamilton's own account matches Rees-Mogg's, although Hamilton in retrospect thought the Rees-Mogg editorship a failure:

William undoubtedly lacked the sort of drive which would have made the *Times* take off, but I defended him before Roy [Thomson] and others because I admired him for the qualities he did have, and which gave the newspaper a solid, dependable feel . . .

. . . It was obvious that he was most at home with those who had good degrees from Oxbridge or shared his interests in antiquarian books, for instance—and he didn't really put himself out to get to know the rest. This didn't adversely affect the paper—many reporters like to be left alone to get on with their job—but it didn't give *The Times* the sort of collective cutting edge it needed if it was to claw back readers from the *Guardian, Daily Telegraph* and *Financial Times*. His great strength was the leader page, especially when he was on form—you might not agree with what he said on economic affairs or the Common Market, but he had a wonderfully incisive pen. . . . But he was largely uninterested in news and sport, which put a brake on what was and wasn't possible in pushing up the circulation.[18]

It did not occur to Denis Hamilton that he himself might be responsible for this failure. Up to 1966 William Rees-Mogg had been officially 'deputy editor' of the *Sunday Times*, but he in practice edited that newspaper. While Denis Hamilton was officially the editor he was already somewhat at arm's length from the *Sunday Times*. He had long been (as Lord Kemsley's personal assistant) a manager rather than a working journalist. But this working arrangement, when carried over into *The Times*, meant that neither Denis Hamilton nor William Rees-Mogg had responsibility for a long-term editorial plan.

The other main sovereign editorship of the day at the *Observer* took a different form. Here David Astor was indeed sovereign because he was the *Observer*'s owner-editor for twenty-seven years (1948–75). When Astor became editor in 1948, he was taking over a primarily arts-and-opinion weekly, which during the war years had employed such writers as George Orwell. It was David Astor who turned the *Observer* into a general newspaper. He was interested in world news, domestic politics, and the arts; but mainly in terms of comment and discussion rather than of hard or exclusive

---

[18] Denis Hamilton, *Editor-in-Chief* (London: Hamish Hamilton, 1989), 143–4.

news. *The Observer* in its golden years after 1948 was greatly helped by the then weak (Kemsley) regime at the *Sunday Times*.

David Astor believed in hiring intellectuals who could write well; they were then loosed off to provide readable discussions of current events and issues. He believed in the 'Exclusive by Interpretation'. In his early days Astor hired mainly amateur, not professional, journalists. In the 1940s the *Observer* was especially well supplied with emigré intellectuals such as Isaac Deutscher. In the 1950s his journalists were often hired straight from Oxford or suggested by his friends in the liberal establishment; a few were suggested by the British Foreign Office, including the spy Kim Philby (who was shared with *The Economist*) before he defected to the Soviet Union. By the 1960s Astor was taking on more journalists who already had newspaper experience.

The *Observer* is now spreading out because it has to. Astor says that when he took over, it was just politics, foreign, books and arts. In the last 20 years he has added, or greatly expanded Features, Sport, Business and Fashion, as well as the colour magazine. . . .

He likes Roy Thomson as a person, but Roy is commercializing the *Sunday Times* and being brazenly honest about it. He (Astor) is following the *Sunday Times* part of the way. But he still insists on more public integrity and will not allow *Observer* journalists to write advertising-related 'puff pieces'.[19]

David Astor was unusually relaxed, compared with other editors, about his staff swapping material with competing journalists. Astor said that his star colour writer, Patrick O'Donovan, had one major reporting technique—talking to other journalists.

The *Observer*'s first editorial (Tuesday) conference of the week was more like a rather noisy academic seminar than an editorial planning meeting. New arrivals wondered at, and old hands complained about, the endemic state of chaos. David Astor claimed to believe that a lack of discipline and order was necessary in order to keep the creative juices flowing in his writers.[20] David Astor in 1968, while admitting his anxiety about competition from the Thomson *Sunday Times*, also told this writer that the main casualty would be the *Sunday Telegraph*, which would close within five years. But in fact within seven years David Astor's own editorship

---

[19] Author's interview with David Astor, 10 Sept. 1968.
[20] Richard Cockett, *David Astor and The Observer* (London: Andre Deutsch, 1991).

was at an end, and two years later the heavy losses led to the sale of the *Observer*.

The 1970s was the last decade for the old style of sovereign editorship.

III

At the *Telegraph* papers another variant of the sovereign editor idea lived on through the 1970s and died in the 1980s. The sovereign editor here was the owner, Lord Hartwell, who called himself 'editor-in-chief' and who was the chairman of the Telegraph company. But there was also an 'editor'. Figure 6.1 uses the description 'Editor (Policy)'. This editor was then really an 'Editorial Page Editor' as found in the USA and some other national systems. At the *Telegraph*, however, while of course all journalists and other employees understood the reality, the outside world including politicians found in 'the editor' a rather grand personage who may have seemed to be similar to the editor of *The Times*.

At the top of the chart (and at the top of the Telegraph building) was Lord Hartwell, the owner and Editor-in-chief. Below Hartwell were three key executives—one in charge of the business side, one the news, and one the opinion and political side. In the 1960s the *Daily Telegraph* placed a massive emphasis on news and devoted relatively limited space to the expression of (Conservative) opinion. In the late 1960s the editor was Maurice Green, who like his predecessor (Sir Colin Coote) was a product of Rugby School, Oxford University, and *The Times*. Maurice Green was an extremely able and straightforward man who when interviewed in 1968 made no attempt to hide the fact that though 'editor' he was only in charge of the small fraction of the *Daily Telegraph* devoted to leaders, letters to the editor, and the then very thin features provision. Also present at this interview was S. R. Pawley, the managing editor in charge of news and production; Pawley answered most of our questions—which largely concerned his massive areas of responsibility and his oversight of at least 80 per cent of the paper's journalists.

The same *Daily Telegraph* editorial system was still operating in 1976, although by now the managing editor presiding over most of the journalists was Peter Eastwood, the former chief sub-editor and night editor. The editor now was William Deedes, the

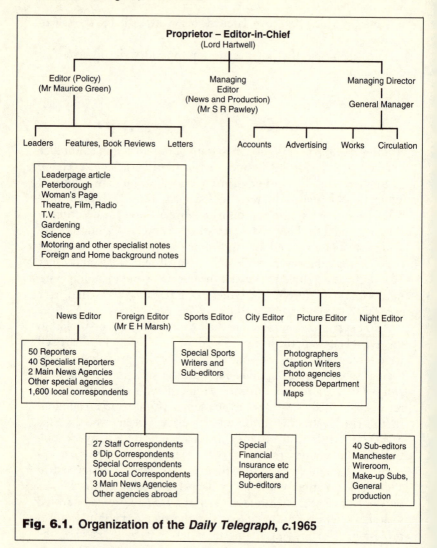

Fig. 6.1. Organization of the *Daily Telegraph*, *c*.1965

distinguished journalist-politician. Deedes became editor in 1974 at the age of 61 and edited the *Daily Telegraph* until the Black take-over in 1986. Bill Deedes was on the old *Morning Post* in the 1930s as a war correspondent in Abyssinia and briefly as a political (lobby) correspondent. He spent the years 1950–74 as a Conservative MP (and Cabinet Minister, 1962–4) before returning to journalism.

Lord Hartwell in 1974 chose him as his *Daily Telegraph* editor and envoy to the political world. For twelve years Deedes cheerfully put up with Hartwell's restricted definition of the editor's role; there was some minor disputation over border areas, but throughout this period at least 80 per cent of the pages and journalists (including their recruitment and deployment) remained under the control of Peter Eastwood, the managing editor. Peter Eastwood had a classic Fleet Street sub-editor's North of England background; educated at Batley Grammar School, he worked on the local *Batley News* and then the *Yorkshire Evening News*, before two years on Arthur Christiansen's *Daily Express* and then the *Daily Mail*. After some colourful war service in South-East Asia, Eastwood spent twenty-four years on the *Daily Telegraph*, before becoming managing editor in 1970:

he demonstrated unrelenting concern for production standards which made him admired, feared, even hated by colleagues. . . .

Under the ownership of Lord Hartwell, a system of divided command, with the Editor adopting a reflective, relaxed approach to the pages of opinion, and the Managing Editor exercising rigorous control over the tightly packaged news columns, gave the Telegraph an unchanging yet supple formula.[21]

Thus spoke Peter Eastwood's obituary in the *Daily Telegraph*. Another account describes him as 'the most hated man' ever to work at the newspaper.[22] This aggressive and hated, but extremely effective, managing editor ran Lord Hartwell's news machine inside the Telegraph building; meanwhile Bill Deedes, whom Duff Hart-Davis quite fairly describes as 'intelligent, civilised, amusing, with an intimate knowledge of politics', was the public face and opinionated voice of the *Daily Telegraph*.[23]

In 1976 Deedes confirmed that he was only in charge of the anonymous editorial 'leaders', the letters to the editor, the obituaries, and the features. At that time the *Daily Telegraph*'s features were still very limited, but he did control such political and humorous items as Peterborough, Peter Simple, and the cartoonist (Nicholas Garland). In 1975–6 the *Daily Telegraph* was averaging about 30 weekday pages; 16 full-page equivalents were devoted to

---

[21] 'Peter Eastwood', obituary, *Daily Telegraph*, 10 June 1991.

[22] Duff Hart-Davis, *The House the Berrys Built: Inside the Telegraph 1928–1986* (London. Coronet Books, 1991), 261–4.

[23] Ibid. 314.

editorial[24] and of these Deedes controlled about three whole pages. He had recently tried unsuccessfully, he said, to acquire control of the news page opposite the editorial page.

One of Bill Deedes's major concerns in his first two years as editor had been to shake up the letters to the editor. Too many published letters in the recent past had been 'just one long moan' of readers complaining that things aren't what they used to be. I was allowed to attend one of Deedes's weekly letters conferences;[25] the meeting was attended by the letters editor and deputy, the features editor, and one leader writer. Deedes encouraged discussion and jokes on a wide range of international and domestic political issues. He observed about the Loch Ness Monster that only those who were trying to be serious could be funny about the Monster.

Bill Deedes did not attend the main 5.30 p.m. editorial conference (which was presided over by Peter Eastwood). Deedes was not a director of the Telegraph company and he did not know whether the paper operated on a fixed formula of advertising to editorial pages. He was, however, widely consulted by a range of senior editorial and business personnel; he worked a five-day week, commuting each day by train to and from Ashford, Kent; he was not chauffeured in a company car and other journalists recall seeing the editor of the *Daily Telegraph* at the bus-stop in Fleet Street, waiting for a bus to the station. Mr Deedes came to town on the 9 a.m. train from Ashford, reading *The Times*, *Guardian*, *Express*, and *Mail* on the journey. He arrived at the Telegraph around 10.40 a.m. and departed at about 10.15 p.m. He saw Lord Hartwell at around 6 p.m. each day. Deedes described Hartwell as being 'a bit lonely' on his top floor with his news agency ticker machines. Deedes was always involved in choosing the front-page lead story and picture.

While he did lunch and dine out politically, Deedes said he preferred to invite politicians and others the short distance to Fleet Street; on most weekdays at either midday or mid-evening a promi-

---

[24] Denis McQuail, *Analysis of Newspaper Content* (London: HMSO for the Royal Commission on the Press, 1977), 15–16.

[25] This passage is based on the author's and Colin Seymour-Ure's interview with William Deedes on 20 May 1976, and on my separate visit to a *Telegraph* letters conference which was followed by a discussion with Deedes. Following this I had a brief meeting with Peter Eastwood: 'The Managing Editor tells me that he is responsible for the entire news coverage, including the foreign news, and also for the whole sub-editing side.'

nent visitor would be found in the editor's office talking to the paper's leader writers and one or two other journalists. Deedes said that he mainly invited Conservative politicians, but also Labour politicians and trade union leaders. Two recent drinks guests in 1976 had been Anthony Crosland (then Foreign Secretary and just back from a visit to China) and Margaret Thatcher (then Opposition Leader).

While this variation on the sovereign editor theme did combine editorial and business decisions in one place, the approach shared some weaknesses with *The Times*. There was too much emphasis on editorial sovereignty, separate from business planning, and Lord Hartwell allowed the business position to deteriorate. Editorial power itself was too rigidly split between a lofty editor-in-chief, an editor of opinion, and the dictator of the newsroom and the sub-editors. Finally the Telegraph sovereign editorship did not know when to hand on to the next generation: 'by 1984 he [Hartwell] was seventy-three; his brother Camrose was seventy-five, Deedes was seventy-one, Eastwood seventy-two, Stephen [managing director] sixty-eight, Holland [finance director] the same'.[26] Journalists tend to believe that personalities are crucial. Here the system broke down because the personalities and personal chemistry were too inflexible. Two years later this seventies-plus team—together with their elderly journalists and elderly readers—collapsed into the arms of Conrad Black.

IV

Three new 1970s patterns of editorship will now be considered; two of these were in upmarket papers, the *Sunday Times* and the *Guardian*. The third was in the *Daily Mail*.

At the *Sunday Times* Harold Evans further refined an editorial product which had already reached and passed its peak of circulation success before he became editor in January 1967. I first interviewed Harold Evans a year earlier, when he was editor of the *Northern Echo* in Darlington.[27] Although he had not yet worked in

---

[26] Hart-Davis, *The House the Berrys Built*, 356.

[27] Author's interview with Harold Evans in Darlington on 10 Dec. 1965, the very day on which he was telling the *Northern Echo* journalists of his imminent departure to the *Sunday Times*. I was present in the *Sunday Times* during the General Election campaign period of Mar. 1966, and also interviewed Harold Evans on 18 Sept. 1968, during his second year as editor.

London, he was known for two things—for his editorial campaign to achieve a pardon for Timothy Evans (no relation), who had been executed for a murder he did not commit; secondly for his appearances on national television presenting *What the Papers Say*. He came to the attention of Denis Hamilton, who himself came from the North-East of England and (who told me that he) had maintained contacts in that region with politicians and journalists. Harold Evans went to the *Sunday Times* initially as 'chief assistant' to Hamilton. One of Evans's first tasks was a new design for the sports pages.

Harold Evans's main achievement was to keep fresh an editorial formula which already existed. The *Sunday Times*, as market leader with a huge recent circulation increase, was already well supplied with young readers and talented young journalists. 'Insight', edited in 1966 by Bruce Page, had already seen its most innovative days before Harold Evans arrived. Harold Evans was outstandingly successful in two areas. One was in the role of editor-as-promoter—the *Sunday Times* and its ebullient editor were always in the news. Secondly, Harold Evans had a special talent for the 'big read' which was the *Sunday Times* core offering. He was skilled at choosing investigations which would make high-selling books; these were expensive—in that several journalists were typically away for several months—but the investigations were no more expensive than buying the serialization rights to existing books. In this *Sunday Times* case the divide between the editor and Hamilton (as chairman and editor-in-chief) worked well because the successful editorial formula was already in place.

The situation at the *Guardian* was very different; here Alastair Hetherington was involved in radically altering the newspaper, which led him also to recreate the concept of upmarket editorship very much in his own image. When Hetherington became editor the paper was still the *Manchester Guardian*; it was the home of the most potent non–London tradition of editorial sovereignty. The paper's unique history included the unique sovereign owner-editorship of C. P. Scott, who was editor for the almost unbelievable span of fifty-seven years (1872–1929)

Becoming editor in 1956 at the age of 37, Hetherington had to survive four major crises. First, he was very quickly confronted with the Suez crisis. He led the newspaper attack on the British government's invasion (with France) of Egypt. Many of the *Guardian*'s local Manchester readers left in droves, but many new readers were gained, especially in London and the South of England.

Secondly, the *Guardian* began to print in London in September 1961. Initially Hetherington continued to edit from Manchester, but gradually he came to spend more and more time in London and less time on trains between the two locations. The management had believed they were merely printing a London edition. By deciding to edit the paper from London, Hetherington in practice turned the paper into a London daily, with a Manchester printing.

Thirdly, the *Guardian* was badly hit by the 1966 financial crisis surrounding the Wilson government. Laurence Scott, the chairman and effective chief owner decided that the *Guardian* would have to merge. *The Times* management also considered three other merger partners, but the *Guardian* merger went very close to happening. The Scott family—as most newspaper-owning families eventually do—became bitterly divided over the issue of whether or not to sell the old family newspaper. Laurence Scott in Manchester wanted to merge with *The Times*; Richard Scott (son of a previous editor), who was then the Washington correspondent, opposed the merger. The *Guardian*'s destiny was controlled by the Scott Trust, whose journalist members, led by Richard Scott and Alastair Hetherington, voted down the merger proposal.

With the merger solution thus rejected, Alastair Hetherington faced a fourth major trial—staying afloat in the depressed economic conditions of the late 1960s. The solution was to tighten belts, including sacking one-quarter of all journalists. Interviewed in 1968, Hetherington[28] evidently believed that he was coming through this fourth trial as well. The company had clearly been racked by conflict and dissent; the move to London had been badly handled, the advertising sales were in a very low state and the Scott family finances were also in bad shape. But the picture improved, especially from 1967 with the appointment of a new advertising director.

Hetherington was forced to take big decisions from his earliest days; and, because in those early days, the *Manchester Guardian*'s team of journalists was quite small, he also played a major part in deploying the specialist correspondents. Subsequently there were many problems with the editor in London, while other key execu-

---

[28] This passage is based on interviews during 1966–8 with Alastair Hetherington, Harford Thomas, John Cole, Brian Redhead, Harry Whewell, John Putz, Richard Gott, and several specialist correspondents.

tives remained in Manchester. The foreign editor stayed in Manchester for a remarkably long time. But Alastair Hetherington continued as an extremely forceful editor and he played a major role in putting the paper together in the evening. He gradually built up a strong team of senior journalists. In 1968 these included Harford Thomas (deputy editor), John Cole (news editor), Peter Jenkins (who had just moved from industrial correspondent to columnist), Francis Boyd and Ian Aitken (political lobby), and Alistair Cooke (New York). Some *Guardian* journalists found Hetherington a somewhat distant and awkward figure; a number of left-inclined younger journalists found him too close to US policy in Vietnam, and too friendly with Prime Minister Harold Wilson. Michael Frayn complained of the acute problems posed for a humorous columnist by an editor with no sense of humour. But these were mild criticisms.

Alastair Hetherington radically changed an already famous newspaper, dragging it after him into a new market niche. In so doing he also showed the possibility of a more activist type of editing style. In particular Hetherington showed that a defence and foreign-policy intellectual could also be a hands-on editor. Hetherington shared this combination of writing and layout/design skills with Harold Evans and also with a *Daily Mail* editor, David English.

V

The editorship of David English at the *Daily Mail* was the most influential London editorship in the final one-third of the twentieth century. He edited the *Daily Mail* for twenty-one years (1971–92). During that time it took over the midmarket leadership from the *Daily Express*. But English also worked out a new style of the activist entrepreneurial editor, which became the common 1990s pattern (and is the subject of the next chapter).

David English edited the tabloid *Daily Sketch* for two years until it was closed down in 1971 by its owners, the Associated/Mail group. English was then switched to edit the *Daily Mail*, which, at the same time was relaunched in tabloid size. David English had what the Associated/Mail group at the time regarded as a conventional background for an editor—he had been a *Daily Express* foreign correspondent, celebrated for his coverage of the 1963 Kennedy assassination. He had then been foreign editor of the *Daily Express*. His predecessor as *Daily Mail* editor, Arthur Brittenden, had been a foreign correspondent, as had the then *Evening News* (1967–73) editor, John Gold.

When I interviewed David English he had been *Daily Mail* editor for five years and already had an extremely forceful editorial style:

He normally works a 5 day week—about 3 are of the 13 hours' variety and 2 are much shorter days. Another way of describing it is that he works 5 days but only 3 or 4 nights. Sometimes if he has worked some unusually long hours he takes a day or even two days off. He also has 8 weeks' holiday a year. Consequently his deputy edits the paper on nearly half the nights of the year. He starts to read the other papers at home at breakfast time. He lives nearby. His deputy is Peter Greville and they work very closely together changing at short notice who is going to edit the paper on a particular day.

There are 4 editorial meetings a day. First, a small informal meeting between the editor, deputy editor and the associate editor, at about 10.30. Then there is a features conference which is led by the features editor and the editor. Then the main conference at 11.15 a.m., which is concerned with the whole of the paper. And then at 5 p.m. there is the main afternoon conference.

He also has a weekly meeting with the woman's editor. He sees the political editor for lunch about once a week and various specialists come in to see him about particular stories. From 5.30 onwards he is on the back bench. He sees the bulk of the copy, some of it in proof and some in raw copy. The only things he does not normally see are the sports stories. He usually goes home immediately the first edition is finished, takes the paper home with him, and reads it there. If he has any points, he then phones back into the office with things that he wants changed. He plays quite a big part in initiating and gathering stories as well as being a back-bench editor. Emphatically he believes in both gathering and processing as the editor's responsibility.

The most wearing thing certainly is staff appointments and keeping the hierarchy balanced. Also 'holding the hands of temperamental journalists' and 'massaging their egos'. As an example, his features editor is currently leaving and he is filling the features job with the woman's page editor. The Money Mail editor is moving across to edit the woman's page and somebody else has to come in to edit Money Mail. There is thus a slot for a deputy features editor. These people all have to be seen, their salaries have to be discussed, a number of other people want to know why they have not been chosen, and what the implications are for them. You have to see about 20 different people to make one appointment, and a lot of people are in rather an emotional state.

The news editor would hire reporters although he would inform the editor as to whom he was hiring. There is an editorial annual budget, which is taken quite seriously within Associated Newspapers. They tend to run 3 or 4 journalists below establishment. Major heads in the budget are foreign travel, buying material from outside specialists, and there is an extensive general budget which covers buying of series including books. He has quite a lot of money which he can switch about in various directions.

Public relations are important in this job but you can do too much of it and cease to be the editor. The Advertising Department is especially pressing with invitations and the circulation people want you to meet the wholesalers and so on. He tries to keep in touch with some prominent politicians—because politicians are a great source of news.

English as editor controls the leaders. The daily leader conference involves the editor, his two immediate deputies plus one or other of the leader writers. Sometimes, if relevant, a specialist is called in. The leader, when written, comes back to the editor who often makes alterations. The letters to the editor are also under him but are controlled primarily by one of the features executives and a letters editor. He sees all letters before they are published at the proof stage. As editor he writes a few leaders from scratch himself, perhaps 7 or 8 a year, and these are quite often done at election time. Sometimes these are 'special pronunciamentos' and tend to appear as front page leaders.

He talks on the telephone every day to Vere Harmsworth (Lord Rothermere). English is a director both of the Daily Mail and also of Associated Newspapers, which he thinks is very important. His contractual position originally was that he had an 8-year contract—this was made up of 5 years plus a three-year rolling clause. He is not quite certain what the contract would now be but the rolling three-year clause is certainly there. He thinks that there is a real problem of it being inhibiting if you wish to go.

In the days when he was at the Daily Express its board hardly ever met. The Daily Mail board is quite active and meets once a month. The Circulation Director belongs, as does the Advertising Director, and they discuss the business strategy of the month—especially the amount of advertising and paging level over the coming month. They discuss things like the possibility of a circulation drive and a series to go with it. They also discuss price rises and their timing.[29]

---

[29] Author and Colin Seymour-Ure interview with David English, May 1976.

This was David English only a quarter way through his twenty-one-year editorship; he subsequently evolved as a still more dominant editor (before becoming chief executive of Associated Newspapers). But the outlines of a new pattern of entrepreneurial editorship are already visible here.

7 Entrepreneurial Editors

A newspaper should be run on the assumption that the editor is a genius.

Bruce Rothwell, *Daily Mail* assistant editor (1966)

In a way probably unique for a company of this size, a national newspaper is very much a one-man show. The paper reflects the editor's interests in a way that, if you were a company this size manufacturing soap powder, it would not. . . . Newspapers are led by the man at the front. If the editor gets it wrong, then the paper gets it wrong. . . . If the editor doesn't find something interesting, it won't go into the paper.

Ross Benson, *Daily Express* diary editor (1994)

NEITHER of these two statements—both made to me, but separated by twenty-eight years—was intended as criticism of the current editor. Bruce Rothwell was saying in 1966 that a dominant editor was desirable; Ross Benson was saying in 1994 that a dominant editor was standard. Between these dates a series of developments occurred in British national journalism which led to a more dominant pattern of editorship. The term 'entrepreneurial editor' is used here to reflect the increased business involvement of the editor; the editor today is expected to lead, to innovate, to do new things, to take creative risks.

Decreased trade union power is one important change since the 1960s. Chief executives of newspaper companies have increasingly taken a more strategic interest in the business, leaving their highly paid and (they hope) highly skilled editors to take the editorial lead. Some chief executives and chief owners reside most or some of the time outside Britain and recognize the unwisdom of excessive interference in editorial detail.

Crude political and business interference with editors by chief executives appears not to have been too successful in recent decades. The Lord Beaverbrook and Cecil King styles of the 1960s or the Robert Maxwell front-page self-adulation of the 1980s were generally regarded as being inept and best avoided. Chief executives who wish to be politically involved can, and do, deal with politicians direct. But being able to say 'I'll mention it to the editor, but he may not agree,' may be a not inconvenient bargaining device. Chief executives, these days, are often most interested in detailed regulatory or taxation benefits. Thus editors and owners may each cultivate somewhat different political contacts, interests, and ideas.

Editors also say that recent changes—in technology and competition—require quicker responses than previously. Comparing 1994 conditions with 1975, when he first edited the *Guardian*, Peter Preston mentioned three linked elements of speed-up. 'There has been a dramatic increase in the quantities of material coming in from news agencies and other services'; the size of each day's paper is at least twice as big, while the number of journalists is the same or less; and thirdly there is heightened competition from press, radio, and TV. All of this, said Preston, means that the editorial day moves more quickly than in the past; 'if you lose an hour in the morning, you never get that hour back.' Chief executives are aware of this and do not want needlessly to waste the editor's time.

The managing director does not see the editor as a remote being; quite the contrary, the editor and the managing director typically work very closely together. The editor is seen as a highly paid creative manager, who will expect to be in complete charge of the editorial department. He expects to be judged primarily on circulation figures.

Most editors last either for about two years or for ten years or more. If the management are unhappy with the editor's and the newspaper's performance the editor is sacked and a new one hired, usually from outside. When a successful editor eventually is removed or promoted, the new editor is often chosen internally. Chief owners and chief executives recognize that much of the editorial control they can exercise is involved in their choice of a new editor. They thus look carefully. Rupert Murdoch tended to choose his editors from among British journalists he had already seen operating in New York. The people who appoint editors usually have some set of editorial goals and changes in mind—

typically they want more readers in general and more young, female, and affluent readers in particular. The prospective new editor may well be asked about desirable editorial changes; as they arrive, new editors typically seek to make dramatic changes in people and pages.

Editors have also become public figures to a greater extent than was the case previously. In the 1960s one of the editor's duties was to get his talking head onto television, but by the 1990s there were more TV channels, and more radio stations inviting more editors onto the airwaves. Being a public figure has given the editor more internal company prestige. All of this has led company managements normally to support and to promote their editor as a star, rather than telling him or her what songs to sing.

I

Editors can be compared to prima donnas, or orchestra conductors, or film directors; in film terms these newspaper editors would perhaps best be seen as 'hyphenates', as people who do two or three creative jobs, like the producer-director-writer.

The trend has been for the newspaper editor to play a more active part in a wider range of activities than in the past. Today's activist entrepreneurial editors tend to engage in all nine of the following list of duties:

1. *Hire and fire* may well be the single most important prerogative; often the arrival of a new editor is quickly followed by half or more of the senior journalists being fired or moved. The editor then typically brings in several colleagues (from his previous jobs) into the top positions. This process may then be repeated once more or several times.

2. *Opinion.* The editor controls the formal policy of the newspaper, in particular the writing of the anonymous editorial 'leading articles'; most 1990s editors write some themselves and instruct leader writers each day. The editor also controls the letters to the editor and chooses between sketches offered by the cartoonist. Even if ignored by most readers the anonymous editorials are not ignored by politicians and have their biggest impact on journalists in the paper; these editorials constitute a daily bulletin board as to

what the editor thinks about current public issues. These opinions automatically flow into, and colour, reporting and feature-writing throughout the paper.

3. The *editorial budget* is controlled by the editor, via a managing editor. The budget is agreed each year and the finance department checks on each month's editorial expenditure. The editor holds sway over a budget of say £15 million; the editor in a fairly short period can make big changes in how this money is spent—less on foreign news, more on book serializations, and so on.

4. *Gathering of news and features.* The editor normally chairs a morning meeting at which the day's news menu is discussed. The editor also talks individually with senior news executives before or after this meeting.

5. *Processing of news and features.* The editor oversees the sub-editing and preparation of material for placement in the paper. Especially on tabloid papers, he is close to the 'back-bench' of processing executives, and—in discussion with them—he chooses the main front-page 'splash' story and decides which stories will be page leads on the main news pages.

6. *Presentation and design.* The general appearance and design is regarded as being salient in the newspaper's competitive effort. The editor typically has in train some planned redesign of some area or section of the paper. A major redesign is a matter of endless agony and effort; it needs the editor's approval.

7. *Systems.* The editor, these days, must make decisions (with production and information technology personnel) on the editorial computer system, the new page make-up system, the new computer graphics, the new electronic picture desk. Closely related to this are:

8. *The sections of the paper.* New sections often involve a different type of printing from the main paper. Merging old sections and creating new ones are major decisions which must be planned and discussed at length with advertising and other departments.

9. *Promotion and marketing.* This involves a range of activities. In recent years London newspapers have spent many millions of pounds on television advertising; the editor is closely involved in the creative message of such advertising campaigns. There is an increasing number of promotional games, co-promotions with television programmes, and so on, all of which involve the editor in issues of editorial compatibility, taste, and benefits.

In practice tabloid editors tend to be involved in all nine of these activities, while some broadsheet editors do not. However, an editor such as Max Hastings at the *Daily Telegraph*—who had little previous news executive experience—surrounded himself with a small team of senior colleagues, including one senior man (Don Berry) who was a design and layout expert.

The editorship which at first glance looks like a one-man band may on closer inspection consist of an editor, a deputy (who edits a daily paper perhaps on 100 days against the editor's 200 days a year), a managing editor (who runs most of the editorial finances), and two or three other assistant editors. There is usually at least one area (such as sport or finance) which the editor largely ignores. Nevertheless it is the editor typically who has chosen this editorial high command (and has decided to leave sport to the sports editor).

II

The previous chapter's account of David English as *Daily Mail* editor referred to the year 1976. David (later Sir David) English continued as *Mail* editor until 1992, by which time he had become a still more commanding force. Gradually the *Daily Mail* won the circulation battle with the *Daily Express*; gradually Lord Rothermere reduced his direct involvement. Then the industrial changes of 1986 allowed David English—like other editors—more leeway to enforce his will.

The *Daily Mail* became celebrated for its 'unique culture'; even an adulatory trade press article, celebrating David English's twenty-one years as *Daily Mail* editor, commented: 'Anyone who has done so much as a shift on his *Daily Mail* knows that there is a unique culture within his editorial department. It's a mixture of surging adrenalin, sweat, fear and excitement.'[1]

By 1992 Paul Dacre was editor of the Mail group's London *Evening Standard* (having previously been English's deputy at the *Daily Mail*). Dacre was then offered the editorship of *The Times* by the Murdoch/News management. Sir David English quickly pulled off a dramatic transformation; he became chief executive of Associated Newspapers, while Dacre was offered—and accepted—

---

[1] 'Machiavelli or the prince?', *UK Press Gazette*, 8 July 1991, 16–17.

the editorship of the *Daily Mail*. Paul Dacre thus took on his editorship of the *Daily Mail* in 1992 with a unique record behind him. He was the first person in 200 years to turn down the editorship of *The Times* and to prefer a popular newspaper editorship.

Under Paul Dacre the extraordinary dominance of the *Daily Mail* editorship continued, and also continued to be an example across all three market levels. Sir David English himself honoured the Mail/Associated tradition that 'editors edit, managers manage'. Two years later (in 1994) Dacre was well established in the job. He had presided over some major section changes which, according to Mail tradition, are editorially, not advertising, led. Under Dacre the *Daily Mail* was much more sceptical about the European Union than it had been under David English.

Paul Dacre was to be seen all day on the main editorial floor, working a thirteen-hour day, five days a week. He arrived at 9 a.m. (having listened to BBC radio's *Today* show and read the other papers); he left for home at 10 p.m. (to look at his own paper's first edition and to watch BBC TV's *Newsnight*). Once or twice a week he went out to lunch, typically with a Conservative Cabinet Minister.

The Dacre morning was devoted to a sequence of meetings. First a proverbially severe inquest meeting on failings in last night's paper. Then a long meeting about the major features (some of two tabloid pages). Then the usual news meeting for the main editorial department bosses; finally a leader-writers' meeting. During the day Dacre also had numerous quickie *ad hoc* discussions with the managing director, the cartoonist, and senior journalist executives, with the circulation manager and the literary editor (mainly about buying book serialization rights).

The evening sequence began with the Night Conference at 4.30 p.m. Here the night desk/back-bench executives offered the editor their suggestions for the 'splash' on page 1, the light story on page 3, the location of the main features, the page leads especially through the first 36 or 40 pages. Paul Dacre tended to leave the back end of the paper to the finance and sports desks. But he himself took a very active part is discussing and agreeing with the back-bench all the major page lead, layout, and picture decisions.

Between 5 and 10 p.m. Dacre's attention focused on the back-bench executives and the final putting together of the newspaper.

In line with the David English tradition of the 'tightly edited' *Daily Mail*, much Dacre attention focused on the overall sequence of the paper—balancing heavier items with lighter, more amusing, and more enticing features. Dacre also tried to balance the new and amazing story with old, amusing, and friendly items such as the Keith Waterhouse column, always on page 10. Extreme importance in this balancing operation was also attached to choosing the best pictures from the picture desk's offerings and melding the chosen pictures with just the right words.

In 1994 the *Daily Mail*, was especially anxious to retain its leadership in the midmarket while seeking to defend itself against a price-cut *Daily Telegraph*, possibly being pushed somewhat downmarket by its price-cutting competitor *The Times*. One casualty here was foreign news—not seen as something which 'sells the *Daily Mail* on a wet day'.

The active entrepreneurial editorship was also to be found at the *Daily Mail*'s stable companions. The 1982 launch editor of the *Mail on Sunday* was quickly sacked; David English then installed a new team of journalists under a new editor, Stewart Steven, who was an outstandingly successful editor (1982–92) and was certainly no less dominant an editor than David English. The *Evening Standard* editorship was run in the same way.

Over at the *Daily Express*—the other main midmarket paper—much the same thing was happening. Nicholas (later Sir Nicholas) Lloyd took on the *Daily Express* editorship in 1986, which enabled him to extend his editorial prerogatives. He became the longest serving *Daily Express* editor since Arthur Christiansen's reign ended in 1957. Nicholas Lloyd was not blamed for the sliding circulation. He had an exceptionally wide range of previous experience (from *Sunday Times* education correspondent to *News of the World* editor) and he was well capable of the activist-entrepreneurial role required at the *Daily Express*. In addition to his well-known enthusiasm for Conservative politics he—like other latter-day editors—had a strong interest in the business world and lunched with captains of industry almost as often as with politicians.

At *Today*, the third midmarket daily, the entrepreneurial editor concept went perhaps the furthest of all—mainly because *Today* lacked tradition, sales, finance, and adequate numbers of journalists. David Montgomery (1987–91) was an exceptionally dominant editor, and for part of his editorship was also managing director.

BOX 7.1. A DAILY EDITOR'S DAY

Richard Stott had edited the *Daily Mirror* (twice) and the *People* (twice) before becoming editor of *Today*. In 1994, after ten years of national editing, this Murdoch-appointed editor of a Labour-supporting newspaper had this daily schedule:

7 a.m.	Listens to BBC radio *Today* programme.
	Goes through the other newspapers.
8 a.m.	(Still at home) Phones news editor about pages 6 and 7; 6 is leader page with 'issue' feature, 7 is personality-led feature page.
	Centre spread (two pages) has been done overnight.
	Talks on phone to political editor.
10 a.m.	Arrives in office.
10–11.30 a.m.	Fielding queries from news desk; more discussion of pages 6 and 7.
	Looking through overnight feature and tomorrow's special section (Money).
	Looking through other stories.
	Deciding page 1 puff (about following day).
	Discussing page 14, 'World Today', a picture-driven page.
	'That's features mostly taken care of.'
11.30 a.m.	Chairs main conference of departmental heads.
12.00 noon	Chairs leader conference.
1.30 p.m.	Focuses now on news pages, especially 1, 3, 4, 5 and 'any big production number we're doing'.
	Night editor is getting on now with early (deadline) pages.

Richard Stott describes himself as 'not much in my office' (which looks out across the newsroom) 'except to read things or to scribble a page. I always spend a lot of time out on the [editorial] floor—always have done, it's good fun. Yes, editing by walking about.'

3.00 p.m.	Editor chooses one of five sketches offered by cartoonist.
5.45 p.m.	Chairs conference. Night editor goes through his list, as to where he's putting everything.

Continued

6.30 p.m.	Works out page 1 with night editor and art director. Also page 3 which is an on-the-day picture-led page.
6.45 p.m.–7.00 p.m.	Reads, in proof, pages 6 and 7 and leaders.
7.30–7.45 p.m.	Sees first draft of page 1 splash.
8.00 p.m.	'If someone on staff wants to see me we discuss it, usually over a drink.'
8.00–9.45 p.m.	If there's a big running story, or if he wants especially to see something in print, waits until 9.30–9.45.
8.00–8.30 p.m.	Most nights, heading home.
9.00 p.m—midnight	At home, but phones into office several times to 'check on what the opposition's running and that we're running okay.'
12.00–12.30 a.m.	Last phone call to paper.

'A long day? Well, it doesn't seem an especially long day. It has a natural cycle, from creating the paper to waving it bye-bye in trucks.'

The above schedule operates five days a week. Saturday is his day off. On Sunday (for Monday) the deputy editor is in charge; Richard Stott stays at home but the 'day still starts the same way' with discussions about pages 6 and 7 and the leaders; and any other scheme he wants to see comes to him at home by fax.

Based on: Author's interview with Richard Stott, Monday, 20 June 1994.

Richard Stott (editor from 1993) persuaded Rupert Murdoch to let *Today* support the Labour Party; Stott also brought in a team of his former colleagues from the *Daily Mirror*. As the only editor successfully to have dictated his conditions for editorial autonomy to both Maxwell and Murdoch, Richard Stott—despite his failed buyout attempts at Mirror Group—was the very model of a modern entrepreneur-editor, until *Today*'s closure in November 1995.

III

Two other decade-long editorships of market-segment leaders helped to develop the new entrepreneurial editor pattern. These were Kelvin MacKenzie's editorship of the *Sun* (1981–94) and Andrew Neil's editorship of the *Sunday Times* (1983–94).

The *Sun*, which Kelvin Mackenzie edited, was a slim down-market daily tabloid and it looked very different from the fat once-a-week multi-sectioned upmarket *Sunday Times*. But the chief owner in both cases was mogul Murdoch and the manner in which he related to these two editors was very similar. These two editors were clearly regarded by Rupert Murdoch (and most other people) as successes and—after a trial period—they were granted steadily more powers.

In both cases there was an overwhelming emphasis on profitability. Both editors were successful at maintaining circulation and the *Sunday Times* was even more successful in expanding into ten advertising-laden sections. By the late 1980s the two papers together were probably making enough profits to provide between $200 and $250 million each year for investment in Fox television activities in the USA. These two commercially successful editors were given untrammelled power within their editorial departments.

Both Kelvin MacKenzie at the *Sun* and Andrew Neil at the *Sunday Times* were recruited personally by Rupert Murdoch before their 35th birthdays. Murdoch had already observed both young men when they were in New York; Andrew Neil was in New York for *The Economist* and Kelvin MacKenzie served a term as managing editor of the then Murdoch-owned *New York Post*. Both men, plucked from relative obscurity into these high-profile jobs, were utterly dependent on Rupert Murdoch's personal approval. Both seem to have modelled themselves on Murdoch's style of Aussie-New York personal directness and business pugnacity.

Murdoch was, of course, not an admirer of the traditional British establishment, and in Neil and MacKenzie he chose two middle-class but still very non-establishment journalists. Neil was a Scot who attended Glasgow University; MacKenzie, despite his Scottish name, was the son of two South London journalists and, as for many Fleet Street journalists, local London weekly papers and a local news agency were his journalism school. Both Neil and MacKenzie cultivated an aggressively street-wise 'common man' personal style.

Neither Neil nor MacKenzie favoured the lowered voice. Kelvin MacKenzie soon became celebrated for his habit of frequent 'bollockings' of his journalists; these were loud and obscenity-laden public denunciations of individuals which even in most manual occupations were a thing of the past by the 1980s. Even an in-house account of the *Sunday Times* describes one habit of Andrew Neil as follows: 'All too often, since he is a demanding editor, they are found wanting. Nobody wants the humiliation, so enjoyed by all their colleagues, of a public dressing-down at the conference.' And also: 'When Neil is dissatisfied with a list he lets his assistant editors know, often in savage terms.'[2]

Both Neil and MacKenzie were hyperactive workaholics. Both editors were deeply involved in the news gathering as well as the presentation sides of their newspapers. Both were concerned to compete remorselessly against the market share of key rivals. Under Andrew Neil, the *Sunday Times* did win back the market share it had lost under Harry Evans. Under Kelvin MacKenzie the *Sun* fought back successfully against the *Daily Star*.

Both Neil and MacKenzie played very active parts in the migration of their newspapers eastward to the Wapping docklands in 1986.[3] Both also found that the new technology (and weakened trade unions) after 1986 increased their powers. Both had now successfully completed a major test of macho management. Both found themselves buoyed up by the entrepreneurial excitement— and high newspaper profitability—of the late 1980s Lawson–Thatcher boom.

Both men were vigorous editorial promoters of Murdoch and News International interests. Both the *Sun* and the *Sunday Times* engaged in massive boosterism of Murdoch's Sky Television (and later BSkyB)—which led to accusations from competitors of abuse of monopoly power. Andrew Neil in 1989 was chief executive of Sky Television as well as *Sunday Times* editor. Both editors also gave huge editorial space to entertainment hoopla; the *Sun* was obsessed with showbiz, sex, and Hollywood—as was the *Sunday Times*. In 1992 Neil was willing and eager to fly to Los Angeles and—without reading the book first—to interview Madonna about her soon-to-be-released book, *Sex*.[4]

Both Andrew Neil's and Kelvin MacKenzie's style of journalism was heavily criticized by fellow professionals in the competing publications. This criticism performed the function of completing a circle. Both Neil and MacKenzie, in their editorial columns as in

[2] Brian MacArthur, *Deadline Sunday: A Life in the Week of the SundayTimes* (London: Hodder and Stoughton, 1991), 27, 69.

[3] Linda Melvern, *The End of the Street* (London: Methuen, 1986), 38–44, 52–70, 95–112.

[4] 'Laid Bare: Unmasking Madonna, by Andrew Neil', *Sunday Times*, magazine, 18 Oct. 1992, 18.

their personal pronouncements, 'answered back' at their critics. Both had a well-developed line in personal abuse and vituperation. Kelvin MacKenzie, with his South London weakness for Cockney rhyming slang, made up insulting-jokey nicknames for his numerous enemies. Andrew Neil was not far behind in similarly childish abuse of competing editors, his numerous critics, and public enemies.

The dominance of Kelvin MacKenzie at the *Sun* became well known; it was regularly chronicled in *Private Eye*, and in many trade press and newspaper articles. The MacKenzie reign also became a central theme of well-informed books.[5] Moreover journalists who had worked on the *Sun* went on to edit all three downmarket Sundays; and two subsequent editors of the *Daily Mirror* were also graduates of the *Sun*.

It was well recognized that the industrial changes of the 1980s encouraged dominant editorships within the downmarket tabloids to an even greater extent than in the other market levels. The *Sun*'s diaspora of editors only served to support these basic trends. Two very basic characteristics of the downmarket tabloid allowed the editor to adopt a hands-on style of editorship to a greater extent than elsewhere. First, the downmarket tabloid had relatively few words and stories. Secondly, the choice of major stories was not externally driven but lay mainly within the arbitrary choice of the editor.

These basic characteristics took their most extreme form on the downmarket Sunday papers. It was here that women editors made their first appearances in charge of British national newspapers. By 1994 each of the three downmarket Sundays had had not one, but two women editors. Most of the comment about the women editors focused on the theme that they were 'only' accepted as suitable for downmarket Sundays and that they seemed to be sacked at least as quickly as male editors. Less noted was the point that these Sundays have the fewest words (per week) of any British national paper. The choice of many stories is even more arbitrary (and thus within the editor's choice) than elsewhere; the downmarket Sundays specialize in the 'Exclusive' investigation. Consequently Patsy Chapman, who edited the *News of the World* (1988–94) was perhaps the dominant individual editor in the years following 1986. These

---

[5] Peter Chippindale and Chris Horrie, *Stick It up your Punter! the Rise and Fall of the Sun* (London: William Heinemann, 1990). S. J. Taylor, *Shock! Horror! The Tabloids in Action* (London: Bantam Press, 1991).

women editors of downmarket Sundays tended to have extensive previous experience of weekly (magazine) editing. One such was Bridget Rowe, who before becoming editor of the *People* in 1992 had edited numerous publications, including *Woman's Own*, *TV Times*, and the *Sunday Mirror*. She told me in 1994 that she aimed to read every word that went into the *People*, including all of the extensive Saturday sports coverage. A Millwall supporter, Rowe spontaneously compared herself to the professional football manager.

The downmarket daily is the thinnest of the British national newspaper offerings. A daily paper of perhaps 48 tabloid pages has about 32 editorial and only about 25 non-sports editorial pages (equal to 12 or 13 full broadsheet pages). Although Colin Myler at the *Daily Mirror* admitted that he could not read all of this material each day, he could and did read all the bigger stories, such as page leads at the front of the paper. He also emphasized that with the once-a-week sections (which operate on earlier timetables) he also read the major stories and approved the main pictures.

The few biggest stories (which the editor monitors) are more dominant in downmarket tabloids. Bigger stories routinely are 'spread' across two pages, and the biggest stories often run across six or more pages. The choice of both feature and news stories is much less driven by outside agendas than with the broadsheets. The downmarket tabloid is not much affected by the agendas of politics, finance, and serious news generally. The editor is especially looking out for melodramatic human interest stories from a number of candidate stories being offered by features and news executives each day and each week.

Exclusive human interest and exposé stories often have legal and taste problems; the editor gets quick legal advice but he (or she) must decide whether to take the risk or send the story back for more research or rewriting. Once it has been decided to go big on a particular story the editor can dictate or adjust the angle. The editor in effect often decides which character is the hero and which the villain, and also approves (or vetoes) the big headlines. Humour is often crucial to the headline and the story, and as always with humour there is the awkward question as to whether it really is funny; the editor's sense of humour is final.

Another key aspect of downmarket tabloids is that they revere youth and are suspicious of expertise. There are few editorial experts on serious subjects; the story subject expertise is in sport and entertainment where again youth is emphasized. Kelvin MacKenzie sacked many journalists who were aged over 40 and favoured '25 and 25'—25-year-old journalists who could be paid the junior reporter's salary of £25,000. With the emphasis thus on youth, inexperience, and entertainment, there were few outside forces or agendas to interrupt the flow of arbitrary editorial decisions.

All of these factors were equally prevalent on the *Daily Star*, where Brian Hitchen was an especially dominant editor (1987–94). Hitchen had a small staff and also wrote a column; he may well have been even more dominant at the *Daily Star* than was Kelvin MacKenzie at the *Sun*. But it is the *Daily Mirror* editorship which has been least understood; the outpouring of stories and books about Robert Maxwell has created a widespread impression that Maxwell dominated and terrorized his editors. Roy Greenslade, editor of the *Daily Mirror* for fourteen months (from January 1990), in his highly informative *Maxwell's Fall* has unintentionally contributed to a false impression. The *Daily Mirror* had a strong editorship from 1985, especially in the person of Richard Stott (editor 1985–92, minus the fourteen months of Greenslade).

Most of Maxwell's front-page ego trips and other editorial invasions happened in his first year; and the *Mirror* lost 8 per cent of its sales in that year (1984–5). When Richard Stott was offered the *Daily Mirror* editorship in 1985:

I had to say to Maxwell, 'Look, I've got to have control of it, otherwise it won't work. You should know before we start, if I don't have control, we'll fight and things are going to go further downhill.' . . . So Maxwell agreed to all that . . . and most of the time he stuck to most of it . . . Not always . . . occasionally one lost spectacular battles with him. . . .'

Richard Stott also told this writer that Robert Maxwell—who was the British pioneer of mass sale daily colour printing—accepted the editor's advice to introduce colour slowly and cautiously. Maxwell accepted this editorial advice, despite the contrary advice of the 'colour technicians' to move rapidly with the (very costly) new colour printing facility. Richard Stott—with his enthusiasm for management buyouts—was one of the most entrepreneurial of editors, a quality which Maxwell probably recognized; the *Mirror* circulation (1986–9) also stabilized and rose slightly.

The general picture of the *Daily Mirror* editorship, after 1985, is of a strong editor (especially Stott and Myler) given sweeping powers by a strong chief executive (Maxwell and Montgomery). The situation at the *Sun* of a strong editor and chief executive (MacKenzie and Murdoch) was not the exception, but the standard downmarket pattern.

IV

Major extensions of editor power occurred in the upmarket newspapers between the 1960s and 1990s. The clearest example of this was the *Daily Telegraph*, where the biggest changes occurred during 1986. In early March 1986 Max Hastings started work as editor. He was a surprising choice—he had established a unique reputation as a TV and newspaper war reporter (from Vietnam to the Falklands) and as author of solid works of military history, but he had never run anything bigger than the 'Londoner's Diary' in the *Evening Standard*. He recalled:

We took over a near bankrupt company with an enormous number of people who were over age or no good. I sacked fifty journalists in the first two weeks. . . . Nobody likes getting rid of people but we were driven by a kind of desperation. We simply had to do drastic things. . . .

On the way home in the car I used to go relentlessly through the staff list, night after night . . . frequently marking those who, one felt, were just not up to it. The proportion of staff who were not up to it used to terrify me . . . the ghastly collection of deadbeats who then involved huge sums of money and difficulty in unsticking. . . . Jeremy [Deedes] gave me the score recently—in the first four years we got rid of three hundred journalists.

God knows I've sacked enough people. But I went through the list again the other day and there's almost nobody we need to sack. . . . We've also dramatically lowered the average age of our journalists.

Max Hastings in 1994—eight years into his editorship—was recounting to me his exercise of the editorial power of hire-and-fire. He had also hired a fresh team of senior editorial executives, nearly all of whom were still there eight years later. Hastings believed in delegating much editorial power to the heads of major editorial departments and to section editors; his attitude, he said, was that having put a lot of effort into trying to choose the right people, you then let them get on with it. If they failed they were fired, but 'I don't believe in much in between'.

Apart from this major exercise of hire-and-fire, Hastings took a special interest in the anonymous opinions. Most days the leader conference took about twenty-five minutes, with leader writers being assigned to topics and the general direction agreed. Hastings himself wrote one or two a week:

I write leaders on the big things—you know, whither the government, should the Prime Minister stay or go, and some Election ones. I sometimes write a leader to amuse myself, like one I did on unemployment last week. . . .

If it's something big or sensitive, it's quicker to do it myself. I can write a leader on anything in 40 minutes or under an hour. If you ask a leader writer to do it, he has to go through a lot of agonizing about what the *Daily Telegraph* ought to think about it, whereas I only have to think what I think about it. . . .

When I'm on holiday I reckon to speak to the paper every day, mainly because of leaders. I was on a fishing holiday when we fell out of the Exchange Rate Mechanism [1992], so I sat in the gillie's house watching the debate on television, and then I sat on a river bank, writing the leader myself.

Max Hastings had one other major area upon which he focused—the news coverage; it was agreed early in his editorship that the *Daily Telegraph* would continue to focus on news as its big strength. Having done a wide variety of reporting (and being a professional author) he tried to have 'a clear idea on the literary merits of all writers on the paper'. This notion of editorship amounted to a huge change from the previous regime. Here was a much more activist and entrepreneurial editorial approach than the *Daily Telegraph* had had previous to 1986.

Another event which had occurred in 1986 and had *Telegraph* links was the launch of the *Independent*, which also operated with its own conception of the strong editor. This was Andreas Whittam Smith (who had been the *Daily Telegraph*'s city editor). The three founders were intending forcibly to reject the pattern of editorship which they had closely observed at the *Daily Telegraph* in the years up to 1986. The key activity was fund-raising for the launch, and Whittam Smith—with his financial contacts and track record—became the chief fund-raiser and the key individual at the *Independent*. The pattern of the dominant chief-executive-and-editor—supported by his two eager colleagues—proved to be a flexible and creative management in the early months and years. Paradoxically this editor was perhaps too entrepreneurial initially and not enough subsequently.[6]

For a decade before the *Independent* appeared, the *Guardian* editorship had also been moving in a more entrepreneurial direction. The *Guardian* editor for twenty years (1975–95) was Peter Preston, who had extensive writing as well as sub-editing and production experience on the paper. As editor he was extremely hands-on in terms of production, but he also continued to write anonymous leaders and occasional signed pieces throughout his editorship. Chosen in 1975 by the Scott Trust's somewhat papacy-like selection process, Preston had an awkward introduction because 1976 was a bad advertising year. But he developed a carefully consensual pattern of leadership, sharing the daily editing duties with various deputy and assistant editors.

Preston played a major role in the *Guardian*'s introduction of a computer system after 1986, and in major redesigns. In particular he committed the paper to greatly increased pagination, funded by classified advertising. And in 1992–3 he was deeply involved in the *Guardian*'s acquisition of the *Observer*. Preston gradually became more directly involved in the overall newspaper business.

The *Guardian*, with its left-of-centre political views, its journalist-friendly traditions and its collegial style was obviously in danger of going stale and being run by a clique of ageing journalists. There was one such period in the late 1980s, but Preston was adroit both in promoting younger people and in reinventing himself. At the end of his editorship in 1994, Peter Preston was still working an eleven-hour day at the *Guardian* and chairing about thirty meetings a week within the editorial department and in the company. In 1975 he had 'never seen a balance sheet', but by 1984 (in close alliance with his chief executive) he had dragged a left-wing newspaper towards commercial success.

Preston's successor, Alan Rusbridger, was very much in the *Guardian* tradition; he had been features editor, presiding over what he told me in 1990 was a 'subbing empire'—processing all the sections as well as features. Like previous *Guardian* editors, Rusbridger was young (40) when appointed, and looked even younger than his age; he was also ideally equipped to continue the

---

[6] Stephen Glover, *Paper Dreams* (Harmondsworth: Penguin, 1994).

Guardian's ancient tradition of editorial sovereignty and its new tradition of entrepreneurship.

In 1995 Peter Preston moved upstairs, with the future of a recent acquisition, the *Observer*, as his leading problem. The *Observer* also had had a long-serving editor in the shape of Donald Trelford (1976–93); through most of this period the effective owner had been Tiny Rowland of Lonrho. Most discussion of this editorship focused on the degree to which Trelford supported Lonrho/Rowland business interests (in Knightsbridge and Africa). Trelford and the *Observer* certainly did lean in Lonrho's direction, but this could not have been more than 2 per cent of the *Observer*'s total editorial coverage. Less noticed were two relevant facts: first, Tiny Rowland, a businessman, not a newspaperman, created a lot of public noise over a fairly small amount of rather inept proprietorial intervention. Secondly, Donald Trelford was remarkably free over the remaining 98 per cent of the editorial output; Trelford broadly fitted the pattern of the entrepreneurial editor, although he perhaps devoted too much of his entrepreneurial energies to his own journalism career and not quite enough to the *Observer*.

And finally, this chapter returns to *The Times*. William Rees-Mogg departed as editor when Murdoch/News acquired *The Times* in 1981; in the next eleven years there were five editors. For once Rupert Murdoch's famous luck deserted him, not least in that Charles Douglas-Home's broadly successful editorship was terminated by his death. The choices suggested that Rupert Murdoch was consistently searching for a formula which could retain some of *The Times*'s old authority while introducing more popular and contemporary elements. The *Daily Telegraph* had always since 1855 been *The Times*'s main competitor, but both the choices of editor and the general strategy of *The Times* suggested uncertainty as to where the main competition was. Simon Jenkins in his brief editorship talked colourfully about clearing the *Independent* off the territory of *The Times*, but he failed to do so.

However, eventually the choice of Peter Stothard as editor in 1992, together with massive price cuts in 1993 and 1994, led to huge (and hugely subsidized) circulation increases. Peter Stothard was not the first choice to succeed Jenkins; he was an unusual choice also because he did not enter journalism until aged 30 and he came direct to the editorship from being a Washington foreign correspondent. However, Stothard had been close to Harold Evans and subsequent editors of *The Times*, including being Charles

BOX 7.2. RUPERT MURDOCH'S CHOICES AS EDITORS OF THE TIMES

		Annual ABC circulation in thousands
1.	*Harold Evans* (1981–2) was much admired by London journalists, but probably intended by Murdoch only as an interim solution. Harry Evans redesigned the paper and brought in some bright young journalists from the *Sunday Times*. Evans subsequently became a leading figure in New York book publishing.	1981—290
		1982—303
2.	*Charles Douglas-Home* (1982–5) was a long-serving journalist on *The Times*, who steered the paper to support of Mrs Thatcher. After a phase of editing from a wheelchair, he died of cancer.	1983—353
		1984—419
		1985—479
3.	*Charles Wilson* (1985–90) came from the *Daily Mail*, the first non-upmarket journalist to edit *The Times*. He captained the voyage to Wapping and made the news pages more popular. His next editorship was the horse-racing daily, *Sporting Life*, before he became a senior Mirror Group executive.	1986—469
		1987—443
		1988—443
		1989—435
4.	*Simon Jenkins* (1990–2), a former *Evening Standard* editor demanded (unsuccessfully) that *The Times* should win back readers lost to the *Independent*. He went back to what he did best, writing a column.	1990—426
		1991—397
		1992—385
5(a)	*Paul Dacre*, who (1992) turned down the job, preferring to edit the *Daily Mail*.	1993—390
		1994—614
5(b)	*Peter Stothard* (1992–) a surprise choice who presided over a big price-cut sales increase and switched *The Times* to attack the *Daily Telegraph*.	1995—647

Douglas-Home's chief leader writer and Charles Wilson's deputy editor.

Despite many surface differences, the pattern of editorship operated by Peter Stothard conformed to the entrepreneurial pattern in general and to the *Daily Telegraph*/Max Hastings model in particular. After Stothard's arrival in 1992 there was yet another cull of senior journalists at *The Times*; a number of new senior editorial executives were brought in, including several from the *Telegraph* stable. Like Hastings, Stothard took a particular interest in the anonymous leaders, in the political coverage, and the whole range of news. Peter Stothard also took a very big interest in features. Stothard seemed in his own skills and interests to combine the dual strategy of *The Times* in its price-cutting phase. Stothard was enthusiastic about news stories and features which would appeal to new young readers coming from the *Daily Telegraph*, but he was also seeking to preserve the strength of the editorial page and the facing 'Op Ed' page with its weighty columns. He regarded being serious and reaching the restless young as compatible editorial goals, telling me:

You have to communicate difficult material reasonably quickly. The days when the typical reader of *The Times* was a bank chairman, who could sit all morning slowly turning the pages, is gone. That person now wants to access information quickly. . . .

Too much in *The Times* was self-serving, it was there for no reason other than to please the person it was about or the person who was writing it. We have squeezed that, and it's not much mourned. . . .

Young new readers like our music coverage . . . something they weren't expecting. Young people accustomed to taking information off screens particularly like the back page digest which directs them to the pages they want.

Peter Stothard had a number of maxims: only talk to politicians if you're sure you're getting more out of it than they are; and 'the editor must look for ways to make the biggest difference'. He also mentioned numerous initiatives—a new television section, a new team to edit the fat Saturday paper, and a new daily meeting for proactive ideas (before the normal formal news conference). Stothard had recently edited *The Times* from Bristol and from Liverpool.

Although *The Times* was carrying on some old traditions, including subsidy, the editorship had changed decisively in the entrepreneurial direction.

8 From Gentlemen of the Press to Journos

IN the 1960s paternalistic Fleet Street employers had offered their journalists fairly secure, and not too demanding full-time employment. The journalists belonged to an aspiring and gentlemanly occupation with some residue of social deference. By the 1990s journalism had become much less secure, with much more work being done by each journalist; gentlemanly values were less evident; there were more women journalists and social deference was largely a thing of the past.

By the 1990s the hierarchy had been stretched both upwards and downwards. While perhaps 300 journalists at the top were more eminent and more powerful than ever before, another 2,000 national newspaper journalists were inclined—in their more cynical moments—to describe themselves as 'journos'; this unlovely term conveyed a new concept of an ungentlemanly technician-with-words. The term 'journo' also perhaps implied that journalism had become more like professional sport, acting, and entertainment—with a small layer of stars and a huge following oversupply of eager seekers after fame, fortune, and stardom.

Between the 1960s and the 1990s the amount of words written and space filled by each national newspaper journalist certainly doubled and perhaps trebled. This was mainly due to the larger number of much fatter newspapers.

Contrary to common journalist belief, the number of national newspaper journalists in London did not greatly alter between the 1960s and 1990s. There were 2,662 national newspaper journalists in London in 1969 and about the same number (or slightly more) in the mid-1990s. It was the big Manchester offices (683 journalists in 1969) which had gone.

But a roughly similar number of London journalists had to do much more work. By the 1990s there were more titles and these had at least twice the number of pages. Also the in-house journalists had to do more to the words, because more outside contributions had to be processed and because journalists now worked further downstream (in areas formerly controlled by compositors) in finalizing pages, integrating editorial with advertising spaces, checking colour, proofing, and so on. Finally the London-based journalists—now without big Manchester operations—had to handle more editions. All of this may add up to a trebling of work.[1]

Against this major speeding-up of the editorial operation all journalists were, of course, in the 1990s operating computer terminals and staring at screens. Only one journalist in this study regretted the loss of the old typewriters, but journalists nevertheless did complain of spending more time embracing the screen and less time talking to people either inside or outside the office. Editorial executives, it is said, like bums on seats in front of them; meanwhile the journalist stares into the screen, operates the keyboard, chatters on the telephone, and can see other screens across the editorial floor. The journalist also sits on an ergonomically designed chair which is supposed to reduce the danger of Repetitive Strain Injury (RSI)—a condition which at one stage seemed to reach epidemic proportions at the high-ratio-of-words-to-journalists *Financial Times*.

News agency material on British national newspapers is used mainly as a back-up and supplementary source. All national papers rely overwhelmingly on their own staff and on various freelance and other additions. Freelances were used in Fleet Street in the past, but they became more widely used especially after 1986. They have probably expanded from around 12 per cent to around 25 per cent of all working British journalists.

There is a tendency for more set-pieces like crosswords and astrology columns to arrive 'oven ready' from an outside contributor into the central computer. Television schedules are increasingly provided by an outside agency or a special unit such as one which does TV schedules for all Mirror Group national titles.

---

[1] Between 1969 and the 1990s some papers, like the *Daily Express*, cut their journalists by about half. But other papers (*Financial Times* and the *Guardian*) increased their numbers. Precise comparison is not possible because 'number of journalists' is now a much more fuzzy concept than in the past. Numbers of words (and pictures) per page add further fuzziness. For 1969, see: National Board for Prices and Incomes, *Journalists' Pay* (London: HMSO, 1969).

Between the 1960s and 1990s there has been a big raising in the average educational level. University graduates in the late 1960s were common on provincial morning newspapers, but still fairly rare on the evenings; by the 1990s graduate entrants were standard on provincial evenings and common on weeklies. Graduates had also largely taken over on the national upmarkets and midmarkets, and were invading the downmarket papers.

The proportion of women in British journalism doubled from about 17 per cent in the late 1960s to about 35 per cent in 1994. Indeed by the mid-1990s women made up about half of all journalists in the younger age groups and in the lower levels of the occupation. In the late 1960s it had been firmly believed by many or most senior male journalists that women were completely unsuited to work as sub-editors. Two main reasons were quoted: first, sub-editors (on morning papers) work late and it would be unfair to expect women subs to travel home from the office at midnight. Secondly, many male journalists argued that women would fail to recognize potential sexual double meanings in the reporters' copy. Male journalists were often eager to quote examples of how women reporters got into this kind of trouble—for instance the young woman reporter covering a society story who began her piece with the words: 'Balls, balls, balls, balls.' In 1960s Fleet Street there was not one female crime or football correspondent; other specialist fields had just one or two women journalists, with fashion as the only woman-dominated field.

By 1994 about 17 per cent of national newspaper journalists were women. Table 8.1 shows a similar proportion of women among editors and deputy editors. But there were no women editors of national dailies and only 5 per cent of political, business, news, and sports editors (some of the most traditionally macho jobs) were women. However, women did better as columnists, as leader-writers, and as attenders at the major daily news conference in the newspaper. The studies from which these data were taken deliberately excluded senior positions in 'softer' areas—such as features editor and women's editor; here the proportion of women would have been much higher. But Ginny Dougary correctly argues that men still dominate in the traditional 'hard news' areas, while women's biggest advances have been in the new features areas and on the Sunday tabloids.

The 20 per cent or so of senior positions held by women in the mid-1990s was a distinct advance on the 2 per cent occupied by

Table 8.1. Proportion of senior positions in UK national newspapers occupied by women, 1993–1994

	% of jobs held by women	Total number men and women
Daily Editors	0	11
Daily & Sunday		
Editors and deputy eds.	17	42
Political, business, news, and sports editors	5	84
Op Ed columnists	19	68
Leader writers	20	45
Attending daily news conference	21	68

Sources: Ginny Dougary, *The Executive Tart and Other Myths* (London: Virago, 1994); Jean Morgan, 'Women still shortchanged on power, says survey', *UK Press Gazette*, 26 June 1995.

women in 1965.[2] But in the mid-1990s a senior team of five people would typically include only one woman journalist. While it is now acknowledged that women can take on any senior job, the increased productivity demands and heightened competition of recent years have in some respects made national journalism into an even more macho occupation than previously. Here British journalism parallels other comparable occupations, but women still probably have better prospects as television producers; this is partly because the BBC has a stronger commitment to promoting suitable women than does any national newspaper.[3]

Across the whole range of British journalism in the late 1960s there were relatively small differences in pay, especially in the minimum (union regulated) minimum rate of pay. For example in 1969 the minimum pay rate on large provincial (English) dailies was 85 per cent of the London national newspaper rate, and large Scottish weekly papers had 73 per cent of the London minimum rate. This gap became wider in the 1970s and was wider still by the 1990s. In 1990 a weekly newspaper senior reporter was earning

[2] Based on 125 senior journalists listed in *Directory of Newspaper and Magazine Personnel and Data, 1966* (WPN and Advertisers' Review), and on 111 senior journalists listed in *Willing's Press Guide 1995*.

[3] Jeremy Tunstall, *Television Producers* (London: Routledge, 1993).

Owners, Managers, and Editors

Table 8.2. Salaries of all UK journalists, 1994

Annual salary 1994	Percentage of UK journalists	Number of respondents	Approximate total numbers of UK journalists
Up to £14,999	23.1	1,153	4,500
£15,000–19,999	22.1	1,105	4,500
£20,000–29,999	29.8	1,491	6,000
£30,000–39,999	15.7	786	3,000
£40,000–49,999	5.6	279	1,100
£50,000 plus	2.2	110	400
TOTAL	98.5	4,924	19,500
No reply	1.6	81	

Source: Jean Morgan, 'Reversal of Fortune', *UK Press Gazette*, 30 Jan. 1995.

only about 35 per cent and a provincial daily senior reporter only about 40 per cent of the national newspaper reporter.[4]

Within national newspapers the hierarchy had also stretched. In 1969 over two-thirds of all national newspaper journalists had been paid between £35 and £60 per week. Taking taxation and journalists' expenses into account most journalists were earning something close to the median. By the 1990s national newspapers had most of the most highly paid journalists, who (as Table 8.2 shows) were earning over £50,000 in 1994. At the same time the starting salary for young journalists on national newspapers was about £25,000. However, these figures by 1994 probably understated the real difference. At the lower end of the national newspaper hierarchy there was a lot of insecurity, such as three- and six-month trials and then short contracts; other people worked as 'regular casuals' employed for, say, three days a week, while yet others were genuine freelances. Meanwhile at the top end of the London system the senior journalists would typically not only be staff (with full pension benefits) but many of them had substantial other journalism income (such as cars, freelancing in addition to their main job, share options, and so on). Highly paid individual stars are discussed in the next chapter.

Both professional and trade union orientations in British na-

[4] 'Pay Survey', *UK Press Gazette*, 5 Aug. 1991.

tional journalism changed drastically between the 1960s and 1990s. In the consensual 1960s British journalism was far from being an established profession; but it was moving in a 'professionalizing' direction—with various attempts being made to raise occupational standards, to control entry, and to improve educational levels. In the 1960s a passive professionalizing lead came from *The Times* and the other upmarket papers; and this was loosely followed by the midmarket broadsheets of the period. Television and radio were strongly 'public service' oriented at the time. The Press Council prospered; efforts were being made to improve the low educational standards. The National Union of Journalists played an active part in this consensual picture.

But by the 1990s all of this had changed and in terms of 'professionalization' had gone backwards. By the 1990s the press was both more commercial and more politically partisan; the occupational consensus had been shattered by sharp antagonism between triumphant managers and a defeated National Union of Journalists. 'Standards' by common consent had declined; the Press Council disappeared. There was less consensus as to the virtues either of upmarket newspapers or of public service broadcasting. In these changes the National Union of Journalists played a central part.

For the twenty-year period, 1966–86, the National Union of Journalists had quite a strong position in British journalism. But by 1986 this power was increasingly under strain and in the late 1980s the union was effectively broken as a significant force. The NUJ, like most trade unions, had pursued such collective goals as raising minimum rates of pay. It had also operated a fairly effective closed shop in many areas and it had helped to make 1960s journalism a relatively secure occupation. Consequently the NUJ's loss of effective power after 1986 contributed to stretching the occupational hierarchy.

The National Union of Journalists, launched in 1907 in Manchester, modelled itself on the National Union of Teachers; its main aim was gradually to improve the working conditions of provincial journalists. For its first sixty years it was a politically moderate white-collar union; its history between 1918 and 1939 reflected the deferential concern for respectability which was still a marked feature of journalism in interwar Britain.

Fleet Street journalists in the late 1960s frequently referred to the insecurity of their work, but would admit that there had been few sackings in recent years.[5] Older Fleet Street journalists of the late 1960s had mostly entered the occupation as teenage indentured apprentices on small provincial newspapers before 1939. Box 8.1 presents an example of the type of apprenticeship agreement which a 16-year-old would have entered into up to 1939.

The majority of all 1960s British newspaper journalists had followed this apprenticeship-and-indentures path into journalism. Only about 27 per cent of newspaper journalists worked on national newspapers; 73 per cent worked on provincial newspapers, where they broadly adopted a white-collar work orientation. The majority of *national* journalists had moved up from the white-collar provincial pattern. A small number of journalists with élite family and educational backgrounds had moved direct into national journalism; and this élite career pattern had also been followed by many of the increasing numbers of radio and TV journalists. However the National Union of Journalists' membership by the 1960s was not confined only to these two—élite and white-collar—strands of newspaper, radio, and TV journalists. The NUJ also had increasing numbers of members in freelance journalism, in periodicals and magazines (plus book publishing), and in public relations.

During the 1960s the NUJ national leadership gradually became more ambitious. They welcomed the arrival of a Labour government in 1964, and the rapid growth of white-collar unionism. The NUJ's leaders also decided gradually to adopt some of the tactics which the printing unions had used so successfully, for example the device of the closed shop to control entry and to bid up the price of their labour. The NUJ turned its energies towards establishing a closed shop. Newspaper managers around 1965 were aware of increased demand for journalists and they agreed to co-sponsor with the NUJ a new entry and training scheme, run by the National Council for the Training of Journalists (NCTJ). As part of this deal the national newspapers agreed not to employ inexperienced journalists; other loopholes—such as the one which allowed young women to work initially as editorial secretaries before becoming journalists—were closed. A few national editors (such as Gordon Newton at the *Financial Times* and David Astor at the *Observer*) objected and continued to recruit new graduates direct into their London offices. *The Times* recruited similarly via the *Times Educational Supplement*; but direct graduate entry to Fleet Street had

---

[5] Author's interview with the then National Union of Journalists General-Secretary, Mr Jim Bradley, Nov. 1965.

BOX 8.1. A JOURNALIST APPRENTICESHIP AGREEMENT, 1939

(1) The apprentice of his own free will and with the consent of his mother having shown during a probationary period of six months a natural aptitude for the profession of journalism hereby binds himself to serve the masters as apprentice in their business of newspaper proprietors and publishers for the term of five years.

(2) (a) That the masters will accept the apprentice as their apprentice during the said term and will during the said term to the best of their power and skill and knowledge instruct the apprentice or cause him to be instructed in the business or profession of journalism in its several branches, that is to say in the reporting of both general news and sporting news and in the sub-editing of the same, in the make-up of a newspaper, and in everything relating to or connected with the editorial production of a newspaper.

(b) That the masters will pay to the apprentice every week during the said term or during so much thereof as he shall continue to be their apprentice wages at the minimum rates of ten shillings for the first year, thirteen shillings for the second year, sixteen shillings for the third year, nineteen shillings for the fourth year, and twenty-two shillings for the fifth year of the term.

(c) The masters will allow the apprentice one and a half days per week free from duty and will in addition and without any deduction from his wages permit him two evenings each week free from duty or equivalent time during the day provided that such time free from duty is used by the apprentice in attending classes with the object of continuing his education in a manner likely to increase his journalistic capabilities. Especially shall the apprentice make himself proficient in the art of shorthand writing. . . .

(3) (b) That the apprentice shall not do or knowingly suffer any damage to be done to the goods or moneys or other things of the masters which shall be put into his care or custody and shall not embezzle or waste them or lend or dispose of them to anyone without the masters' consent and shall not gamble with cards or dice and shall not play at unlawful games or frequent taverns but in all things he shall demean and behave himself towards the masters as a good and lawful apprentice ought to do.

(c) The mother shall during the said term provide the apprentice with suitable clothes and all other necessaries.

(d) That the masters shall be at liberty to deduct from time to time out of the wages to be paid to the apprentice as aforesaid any sum or

Continued

143

> sums of money which may be reasonable for any loss which the masters may sustain by reason of the negligence or misconduct of the apprentice.
>
> (e) That in case the apprentice shall at any time during the said term be wilfully disobedient to the lawful orders or commands of the masters or be slothful or negligent or shall otherwise grossly misbehave himself towards the masters then and in any such case it shall be lawful for the masters to discharge the apprentice from their service.

been reduced to a trickle by the late 1960s. When the national newspapers wanted to recruit a journalist from a local London publication they normally sent him initially to their Manchester office. The NUJ was very strong in Manchester, as well as most of the regional daily centres; and it also became efficient at signing up young journalist recruits when they were at the NCTJ 'block release' courses.

In 1966 the National Union of Journalists was still completing its closed shop strategy. I attended the NUJ Annual Delegate Meeting in 1966 and noted: 'The general approach is of a white-collar trade union which is overwhelmingly concerned with pay and conditions and nothing else. . . . Nor is it a militant white collar union like say ASSET.'[6]

But from about 1966 onwards the NUJ did move closer to the pattern of the white-collar union with 'militant' left-wing leadership. It continued to ride on the mass media and advertising boom. The general NUJ approach was to raise minimum rates. This increasingly assertive tone in the NUJ overall was reflected in more aggressive bargaining by the Fleet Street national newspaper journalists. Fleet Street NUJ chapels within most newspaper companies adopted the printing union device of the 'compulsory chapel meeting', in fact a quickie strike called close to first edition time.

The results of this NUJ Fleet Street militancy were quite dramatic. By the mid-1970s national newspaper journalists had won huge pay increases in real terms; much longer holidays had been won, sabbaticals were now possible, and—most spectacular—many journalists now only worked a four-day week.

[6] Author's notes on attending NUJ Annual Delegate Meeting at Scarborough, Apr. 1966.

The successes of the Fleet Street journalists created new tensions between them and their provincial colleagues. As the NUJ acquired a more left-wing and militant reputation, other tensions also emerged. Intra-union conflict often seemed to focus on the current General Secretary. The NUJ overall also pursued its love-hate relationship with the printing unions. Some favoured a merger with the politically militant, but industrially Luddite, National Graphical Association (NGA). Others—especially many national newspaper journalists—increasingly resented the NGA's high pay, overmanning, and refusal to accept new technology.

Conflict between the NUJ and NGA was an important factor in persuading the News International journalists to move to Wapping in January 1986; in so doing these journalists hammered nails into the coffins of both the NGA and the NUJ. The NUJ immediately expelled all those journalists who had moved to Wapping.

From 1986 the National Union of Journalists entered a phase of rapid decline. It was no longer able to win strikes. Indeed it soon had the experience of strikes in which it handed out strike pay and still lost. One such strike occurred in 1989 at the two Thomson daily papers in Aberdeen.[7] The Thomson management was from early 1988 in the forefront of requiring first senior journalists, and then all journalists, to sign individual contracts of employment. These contracts forbade journalists to engage in quickie unofficial strikes, thus removing the NUJ's key industrial weapon.

After the traumas of Wapping in 1986 most national newspaper managements moved quietly. In 1988 for example journalists at the *Sun* were being paid an average £30,000 for a four-day week. But by 1989 the national managements were ready to attack. In October 1989 journalists at the *Daily* and *Sunday Telegraph* held a 36-hour strike over the seven-day-newspaper economy plans. The winter of 1989–90 saw a series of confrontations with the Mail/Associated management, which was especially determined to impose individual contracts.

These external threats to the NUJ further exacerbated a number of already bitter internal disputes. A succession of NUJ finance officers and General Secretaries made unhappy and expensive exits. The NUJ had never been good at collecting subscriptions and now there seemed to be an increasingly large gap between the number of members claimed and the total sums of subscriptions

[7] James Buxton, 'The real conflict behind the news', *Financial Times*, 24 Nov. 1989.

collected. A 1990 survey found that 66 per cent of national newspaper and 49 per cent of regional newspaper journalists still belonged to the NUJ.[8] But by 1990 the NUJ had already lost most of its negotiating rights and industrial muscle.

Managements by 1994–5 claimed to see the NUJ as a spent force. Managements certainly saw their journalists in terms of a steep hierarchy; at the top the editor, the assistant editors, and other editorial executives; at the bottom the junior journalists and freelances who were insecure and peripheral; in the middle the 60 per cent or so of middling journalists who were 'staff' and still employed on a semi-permanent basis, with pension and other rights.

Between the 1960s and 1990s the old occupational community of Fleet Street was disbanded; career patterns became more chaotic; a 'reserve army' of aspirant journalists was greatly enlarged; and British national journalism became more layered into the three market levels.

The old Fleet Street was certainly not one big happy family; on the contrary it was divided up into numerous warring sub-territories. But the *Daily Express*, *Daily Telegraph*, *Sun*, and *Daily Mail* (and their Sunday companions) were up to 1986 all within three minutes' walk of each other. Each band of journalists tended to have its own pub; nevertheless there was much intermingling. Keith Waterhouse has recorded how—as an old *Daily Mirror* hand—he felt surrounded by numerous people whose lives and printed output he had been acquainted with over the years. There was a certain amount, also, of moving between different categories of newspapers, because—especially before 1970—the middlebrow or midmarket papers were so dominant. It was midmarket papers like the *Daily Express* and *Daily Mail* which had provided many of the print journalists who moved into television in the 1960s and 1970s.

After 1986 and the breaking up of Fleet Street, journalists tended to complain that they no longer met—on the street, in the pub—their old journalist friends and acquaintances. There had before 1986 been some off-Fleet Street ghettoes, such as Times Newspapers in Gray's Inn Road. But after 1986 this became the norm; for example the *Daily Mail*, *Mail on Sunday*, and *Evening Standard* in affluent Kensington. More newspaper groups went

---

[8] '1990 NUJ Survey', *Journalist's Week*, 9 Mar. 1990, 15–18.

east to docklands. At Wapping journalists from different newspapers certainly did meet and did share taxis to press conferences;
but, with the main exception of sport, journalists from the *Sun*
and *The Times* would not usually be covering the same
stories.

In the 1960s not only was Fleet Street a more coherent national
entity, but career paths into national newspapers were much less
chaotic than they subsequently became. My late-1960s study of
specialist correspondents showed a fairly standard previous career
pattern, with average ages as follows:

Age 18: Entered provincial journalism
Age 26: Entered national journalism
Age 30: Entered national specialization
Age 33: Began present specialization
Age 40: Present age

There were many exceptions, of course, but the NUJ requirement
that experience must be gained in the provinces gave a significant
common patterning to careers overall.

In terms of education the 1960s picture was much more polarized. Over half (54 per cent) of 1968 national specialist correspondents had finished formal education by age 17. Only one-third had
finished education at age 20 or later (typically with a completed
university degree). There was thus a marked bipolar distribution,
with most journalists having either less than, or more than, the
normal 18-year-old university entrance level of qualification.
Moreover within the higher education group, no less than two-
thirds had been to Oxford, Cambridge, or London Universities.[9]
This polarized pattern was, however, countered by the requirement that all must go through provincial journalism. But the
graduates had spent only about half as much time in provincial
journalism as had the non-graduates. After arrival in Fleet Street,
careers tended to continue in a relatively ordered manner in
circumstances of effective job security. Of these middling and
upper-middling national journalists, one-third were aged under 35,
one-third were aged 35 to 45, and one-third were over 45. The
main 'second career' possibility at that time was public relations,
an option chosen by some journalists from each of the age
brackets.

[9] Jeremy Tunstall, *Journalists at Work* (London: Constable and Beverly Hills, Calif.:
Sage, 1971), 96–7.

After the mid-1980s the NUJ was no longer able to enforce its wish that all national journalists should previously have worked on newspapers outside central London. Consequently a marked generation gap emerged between those who were recruited into national journalism before and after 1986. By 1995 most national journalists aged in their late thirties or older had been recruited via the provincial route. But there was a new grouping of journalists under 35 who had been recruited under different conditions.

Many of these more recent recruits had entered, not through provincial newspapers, but through specialist (usually London-based) magazines. Specialist financial magazines and women's magazines had previously provided a modest flow of recruits into financial and women's sections of national newspapers. Now this pattern was followed from showbusiness, medical, environmental, listings, and other types of magazines into the relevant specialisms and the burgeoning new sections of national newspapers.

In the 1960s there was a 'reserve army' of journalists mainly on provincial daily newspapers who wanted to move to London. By the 1990s that reserve army had become much bigger; the fully employed members of the reserve army now worked on magazines and specialist publications. Another large element were part-time, casual, and freelance journalists, often working one or two shifts a week, filling in on holidays, and offering freelance contributions to newspaper section editors. Also aspiring to jobs on national newspapers were the traditional battalions on the regional daily newspapers and in the local news agencies.

Clearly the recruitment of journalists to national newspapers was becoming more like the recruitment of actors. Also increasing the total body of 'resting' or aspiring journalists were the products of a hugely increased number of university courses in journalism, media studies, and communications.

Meanwhile British national journalism has become more layered into the three market levels, with experience at the upmarket level now being seen as a disqualification for employment at the downmarket level, and vice versa. The former pattern of journalists who worked at all three levels (such as Sir Nicholas Lloyd) appears to be a thing of the past. There is some movement from midmarket papers (mainly the *Daily Mail*) into upmarket papers (such as *The Times*), but even this has become fairly rare. Experience on the *Sun* is highly valued by the *Daily Mirror*, *Daily Star*, and ·the downmarket Sundays, but is a disqualification in the midmarket and upmarket. The main movement in the midmarket has been between the *Daily Express* and *Daily Mail*. There is much movement within the upmarket newspapers, with the exception of the *Guardian*, where staff jobs are still for life and only a few journalists leave. There has been much movement between the *Independent*, *Times*, and *Telegraph* dailies and Sundays. An illustration of this recruitment within the upmarket is provided by the launch of the *Independent on Sunday* in January 1990. The list of 'Editorial Appointments' of full-time journalists and major 'contributors' indicating previous locations appears in Table 8.3. The general tone was upmarket to a perhaps unwise degree; the most downmarket magazine origin was the London listings magazine *Time Out* (its then editor Simon Garfield). International publications included the *International Herald Tribune* and the *South China Morning Post*. The most downmarket single newspaper origin was the *Sunday Express* (in the person of Lynn Barber). Incidentally 23 per cent of these recruits were women, and women accounted for half the Sunday Review and Features section, the most admired part of the *Independent on Sunday*.

Television and radio journalism had by the 1990s largely developed its own direct patterns of recruitment. Senior jobs in television increasingly only go to those with previous experience

Table 8.3. Editorial appointments for the *Independent on Sunday*, January 1990 (N = 88)

Previous locations	%
Independent (daily)	38
Other upmarket newspapers	32
Upmarket and international magazines, and specialist publications	15
Freelance	8
TV and radio	3
Midmarket newspapers	2
Downmarket newspapers	0
Banking, book publishing	2
TOTAL	100

BOX 8.2. SIMON HEFFER: ONE JOURNALIST'S QUICK-STEPPING CAREER

- Read English at Cambridge (1979–82). No undergraduate journalism; I played politics.
- All I could do was write, so for 18 months I was a sub-editor on a magazine for laboratory technicians. They gave us an English grammar test, lucky for me; so I got this job at £6,000 a year—it hardly paid my train fare.
- Now interested in how badly the National Health Service was being run, I became a cub reporter on *Medical News*. Was there one year; after six months, as assistant editor.
- I was introduced to people in Fleet Street pubs, including Peter Utley, then *Daily Telegraph* deputy editor. Peter (who was blind, but prompted by his wife) said, on one occasion, 'Is that a Corpus tie, I see, dear boy?'
- Filled in for features editor of another medical magazine, *GP* (Haymarket), while she was on maternity leave.
- Introduced by Peter Utley to Peter Stothard, then deputy editor of *The Times*; subsequently I wrote leaders on the need for radical national health service and welfare reforms—about two freelance leaders a month. This was 1985 when Charlie Douglas-Home was dying and Charlie Wilson was taking over as editor of *The Times*.
- In March 1986, Max Hastings (just installed as *Daily Telegraph* editor) asked Peter Utley for names 'of bright young men'. I was then nearly 26. When Max phoned I was at a noisy boat race party. I was one of his first hires. I was on the *Telegraph* five years (1986–91), starting as a leader writer.
- Then did six months as number two lobby correspondent at Westminster. With my strong political views, I didn't really like reporting and having to regurgitate the bromides of some MPs I thought were mentally ill.
- So then I did the Parliamentary Sketch quite happily and also one or two leaders a week.
- Later I was a *Telegraph* leader writer and columnist.
- But Max Hastings and I fell out a bit (1990–1); he was happy with the fall of Thatcher and being in the ERM, while I was unhappy with both.
- Charles Moore (then *Daily Telegraph* deputy editor) told Dominic Lawson, his successor as editor at the *Spectator*, about this; and Dominic offered me the deputy editorship there.

Continued

- While at the *Spectator* I also did an *Evening Standard* column (1991–3) under at first Paul Dacre and then Stewart Steven.
- Then Paul Dacre invited me to do the column in the *Daily Mail* (1993–4).
- Then Max Hastings invited me back, so I left the *Spectator* to become deputy editor at the *Daily Telegraph* (1994).
- Back to the *Daily Mail* as columnist (1995).

of television programming, technology, and the relevant genre.[10] However, when television and radio do deliberately recruit from the press they tend to choose from upmarket newspapers like the *Guardian* and *The Times* (which provide ready-made reputations and together provide political 'balance').

This highly layered occupational structure in journalism, of course, reflects not just the British social class structure but that of all industrial countries. However, in, say, the United States or France newspaper sales are dominated by local monopoly dailies aimed at the top half of the population in education and income terms; these industrial conditions are more consistent with a uniformly supported mid and upmarket professionalizing tendency within journalism. In Britain, where the dominant press consists of national newspapers stratified in terms of social class, the conditions are not favourable and have become still less favourable to a professionalizing tendency.

Nevertheless there is some element of integration between the élites of the upmarket and the midmarket newspapers. Although they do not dominate the sales, the midmarkets and upmarkets together constitute two-thirds of all of the daily and Sunday titles. So if one can think in terms of an élite of 100 top journalists within each level, 200 of the total 300 are running the midmarket and upmarket newspapers.

This book is not a study of such an élite. But clearly these 200 or so journalists do have much in common. Their incomes are in the national top 1 per cent; most of them are men. Most are university graduates, and the 1968 finding of two-thirds of graduates being from Oxford, Cambridge, and London universities probably remains true. Even in 1968 there was a skew (in terms of origins) to the South of England; and the South-East and London focus has become stronger since. Personal connections, casual meetings, gos-

---

[10] Tunstall, *Television Producers*.

sip, and job-finding networks were very important in the 1960s and have become even more so since. All of these things correlate with an élite education, followed by working and living in London. This is an extremely London-oriented group, many of whom live in familiar inner-London locations from Islington to Fulham.

Members of this journalist élite work long hours between the BBC's *Today* radio show and television *Newsnight* at 10.30 p.m. They have a strong personal sense of successful achievement in a highly competitive occupation. Self-confident and extrovert demeanours are not in short supply. These people have strong views and express themselves forcefully (even to prying interviewers). These are the people of the written and spoken word; many of them are virtuoso deliverers of the humorous anecdote. But these same people have a marked tendency to regard most politicians, business people, and members of the royal family as poorly informed and ill educated.

They themselves would also insist that they are individuals; the British traditions of individualism and minor eccentricity are certainly still much in evidence. Indeed the national newspaper industry has recently encouraged the development of journalist stars, some of whom we meet in the next chapter.

Part III
JOURNALISM, STORIES, AND READERS

9 Page Power

FATTER newspapers in recent decades have led to more specialization both in terms of pages and people. The 1950s and 1960s saw a big expansion in specialist news reporting. The 1980s and 1990s have seen a big expansion in 'non-news'—in feature coverage and in regular sections devoted to specialist areas and to consumer themes. There has been a huge growth in the phenomenon of the star columnist who is given a set space on perhaps two days a week. There are also star exponents of the Big Interview, the heavily featured agony aunts, and the star astrologers.

This burgeoning of sections and star writers has implications for many aspects of journalism, and not least for the exercise of editor power. A high degree of autonomy is granted to the section head (who has perhaps 20 pages published each Wednesday); the section head typically is left very free from week to week to spend his or her section budget. An even higher degree of autonomy is normally granted to the star columnist or star writer; typically the columnist is required to produce, say, 800 or 1,000 words for Monday and Thursday and to deliver these words by an agreed deadline on Sunday and Wednesday; what the words say is up to the columnist.

But while the editor thus cedes a high degree of autonomy on a week-to-week basis, this ultimately is conditional autonomy. In the longer run the editor retains the strategic power; and editors are always signing new stars, while some columnists' contracts are not renewed or are cut down from two to one per week. There is a steady flow of announcements that one paper is about to merge its television guide and its 'Living' section, while another newspaper is about to separate (perhaps for the second or third time) its business and its sports sections.

The arrival of a new editor is typically followed by the appearance of a new section. The new section, it is announced, represents the new editor's fresh thinking; the new section will be aimed at young readers and will feature the work of star journalists. This, for example, was the trade press on a new Arts and Features section of *The Times* launched by a new editor:

The man chosen to edit what has been a cherished project of editor Simon Jenkins is executive editor (features) Brian MacArthur.

Last week MacArthur told UKPG: 'I hope it will be serious but sharp, entertaining and often controversial. It will give *The Times* a younger and more modern image . . .'[1]

When another editor was appointed two years later the section disappeared in this form, with most of the material and persons being redeployed in new locations.

I

The 1950s and 1960s saw a big increase in the numbers of specialist news reporters and 'correspondents'. Such specialization existed in the Victorian period mainly in the form of political reporters and foreign correspondents. By the 1930s sports reporting was a big specialist field; while defence and industrial (or labour) correspondents were spreading from the upmarkets to all of the other national dailies.

A typical national daily by 1968 had no less than 58 specialist news gatherers (plus specialist sub-editors) from a total of some 300 journalists in London and Manchester. The main categories were:

foreign correspondents	8
sports correspondents and reporters	21
financial specialists	8
other specialists	21
Total =	58

Amongst the 'other specialists' were included old-established fields, such as the political (lobby) correspondents, but also new specialists such as the education correspondents.

In my study the specialists were classified according to the main goal (advertising, circulation, or prestige) served by the field in question.[2] We can list these fields under the same goal classification

---

[1] 'MacArthur edits new Times arts section', *UK Press Gazette*, 20 Jan. 1992.

[2] Jeremy Tunstall, *Journalists at Work* (London: Constable, and Beverly Hills, Calif.: Sage, 1971).

and summarize what happened to each field between 1968 and 1995.

Two fields—crime and football—were classified in 1968 as having an audience or circulation goal. Crime journalism grew larger and more political, while public relations efforts—both by pressure groups and the police—became more sophisticated.[3] Between 1968 and 1995 'sport got bigger' (as one sports editor put it) and football covered more pages in the 1990s. Both of these fields continued to be seen by editors, circulation directors, and by journalists as ones which sold a lot of newspapers.

Two of the 1968 fields—motoring and fashion—were classified as having an advertising goal. While both fields were believed to be popular with significant groups of readers, these fields made greater concessions to advertisers than were found elsewhere. In both these fields the main news sources were also the main advertisers, and these major commercial interests were allowed to dictate lengthy embargoes between when the new cars or new fashions were first seen by the journalists and when the first reports appeared. Both of these fields clearly continue to have advertising relevance; but in both cases the appeal has been broadened further in a circulation direction. Motoring correspondents have increased the coverage they give to broader motoring and political (and environmental) concerns. Fashion reporting has been propelled by colour printing and press hyper-competition into a more prominent place; fashion pictures appear on front pages and in big spreads on centre pages, and fashion is employed as a 'respectable' upmarket device for presenting pictures of female (and some male) models.

In 1968 I classified foreign correspondence as a 'non-economic' or money-losing field. That was the view also of Rupert Murdoch and the other downmarket owners who after 1970 largely dispensed with this prestigious but expensive field of coverage. The final category was classified as 'mixed' in goal. This included political (lobby) journalism, which is discussed in a subsequent chapter (16). The other mixed goal fields were aviation, labour, and education. Aviation continued into the 1990s to receive about the same emphasis. Education was a rising field of the 1960s and it continued to retain at least as much salience into the 1990s.

Specialists in such fields in both the 1960s and 1990s had a considerable degree of autonomy. Once the editor (and news edi-

---

[3] Philip Schlesinger and Howard Tumber, *Reporting Crime* (Oxford: Clarendon Press, 1994).

tor) assign a journalist to one of these specialist roles they ask and expect him or her to acquire specialist expertise. The specialist then quickly acquires a considerable element of control over the day's choice of story; typically the specialist would tell the news desk executives what he or she proposed to cover that day and, more times than not, the desk people would agree. The specialist would also become part of an informal specialist grouping or club. These specialists collectively defined the field in question: it was from the collective output—press, radio, and TV—of these specialists that the national audience largely heard about the field in question as well as the names, sayings, characteristics of the prominent people within that field.

My study also showed that, in addition to competing with each other for exclusive facts, details, and 'angles', these specialists also engaged in co-operation. Most 'club' members would give to any fellow specialist a press statement or a fact which was generally available or would become available well before the evening deadline. But there was also a second, more intimate type of co-operation, which involved regular partners—usually two or three journalists on different papers—who systematically 'worked together'. For example if a particular story required phone calls to twenty separate sources, a *Daily Mail* specialist and a *Daily Telegraph* specialist might make ten phone calls each and share the results (either face to face or by phone). It was widely believed that partnerships between journalists who were not direct competitors (for instance a tabloid with a broadsheet) were more acceptable. However, exchange partnerships between directly competing specialists are more helpful, first, because direct competitors are more likely to be covering the same story in roughly the same way; and, secondly, co-operating with your most direct competitor cuts out one of the most severe competitive threats and reduces the chance of your 'missing the story'. The majority of specialists were aware of competing against such partnerships; and a quarter of all specialists admitted that they themselves engaged in such regular partnership exchanges. My study identified fourteen *Daily Mail* and ten *Daily Express* specialists involved in such exchange partnerships. There were at least two examples each of *Daily Mail* journalists co-operating with specialists from the *Daily Express*, *Daily Mirror*, *The Times*, *Daily Telegraph* and the *Sun* (before Murdoch and Lamb).[4]

---

[4] Jeremy Tunstall, *Journalists at Work*, 205–49.

Editors of these newspapers were also asked about their attitudes to such behaviour. Editors, of course, were well aware of the phenomenon; however, some did not know about some of their own specialists' co-operative partnerships. Several said that they welcomed a moderate amount of co-operation, but strongly opposed partnerships with direct competitors. Alastair Hetherington in 1968 stated that such practices reduced the power of the editor; more than one editor said that he would fire any specialist who co-operated regularly with a direct competitor.

However, although an editor's knowledge and control of such partnerships may be incomplete, the specialist's autonomy is very far from absolute. Indeed specialists resort to these exchange partnerships precisely because so many aspects of newsgathering competition are beyond the correspondent's control. In 1968 specialist correspondents did complain about the way in which their stories were used; some correspondents (especially on the more serious papers) suffered fairly little sub-editing, but especially on the popular papers a specialist's story might be cut by a half or might not appear at all. In 1968 also the specialist correspondents complained that 'by-lines'—the journalist's name attached to the story— were used as a disciplinary device. If a news executive was unhappy with some aspect of the specialist's performance, the by-line was withdrawn and the story appeared without a named author.

Specialist journalism since the 1960s has been greatly affected by the increased polarization between the upmarket and the downmarket newspapers. Broadly speaking, news specialization has been still further developed by the upmarket newspapers, with new specialisms in fields such as architecture, law, the media, and the environment. But the *Daily Mirror* now has fewer news specialisms than it had in the 1960s; this followed a 1969 decision by the first Murdoch-appointed editor of the *Sun*, Larry Lamb, largely to rid himself of serious news specialists:

I have always been wary of specialists, though in some areas—in Parliament, for example—one cannot do without them.

On the old *Sun* there had been twenty-seven. Twenty-seven people with unnecessary private offices and underused secretaries.

. . . many newspaper 'specialisations' are not only unnecessary but also can be a positive handicap, in that specialists become too close to their subjects, form little clubs of their own, and tend to forget that they are in the business of disclosure. And, of course, once they have acquired the distinction of a title of some kind, they feel entitled to refuse work outside their immediate area of specialisation, and are therefore chronically underemployed.[5]

The downmarket newspapers continued with their political specialists and strengthened their sports and crime reporting. They appointed 'Royal Correspondents' after 1980 (see Chapter 19 below), while showbusiness and television also received increased specialist attention.

The midmarket newspapers have here—as elsewhere—experienced contradictory impulses. An example is the question of whether to have environmental correspondents; all three midmarket dailies decided to have environmental correspondents and subsequently changed their minds. The environment specialism has also caused some upmarket editors anxiety.[6] Charles Moore, editor of the *Sunday Telegraph* in 1994 believed that although many readers thought they were interested in the environment, most readers in fact found it boring; meanwhile the *Sunday Telegraph* had an admired specialist operating in this field. The environment, like previous mixed fields—such as labour, education, health, and defence—is a semi-political field, with obvious party political overtones. Thus some editors clearly believed that environment corespondents would be 'captured' by left and green interests. But there is a case also for arguing that the 'environment' is too big and vague a field and is best covered by more sharply defined existing specialists such as science, transport, technology, and health specialists or by correspondents in the relevant foreign countries, in Brussels, at the UN agencies, and in the relevant British regions. The green-inclined environmental coverage is also to be found in significant quantities in television documentaries and some of this seeps across into various newspaper feature offerings.

One of the biggest changes in specialist subjects has been the trend towards consumer, leisure, and life-style areas. The travel, food, and health pages of the 1960s have become the travel, food, and health multi-page sections of the 1990s. Even in a traditionally 'hard' field, such as finance, much of the increase has been in the form of 'Personal Finance' coverage about your bank, your home, and your pension.

---

[5] Larry Lamb, *Sunrise* (London: Macmillan, 1989), 22–3.

[6] On the environment and the press see Robert M. Worcester, 'Are newsrooms bored with Greenery?', *British Journalism Review*, 4/3 (1993), 24–6. David Longman and Colin Lacy, 'Despatches from the doze-zone', *British Journalism Review*, 5/2 (1994), 49–53.

Specialist journalism has also migrated out of the general news pages at the front of the paper into new sections and new columns written by personality columnists. Many of the people who generate this new wave of specialized material are not even on the staff of the newspaper. Some of the most prominent personalities working for a newspaper are columnists who may be non-staffers contracted to write one column per week. Many or most of the people who write for the travel section, the women's pages, or the personal finance section are freelances; they are often journalists working full time on a specialist travel, women's, or financial publication, who also do regular or occasional pieces for a particular national newspaper section. These latter types of specialization also prevail in the downmarket papers.

II

British journalists are inclined to say that the power of the 'back-bench' is the aspect of newspapers which outsiders least comprehend. In Chapter 3 there was an account of the *Daily Mirror* in the late 1960s; here the night editor and his numbers two and three between them chose the lead story and lead picture for each of the news pages. Because of the smallish number of pages and the small number of spaces available, this one individual—the night editor—was able himself both to select the material and to determine the overall look of that night's newspaper. In doing this he was, of course, also acting on the basis of discussions with the editor and other senior people. The night editor and his two assistants—and their team of sub-editors—were also rejecting most of what the *Daily Mirror*'s journalists had written that day. Sub-editors rejected material by 'spiking' typed sheets of paper onto a crude wood-and-upturned-metal-nail device. The back-bench rejected some of the sub-edited material by throwing the pages—and photographs—on the floor.

Today the sub-editor's spikes, pots of paste, and blue pencils have gone. So have the rows of simple tables at which the sub-editors sat. Now, of course, the sub-editors work at desk top computer terminals and their whole operation is much more complex; they are now also doing the final typesetting once done by 'compositors'.

The 'traditional Fleet Street system' requires that the newspaper is assembled, designed, and generally put together by the back-bench. This 'traditional' system really only dates from the 1920s and more especially from the Christiansen/Beaverbrook *Daily Express* of the 1930s. One news editor described this tradition thus: 'The news desk, with its correspondents and reporters, prepare the meal—they cook a big range of available dishes and spread them out on the table; then the back-bench come along, they taste the dishes and decide which ones they like; while the rest are thrown away.' This tradition—of presenting the back-bench with more dishes than they eat—still continues. Reporters and even senior correspondents write stories during the day which the back-bench may reject, or heavily cut, in the evening. The tradition has been weakened in some respects, but strengthened in others.

The rapid arrival of computer technology in late 1980s Fleet Street, followed by the facility for designing whole pages on screen, created something of a 'generation gap' amongst sub-editors. The new technology—and the perceived need to have attractive-looking pages—placed heavy emphasis on sub-editor computer skills at the expense of other, more old-fashioned, sub-editor virtues. A foreign editor said:

A sub-editor who can sub a story very quickly, make a headline that fits, is computer-literate, tends to get given the most important stories; the person who knows how to spell African capital cities and the name of the last President but two and worries about the grammatical structure of the kicker paragraph or whatever—these kinds of skills have been pushed into the background.

A sports editor emphasized the need for speed in Saturday subbing on a Sunday paper: 'A lot of red hot subs didn't cross the new technology divide, they just couldn't handle it. . . . they used to come in until 1987 because Saturday subbing was well paid and very sociable and everybody chatted and laughed in between doing the business with the blue pencil.' Sub-editing has become less sociable and subs become absorbed into the 'blinking green monster'; some executives see a loss of efficiency from the older sociable ways, for example the loss of the practice of discussing a headline—scribbled on paper—with your neighbour on the sub-editors' table.

Fresh waves of still more sophisticated computer terminals seem likely to ensure that computer skills will continue to be vital. The more traditional word and literary skills may catch up; but there is also a common perception that the paper's sub-editors are not using some of the facilities already available in the current system. In newspaper offices—as elsewhere—there are certain individuals known by their colleagues to be able 'to do more' with the system.

There are also other obvious ways in which new technology goes along with back-bench strength. As colour in the early 1990s became universally available there was also an increased focus—in both broadsheets and tabloids—on design and layout; these are areas which traditionally belong to the back-bench—with their traditional titles such as chief night editor, associate night editor, and chief sub-editor.

Back-bench power differs sharply across the broadsheet/tabloid divide, but there are distinctions also within these categories. Back-bench strength is greatest on the downmarket tabloids, the *Sun*, *Mirror*, and *Star*. The *Daily Mail* and *Daily Express* back-benches have been powerful since the 1930s and this has continued into the 1990s. But on both of these papers there are more counterbalancing forces—and more status accorded to leading writing journalists. On all of the tabloid papers it is common practice for the editor either to sit in on the back-bench or to remain in his office and to consult with the back-bench until late in the evening.

Occupying an intermediate position were *The Times* and *Daily Telegraph*. Both of these dailies have continued to take the view that a reader-friendly newspaper requires a strong back-bench. The *Daily Telegraph* gives itself the task of using a large number of separate home news stories, and this inevitably requires a considerable marshalling effort. *The Times* in the 1980s employed in senior positions a number of *Daily Mail* journalists, and there was a continuing effort to liven up *The Times* with some tabloid news presentation skills.

III

After 1986 some newspapers doubled or even trebled the number of sections offered to readers per week. Most of this additional matter was 'feature' material, typically written several days or weeks previous to the day of publication. Although 1986 was the key date, sectionalization had a lengthy pre-history. Back in 1962 the *Sunday Times* had launched its 'Colour Supplement', vaguely copied from the *New York Times* Sunday magazine; but when in

September 1964 the *Observer* launched its Sunday reply and the *Daily Telegraph* launched its Friday version, these three upmarket 'Colour Supplements' came to be seen by the advertising world as separate publications, Britain's leading high-quality high-gloss upmarket weekly magazines. They came to loom large in the total profits and losses of their mother publications. This 'Colour Supplement' phenomenon remained largely fixed for two decades until 1981, when the *News of the World* launched its *Sunday* magazine/supplement, and 1982 when the *Mail on Sunday* launched its *You* magazine/supplement (against the already existing *Sunday Express* magazine).

The three latter magazine offerings all emphasized that these glossy magazine/supplements were a crucial ingredient of market leadership. The *Mail on Sunday* was seeking to use *You* to wrest the midmarket Sunday leadership from the *Sunday Express*; the *News of the World* was seeking to consolidate its leadership in the Sunday downmarket.

The Wapping 1986 industrial changes, by massively cutting costs were, of course, favourable to new sections. This was also a period of cheap newsprint and expanding advertising. Two other factors after 1986 were especially relevant to additional sections. One change was the introduction of a high-quality colour printing capability right through the main newspaper; this colour capability encouraged all papers, but especially the tabloids, to create special sections of 16 or 20 pages folded into the main paper; for example, sport on Monday and television on Saturday. The opening up of television listings for the first time in 1991–2 allowed British newspapers to produce weekly television guides.

In 1988 Saturday was revolutionized as a newspaper day; this change started with the upmarkets but also filtered to the other market levels, turning Saturday from the thinnest to the fattest day of the week for British national newspapers. The Saturday revolution of 1988 was led by the newcomer, the *Independent*; this was followed by the *Sunday Telegraph*'s glossy magazine being switched to the *Daily Telegraph*; a move intended to strengthen the *Daily Telegraph*'s sales leadership in the daily upmarket and also to compete against the *Sunday Times*, the Sunday leader. This competition took several forms, but the *Daily Telegraph* continued to provide extra Saturday offerings; in 1995 it introduced separate motoring and personal finance sections, bringing its total Saturday sections to nine. The *Daily Telegraph* and *Independent* had Saturday sales 18 per cent and 25 per cent above their Monday–Friday levels.[7]

This sectionalization explosion was certainly encouraged by growing advertising expenditure during 1986–8, but it continued when advertising expenditure declined in 1989. The new sections were driven especially by market share considerations and by the observation that some (but not all) sections significantly increased circulation. There was a general management urge to provide a 'reader benefit' of more editorial pages per penny paid.

As newspaper sectionalization developed in Britain there was a big range from the 80-page high-cost Sunday glossy (with a staff of thirty full-time journalists) to a 6-page 'section' inside the main paper on Tuesday (with a staff of one half-time journalist). At the high-cost, high-risk end of sectionalization were the glossy magazines, which were given away free with the newspaper but could have been sold as separate stand-alone glossy magazines. The glossy magazines were financially positive for the market leaders, the *Sunday Times* and *Daily Telegraph*.[8] Its high advertising return was largely taken up by the very high production cost, but was strongly positive overall by boosting the sales and advertising rates of the other much more cheaply produced sections. For the competitors like the *Observer* the colour magazine was always seen as a costly obligation, and was dropped after the *Guardian*'s take-over.

In the midmarket (with lower advertising rates) the glossy magazine/supplements were more problematic. While the midmarket managements succeeded with their Sunday glossies, both the *Daily Express* and *Daily Mail* tried—and failed—during 1986–9 to sustain a glossy magazine on Saturday. The downmarket managements had to struggle hard to maintain rather thin glossy magazines—again on Sunday only. The *People*'s Sunday magazine was said in 1991 to be losing £10 million a year, while the main paper was making £10 million a year.

After 1990 there was a trend for the glossy magazines to switch towards women readers and to redefine themselves as glossy women's magazines. A 1993 move towards the woman's magazine concept by the *Mail on Sunday*'s *You* magazine was followed by, for example, the *People* and the *Daily Telegraph*.

[7] National Readership Survey, Jan.–June 1995.

[8] The *Telegraph* magazine started in 1964 with the Friday *Daily Telegraph*, was with the *Sunday Telegraph* during 1976–88, and from 1988 was with the Saturday *Daily Telegraph*.

These continuing glossy magazine doubts and redefinitions were strongly influenced by the new opportunity to print a separate supplement/magazine on conventional cheap paper. The quality of colour now available on cheap paper was accompanied by other advantages; not only was it radically cheaper (than the glossy), but it could be used in a larger (tabloid rather than A4) size. Finally, it could be produced quickly to normal newspaper timetables, thus avoiding the several weeks timelag of the glossy and allowing the use of up-to-date reviews and news-related material. The pioneer here was the Sunday Review section of the *Independent on Sunday* (January 1990). This 'heat-set' colour magazine approach was quickly copied by *The Times* Saturday magazine and then by several others. These heat-set 'Reviews' provided a much more flexible environment for advertisers, for editors, and for writers. Massive two-page advertisements with high-quality colour were available at short notice; editors of these reviews did not have to be so obsessed (as their glossy counterparts) with the need for dominating pictures; and these new reviews offered slots for ambitious journalists to show their paces over 3,000 words.

Moving down the section offerings there was an expansion after 1986 of the second sections of the upmarket Sundays. The *Sunday Times*, under Andrew Neil's editorship, changed into a ten-section product. Meanwhile the upmarket dailies moved towards multiple-section Saturdays and two or three weekday sections. The *Guardian* was a pioneer of the second (and third) weekday section in tabloid format, with a different editorial (and classified advertising) theme for each day.

The final type of section offering is the 'internal section'; this solution was especially favoured by the downmarket dailies—with internal sections devoted especially to women, Saturday and Monday sports, and television. Some midmarket internal sections have become quite large—for example the *Mail on Sunday*'s 40 or more pages of finance from 1994 onwards.

Since 1986 sections have continued to change, expand, and contract in such a way as to mean that any general statement becomes quickly outdated. But this very element of constant change also means that the sections have become a continuing research-and-development and test-marketing mechanism. Sales vary from day to day, showing the changing sales appeal of the Money section against the Health section, and so on. Sales also vary according to month, season, and year—again in line with sectional offerings.

Like the extra channels in television, these extra newspaper sections have become a forcing house for new commercial formulas as well as for new creative talent. One cheap commercial formula is to allow young staff journalists to offer long feature articles to a section editor; the section editor gets a long piece at little or no extra cost, but the young journalist experiments with the newspaper's longest writing form. The sections provide editorial executive experience for journalists. The section editor typically has a small journalist staff and a budget for commissioning freelances. Here is an opportunity to learn editorial-plus-entrepreneurial skills.

The sections also contribute strongly to the personality, the overall character, and the image of the newspaper. Following and copying the multi-section *Sunday Times*, the Saturday *Daily Telegraph* has also steadily put on weight; in pursuit of the British super-heavyweight crown both papers have used their multiple sections to establish a new kind of supermarket reputation. The *Guardian*, with its more cautious and cheaper expansion into tabloid second sections, has strengthened its image as the paper of the youngish and leftish reader of classified employment advertising. The *People* has deployed its three Sunday sections in line with its ambition to move somewhat upmarket. The *Daily Mail* and *Mail on Sunday* have developed sections with an appropriate element of enticing midmarket polish. Meanwhile it is also noticeable that newspapers which are unsuccessful and confused as to their target market tend to be uncertain and confused in their sectionalization strategy.

IV

Although freelance journalists may perceive newspaper section editors as being hard-faced and commercially minded managers, the section editors see themselves as journalists relying on their personal flair and instinct to choose suitably riveting reads for their customers. Like many other journalists (and television producers) these section editors are highly sceptical about research findings. The editor of a magazine which attracts £1 million worth of advertising per week happily claims ignorance as to what proportion of the readers are male or female, but 'you could ask our advertising people'. The very fact that research data are associated with advertising may lead to their rejection. Magazine and section editors indeed have a double commitment to creativity—they share the normal journalist's concern with words, but their concern with pictures, page layout art, and the visual in general is greater than that of most journalists.

The conditional autonomy of the section editor largely excludes politics. This is simply because politics is handled by the day-to-day political correspondents, various other senior journalists, and the editor. But although the section editor does not deal with the most overtly political type of material, many newspaper sections do deal with major semi-political areas such as education, social services, local government, property and housing, the environment, agriculture, and transport. Even travel can be quite political. The *Guardian* on the left and the *Daily Telegraph* on the political right both carry a lot of sections dealing with such semi-political material. There is also, of course, a strong 'semi-political' element in much arts, theatre, and book reviewing.

Thus, while section editors do not usually impinge on day-to-day national politics they do commission pieces from political figures and the heavy emphasis on celebrities as subject-matter does encompass elected politicians, business, and trade union leaders, and other semi-political persons. One Murdoch/News section editor said:

The individual writer might go to meet somebody and get such an unfavourable impression, they might say, 'Gosh this is such a pompous ass, I'm going to expose him or her as such,' and I would say 'Fine, let's do it'; the editor might occasionally say 'I think you've run too many showbiz people, or too many politicians, lately'—but that would be a question of balance, not attitude.

The section editor's external power, however, primarily takes the form of cultural power—encompassing the huge areas of 'popular culture', pop music, and television through to serious culture, music, television, and the arts. The section editors collectively also are arbiters of 'celebrity'; part of becoming more than just a singer or a sportsperson is to become the subject of lengthy articles in newspaper magazines and sections.

At the high culture end of the spectrum section editors employed especially by the *Guardian*, *The Times*, and the *Independent* see themselves as performing some kind of cultural leadership. It could be argued that these sections have taken over the role once performed by the 'weekly journals of opinion' like the *Spectator* and *New Statesman*.

There is a kind of metaphysical goal. . . . it's important to do ground-breaking work . . . sometimes we do pieces that affect the way people think; this is not like the *Sunday Times* glossy magazine which you can read on Sunday afternoon and then bin it; we do more substantial stuff and people keep it on their bedside table throughout the week, you can feel people reading a particular piece during the week and they will talk about it a lot.

Both *The Times* and the *Guardian* have long seen themselves as vehicles for good writing across a wide range of subjects from politics to sport. As one senior executive at the *Guardian* said, 'The *Guardian* has always been known as a writer-friendly newspaper; this has been the place where your words are lovingly massaged into print; now others are offering the same service.' The *Independent* was the chief new loving word-massager, but one 1990s editor of *The Times*, Simon Jenkins, especially emphasized that part of the paper's tradition.

Section editors at the *Sunday Times*, *Daily Telegraph*, and *Mail on Sunday* say quite similar things. One emphasized the centrality of 'incredibly stimulating or amusing words', and another said, 'The key to a magazine is just having good ideas which you can translate onto the page and which are memorable, or interesting or amusing or fascinating or totally revelatory or whatever.' These latter section editors are aiming at a larger slice of the British public and in practice their definition of a gripping read is more middle-brow and best-sellerish.

The tabloid Sundays have another definition again. For example the *Sunday* magazine section of the *News of the World* deliberately cultivates a more family and bland atmosphere than the main newspaper; since much of *Sunday* is designed to appeal mainly to women and children, the editorial policy is to include one longer piece in the middle—often a true life crime story—which is intended as a riveting read for the man in the family.

Cultural power is exercised in the most pointed manner in the editorial choice of freelance writers. The biggest decisions of this kind are the editor's choices of regular weekly columnists. But since successful columnists typically last for decades, most day-to-day choices focus on freelance contributors. Each publication and each section has its list of frequently and occasionally used freelance contributors. Each section editor also receives a steady flow of unsolicited ideas; one such editor calculated that of about 100 unsolicited ideas per week he typically rejected 99 and accepted one. Section editors pointed out the potential waste of scarce time. 'Lots of people phone with an idea and I nearly always say "Send me two paragraphs", because two paragraphs I can deal with in about ten seconds, I put a No on it and a polite letter gets typed by the secretary, or—less frequently a Yes, I'd like to see a longer outline or I phone the person to discuss it.'

The unequal balance of power between the section editor and the vast majority of freelances is illustrated by what happens when newspapers are hit by bad economic times, as in 1990–2. When their commissioning budgets are cut, section editors find themselves doing several things, each of which is bad news for freelances. Declining advertising revenue will result in fewer editorial pages and there may be a disproportionate cut in the budget for freelance work. The section editor uses more material from staff journalists, who do not have to be paid anything extra. Most section editors have a backlog of material which they previously commissioned (and paid for) but did not use; thus the editor can 'run down inventory', which again costs nothing. With less space, less money, and less need for freelance material, there is also likely to be a cut in the amounts paid. What would have been a £500 commission is cut to £400; and special high rates (for star freelances or to include research or travel) may be eliminated altogether. Consequently a 20 per cent cut in advertising revenue might lead to a 50 per cent cut in money available for freelance writing in a specific newspaper section.

Any section editor, arts editor, or book editor has his or her favourite freelances and reviewers. But section editorships change; the new section editor may not agree with the previous editor's choices. A long-established film reviewer, opera critic, or pop music writer may suddenly be fired by the new 30-year-old section editor:

You do need to have critics who work on the paper for a long time and become identified with the paper . . . but, if someone's not coming up to scratch, you have to get rid of them; you're under a lot of pressure yourself to produce the best. . . . so there's a lot of not being diplomatic. . . . it's very brutal . . . but you can't hide people, you've just got to get rid of them and that's very hard to do.

Under the prevailing competitive conditions, section editors are constantly reminded that they are exerting power within a cultural market. Talking of freelances, one section editor said 'It's the "if

you don't want to do it at that price, I know others who will"
syndrome'. But section editors are also aware that they themselves—in operating the section—occupy a specific market slot.
For example section editors at the *Guardian* and *Independent* complain that the *Sunday Times* will pay more—in some cases several
times more—than they can pay. *Sunday Times* section editors operate on the assumption that their paper is 'the market leader' exercising a magnetic attraction on writing talent of all kinds; but the
Sunday Times section editor is especially aware of the need to
appeal to a semi-mass readership. Among the tabloid newspapers,
Mail and *Express* section editors also see themselves as in a strong
market position.

Finally there is a market, not only in columnists and freelances,
but in the section editors themselves. If a section editor has built up
his or her section, this will have been reflected especially in advertising revenue, but perhaps also in circulation figures—the Tuesday circulation figure may have increased recently. Successful
section editors are recognized as having editorial-entrepreneurial
skills and the head-hunting of section heads is a growth activity.
This phenomenon has not only market, but also power and
autonomy, implications. The section editor, who is in demand
elsewhere, may be accorded more autonomy—and thus becomes
one of the senior power-wielders within the newspaper's editorial
department.

10 Star Power

ADAILY newspaper which in 1965 had just two or three prominent personalities was by 1995 giving the big promotional treatment to perhaps twenty or thirty columnists and other journalist stars, who now appeared both at the front of the paper and also throughout the various new sections.

Terms such as 'columnist'—like much else within journalism—lack agreed definitions. For this book the 'star' journalist is one whose work appears regularly—such as on Monday and Thursday—at a standard length and location in the paper; the star journalist's name appears prominently at the top of the piece, usually accompanied by a photograph. Normally the star or columnist has complete control over this space and is subject to only the most minimal sub-editing; the star can write what he or she likes and is not subject to normal editorial constraints.

The emergence of the star journalist in Britain is a topic which awaits its historian. But the midmarket dailies in the interwar period did project a very small number of stars; there were certainly some transatlantic and Hollywood influences involved. The *Daily Mirror* in its pioneering late 1930s phase absorbed some advertising influences from J. Walter Thompson. From this one advertising agency came the *Mirror*'s leading sports columnist, Peter Wilson, and also William Connor, who as 'Cassandra' was the most high-profile popular newspaper columnist of the mid-century. Cassandra wrote his pungent column in the *Mirror* between 1935 and 1967 with a gap during 1942–6. He continued to criticize the British government for its inadequate conduct of the war for the first thirty months of the conflict.[1]

There was already in the 1930s a transfer market in personality columnists. For example in 1936 Godfrey Winn began a daily page in the *Daily Mirror* called 'Personality Parade'. The *Mirror* pro-

---

[1] Robert Connor, *Cassandra: Reflections in a Mirror* (London: Cassell, 1969).

moted Godfrey Winn himself as a personality and after only two years he was enticed across to Beaverbrook's *Sunday Express*; he later moved to the *Sunday Dispatch*. But during the 1940s and 1950s newspapers were thin and the current popular newspaper approach was to have just two or three big personality names. The star phenomenon was associated with entertainment and the heavier newspapers did not have stars. Right into the 1960s the *Daily Express* was quite grudging even with the number of by-line names it allowed to reporters. In retrospect this was perhaps part of the deference which the midmarket papers still paid to the upmarket papers.

The Times remained almost completely anonymous until 1966. In fact William Haley, the last anonymous editor (1952–67) himself wrote a highly eccentric weekly literary column under the name of Oliver Edwards. But it was only in early 1967 that the new editor, William Rees-Mogg, both abolished anonymity and began to promote a few selected star journalists. Even this was done very sparingly. Apart from regular weekly columns given to the existing Washington and Moscow foreign correspondents and to the chief political correspondent, Rees-Mogg[2] appointed just two fresh columnists, Ian Trethowan and Auberon Waugh, to write a political and a humorous column respectively; a third regular columnist was added four years later in the shape of Bernard Levin and his arts-oriented column. After Rees-Mogg's arrival the next significant expansion in columnists did not occur until fourteen years later, when Harold Evans became editor.

The other upmarket papers were equally cautious with prominent personality columnists. The *Daily Telegraph* continued to believe in news rather than personality views. The *Guardian* from 1959 had a humorous column by Michael Frayn but its first political column was not launched by Peter Jenkins until 1967.

Right through until 1986 the number of columnists and star writers remained small. After 1986 several factors—the extra pages, the extra competition, and the perceived need for more aggressive newspaper promotion—all came together and ignited into an explosive growth in star journalism. Editors and section editors elevated existing staff journalists to new celebrity status and also signed numerous fresh stars and starlets. This meant that a number of quite junior journalists were given instant star status.

[2] Iverach McDonald, *The History of the Times*, v: *Struggles in War and Peace, 1939–1966* (London: Times Books, 1984), 223–5 and 453–4.

BOX 10.1. KEITH WATERHOUSE

Keith Waterhouse was the successor to Cassandra as the main *Daily Mirror* columnist; the immediate (brief) successor was George Gale, who was too right wing for the *Mirror*. Waterhouse's column first appeared in the doomed *Daily Mirror* magazine in 1969–70 and then transferred to the main newspaper.

Waterhouse was born in Leeds in 1930 and was a reporter on the *Yorkshire Evening Post*. He joined the *Daily Mirror* in London at the then unacceptably young age of 22: 'I did it by lying'. He always wanted Cassandra's job, 'but it was occupied, so I went freelance. I was young and stupid'. He became a star feature writer for the *Daily Mirror* and a Hugh Cudlipp favourite. He wrote novels including *Billy Liar* (1959) which he also scripted into a successful film.

Keith Waterhouse became one of Britain's most successful and most prolific writers. Despite his numerous novels, stage plays, and screenplays, he continued to write a twice-a-week column. His column satirizes the passing political and social scene between Brussels, London, and the local Town Hall.

Waterhouse has strong views on columns. You need to have a background as a hardened hack; you need to have been out reporting, talked to politicians, and travelled. It helps to mix not only with politicians but also with literary, stage, and screen people. His *Waterhouse on Newspaper Style* was originally written for the *Daily Mirror* but was published by Penguin in 1993.

When Robert Maxwell acquired the *Mirror* Waterhouse took a dim view of the man he called Cap'n Bob. David English pounced and Waterhouse moved (with his leftish opinions) to the *Daily Mail*. Waterhouse explained his working habits to me in 1994: 'I write only in the morning. Each year I do one book and something for television or a play. The *Daily Mail* columns for Monday and Thursday I write on Sunday and Wednesday morning. At 9 a.m. I have not yet decided on either the topic or the characters in the column; but I'm sitting there with all the newspapers. I use an old manual typewriter. By 10 a.m. I've decided what to do and by 1 p.m. the column has been faxed. I'm a newspaperholic and also read a lot of trade magazines—each one takes you into a private Wellsian world—for example I read *The Grocer*, *Fortean Times*, and *The World's Fair*, which reviews new rides and has wonderful obituaries.'

BOX 10.2. SIR JOHN JUNOR

John Junor followed John Gordon both as editor of and columnist in the *Sunday Express*. John Junor was aged 35 when in 1954 he was appointed editor of the *Sunday Express* by Lord Beaverbrook, and he continued as editor for over thirty years. John Gordon, a previous long-time *Sunday Express* editor, contributed a column to the paper over two decades until he died in 1974.

From 1974 onwards John Junor himself wrote the *Sunday Express* column, initially for over a decade of his own editorship and then under his successor. In 1990 he was persuaded to move to the *Mail on Sunday*. John Junor is known for his pugnacious writing style and in particular for his pugnacious comments on politicians and other public figures. Originally a Liberal, as a Beaverbrook editor he moved to the political right. He was an ardent supporter of Margaret Thatcher and was knighted, on her advice, in 1980.

Junor told me in 1994 that many 'columnists' were really 'essayists' who wrote on a single topic each week. The genuine column had to have several different items. Junor himself saw the column as having a political core. But typically the one or two key political items were accompanied by three or four other items, on television, the royal family, and much else; usually there was a picture of an attractive woman in the top half of the tabloid page ('I think a lot about women').

At 75 John Junor did not seem much older than he had at 49. He was appearing regularly in his comfortable *Mail on Sunday* office where he had a secretary to handle his 40 to 50 letters a week. ('Half of the letters are from people who say they followed me across from the *Sunday Express*'.) He was still regularly going out to lunch with prominent politicians as well as showbiz and television people: 'You need to watch quite a bit of television; and you must be constantly plucking out ideas. To be a columnist is to work 24 hours a day. I used to carry a notebook and when I was on the train, if something in one of the newspapers made me angry, I'd make a note. But now I carry a tape recorder which enables me to record my indignation while it's fresh.' During over forty years as editor and columnist John Junor handed out many harsh judgements; he himself was also fiercely denounced in print by a succession of politicians and journalists.

BOX 10.3. AUBERON WAUGH

Auberon Waugh suffered from some early disadvantages. His father was the novelist Evelyn Waugh, and Auberon published four novels before his thirtieth birthday. While in Cyprus as a national service officer in the British Army Auberon Waugh experienced a near fatal shooting accident with six bullets passing through his upper body. Thirdly—like a character in one of his father's novels—he spent only one year at Oxford, having failed the first year exams.

Now luck and family connections proved positive as Auberon Waugh wheedled his way into *Queen* magazine and the *Daily Telegraph* before 'taking advantage of my mother-in-law's acquaintance with one of Mr Cecil King's daughters'; via Cecil King and Hugh Cudlipp, Waugh acquired the perfect 1960s Fleet Street job as 'special writer' on the *Daily Mirror*; Waugh just sat in the newsroom writing away at his novels.

His first column was in the *Catholic Herald*, starting in 1963. From then on 'I was to be writing at least one weekly column every week ever after, sometimes four or five a week.' Waugh subsequently columned for the *Spectator* and both the *News of the World* and the *Sun* (in the first year of Murdoch). He was sacked from the *Spectator* by its then editor, Nigel Lawson, and acquired three new columns. He became the first political correspondent of *Private Eye* and for the next sixteen years made scurrilous attacks on many politicians both decent and indecent. Waugh was also invited to do a Saturday column in *The Times* by the editor, William Rees-Mogg 'whom I had met at the christening of a shared godson'. Thirdly, also while at *Private Eye*, Waugh wrote a column on 'country topics' for Charles Wintour of the *Evening Standard*.

Auberon Waugh's columns were always—like the person himself—a bizarre mixture. Politically he combined devastating insights and criticism with childish abuse and loony-right self-caricature. As a columnist he gave much delight to many readers, and he also deliberately insulted women, and virtually all minorities, including the physically handicapped.

His 1991 autobiography *Will This Do? The First Fifty Years of Auberon Waugh* was his sixteenth book. In his fifties—but still both much older and much younger than his real age—Auberon Waugh seemed to have entered a quiet phase. In 1994 he was only doing three columns a week in the *Daily Telegraph*, plus columns in the *Spectator* and the *Oldie* and editing something called the *Literary Review*. A fellow star writer (Hunter Davies) estimated his income at about £125,000 from writing plus extra from his father's estate.

Meanwhile there was greatly increased demand for the small number of established stars who had been plying the column trade in the years and decades previous to 1986. Perhaps the three most prominent of these were Keith Waterhouse, John Junor and Auberon Waugh. These three very individual individuals (and a few others) have had a huge influence over the British development of the newspaper column.

Because their columns crossed the divide of 1986, Keith Waterhouse, John Junor, and Auberon Waugh by the 1990s were seen by many younger journalists as the old fogeys of column-writing. Most of the established column-writers were cantankerous males of fairly mature years; these three and others had distinguished careers of editing, book-writing, and column-writing behind them. Their energy, if diminished, was still there in good supply as they continued to ride their favourite hobby horses, to attack their favourite enemies, and to charm their loyal readers.

Many of the columnists appointed after 1986 and after 1990 were very young and in other respects also the mirror image of the established old fogey columnists. A substantial number of new columnists were both young and female; with the ever-present urge to attract more young female readers, editors were naturally anxious to find the latter-day successors to star women columnists such as Jean Rook, who was the leading journalist at the *Daily Express* until her death in 1991. Meanwhile Lynda Lee-Potter remained a truly stellar performer at the *Daily Mail*; Lee-Potter's combination of big interviews and columns effectively utilized her exceptional writing and interviewing skills.

II

For the young or relatively inexperienced journalist the twice-a-week column can be a formidable challenge. The established old fogey columnists are inclined to complain that young columnists in general, and young women columnists in particular, don't know enough, haven't had enough experiences, and have nothing interesting to say. There is indeed a good deal of columning about what I saw on television, at the supermarket, in the car park, and at my children's school. This is true of young male as well as young female columnists. In past times of fewer columnists and more money, young columnists were sent off on world tours and thus acquired easy subject-matter.

Opinion is basic, and the columnist needs the self-confidence to express opinions with vigour. Other journalists comment on the columnists' oversize egos—their tendency to excessive use of the first person singular, the flattering and dated picture alongside the columnist's name, the general air of self-importance. But the British columnist is a one-person act; only the most prominent columnists have a secretary.

For the journalist, launching a column is a significant career move; it may all begin with standing in for a holidaying colleague. Then, perhaps, the editor offers one column a week, which enables the journalist to go freelance. New columnists tend to find that they are moving direction, perhaps both in character (short items to essay) and content (less showbiz, more politics); there are also moves between publications (magazine to newspaper).

Julie Burchill was aged 17 when she joined *New Musical Express* in 1976. She then migrated from pop music to a succession of other publications, such as *The Face* and *Arena*. She went through a punk feminist phase, moving from admiration of Stalin to admiration of Mrs Thatcher. By the early 1990s Burchill was (she said) being paid £120,000 for her weekly *Mail on Sunday* column; this was a multiple-item column, mainly feminist comments on items from · the week's newspaper and TV news. Later she moved to the *Sunday Times* and switched her subject-matter to films. She also wrote books and cultivated a media reputation for Greta Garboesque reclusivity.

Like audio-visual stars, these newspaper stars tend to cross over into other media. Some columnists also have 'my TV show' or 'my radio show'; columnists are an obvious choice for TV and radio producers who need articulate opinions from a known public personality. Columnists have the advantage of being available, since they tend to see TV and radio appearances as part of their career strategy and the most obvious way of publicizing themselves and their column.

Column-writers are also book-writers; again books fit into the standard columnist's career game plan. Columns can be directly recycled into books; something which especially attracts the columnist's attention can be treated at greater length in a book. The book is a way of consolidating one's appeal to the loyal I-read-every-single-column readers who write letters to the columnist. Books are a mechanism also for establishing expertise and reputation as a heavyweight opinionated thinker. Brian Appleyard said that his 1993 book about science, *Understanding the Present*, established him as 'a pundit'.

Columnists maintain uneasy relationships with each other. Naturally there is competition between columnists in the same line of country; there is also rivalry for the best spots in the particular newspaper—for example most heavyweight and political columnists want star billing on the main comment, or Op Ed, page. Most columnists want to be at the top of the page (although Keith Waterhouse claimed that Alan Watkins made a mistake in leaving his bottom-of-the-page *Observer* location). Some columnists conduct open warfare with each other through their columns.

All columnists are critics, and since all columns tend to emphasize personalities, columnists can become professional character assassins. This is, of course, a problem for which most writing journalists and columnists evolve their own solutions; most columnists have a few public friends as well as enemies. They also become expert and adept at avoiding libel.

Columns are, from an editor's viewpoint, one of the bedrocks of the newspaper. It is comforting to the editor to know that these particular slots are always taken care of in advance by selected and seasoned performers who can be relied on to observe the disciplines of time, length, and reader appeal. In evaluating columnists, editors seem to rely generally upon their own opinions and the opinions of others around them. Some circulation directors hand on the opinion that Thursday's good sales are boosted by a couple of columns which appear that day; but any such sales boost is unlikely to be more than 1 per cent. Columnists who receive a lot of letters tend not to keep this a secret from the editor; prominent columnists also receive prizes. An editor may even commission some research. Roy Greenslade did this when his *Daily Mirror* boss, Robert Maxwell, wanted to get rid of a new columnist, John Diamond. Greenslade was himself sceptical about the research, but pleased that it tended to confirm his editor's wise judgement against Maxwell's blind prejudice.[3]

Another factor which influences editors is the strength of alternative job offers. The columnist transfer market became more and more active in the late 1980s and early 1990s. Several columnists made several moves, with the *Sunday Times* (under Andrew Neil) being the publication most determined to corner column talent

---

[3] Roy Greenslade, *Maxwell's Fall* (London: Simon and Schuster, 1992), 212–13.

from both the other upmarket and midmarket papers. By the early and mid-1990s an average fee was probably about £1,000 per column, fees of between £25,000 and £75,000 being the standard range for one column per week. Two and three columns a week were paid more. William Rees-Mogg was paid £60,000 for one column by the *Independent* and £120,000 for two columns a week by *The Times*. Editors can also offer other frills—display on the page, length, travel expenses, and the right to do occasional pieces for competing papers. But the transfer market in columnists is more arbitrary than the transfer market for footballers. Even when there are rival bidders, there may only be two or at most three. Moreover, columns often do not transfer well into rival publications. A columnist from the *Guardian* may be offered twice as much by the *Sunday Times*, but would the column really belong and would the columnist be comfortable?

The column is a platform in public life. The British column is not syndicated or networked into every home in the land. In fact it typically appears in only one national publication. But the columnist can use the main column to spread his or her views elsewhere as well. The *Daily Mail* columnist can stretch upmarket by also writing in the *Spectator*; and *The Times* columnist may do the occasional piece in the *Sun*. The main column deals the columnist into the game of national debate. Politicians and radio/TV producers will see the column either in the paper or in photocopy.

A national newspaper column provides a platform envied by many politicians, business people, writers, academics, priests, and other professionals. The columnist has a base from which to address a national audience once or twice a week. The successful columnist's platform seems to be there for life; editors, Prime Ministers, and many others come and go, but columnists march onwards through the decades.

III

Columnists constitute the biggest category of star writer in British journalism not least because there are political, sports, showbiz, and financial columnists as well as the general variety. There are also several other types of star, including the Big Interviewers, the Agony Aunts, and the Astrologers.

'Big interviewers' typically contract to produce perhaps two or four big interviews per month. These interviews may occupy a

whole newspaper page or several magazine pages. Some big interviewers have acquired a reputation for aggression and unremitting
hostility, which can lead to a shortage of willing interviewees.
Hunter Davies established his reputation with books about The
Beatles and Tottenham Hotspurs and he, probably rightly, thinks
he is as interesting as his interviewees; consequently his interviews
have tended to be part column of opinion, part straight interview,
and partly a sort of duet in which interviewer and interviewee are
presented as a double act.

Other star freelance journalists specialize in the foreign visit,
often to interview some larger-than-life personality. Russell Miller
has been a leader in this type of journalism, specializing in 4,000-
and 5,000-word pieces for the *Sunday Times* magazine. These are
elaborate exercises requiring extensive previous reading and research; much more than just the usual hour or two with the subject;
and a substantial picture input.

Marjorie Proops, the 'agony aunt' of the *Daily Mirror* was one of
the best-known British journalists of the 1970s and 1980s. The
agony aunt who dispenses advice primarily about sexual and marital problems is a relatively recent phenomenon. Contrary to popular belief, Marjorie Proops began her famous advice column in the
Daily Mirror as recently as May 1971. The kind of explicit advice
which she gave would not have been accepted by any national
newspaper editor much before 1970.

The Second World War had generated other types of advice
services, including a Mirror service which overlapped in time, but
not in subject-matter, with 'Dear Marje'. In the mid-1970s 'Mirror
Group Newspapers' Readers Services' was still dispensing serious
advice; it employed four specialists on housing, health, social services, and tax; it was based in Camden Town with a staff of forty-
two people and a then budget of £200,000. It was giving individual
answers to about 70,000 enquiries per year. There had been a
comparable service operated by the *News of the World*; named after
John Hilton (Professor of Industrial Relations at Cambridge University) it operated from 1942 until it was closed by the Murdoch
management in 1974.[4]

The switch from these serious (and expensive) advice bureau
services to the agony aunt columns obviously had several elements.
Commercially the newspapers were saving money and introducing
a new operation which—while it still gave some advice by mail—

[4] Jeremy Tunstall, 'Letters to the Editor', in Oliver Boyd-Barrett *et al.*, *Studies on the Press* (London: HMSO for the Royal Commission on the Press 1977), 219–20.

had high readership value and had strong elements of titillation and entertainment mixed in with the sensible auntie advice. Marjorie Proops had had a lengthy star career previous to her agony aunting. She was woman's editor of the *Daily Herald* in 1950 and became a columnist in 1953, following the then common columnist pattern of world travelling.[5]

A somewhat similar pattern was followed by another much-loved agony aunt, Unity Hall, who was woman's editor of the *News of the World* for ten years before being officially designated as agony aunt. Hall spoke to us not long before her death in 1992. She had written ten novels and several royal family books as well as ghosting books by the model Jean Shrimpton and by Prince Charles's valet. She edited the teen magazine *Fabulous* and she also led a feminist crusade against the male chauvinist rules at El Vino, Fleet Street's most famous drinking hole. Unity Hall was still writing (she said) two books a year, but she took her *News of the World* duties seriously. She explained the formula as one lead letter, sub-edited to be a good read; a balance of letters from men, women, and teenagers: and reassuring advice appended to the published letters. Some tragic and heartrending letters came without name or address:

I could show you some letters. You just wish you could do something. For instance, a 15-year-old girl writes that her father is sexually abusing her and he's bringing in his friends to do the same. . . . But you're absolutely helpless because there's no address—although you know the area from the postmark. I always keep that kind of letter. But you can't do anything. It makes me very angry.[6]

The rise of the agony aunts as stars has been paralleled by those ultimate star writers, the astrologers. Astrology plays no part in the life of most newsrooms, although one columnist reports:

I know better than most that astrology is rubbish because my very first job in journalism was writing horoscopes for a stable of women's magazines. It was the office task always given to the newest recruit because it was so stupid, so easy, that even a wet-eared geek like me could do it. There was a simple formula that you had to follow. You had one paragraph, a maximum of four sentences and you had to write something positive, something negative and something maybe.[7]

---

[5] Angela Patmore, *Marje: The Guilt and the Gingerbread* (London: Little, Brown, 1993).
[6] David Wood interview with Unity Hall.
[7] Jan Moir, 'Stars in their eyes', *Guardian*, 6 Oct. 1994.

By 1995 all of the national downmarket and midmarket papers were carrying astrology columns, as were the *Daily Telegraph* and *Sunday Times* magazines. Astrology columns are extremely profitable all round;[8] readership is high and the special phone numbers generate generous piles of cash to be divided between phone company, newspaper, and astrologer. Editors are a trifle embarrassed that something which contains so little journalism and so much commerce should be so popular.

[8] Veronica Lyons, 'Prophet Margins', *Newspaper Focus*, Sept. 1994.

11 Television and the Press

SINCE 1936, when British television began, the newspapers and television have been involved in a continuing love-hate relationship. But over six decades they have also learned to live with each other. Television is primarily an entertainment medium; its most popular output is drama/fiction, sporting contests, and other spectacle and comedy, while radio's main offering is music. All of these offerings have a broad appeal across the demographic variables. The press has its main strength not in this broad middle range but at the most serious extreme and at the least serious, most sleazy, and most disreputable end of the range.

The British national newspapers were quite slow to report on television as an industry. The showbusiness column of the *Sunday Express* in the early 1950s still focused only on theatre and films, not on television.[1] But by the mid-1950s the cross-over pattern was already being established by which rising media stars move between press, television, and other media. The 'Angry Young Men' (Kingsley Amis, John Osborne, Colin Wilson, and Alan Sillitoe) were 1950s authors of books and plays; the collective tag was first awarded by the *Daily Express* on 26 July 1956, and was quickly taken up by the *Daily Mail* and the rest of Fleet Street. In 1956 both newspapers and television needed new material. These authors had their biggest sales of books and theatre tickets, when television coverage followed in the wake of press comment.[2]

Subsequently many new types of complementary cross-over relationships were discovered. Some books appeared as both

[1] Logan Gourlay (ed.), *The Beaverbrook I Knew* (London: Quartet Books, 1984), 116–62.
[2] Harry Ritchie, *Success Stories: Literature and the Media in England, 1950–1959* (London: Faber and Faber, 1988).

television programmes and newspaper serialized extracts. BBC television programmes often had associated magazines; and by the 1990s the old Fleet Street practice of 'buying up' a national character had evolved into a combined operation between a Murdoch newspaper (the *Sun*) and a Murdoch TV system (BSkyB); it was this uniquely complementary *Sun*–Sky partnership which in 1994 flew the fugitive criminal Ronnie Knight from Spain to London to face trial and imprisonment.

I

The downmarket newspapers in Britain reacted to television by broadly placing themselves 'below' television. The downmarkets provided various kinds of additional information along the lines of: 'You've seen the programme/soap episode/comedy show, so now listen to the gossip, and scandal behind the scenes.' In particular, the downmarkets focused on the most popular of all TV programmes which in Britain were the early evening soap operas (like *Coronation Street* and *EastEnders*), plus other fictional and comedy series. In addition the downmarket papers searched out fresh examples of melodramatic human interest stories—such as kidnapped baby stories. Another focus was on stories which were too perverse or sadistic to appear first on television; for example, the downmarkets focused on cruelty to children and sex scandals of all kinds. Some of these latter downmarket stories would later be followed up by television and other newspapers, thus confirming the initially proclaimed status of 'Exclusive'.

The midmarket papers, as already suggested, had the greatest difficulty in competing with television. The successful *Daily Mail* formula focused very strongly on feature stories in narrative form, often running over two or more pages, and deftly angled towards the *Daily Mail* target reader:

> Lizzie is incapable of lying or dissembling. Her loving childhood growing up in Eastbourne and her powerful Catholicism have given her a formidable strength. She's fundamentally an optimist, a survivor, a warm and lovely person. I have no doubt that whatever the final outcome of this sad triangle, she will ultimately come through intact.[3]

[3] Lynda Lee-Potter, 'How Michael Betrayed Me: concluding Lizzie Aspel's extraordinary testimony about her husband's secret affair', *Daily Mail*, 27 Apr. 1994.

The upmarket newspapers had less to fear from television because they were focusing on a breadth and depth of serious (politics, foreign, financial, arts) news and features, which cannot be found so neatly packaged and in such generous quantities in television.

II

Although newspapers have become very dependent on television, the reverse is also the case. The prominent position of newspapers in policy-making for television is dealt with in another chapter (24). But in terms of simple news coverage, both television networks and individual producers are highly dependent on the press. Most television programmes get quite small audience ratings—such as 2 or 3 per cent of the population watching; and their producers, typically, see newspaper journalists as the main potential source of publicity. There are at least six different types of coverage which newspapers devote to television.

What is in many ways the most influential press coverage takes up the least space and the least journalist input. This is the anonymous editorial leading article carried in the prestige newspaper. A mere five editorials carried by *The Times* in two months in 1985 certainly made a deep impression on the then BBC Director-General; they seem also to have had a marked impact on government policy. The anonymous editorials on broadcasting issues would normally take up only a small fraction of the working time of one journalist.

On the other hand major press conferences—such as the launch of the BBC or ITV autumn schedule—may attract 150 journalists. Of that number, half or more are freelances. Partly because of these freelances, the total number of British TV journalists is uncertain. But, especially if provincial newspaper and trade paper journalists are included, the total is probably nearer to 300 than to 150.

One small but influential group are the media correspondents. They cover broadcasting and the press as industries and as policy areas. They normally report to the home news desk and their stories usually appear on the news pages, or occasionally on the business pages. Some media correspondents (mainly of broadsheet dailies) also edit weekly special media pages. These pages have become a forum for the discussion of current television industry issues. Directors of Corporate Affairs at ITV companies and senior BBC executives write articles for these media pages which are copied and read in all the places where TV policy is discussed.

All daily and Sunday newspapers employ previewers and reviewers. The 'previewer' is the journalist who makes the newspaper's choice of programmes recommended for tonight or the next seven nights. The previewer recommends thirty or forty programmes per week. A sub-editor will be in charge of the overall schedule which needs to be subbed into house style and regional variations. Into this overall TV schedule format are slotted the film choices by a film writer and the TV previewer's choices. Some previewing of programmes is done physically at the BBC TV centre in West London and at ITV companies, but this means time wasted on travel. Some previewing is done from press handouts, and phone calls to the producer, writer, or star. In recent years, however, previewers have increasingly relied on being shown advance tape copies of the programmes. Previewing obviously rules out all live programming such as news or sport. Most current affairs programmes (being part of journalism) are still being edited right up to transmission time. The previewers focus on what is available and preferably what is not too routine. Consequently the previewers focus heavily on drama and documentary.

Certainly the previewers collectively have some power to influence the size of audiences; research indicates very high readership of these recommendations. Nevertheless it is the reviewers who tend to carry the higher prestige within journalism. Reviewers are not able to influence the audience size of the specific programme they are critiquing, because the programme has already been transmitted. Nevertheless they are more highly regarded within newspapers; while the previewer is a highly pressured provider of snippets about tonight's TV offerings, the TV reviewer has the status of at least a critic and may have the prestige of a columnist.

Both previewers and reviewers are left remarkably free to decide what they write and which programmes they write about. Even an editor who writes editorial leaders about television policy will normally allow his previewers and reviewers to say quite contradictory things in their signed pieces. Television writing is broadly regarded by newspaper editors as soft entertainment material; television previewers and reviewers are encouraged to develop a personal style which will be attractive to the readers.

Especially in the broadsheet papers, television reviewing spills over into art criticism. Large articles, or lengthy interviews on the broadsheet arts pages, may turn out to focus on a TV drama producer, the presenter of a new art or music programme, the writer of the book-of-the-TV series, or the architect who contributed to that recent architecture TV series. There is also increasingly the broadsheet arts page piece on the deeper meanings of current music videos or the semiology of Australian soap operas.

Of course, the tabloids give the largest coverage to television. Some newspapers operate a special showbusiness desk; but most tabloids have a number of television journalists who work within a much larger features department. Half, or even more, of the entire features output may deal with television, music, and films. A significant mistake or computer error in the day's TV listings can, say tabloid journalists, generate several hundred complaining letters and phone calls.

These journalists agree that they do focus primarily on the most popular programmes and the current top twenty in particular. This leads to a continuous flow of stories about *EastEnders* and *Coronation Street* performers and their relatives (both near and distant); there is also a big focus on any newly successful British series and on the most popular one or two American series of the year. The ideal tabloid story about television needs either a highly rated programme or a major star; it also needs an additional human interest element, which will usually be negative. One downmarket journalist said there were really only four types of newspaper TV story—Previews, Reviews, Positive Features or Soft Interviews, and (much the best stories) 'Legover Situations, Sex and Sniffing'. The 'best' downmarket story, then, is a negative story about a star performer. There is the usual specialist journalist problem of generating negative stories while retaining friendly relationships with news sources.

One partial solution to this latter problem lies in a division of labour between staff and freelance journalists. The positive feature or soft interview is more likely to be conducted by 'Our Showbusiness Correspondent' or one of our staff feature-writers; stories about the ill health or extra-marital relationships of stars are more likely to be provided by freelance journalists, or general reporters.

Most television stars are understandably cautious about talking to tabloid newspaper reporters; if they do agree to be interviewed, their publicists may insist on conditions intended to ensure that the end-product will be positive rather than negative. On the whole, the bigger the star currently is in terms of public popularity, the less likely the star is to grant interviews to any newspaper, let alone a British tabloid. These journalists are able and resourceful; they employ numerous tactics and devices for getting at least some authentic bad news out of British television. Some of these journalists began covering television in newspapers in Manchester, Birmingham, or Leeds, where they got to know the producers and stars of nationally networked shows. A common device is payment for tips. Quite often a freelance journalist is paid for the original information, which a staff journalist follows up. Some show-business reporters are adept at persuading young stars to say more than they intended. The agreed arrangement may be for a positive audio-taped interview during a restaurant lunch. The reporter may then ostentatiously switch off the tape recorder and—over coffee and brandy—may ask some more intimate questions which the young star answers, assuming that this part of the interview is off the record; but the reporter has a second tape recorder in his pocket and hence a complete record of the young star's more spicy revelations.

Rising stars get the most favourable coverage because the novelty makes a story; because their bargaining strength allows the publicist to fix conditions; and because the journalist wants to build goodwill for the future. But a journalist who does positive interviews with a rising star can also recycle the earlier material into negative stories once the star is falling; now it is revealed that the star has long had a problem with drugs, drink, stage fright, marriage, or parenthood. This sequence can run still further; having savaged the star in mid-career, it may be possible for the journalist to return later for stories about the old star who has kicked the wicked habits and is on the comeback road.

One downmarket journalist was a committed believer in public service broadcasting and claimed that his proudest achievement to date was getting the two words 'King Lear' into a British tabloid newspaper. But the predominant view of popular television reporters was critical of public service broadcasting in general and of the BBC in particular. They expressed resentment at what they saw as the BBC's snobbery, its attempts to exercise 'cultural power', and its reluctance to let them view BBC programmes ahead of transmission. The BBC was compared unfavourably with ITV companies such as London Weekend Television; LWT was positively eager to supply advance tapes of all available programming and much more active in providing meetings with, and press conferences by, star entertainers.

One senior television producer who had also worked in newspapers said that the reputation of particular programmes tended to be shaped by press coverage: 'The initial press reaction to a new programme tends to establish the conventional wisdom and to fix that programme's reputation on a permanent basis.' Senior television executives have to deal with hundreds and thousands of hours of output; the head of a channel cannot view the full output even of his own channel. When, for example, the decision has to be taken as to whether a new TV series should have a second season, there are several possibly relevant forms of evidence. One is the audience rating, but this is heavily influenced by the time of day and the surrounding and competing programmes. Meanwhile there will normally be a file of press comments—previews, reviews, news stories, performer interviews—resulting mainly from the launch publicity effort and the first one or two programmes transmitted. This file of press cuttings constitutes the only available batch of independent opinions; it is also the batch of opinions which went out to the public. Consequently these early comments are a key piece of evidence in influencing the decision as to whether to cancel or to continue the series. Even if the series does continue into a modestly successful second and third year, it will probably never again generate such a large batch of press comment. Not only do press journalists give much less attention to continuing series, so also do senior television executives. If the series is successful enough to be reshown, the press previewers will return to the original press comment.

Senior television executives and their publicists know that the print journalists are mainly interested in novel human interest, new shows, and current stars. Consequently the biggest publicity effort is put into promoting new shows and putting star personalities on display. Some television executives have themselves become famous for providing quotable quotes on current controversies; rising TV executives tend to copy the Michael Grade style, which involves a few hard-hitting speeches per year, designed to attract press attention.

But not all corporate publicity is 'offensive'; senior BBC television personnel told us that the BBC devotes about one-third of its publicity effort to 'defensive' measures. The BBC is defensive for the very good reason that it has been attacked so many times in the past. One tabloid newspaper TV specialist said that the BBC was mainly concerned 'to defend its comedies; the Beeb wants to eliminate divorce, drink, drugs and deadly illness stories about its top comedians.'

According to one senior BBC press relations person the tabloids reached new depths in the mid-1980s:

The TV reporters on the tabloids and middle-market papers hunted in a pack and they would confer and decide what the story was, and some of the slightly weaker minded members of the fraternity would go along with these agreed distortions and misrepresentations; this tabloid rat pack didn't just fly kites, they flew Zeppelins and we used to get the blow-back from them at first edition time.

There are also full-time publicity people at the department level in television; and a few very prominent specific programmes are allocated a full-time publicist. But most executive producers and series editors themselves make the main publicity effort on behalf of their programme. Television journalists receive a continuing stream of phone calls and messages offering information, interviews, and pre-recorded taped programmes.

Drama series typically generate a larger collective publicity effort, because individual actors have their own agents and some have their own publicists. Independent producers employ publicists in order to establish their company names and to strengthen their reputations. But across the television genres the documentary and features producers are probably the most dedicated and successful self-publicists.[4] Print journalists seem to be irresistibly attracted by the documentary genre's offerings of human emotion and melodrama-in-real-life. Documentary producers tend to identify passionately with their human subjects—another quality which probably attracts print journalists. One documentary producer, however, commented more sceptically: 'The journalists seem desperate to find anything that's sort of worthy of their attention.'

There was some acknowledgement by print journalists that the rat pack of the mid-1980s had invented, or at least grossly inflated, some stories. The self-regulation debate, the two Calcutt commit-

---

[4] All information on television producers is from Jeremy Tunstall, *Television Producers* (London: Routledge, 1993).

tee reports, and the Press Complaints Commission were quoted by some as having led to better standards of reliability and accuracy. But on the television side of the fence there is still a very strong feeling that much or most press reporting on television displays ignorance of the television industry and a disregard for truth, fairness, and objectivity. Television producers and newspaper TV reporters are remarkably bitter about each other. British television producers regard themselves as national leaders, or indeed world leaders, in their profession; they resent being so dependent upon the writings of relatively junior and predominantly tabloid newspaper journalists. To the producers it seems perverse and wrong that such journalists and such newspapers should play such a big part in the destiny of British television.

III

Because there is much difference between television genres and there are also major differences between specialist fields, and sections in newspapers, there is also considerable variety in the ways in which TV and press compete with, and complement, each other. Looking at the television side three major types of factual, or actuality, television are offered—news, current affairs, and documentary. In news British television is required to be objective and to 'balance' partisan views. There is also only room for a small number of short items in a half-hour TV news. These restrictions combined—neutrality plus brevity—lead to a very abbreviated style of quick establishing shots, sound-bite interviews, and neutral comments to camera. In hard news, by comparison, the newspapers are relatively unrestricted in terms of balance, or number and length of item. The TV news is really a headlines-and-pictures service; the newspapers broadly assume that their readers have already seen this service (or heard a radio version).

With 'current affairs' the situation is quite different. There are only half-a-dozen or so of these shows per week or—because of holidays—only about two hundred a year on the four conventional channels. The newspapers together produce vastly more longish feature articles per year. But whereas the 2,000-word press article may represent only a few days' work, the TV current affairs programme has often done between ten and twenty person-weeks of research before filming begins; filming and editing again involve significant amounts of the time of several people. Thus British TV current affairs programmes are few and overresearched, while the press equivalents—long feature pieces—are numerous and underresearched. 'Investigative journalism' in Britain is alive and well, and living in television; but quite often the TV current affairs team write an article for one of the upmarket newspapers.

In documentary the situation is different again. The people who make documentaries are not journalists, but instead regard themselves as 'film-makers'. This is a prestigious area of television in which both film art and artistic freedom are to the fore. General documentaries film 'spontaneous' human life, which is then edited according to dramatic and artistic criteria. There are also, in British television, more specialized types of factual programming which follow a broadly documentary approach; these include Natural History (another high-prestige TV area) and programmes which deal with art, music, architecture, and science/medicine. All of these programming areas have their distinctive genre characteristics and world-views; natural history programming, which back in the 1960s was largely about exotic animals, by the 1990s had adopted a much broader environmental approach with a distinctive underlying 'green' ideology. These same areas have proved to be attractive elsewhere—with teachers and children, as well as with the press. The newspapers also have gradually strengthened their coverage of the environment, art, architecture, and science/medicine. But in the press these are still relatively marginal areas, while in television the same areas are central to the public service broadcasting project (especially as seen on BBC2 and Channel Four).

In some other areas the offerings of TV and press are more evenly balanced:

- *Crime* is, of course, a staple of television, but mainly in a fictional form. Factual crime is more strongly covered on a day-to-day basis by the press, not least because under British conditions the press is better suited to reporting court cases, as well as the politics of crime. Television's main 'factual' coverage of crime is restricted to a very few programmes.
- *Sex* is a staple of both TV and newspapers. Here again television gives the most, and the most explicit, attention to sex in fictional programming, while the popular news-

papers are the leaders in claimed factual coverage of sexual gossip.

- In *sport* television has the advantage, where it can present the sporting event in full or in part. But of course only one contest can be presented at a time; television coverage tends to stress the positive not least because of its financial involvement in exclusive contracts. The newspapers cannot present the events but their strength lies in the breadth of their daily coverage, in their presentation of detail (such as race cards), and in their more negative coverage of both the politics and the gossip of sport.

- *Disaster* coverage is another classic news field in which television has certain obvious advantages. Its immediacy allows it to bring early news and its coverage of these highly negative events tends to emphasize the positive—the wonderful work of the emergency services, the brave survivors, and the Prime Minister's quick visit. The newspapers' strength typically lies in their greater detail and their stamina in pursuing the causes and politics of the disaster.

- *Celebrities* of all kinds—actors, comedians, musicians, politicians, sportspersons, business leaders, and royals—tend to be shown in a more positive light by television, which mainly covers them as they make their pre-planned public appearances. Newspapers cover these as well, but the papers' strength is in presenting the personal, the informal, the secret or private, the motivations, and the negatives which lie behind the scenes and behind the celebrity's intended public persona.

We will return to most of these points in subsequent chapters.

IV

A substantial fraction of British newspaper coverage of the audio-visual media focuses on American film, television, and music in general and upon Hollywood stars in particular. The British newspaper attitude towards Hollywood is ambivalent. On the one hand Hollywood means glamour, stars, glitz, and gossip. But also British newspaper executives share the television executives' perception that Hollywood is cheap; just as expensively made Hollywood TV series can be cheaply acquired for showing on a foreign network, so newspaper coverage of Hollywood can be cheaply acquired from agency services and stringers based in Los Angeles. In recent years the main location of British foreign correspondents has been Washington; even for TV and showbusiness coverage the few relevant British staff correspondents have been based not in Los Angeles but in New York. The significance of New York is that it is the main US location for predigested showbusiness material—it is the home of American tabloid and magazine journalism, the headquarters of the TV networks and advertising agencies, and the better location for the vulgar rich, for fashion, for politics as showbusiness, religion as showbusiness, and 'Americana' in general. A common British newspaper pattern is a correspondent based in New York who deals wholly or partly with television and showbusiness; meanwhile Los Angeles is covered by perhaps a regular (half-time) stringer and several irregular stringers and freelances.

In the case of television, there are usually only two or three American series in the British top fifty. The newspapers do then give coverage to the stories of these few current hits. Some of the US shows which have been most popular in Britain have been deliberate fantasies (such as *Dallas* or *Baywatch*); these allow for much British speculation as to how factual the fiction may be.

In music the balance of trade is presented as if it were more even; there has been much emphasis on British music in the USA and on long-established superstars such as Mick Jagger, Elton John, and Rod Stewart. In film also British newspapers focus on British actors who are currently starring in Hollywood films. There is again a nostalgic interest in long-established superstars with British connections, such as Elizabeth Taylor. But in film the American product really is dominant in Britain, and consequently a good deal of attention is devoted to Hollywood stars and films.

The different categories of British newspapers naturally have slightly different perceptions of Hollywood. The upmarket newspapers tend to have reliable stringers who provide a rather serious view of Hollywood, focus on avant-garde directors, and do occasional pieces on Californian politics and life-styles. Both the midmarket and the downmarket newspapers are more committed to full-blown star worship and star denigration. Hollywood publicists both in Los Angeles and London are well aware of the aggressive habits of the British tabloids. Stars who are reluctant to give interviews to any journalists are even more reluctant to talk to British tabloid journalists. When Hollywood stars are in London promoting a film it is common practice to plan one interview with each of several media categories—such as one with the BBC, one with ITV, one magazine, one broadsheet newspaper, and (maybe) one tabloid. This restrictive approach is accompanied by negotiations designed to ensure favourable coverage. A tabloid journalist told me how he asked Michael Jackson on the telephone one question: 'Did you have a good flight?' Although Mr Jackson's entire contribution to the interview before replacing the receiver was one word ('Yes'), the journalist still managed to get an 800-word piece into his paper.

The British tabloids thus largely rely for their Hollywood star coverage on publicity handouts, the offerings of stringers and freelances, and upon copying from—or buying UK rights to—American articles. Publications of the *National Enquirer* type are closely followed, as well as the weighty trade papers like *Variety* and the New York tabloids. As is the usual pattern, some stringers either work for these publications or are closely involved with them. This provides a steady flow of highly negative material about the sleazier aspects of Hollywood. Since the London tabloids will not be trusted whatever they say, they have nothing more to lose by uninhibited negative coverage.

One category of London publication is, however, especially dependent on Hollywood. These are the glossy magazines, both the free-standing magazines and the glossies supplied with newspapers. They depend upon a lengthy production cycle of at least one month; for their long articles they need to choose the topics some two months in advance. Thus they need a subject for glamorous glossy photographs (to go alongside glossy advertisements) that is guaranteed still to be fresh and timely in two or three months' time. What subject area provides fresh and genuinely new and usually glossy events which are pre-scheduled two or three months in advance? There are a few things such as Wimbledon and other sporting events, the opening of Parliament, anniversaries of 50 and 100 years ago. But the biggest, most reliable supplier of these pre-arranged glossy events is Hollywood's London release of new films. The London office publicists, of course, know the strength of their bargaining position; the newspaper's glossy magazine editor wants advance pictures from the film, plus an interview and photo session with a star or stars. The publicist, in return, makes conditions, one of which London editors find particularly repellent—namely 'copy approval'. Many angry words and much professional bitterness result.

V

Newspapers have long been a story-telling medium; journalists have long been tellers of factual stories. The news sense equates with the 'good story'. Television also is a story-telling medium; its dominant form is fictional and/or comedy stories and television's factual coverage tends towards a narrative form. Consequently the influence of television on the press is not out of line with the newspaper's own history.

But the pressure in recent decades has been towards the newspaper medium redefining its own story-telling strengths. Each particular newspaper, also, moves towards the 'good story for us'; journalists from the *Sun*, *Daily Mail*, *Guardian*, or *Sunday Telegraph* are all aware of certain types of stories which fit especially well with their particular paper. As part of their distinctive types of story, as part of their distinctive voice, particular newspapers each have their own house version of the English language and the British sense of humour. These are senses of humour, perhaps influenced by television, but suited to the newspaper. The *Sun*'s sense of humour emphasizes bold punning headlines, cockney rhyming, and raucous overstatement. The *Guardian*'s sense of humour by contrast is youthful (or student) intellectual and flippant, the *Sunday Telegraph*'s wry and whimsical.

Journalists on particular newspapers seek the 'good stories for us', stories which have a suitable 'angle' for us and stories which fit with our political slant. 'Objectivity' in 1990s British journalism, even for the upmarket newspapers, is only one desirable ingredient among several; it is possible to have a story which predominantly is a good story for us, with our angle and slant, but which also does a bit of objectivity in the form of two or three paragraphs for an opposing viewpoint or spokesperson.

There is a perception among many press journalists that 'objectivity' is less important now than in the past. Objectivity and objectivity rituals are observed by the BBC and the British broadcast media in general. But even in broadcasting objectivity only has to be observed over several programmes, not within each separate programme. Newspapers, in any case, need to 'take it further' than TV and radio. They need to go beyond the neutral and objective rituals of balance.

12 The Big Story

SINCE the birth of the British daily press in 1702 editors and journalists have always been looking for celebrities, drama, conflict, 'human interest', and 'good stories'. Already in the eighteenth century there was a strong focus on actors, the theatre, and gossip about the king and the royal court. The advertisements focused on the theatre, crime, and stolen property and patent medicine cures for venereal disease.[1] War then as now was the best news story, but a problem for London journalists has been that Britain in the second half of the twentieth century has been a comparatively dull, undramatic, unviolent place. Even the violence in Northern Ireland was on a modest scale and left newspaper readers largely indifferent and bored.

Britain since 1945 has been a country with a rather low level of conflict and drama, while its press has been exceptionally competitive and hence in need of strong doses of dramatic news. The journalists' demand for violence has been greater than the supply of drama and violence generated by British society. In the 1960s the two main sources of violence and conflict stories were foreign countries and domestic industrial stories. In the 1960s and 1970s the 'industrial' or 'labour' specialism reached its highest peak of prominence and prestige in British journalism. A detailed content analysis[2] conducted in 1975 found that an industrial relations story was typically the second or third story on the front page; a typical front page would carry two sizeable (20 column centimetres) industrial relations stories. As the newspaper editors of 1975 inspected the available supplies of drama and conflict, they would typically allot the first two headlines to one foreign story, one British political (or other) story, and the third position to an industrial relations

---

[1] Michael Harris, *London Newspapers in the Age of Walpole* (London: Associated University Press, 1987).
[2] Denis McQuail, *Analysis of Newspaper Content* (London: HMSO for Royal Commission on the Press, 1977), 99–214.

story. Once or twice a week the industrial story would have the front-page lead.

The assumption appeared to be that strikes, trade unions, and industry were (apart from national politics) the best source of British conflict stories. My earlier study showed that industrial correspondents also carried high prestige within British journalism, only just behind foreign and political correspondents.[3] However, something funny happened to the strikes and violence on the way to newspaper front pages. Contrary to prevailing opinion, the bulk of these stories were not about strikes; they focused instead on trade union leaders engaged in other activities such as negotiating with the government. A television analysis of part of the same year (1975), *Bad News*, also showed that industrial relations coverage was dominated by individual trade union leaders.[4] The Thatcher government after 1979 largely stopped talking to trade union leaders, thus robbing them of much of their star status. As trade unions were also weakened by legislation and loss of membership, and as strikes become less common, the status of industrial correspondents and labour news also declined in British newspapers.

The increased prominence of tabloids and newspaper sections led to a re-emphasis on traditional themes—such as star and celebrity personalities, picture stories, crime, sex, sport, and disasters. As these traditional 'human interest' and 'good story' approaches were re-emphasized, there was an increased tendency for the lower tabloids to lead the popular news agenda. The choice of one human interest story to dominate a front page (and several inside pages) is an essentially arbitrary choice; it is not the kind of choice which a television news editor—concerned with balance, respectability, and caution—can make. Consequently the 'human interest' agenda is typically led by a downmarket tabloid 'exclusive'; this is then followed by the midmarket dailies and the more popular broadcast media (breakfast and early evening BBC and ITV, Sky, and popular radio channels). Finally the heavier media (upmarket newspapers, BBC Radio 4, and BBC2 and Channel Four television) follow up the tabloid lead; these heavier media report 'what the tabloids are saying' and also emphasize more weighty angles (such as the legal and political implications of this latest shock and horror).

---

[3] Jeremy Tunstall, *Journalists at Work* (London: Constable, and Beverly Hills, Calif.: Sage, 1971), 110.

[4] Glasgow University Media Group, *Bad News* (London: Routledge, 1976).

I

The standard ingredient of the Big Story is the big individual personality; this can either be an already established media star or an as-yet-unknown. Different newspapers favour different individuals. An example of suitable upmarket material was the actor Stephen Fry, who in early 1995 walked out of his part in a West End play, apparently due to two bad newspaper reviews. In the next six days 5,365 column inches (or 136 column metres) of national newspaper copy were devoted to Mr Fry; most of this was either favourable or neutral and nearly all of it was in the upmarket and midmarket papers.[5]

Downmarket papers have their own favourite stars—often drawn from sport and TV soaps. The *Sun* for example, carried on a long love-hate relationship with the wayward footballer Paul Gascoigne, conducted in its very own pet language such as: 'BOOZA GAZZA THROWZA WOBBLA!'[6] The *Sun* cultivated a special relationship with stars of the BBC soap opera *EastEnders*. It quickly revealed that 'EastEnder Star is a Killer'—Leslie Grantham, the show's early villain, had been found guilty of murder and had served ten years in prison. All of the downmarket papers have woven numerous stories linking the soap stars' fictional and real lives.[7]

The other type of instant press star is the unknown in real life drama. This is the ordinary person suddenly confronted with extraordinary circumstances—the mother whose child has disappeared or the miraculous survivor of an accident. Many of these stories concern babies and small children—the snatched baby, the sexually abused or the physically handicapped child.[8]

Many of these stories go through the hands of intermediaries. For stars there are, of course, professional publicists, and it is increasingly the individual stars—not the football team or the company—who engineer the publicity. There are also intermediaries working for many human interest unknowns, because competing newspapers want to run 'my story' pieces or long interviews. This

---

[5] Alexander Games, 'A bit of Fry and worry', *Evening Standard*, Mar. 1995.

[6] *Sun*, 9 Apr. 1994, 1.

[7] David Buckingham, *Public Secrets: EastEnders and its Audience* (London: British Film Institute, 1987).

[8] Meryl Aldridge, *Making Social Work News* (London: Routledge, 1994), 43–103. Pauline Illsley, *The Drama of Cleveland* (London: Campaign for Press and Broadcasting Freedom and the Standing Committee on Sexually Abused Children, 1989).

BOX 12.1. SOME WORDS FROM SENIOR JOURNALISTS AT THE *SUN* AND THE *NEWS OF THE WORLD*

'Actors now are more money-grabbing. Two TV series stars recently were trying to sell the secrets of their romance to the *Sun* for £20,000. We did a tactical wrecking operation. . . . some of the romance details leaked out, and they got £10,000 for a two parter later in the week in the *Sun*'.

They tend to go for lots of womb tremblers, dying babies or miracle babies; we have the occasional miracle baby but only if it's a miraculous miracle baby. They churn up a miracle baby most weeks, they do more relationships than we do, we tend to go for sex in relationships. Don't forget their readers are older than our readers, our readers are young; theirs are old so they tend to go for 'Is your man suffering from a mid-life crisis' whereas I go for 'How to pull the guy you fancy.'

'We have very long lists of investigations, stuff we're working on and only a very small proportion is used each week. . . . If the editor decides to use it this week, we do the showdowns on Friday; if we're going to say something very strong about somebody—this is criminal thugs, bent bailiffs and stuff like that—we always try to talk to them on Friday. Also in the case of showbusiness we do ask the stars, for their quotes—or an agent. So there'll be slightly more copy to come on Friday evening . . . it has to go that week, because you raise the dust when you go on these stories.'

'Celebrities and stars are hugely important to the *Sun*; we're a showbiz celebrity paper, so of course celebrities in showbiz and royals are hugely important to us.'

'I video stuff and watch it, sure all the soaps, all the stuff our readers will watch; if there is a certain soap story-line, then yes we do spin stories off it.'

'At the *People* if you've got just three quotes—just half a story—you flutter it up and spread it out; but the rest will be fairy writing. At the *News of the World* we are more direct and much more straightforward.'

'People come to us from other papers who have great reputations and last one week; because we do demand a very high standard, very fast, very accurate, very exclusive. . . . I still think that at the *Sun* we've got the highest standard of journalism in Fleet Street. . . . We are the best and to stay the best you've got to put in the hours.'

'I enjoy my job and I like the editor and I think Rupert Murdoch is a fairly remarkable guy, and I love the *Sun*, I'm working for the biggest selling English paper in the world.'

Continued

'I've got to say that when it comes to freelances, then the freelances will generally come to us first because at the *News of the World* we will pay you better money than people like the *Mirror*.'

'Here you're offering £100 just for a tip, but at the *Daily Mail* we only paid £50 for a page lead.'

Fig. 12.1. The *News of the World* reminds its readers of some of its 1994 front pages

sets in motion the 'Buy-Up', which itself has a well-established sequence of phases. First the offers are made, quite often in sealed envelopes to be scrutinized by the unknown's newly acquired lawyer. There may then be negotiations and/or an auction. By the 1990s combined bids were common, often between two News International entities (usually the *Sun* with either the *News of the World*, or the *Sunday Times* or Sky television). After the successful bid has been identified, an agreement is signed (although some unknowns unwisely miss out this phase). The bought-up person is typically moved to a secret hotel (or other location) and intensively interviewed; this is usually done by pairs of journalists (one reporter, one feature-writer), sometimes by several pairs in succession. The story is then written up in several instalments; speed is of the essence because the competition may be planning spoilers—and since the spoiler story is usually more negative than 'my story', it can be more readable. During the secret debriefing and writing phase, new technology—such as mobile phones and remote keyboarding into the newspaper computer—have made it easier to maintain secrecy. The sums paid for buy-ups can easily be exaggerated. Most buy-ups only pay between £1,000 and £5,000; but a story which has been in the national headlines for many days—such as a protracted kidnapping—may be worth several hundred thousand pounds; in this case there may be the prospect of additional revelations in the future.[9]

For the midmarket newspapers the ideal 'unknown' central character is one who has some kind of elevated connections; a doctor or lawyer is ideal. A judge and a super-rich upper-class politician, plus three women is even better: 'Minister bedded Judge's wife and daughters' (see *News of the World* headlines, Figure 12.1).

II

By the 1960s British newspapers had already been using photographs for over half a century; the *Daily Express* and *Daily Mirror* were the leaders in newspaper pictures. But since the 1960s pictures have become more central to all types of newspapers. Major trends towards tabloids, sections, and more competition all encour-

---

[9] Andy Beckett, 'I want to sell you a story', *Independent on Sunday*, 25 Sept. 1994.

aged greater use of pictures. The availability of colour for news pictures took this trend even further.

In the 1990s tabloid editors wanted pictures either to lead or at least to accompany all longer stories. Both tabloids and broadsheets carried 'picture-led stories'—stories which might not be used at all without the pictures. *The Times*, which in 1965 carried only classified advertisements on its front page, by 1995 often carried pictures of fashion models or entertainment stars in colour 'above the fold' to attract the casual purchaser.

The picture desk—along with the home news desk and the feature desk—is at the centre of the action on the editorial floor. The picture desk is atypical in that it services all areas of the newspaper, including the business, foreign, and feature pages. Picture desks, like other desks, conform to the house style, values, and also to the political stance of, for example, a midmarket newspaper: 'We're not into stunt pictures, we like tasteful middleclass pictures. . . . the *Mirror* and *Sun* like brasher pictures and in trying to sell their product they use photographs bigger than we will. . . . we like a more sedate style.' Another picture editor on a Conservative midmarket paper discussed one of the day's picture assignments which had added salience because of his paper's suspicion of a current trade union campaign: 'We're watching Princess Diana on her hospital visit today. . . . we've got a special interest because of the current union campaign about the poor state of the National Health Service. . . . we have a story to show that one main part of this trade union case is untrue.'

Like other journalists in charge of desks, picture editors tend to start early and finish late: 'My radio alarm will go off at 6 a.m. I listen to the 6 o'clock news and if there is something new and important that's happened overnight, I'll assign photographers from my home—phoning them at their homes. I reach the office at 9 a.m. and leave around 8 p.m., having assigned photographers to things we already know about for tomorrow morning.' The picture desk is unusual not only in serving all parts of the paper but in the range of its output; this varies from large pictures for prominent front, back, and centre pages to small mug-shots of individuals involved in shorter stories. Including pictures specific to particular regional editions the daily paper may print over 100 separate pictures per night.

Working for a typical 1990s daily picture desk staffed by four journalists (plus secretaries) would be about twenty staff photographers; the desk would also employ 'regular freelances' on a virtually full-time basis, plus other photographers varying from two or three days a week to two or three pictures per year. The picture desk also relies heavily on news agency picture services; in the 1960s these agency pictures were delivered around Fleet Street by a small army of messengers. Today agency pictures arrive by motorbike and also through the electronic picture machine. Each day the picture desk personnel will consider hundreds of separate pictures from their own staff photographers and stringers, from outside agencies and freelances, and from the newspaper's own picture library. In addition there is a 'picture-grabbing' facility for taking still pictures off television.

The picture desk often works in an atmosphere of considerable excitement; the picture editor is especially concerned about the choice of the main front-page picture and anxious about having perhaps missed pictures which competitors have got. There is a version of the familiar Fleet Street tradition which encourages journalists to beat the opposition but not to kill it. A picture editor who has missed a picture, which everyone else will have, can usually appeal to an opposite number. The other picture editor will, of course, keep his best pictures for his own paper, but may be willing to give one of his rejects to a colleague across town.

The picture desk differs from most other desks in that it does not control its own pages with its own sub-editors. The picture desk's function is to gather pictures for use on other desks' pages. Picture editors repeatedly discuss with the news desk and other desks as to their picture needs. But there is considerable variation in the weight given to the picture editor's preferences in the final selection. In some newspapers the picture desk selects perhaps the ten best pictures for another desk to choose from. The other extreme is for the picture editor to make the choice and to offer a single photograph to the relevant desk.

The onward march of both technology and competition have posed many difficult questions as to what is and is not acceptable in terms of editing or 'improving' photographs. Back in the 1960s it was already common practice to employ 'retouching artists' whose main task was to strengthen and sharpen the reproduction of black-and-white pictures on low-quality paper; this was done by, for instance, cleaning or whitening the background and sharpening the profile of the photo subject's face and body outline. With electronic picture equipment it is now possible to use newspaper versions of facilities available to television producers; colours can be lightened, darkened, or completely changed, and so on.[10] Picture editors are aware that newspaper readers may already have seen colour television film of the same events; this emphasizes the search for the most striking and dramatic possible pictures. Some of the biggest alterations to pictures involve 're-posing' the picture by, for example, reducing the empty space between two figures. From time to time there is outright fakery. One notorious example occurred in May 1990 with the picture of a British truck driver called Paul Askwell, who was wearing a *Daily Mirror* T-shirt; the *Sun* picture desk simply transformed the T-shirt to say the *Sun* instead.[11]

III

British national newspapers have always looked towards crime to generate a strong supply of 'good stories'. But during the twentieth century there have been two major inhibitors to crime reporting. First there has been the rather restricted nature of the formal regime; the British Police have followed the British central government's highly secretive traditions. Moreover, the British courts in general and the judges in particular place severe restrictions upon court reporting; *sub judice* rules, for example, strictly forbid pre-trial speculation as to guilt and innocence. These formal restrictions are, however, undermined in typically British ways; senior crime journalists do establish friendly relationships with senior policemen. Restrictions on pre-trial coverage lead to massive coverage during and after the trial.

A second problem is that while Britain has a lot of crime, much of this is petty theft. Guns are only carried by a small minority of both criminals and police. The newspapers have, however, evolved some simple means for confronting these awkward problems. Whilst most murders and rapes are committed by people known to the victims, the newspapers focus on the atypically dramatic cases, such as mystery rapists and the fairly rare British cases of serial murder. This still leaves the newspaper crime offerings looking regrettably dull and sparse compared with the fictional crime offer-

[10] Roy Greenslade, 'How to turn a frog into a prince', *British Journalism Review*, 5/1 (1994), 23–9.

[11] Peter Hillmore, 'Sun of a gun reflects Mirror image', *Observer*, 13 May 1990.

ings of British television, let alone the offerings of Hollywood. However, in the age of television, British newspapers have copied a radio and television practice—namely the replay of the golden oldies. In the 1990s British national newspapers were running frequent stories about some favourite crimes of the 1960s. 'The Great Train Robbery' of August 1963 involved the then large sum of £2 million; the men involved in this train robbery became hero/villains whose exploits were covered in films, TV programmes, and above all newspapers for the next three decades.

'The Moors Murders' was the newspaper tag attached to a series of child killings which took place in the Manchester area in 1964; as a result Colin Brady and Myra Hindley were in 1966 sentenced to life imprisonment. Hindley became a focus of endless newspaper attention; David Astor (former editor of the *Observer*) argued for Hindley's release, while a chorus of fierce tabloid voices demanded that 'life must mean life'. In 1994, the thirtieth anniversary of the Moors Murders, there were several TV programmes and many newspaper column yards devoted to Hindley. Over thirty years after the grizzly events (when Hindley had been in prison for twenty-eight years), the *Daily Telegraph* could still devote its main front-page splash headline to a minor development in the endless Hindley saga.[12]

Another 1960s favourite criminal pair were the Kray brothers. As with the Brady–Hindley pairing, the more forceful of the two Krays was suffering from incurable mental illness. But no matter; before they were locked away, the Kray brothers were presented by newspapers as colourful characters on the swinging London scene with some then fashionable overtones of working-class culture. The Krays lived in the East End of London and both became professional boxers at age 16. Obsessed by Hollywood gangster imagery, they began a protection racket business in Bethnal Green; they later moved to a fashionably swinging West End of London and photographs show them posing with countless British and American showbiz stars. They wore the dark suits and grim countenances required by gangster cinematic tradition, and claimed to have murdered only rival criminals, never decent law-abiding folk. The Krays also inspired a feature film, a dozen books, and a steady stream of newspaper stories. Ronnie Kray suffered from schizophrenia and spent twenty-five heavily sedated years in

---

[12] 'Hypnotism for Hindley is approved', *Daily Telegraph*, 25 Jan. 1995.

prison, but when he died in 1995 the upmarket newspapers, as well as the tabloids, gave him full-page obituaries, with nostalgic headlines.

In the 1960s there were twenty full-time national crime correspondents, with the *Daily Express* and *Daily Mirror* having three each. The *Daily Telegraph* had two but it was an exception among the upmarkets; *The Times* in the late 1960s had in Norman Fowler[13] a Home reporter whose job was defined in terms of the Home Office, and who thus covered prisons and the politics of law and order. By the 1990s this type of coverage had greatly expanded, and most of the upmarket papers now had both crime and legal specialists. There was also an expansion of organized pressure groups and publicity concerned with crime, the prisons, and law and order.

The news reporting of prisons had long been one of several on-and-off topics—depending on newsworthy happenings like executions, escapes, and riots. Reporting on the police themselves had changed somewhat in that by the 1990s the police were much more given to press conferences and public appeals for help in apprehending criminals. But on a day-to-day basis Scotland Yard still appeared to be more devoted to keeping information in, rather than letting it out. John Weekes of the *Daily Telegraph* complained to me in 1966 about the inadequacies of Scotland Yard's output and the same journalist, still on the same paper, made a similar complaint twenty-five years later.[14]

But in both the 1960s and 1990s experienced journalists had developed their own extensive relationships with senior police officers. Percy Hoskins, the *Daily Express* senior crime correspondent in 1966, was clearly a close friend of the Scotland Yard high command. Hoskins lived in a small but convenient flat in Park Lane where he entertained his police friends; he had written a book called *No Hiding Place* which became a BBC television series. The 1960s crime correspondents were very committed to the police world-view and they were the most Conservative-inclined of all the specialist groups studied at that time.

A common factor in both periods was that British conditions placed major emphasis on the reporting of court cases; journalists with good shorthand had been doing this well back into the Victo-

---

[13] Who later became a politician.
[14] Philip Schlesinger and Howard Tumber, *Reporting Crime* (Oxford: Oxford University Press, 1994), 174–5.

rian period. One change from the 1960s to the 1990s was the tendency of the tabloids to accord ever more massive coverage to especially sensational cases. On the day of the verdict a tabloid newspaper will devote perhaps its first three pages to the final day in court, plus a pre-written 'Eight-page Pullout Inside' in which the shocking details are lovingly described. Some murder cases, of course, result in acquittal and the downmarket papers have become expert in running deliberately ambiguous front-page headlines which initially suggest that the accused is really guilty.

Each year seems to produce its serial-killings-of-the-year. In January 1995 Frederick West committed suicide while undergoing trial, accused of murdering twelve young women. Meanwhile a 1975–8 series of thirteen killings had entered the British classic crime repertoire; this serial murderer had been dubbed by the press the 'Yorkshire Ripper' because most of the women were prostitutes—an echo of the Jack The Ripper case which also involved prostitutes. The behaviour of both the police and the journalists in the 1981 Yorkshire Ripper (Peter Sutcliffe) trial seemed to breach both the relevant rules and law.[15] Similar things have happened in several subsequent serial-killer-of-the-year cases.

Serial murders tend to have overtones also of perverse sexuality, which add to both news and 'good story' value. Rape is obviously relevant here and newspapers tend to choose from available rape cases those which are atypically dramatic. A 1990 study of national newspapers showed that the *Sun*, *Daily Telegraph*, and *Daily Mail* (the three daily market segment leaders) carried the most rape stories. The cases selected for newspaper treatment were atypical because about two-thirds were cases in which the rapist was a stranger to the victim; however, the latest official data showed that in 61 per cent of rape cases the rapist was known to the victim.[16]

A sexual dimension also adds to the news value of a story about a sports celebrity or an entertainment star. Indeed this is the foundation both of gossip journalism as practised by the mid-market papers and also of the exclusive investigation of the downmarket Sundays. In recent years it has also become a staple of royal reporting.

[15] Press Council, *Press Conduct in the Sutcliffe Case* (London: Press Council, 1983).

[16] Lorraine Heggessy and Jacqui Webster, 'News warped by the lust for a sexy story', *Independent*, 14 Nov. 1990.

IV

'Sport has got bigger' said one 1990s sports editor. Sport got bigger mainly, however, because the newspapers got fatter. Already in 1975 the downmarket dailies devoted 28 per cent of their editorial space to sport, the midmarkets 22 per cent, and the upmarkets 14 per cent. Already in the 1960s the star sports columnists had arrived and were cultivating not only their prose but their appearance. Peter Wilson, the *Daily Mirror* sports columnist, wore a cloak and carried a silver-tipped cane, while Desmond Hackett of the *Daily Express* was known for his brown bowler hat. When I interviewed Fleet Street football correspondents in 1967 they were still living in the warm glow of England's having won the World Cup the previous year.

In talking to sports editors in the early 1990s it was apparent that much remained the same. Sports journalism has always had distinctive aspects, including a very uneven flow of news through the week. The most demanding single experience for a sports desk is handling all of the Saturday football and other matches which finish very close to the (early) first edition times of Sunday papers. Daily papers have a lesser version of this problem on midweek evenings. On these busy days some newspapers print as many as eight separate regional editions; whole pages are rapidly altered to provide separate editions containing reports on Scottish, then North-East, then North of England football, and so on. This editionizing of sport is part of what sports desk personnel perceive as a fiercely competitive field. One sports editor quoted research showing that among male readers as many started reading at the back (sports) pages as started at the front (news) pages. Sport, in the tabloid papers, tends to be the most expensive department. A typical daily sports desk in the early 1990s had an annual budget of £4 million and a staff of some sixty journalists. Foreign travel—with British teams playing abroad—is a major cost item.

Another aspect of competition is the general air of belligerence and antagonism surrounding sports journalism. British sports managements are seen as defensive and evasive in dealing with the press, and especially the tabloids. Given the ferocity of much of the reporting this is not too surprising. Sports editors complain about the double standards of some star players who refuse to give interviews but nevertheless 'write' regularly for certain popular newspapers. In practice a few tabloids—especially the *Sun*, *Daily Mirror*, and *News of the World*—have 'bought up' not only most of the leading football players, but also the leading managers. Whether this is on a contractual or a more *ad hoc* basis, the other sports editors say that they are thus denied access to the personalities. The resentment of these other sports editors finds expression in some extremely negative reporting of the personalities 'owned' by richer competing newspapers.

The sports editor also receives phone calls from players' agents who are in effect auctioning off single stories to the highest bidding sports desk: What will you pay for an exclusive interview with a particular player? One news desk buys the story, but the competition—who did not bid, or did not bid high enough—know about the story and are ready to run counter 'spoiling', or contradictory, versions of the same story. Additional negative 'angles' are provided by the news desk; when the story is a player's personal life, the news desk may assign general reporters who deal 'with the divorces, girlfriends, personal stuff'. One of the main casualties of this belligerent competition has in the past been the manager of the England football team. Some of the pent-up frustrations of tabloid sports reporting are expressed in venomous stories about this frail human being.

The sports editor is like other desk bosses in having a substantial degree of autonomy. Several sports editors say that the editor takes little interest in sport. The sports editor has his (he is always a man) pages and his discussions with the editor may focus on the inadequacy of the current page provision. There is normally a standard ration—such as seven weekday pages on a tabloid—and within these pages the sports editor is remarkably free. The typical sports desk runs a sort of newspaper-in-miniature, with its own specialists as well as general reporters, its own regional reporters (in Manchester, Glasgow, Birmingham, and so on), its own columnists/chief reporters, stars, and its own team of sub-editors. One typical early 1990s daily sports desk had six desk staff, twenty-seven correspondents and reporters, and twenty-eight sub-editors. Feeding into the sports desk would also be the work of regional freelances and a steady flow of domestic and international agency material.

Although relatively autonomous, the sports editor does experience several constraints in addition to what he sees as an inadequate ration of pages. The key constant is the size of the budget and the staff. Another constant is the need to carry certain standard 'furni-ture' items; the largest pieces of sporting furniture are the racing cards for what, on some days, can be several race meetings. The sports editor complains that he must devote two of seven tabloid pages—and sometimes an even higher proportion—to racing cards which only 3 or 4 per cent of the readership would miss. If say 7 per cent of the newspaper's total space can be devoted to something read by only 3.5 per cent of the readers this shows how powerful a sporting interest group can be. Sports editors complain that on the rare occasions when the racing card of a major meeting is left out, the phone and fax lines became clogged with irate messages.

A tabloid sports editor may control up to one-quarter of the newspaper's journalists and one-quarter of its non-advertising space. But it is the sports desk's combined control of sub-editors as well as reporters which gives the sports editor such a high degree of page power. Those pages at the end of the newspaper are his in two crucial interlocking ways: he controls the newsgathering spec-trum—which stories will be covered and by which journalists; he also controls the sub-editing operation—which stories are rejected, which stories become page leads, which story gets the big back-page headline.

The big change between the 1960s and the 1990s is the increased coverage, now in colour, provided by both television and news-papers. In horse-racing, for example, Channel Four has greatly added to the television coverage; the newspapers have extended their coverage of this unique world. Horse-racing has generated a team of ex-jockeys and old Etonians who combine colourful per-sonalities with prodigious expertise, and a number of these stars appear in newspapers and on television. Cricket is a sport which is called upon to fill more sports pages when football has its summer rest; it now goes on for more hours per week and more weeks per year than previously. Cricket journalists have been encouraged to focus on colourful stars and their colourful personal behaviour; this in turn has generated a fresh supply of stories about the extra-marital sexual adventures of cricketers.

If sex and sport sells newspapers, so also does crime and sport. It is, of course, television which has provided greatly increased finance for football, athletics, rugby, cricket, and other sports. Drugs also have become a big issue. This has generated a wave of corruption stories which enable some sports journalists to point the finger at several categories of sports potentates. Athletics organizers, football managers, sports agents, and Sky television have all been portrayed as villains who are corrupting British sport.

V

Other traditional news themes have also been pursued with renewed vigour. The big disaster is a classic type of news story, but a disaster like the December 1988 crash of Pan American flight 103 in Lockerbie in Scotland received extraordinary coverage both at the time and subsequently. Big disasters now seem to have layer upon layer of additional significance—intelligence, international terrorism and politics, the viability of huge industrial companies, the environmental consequence of high-technology projects, and so on.

Food is one other traditional news area which now has added news appeal. News and feature desks can safely assume that all readers care about food. Food stories touch many of the newly important feature areas—health, environment, science. British newspapers since at least early in the twentieth century have linked stories about food imports and exports with the British prejudice that continental Europeans are insensitive enough to eat horseflesh and in general are willing to sacrifice animal welfare to gastronomy. Such stories have been given new vigour by the common agricultural policy of the European Union and the growth of vegetarianism. The *Sun* in particular has called upon its peculiar sense of humour to denounce French cruelty to snails, while other newspapers criticize both the French and the Italians for their cruel habit of eating veal.

13 Readers and Viewers

THE behaviour of readers with their newspapers is another case of everything changing, while everything stays the same. Everything has changed from the stability of the 1960s when the British were still loyal to their chosen newspapers, which were home delivered like the milk and the bread. By the 1990s newspaper readership was much less stable, there was much less loyalty, and home delivery was now a minority pattern. By the 1990s it was much more common to read one daily on Monday, a different daily on Tuesday, and no daily newspaper on Wednesday. The newspaper reader is the same person as the supposedly loyal TV viewer, who actually only watches every second episode in a television series. There is now a much more volatile pattern in both press and television, involving a major element of channel hopping and newspaper hopping 'promiscuity'; but this is combined with an opposite and quite strong element of conditional—perhaps three or four times out of six—loyalty.

Newspaper readership research also changes and yet stays the same. More than one person has always read the typical newspaper, so sales or circulation never tell the whole story. British readership research, using respectable national samples of the public, began in the 1930s; since then the research has become much more sophisticated and much more extensive. But readership research remains the same in basic respects. It is expensive and takes two main forms. Either it is very big and broad in scope like the National Readership Survey, which is oriented towards national advertising; or it is aimed at very narrow questions, such as the readership of the new sports section of a particular newspaper.

The attitudes of journalists towards research have not greatly changed. In the 1990s, as in the 1960s, journalists were defensive and sceptical on most research issues; journalists (like TV producers) tend to say that research either shows what they know already or gets silly answers because it asks silly questions. There is

Table 13.1. Average through readership of four popular dailies (*Daily Express, Daily Mirror, Daily Herald, Daily Mail*), 1963

	Men	%	Women	%
1	Cartoons	52	Horoscopes	58
2	'Tragic'/ordinary people	50	'Tragic'/ordinary people	55
3	Celebrities	48	Ordinary people	52
4	Sports	47	Letters	51
5	'Light'/ordinary people	42	Celebrities	50
6	Domestic politics	41	Cartoons	48

Source: James Curran *et al.*, 'The Political Economy of the Human-Interest Story', in Anthony Smith (ed.), *Newspapers and Democracy* (Cambridge: MIT Press, 1980), 288–347.

Table 13.2. Readership 'right through' stories in the *Daily Mirror*, 1971

	Men	%	Women	%
1	Laughter	70	TV programmes	73
2	TV programmes	69	Laughter	69
3	Andy Capp cartoon	69	Stars (horoscope)	67
4	Sport	53	Andy Capp cartoon	65
5	Other cartoons	51	Letters	65
6	Picture stories	50	Picture stories	62

Source: *What People Read in the Daily Mirror* (IPC Surveys Division, 1971).

some truth in both these points. British national newspapers are so enormously varied as to defy the effective use of standardized questions and categories. It is also broadly true that readers today still have the same preferences as readers had when readership research began in the 1930s. Both upmarket and midmarket papers have for the last 150 years been adding more light material; but it has probably always been the light material which attracted most readers. The popular Sundays of the 1840s and the *Daily Telegraph* of 1855 recognized the newspaper reader's wish to be entertained.

A March 1934 national survey found that among all readers of national newspapers the most popular news category was 'acci-

Table 13.3. Items which newspaper readers 'specially choose' to read, 1993–1994 (%)

Items	All Adults	Readers of		
		Sun	Daily Mail	The Times
TV programme details	42	48	48	42
UK/British News	34	33	46	54
Weekly entertainment guide	22	26	26	18
Sport	21	29	25	24
Puzzles and crosswords	20	24	24	18
Jobs/appointments	13	17	10	13
Women's pages	12	13	15	10
Home and Garden	12	11	18	11
Medical/health/fitness	11	10	15	13
Food/drink/cookery	11	9	14	14
Film and video	11	15	12	11
European news	10	6	14	25
Relationships	9	13	8	7
Travel & holiday	9	8	13	10
Non-European foreign news	8	5	12	21
Newspaper editorials	8	5	14	21
Cars and motoring	8	10	11	13
The environment	8	6	8	11
Arts/books/music	7	13	11	17
Education	7	5	6	16
Science & technology	7	6	9	17
Personal finance	6	3	12	14
Business/company	4	2	8	12

Source: TGI GB Target Group Index Oct. 1993–Sept. 1994.

dents', followed by weather (not forecasts but including accidents due to the weather), local news, crime and divorce, trade union and labour, municipal (the 1934 London County Council elections were in progress), personal gossip, and royalty. Among the readers of *The Times*, *Daily Telegraph* and *Morning Post* the most popular single category was Crime and Divorce.[1]

The accompanying tables indicate several continuing themes:

- The most popular items tend to be things which are not really part of journalism as traditionally understood—the

[1] Political and Economic Planning, *Report on the British Press* (London: PEP, 1938), 152–3.

television guide, the strip cartoons, and the stars (of both horoscope and entertainment). Also popular are human interest, especially negative human interest, stories. All of these tend to appeal across sex, class, and age.

- Sport and women's items are popular with many (but not all) men and women respectively.

- Upmarket readers like the kind of light and human interest material in which the downmarket papers specialize; but this does not apply the other way around—readers of downmarkets generally are not interested in foreign and financial news.

- Readers respond to price and other inducements to try another paper. Price-cutting worked in the 1990s as in the 1930s. Expensive promotions—money-for-life competitions, bingo, win-a-free-holiday, and so on—continue to attract both upmarket and downmarket readers.

I

Television obviously played its part in transforming the 1960s pattern of stable readership to the 1990s pattern of readership volatility and promiscuity. The typical British adult went from two hours plus of TV viewing in the 1960s to three hours plus in the 1990s. There was a huge expansion in the hours of television in general and of news in particular, including breakfast news, news on the hour, and late news. There were also video, satellite and cable. In addition there was greatly increased availability of radio and recorded sounds—including car and Walkman sound equipment. Newspapers found themselves up against ever higher tides of viewing and listening competition for scarce audience time.

Advertising and circulation executives quote contradictory evidence as to whether the time spent reading the newspaper each day has declined. There is some evidence of weekday decline, partly outweighed by a weekend increase (involving Saturday and Sunday with more weekend sections still being read into the next week). Instead of the regular twenty or thirty minutes of yesteryear, newspaper reading has probably become more difficult to research, because more uneven—a combination of very short bites (or quickie impulsive reads while looking at the TV schedule, crossword puzzle, weather forecasts) combined with irregular long reads of that gripping two-page spread or five-page magazine feature. There is probably also more newspaper reading as a secondary activity—while watching TV, listening to music, cooking, and driving.

The drop in sales of newspapers has been matched by a somewhat bigger expansion in the size of newspapers and the amount of editorial (non-advertising) material. Faced with a newspaper which is now two (or more) times as fat, the reader has inevitably become more selective. The most obvious form of selectivity is the non-reading of whole sections. There is a 'his' and a 'hers' path especially clearly demarcated in some papers—for example sports sections and sections which are really women's magazines. There are also alternative serious and entertainment-and-sport paths.

The drop in sales has been accompanied by a big increase in the total number of households since the 1930s and the 1960s. Consequently the drop in daily newspapers per household is much bigger. Whereas a four- or five-person household took two daily newspapers in the 1950s or 1960s, the 1990s pattern is of just one daily paper going into a smaller household of two or three people. (There are also many more one-person households.) In the past the larger household may have had one paper chosen by him and a second paper chosen by her. Now it may be that he chooses the paper on some days in the week, while her choice prevails on other days. This latter pattern is also encouraged by the big increase in part-time work by women. Women probably make more of the newspaper-buying decisions than previously; obviously, also, male unemployment discourages regular male newspaper purchasing.

A decline in home delivery is acknowledged by newspaper executives. The National Readership Survey for the mid-1990s shows home delivery at about one-third of all sales; there is uncertainty as to the previous figure but it may have been as high as two-thirds. The traditional British retail newsagents still exist (often with an Asian owner), but some have found it difficult to deliver the papers by 7 a.m. each morning. Some people now leave for work earlier. There are fewer letter boxes reachable from the street (and more security). There is now much wider availability in supermarkets, filling stations, corner groceries, and multiple stores; there is also a bigger spread in time of purchase. Under 'sale or return' conditions wholesalers keep at least some local retailers topped up with copies of morning papers right through the day; some people when picking up the children from school, or returning from work, are still buying morning papers at 4 and 5 p.m.

Sunday newspaper-buying habits have always differed from the weekday; this pattern continues. But by dropping daily delivery, the weekday consumer has acquired total weekday flexibility. There is now the choice not only of which paper or papers to buy, but also the second choice of which day or days—how many times per week. Some selection is clearly oriented to particular days when a paper carries certain sections. For example a male football enthusiast may focus his newspaper buying upon three weekend and midweek football days; his wife may buy a paper with specific sections which appeal to her on another two days of the week. Some people undoubtedly choose the health, educational, or personal finance days of more than one daily. The obvious basis for selection is the individual's or the household's weekly routine; when he visits the branch plant on Tuesday he sees a different daily paper; while she always sees her mother's choice of paper on her regular Saturday visit. Or the weekly supermarket trip means another once-a-week purchase.

Many of the short-term sales increases are—according to industry executives—due to two-day-a-week customers temporarily moving up to four-days-a-week and like changes. There is also some suggestion that individuals take quite long periods to make a change. For example, when the *Independent* appeared in 1986 it considerably increased total upmarket sales; many purchasers added it to their previous purchasing pattern. It can take individuals two or three years to make a more permanent choice.

II

Expensive survey research is treated sceptically by senior journalists, partly because it is only one of several kinds of feedback which reach the newspaper. Advertising, a major source of newspaper revenue, is also an early indicator of how the economy is performing. In worsening market conditions companies often cut their advertising spending before they announce their reduced profits; consequently newspapers (and editors) tend to be aware of changes in the economic climate at least as soon as—and often before—politicians and businessmen. Newspaper circulation departments are also well attuned to unemployment; the closure of a big employer will mean an immediate drop in newspaper sales in the relevant area.

Circulation, however, is the most sensitive indicator of newspaper performance and the one which is taken more seriously in editorial and business departments. Audited circulation figures are published each month; but daily and weekly figures reveal a much more volatile detailed pattern. Each day in the week has different levels of sales, with Saturday—in the 1960s the worst day—having been boosted into the highest selling day for national newspapers. Circulation managers now attend the main editor's morning conference each day; they report current trends and are on the lookout for stories which may sell extra copies, either locally or nationally, tomorrow morning.

Apart from wars and General Elections few political or foreign stories sell extra copies of British newspapers. The 1963 assassination of President Kennedy was an exception; the shooting occurred about three hours before London first edition times—all Fleet Street papers gave massive coverage to the event and the *Daily Express* printed and sold 250,000 extra copies. The Kennedy funeral (and the Winston Churchill funeral) sold even more extra copies. In 1994 the death of John Smith (leader of the Labour Party) increased sales. But most sales increases are caused by special promotions (especially TV promotions of serialized books) or regular events such as the start of the football season, the house astrologer's quarterly special, or the beginning of the school year. In recent years the most sensational royal stories have sold extra copies. Sales alterations for the most part, however, involve either obvious local interest or tremors so subtle that their origin is uncertain.

Circulation figures are important partly because they are so immediate and because each day carries the possibility of some dramatic seismic shock. One such example occurred in April 1989 when the *Sun*, in commenting on 95 deaths at the Hillsborough football disaster, carried an accusing story about drunken Liverpool fans; this and other related stories led to huge sales losses for the *Sun* in Liverpool, which in simple sales revenue cost millions of pounds.[2] But the much more common small circulation tremors have added significance because—with wholesaling reforms and

[2] Peter Chippindale and Chris Horrie, *Stick It up your Punter* (London: Heinemann, 1990), 276–94, 336–41.

computer technology—the information flow is both precise and rapid.

The Letters to the Editor feature goes back to the origins of newspapers and is important to the editor who gets a quick return flow of comment about his editorial pronouncements. My research for the 1977 Royal Commission suggested a total of about two million letters per year. In addition to letters to the editor another significant category was letters to the individual named journalists. The 1968 specialists' study showed 200 specialists each averaging about 700 letters a year or 140,000 letters in total.

Since the 1960s there has been a big increase in the number of points at which significant numbers of letters flow into newspapers. There are many new specialized letter sections—for instance in sport, financial, and women's sections. Also the growth in column-writing has generated a large new activity of letters to the column-ist. Columnists say that they pay careful attention to these letters and some prominent columnists have a secretary whose major task is answering letters. Most columnists seem to get only a steady trickle of letters, but a sudden surge of, say, a hundred 'personal' letters on a specific topic is something which cannot easily be ignored. As with the specialist correspondents, it seems, most letters contain routine observations or questions, while occasional letters become the basis of later columns.

Since the 1960s many letters have come by fax and telephone, which makes them more immediate. An important development on the tabloids has been the telephone 'vote'; a current question is put to the readers whose telephone Yes or No can be recorded auto-matically via special telephone numbers. Sometimes the question is facetious. In April 1991 Kenneth Clarke described *Daily Mirror* readers as 'morons'; the *Daily Mirror* then asked its readers to vote on whether Clarke himself was a moron or a prat. By 5.30 p.m. that day 46,000 *Mirror* readers had phoned in their votes, with the 'prat' votes leading the 'moron' votes by six to four. On other occasions the question is one on which the editor is genuinely uncertain. Popular British newspaper editors want to take sides on many current issues and they want to take the same side as the majority of their readers. They often use these telephone votes as a quick sampling of reader opinion. The editor realizes that any telephone voting sample is unrepresentative, but for an uncertain editor it is comforting to have the opinions of at least tens of thousands of readers. No other mechanism can generate such a big response in less than twenty-four hours and consequently no other mechanism is so influential in persuading the editor as to who is the hero and who the villain in the current controversy. The results of these telephone votes are also published in the newspaper and a succession of such votes cannot but influence the way in which all staff journalists perceive their audience.

III

Eighty-five to 90 per cent of British adults were reading a national daily on any day in the 1960s; by the 1990s this same level of 85–90 per cent of British adults still read a national daily regularly—but only at least once a week, not once each day. British newspaper readers are like a nation whose families once bought fresh bread every day but now buy it between once and five times a week.

There still are perhaps 40 per cent of British adults who read one or more national dailies every day; we may now need to call these people 'heavy readers' of national papers, and if we include Sundays, regional dailies, magazines, and local papers, they probably read between ten and twenty newspapers and magazines a week. Next there is another 20 per cent category of 'medium readers' and these are also the median or typical case. They may in addition be the best examples of promiscuous readers—reading national dailies on perhaps four to six days a week. They typically will not have a newspaper delivered and are thus free to switch allegiance during the week. Third comes another 20 per cent of 'light readers' who read a national daily at least once and up to three or four days a week; like most British adults they will read at least one local weekly and, including magazines and local dailies, may still read a newspaper or a magazine of some kind on most or all days of the week. Finally there is another 20 per cent category of 'low or nil' readers of national newspapers. Some of these will be people who prefer regional dailies and weeklies (as many Scots do). Others simply prefer the audio-visual media. But some are the functionally illiterate, who cannot both read and understand even a lower tabloid.

This gradation from heavy to low or nil readers is largely independent of the up/mid/downmarket classification. But not entirely so. The people with the most education and income watch only about half as much television as those with the least education and income. Newspaper reading is the other way about—those with the most education and income do the most newspaper reading; but the correlation appears not to be especially strong.

IV

Since radio listening became a mass phenomenon in the late 1920s, daily, and near daily, newspaper reading has been done by people who are also following broadcasting on a daily, or near daily, basis. In the age of television, newspaper reading has become part of massive amounts of time devoted not just to television and newspapers but to radio, recorded music, magazines, and books. Radio, especially, is often underestimated, although radio listening takes up nearly as much time as television. Newspapers are competing with not just twenty-plus hours of television viewing, but thirty and forty hours of total media exposure per week.

Newspaper reading has come to complement television viewing in particular; radio listening is often a secondary activity to newspaper reading and to a range of other activities. The television guide is the most read (or looked at) part of the newspaper; but the television guide differs from one newspaper to the next. The particular newspaper guides its particular readership as they seek to construct their own viewing schedules.

The daily newspaper has become a guide to life and consumption in general and to media consumption and entertainment in particular. We lounge in front of the television watching our favourite drama, comedy, and sport, and watch perhaps one TV news per twenty-four hours. We follow up this viewing with newspaper gossip about TV stars, with league tables and other sports detail and opinion, and with more or less general news (depending on choice of paper). We also use the newspaper for humour, for the weather, and to check how our politicians or our investments are doing.

Audiences for particular television channels and programmes are falling because—as with newspapers—there is increasing competition. In television, as in newspapers, the least serious programming is the most popular. With newspapers, as with television, audiences graze and zap across large amounts of material before selecting and focusing on some material for more careful scrutiny.

In many countries these similarities are less striking because of

local newspaper monopoly which in practice means little newspaper choice. In Britain, however, the press offers a bewildering
array of choices; even in the depths of the country the undecided
purchaser can choose between eleven national dailies, and perhaps
two local dailies and two local weeklies—fifteen different current
newspapers. Choice, volatility, and promiscuity prevail.

Part IV
NEWSPAPERS AND POLITICS

14 Stronger Media Versus Government

IN many countries the media have become bigger, stronger, and quicker, while governments and politicians have become less popular. The details vary between democratic countries, but television everywhere has more channels which transmit for many more hours than was the case two or three decades ago; there is more news on these channels and there is also more news and political coverage available on radio and in the press.

But the great public tends to find politics boring; television news producers especially focus on political personalities responding to the most dramatic and conflictual of current events and stories. One result is the quickie sound-bite in which the politician typically seeks to combine a few cautious sentences with one quotable phrase. 'Longer forms' of news exist from the half-hour weekly factual show to the all-news channel, but here the audiences are typically small.

Fatter newspapers also generate greater coverage of politics than existed in the past; but much of this coverage focuses on political personalities, often in some kind of negative context. The typical 'long forms' of political news in the press are increasingly either the Big Political Interview, the political column, or the multi-page investigation of what went wrong in the recent political disaster or scandal. Comment, often highly critical and partisan, is to the fore.

Political news has always moved quickly. One hundred years ago the electric telegraph already ensured that yesterday's political speech could be in this morning's newspaper. Nowadays from one day's breakfast news to the next day's there are deadlines, sound-bites, and answering sound-bites through the twenty-four hours. The newspapers increasingly summarize the sound-bites and then add some off-the-record details and some speculative venom of their own.

The relentless speed of modern political coverage quite often catches politicians unawares. The senior politician may emerge from a Cabinet committee, or step off an international night flight, to be told by a press aide or a journalist about some dramatic event which demands an immediate comment. The 'no comment until I know more' response can leave the field to political opponents and it can result in 'Crisis denied' headlines which later require a further and different denial. A politician can thus easily fall into the trap of making an ill-informed and ill-considered quickie statement.

Politicians increasingly believe that the success of their careers and their causes depend upon a steady flow of media publicity. Consequently politicians, both in and out of office, spend a lot of time doing things—making speeches, attending dinners, visiting foreign countries, opening buildings, supporting football clubs—which are intended, wholly or partly, to attract media coverage. Although politicians tend to be gregarious people, they still observe most other politicians most often through the media. Indeed politicians get much, or most, of their political information through the media. The politicians, like the political journalists, watch those low-audience political TV shows in those unpopular Sunday morning and late evening time slots; they are among the small audiences of the all-news channels. Even politicians-in-office presiding over great departments of government still get much of their information about their own government (and even their own departments) by reading the daily pack of press cuttings.

More media competition has probably made political news more negative and more aggressive in most democratic counties. The paradoxical combination of heightened commercial competition with heightened partisan bias may also be a standard international trend. But to content analyse and to prove such an assertion would be a near impossible task, not least because the media in general and the press in particular can change their political emphases quite sharply from one year to the next. The press can seem to forget its supposed watchdog duties for years on end, but after a lengthy slumber that same national press can wake up feeling freshly aggressive and hungry for the raw flesh of politicians. The national presses which went to sleep during the Reagan–Thatcher 1980s, woke up and savaged their same-party successors (Bush and

Major). The national presses of France, Germany, Italy, and Spain have all exhibited massive mood swings in recent years.

I

The love-hate relationship between British journalists and politicians is breath-taking in its intensity. Table 14.1 shows how members of the House of Commons rated the honesty and ethical standards of journalists in 1995; 77 per cent rated journalists' standards as either low or very low. Labour MPs were slightly less critical than Conservative MPs—probably reflecting heavy recent criticism of the Major government. As Figure 14.1 shows, journalists were significantly less admired by MPs than were a number of other occupations. Harris only asked about 'journalists' in general. Probably many of these MPs would have made exceptions for particular individual journalists. Indeed most successful politicians have their especial favourites among journalists; and the political journalists state quite explicitly that—while they inevitably lose some potential sources by criticizing them—they also are careful to retain personally warm relationships with particular well-placed politicians.

The confrontation between politicians and political journalists is in part a battle between two sets of sensitive egos. The politician-journalist Julian Critchley made this comment on the sensitivity of the politician's ego to the printed page:

I am neurotic about newspapers. Like every other MP I can spot my name in an acre of newsprint; it can spring up from the page bearing with it the opinion of friend and foe. I will even admit publicly to a slight feeling of disappointment if the Julian turns out to belong to Ridsdale, Brazier or Amery.

Vanity, however ridiculous, is the fuel of public life, and any public man who tells you otherwise is not speaking the truth. When praised we blush with a maiden's pleasure: when abused we first sulk then shout. There lurks deep inside us all the strong desire to hit back. Show me a politician with a thick skin and I will show you a journalist with decent feelings.[1]

But the politician-journalist love-hate relationship is only part of a larger confrontation between governments and political parties on

---

[1] Julian Critchley, *UK Press Gazette*, 26 Feb. 1990.

Table 14.1. Politicians' (House of Commons) rating of the honesty of journalists, 1995 (%)
(Q: 'How would you generally rate the honesty and ethical standards of the people in these different fields. . . . Journalists?')

Rating: Honesty and Ethical Standards of Journalists	Total	Party of MPs			Region of MP			
		Conservative	Labour	Other	South England	North England	Midlands Wales	Scotland/ N. Ireland
Very High	—	—	—		—	—	—	—
High	1	1	—		1	—	—	—
Average	22	11	33	30	18	18	20	44
Low	38	39	40	20	29	50	53	19
Very Low	39	47	27	50	49	33	27	38
Don't Know	1	1	—	—	1	—	—	—
TOTAL	100	100	100	100	100	100	100	100
Unweighted Number	167	72	85	10	62	48	35	22

Source: Harris Research Centre, Fieldwork 29 Mar.–19 Apr. 1995.

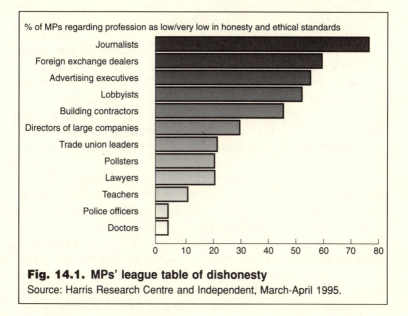

% of MPs regarding profession as low/very low in honesty and ethical standards

Fig. 14.1. MPs' league table of dishonesty
Source: Harris Research Centre and Independent, March-April 1995.

one side and newspapers on the other. Another politician-journal-ist, Lord (Bill) Deedes, made this comment:

The newspaper world is a bit like a pack of hounds: when they've got a tired and bedraggled fox they become merciless. When it comes to a government on the ropes don't expect mercy from newspapers. You don't get the hunt master saying to the hounds: 'Call it off, the fox is tired.'

The press thinks it's essential to have some kind of opposition. And the appetite grows with feeding.

There is a great invisible struggle going on as to who really has the most power—the Government or the newspapers. We don't even admit this to our wives. This rivalry is very strong and it goes back to Stanley Baldwin and Profumo. There's a high sex drive on both sides.[2]

There is, nevertheless, amongst senior newspaper people an urge to put their power in evidence. Television and radio have the opposite urge to hide their power and to neuter their partisan influence. But the attitude of newspapers to political power is one of 'if you've got it, flaunt it'.

[2] Bill Deedes, *The Guardian*, 17 Jan. 1994.

II

British political journalism shares many common characteristics with other democratic countries, but also has its full share of national idiosyncrasies. Not least of these are the extreme age and continuity of highly competitive political journalism in London. No other city in the world has such a long and uninterrupted history of such competitive political journalism. The politically independent London press pre-dated British democracy by several decades.

Some discussions of British political journalism suggest that the government only allows the newspapers to be a half-free press. Such protestations may be good ideology, good lobbying language, or good rhetoric; but they are based on historical ignorance. Even during the two world wars the British government only introduced the amount of censorship which the press was willing to accept. During both world wars press criticism of the government continued.

In Britain since 1855 governments and politicians have always tried to obtain at least the passive approval of the press. In the interwar period this still meant the approval of the press owners. Moreover, the mid-century saw the return of the aristocratic Prime Minister (Churchill, Macmillan, Douglas-Home) for most of the years 1940–64; these politicians, Alastair Burnet told me in 1967 (when he was editor of *The Economist*), felt that 'editors were not really the kind of people you could invite down for the weekend'. After 1964 Harold Wilson changed all this, and since then meritocratic Prime Ministers have courted their favourite meritocratic editors with some determination.

But much of British politics still looks like something out of a BBC costume drama series shot in front of picture postcard sets. Some of the grandest buildings contain players whose power has steeply declined. One such is Buckingham Palace. Another is the Foreign and Commonwealth Office, a grandiose relic of the imperial past, which faces across Downing Street the diminutive but powerful number 10 (Prime Minister) and 11 (Chancellor of the Exchequer). At the Palace of Westminster the main group of political (lobby) journalists occupy what amounts to the servants' quarters—severely cramped shared offices in the north wing under the clock tower (Big Ben). Parliament is like a cross between a neo-Gothic cathedral and a rail station of the same era; both journalists and Members of Parliament have been famously uncomfortable within this building for decades. Recently some of both categories have been moving into more comfortable new buildings nearby. While some MPs will get new offices just to the north of Big Ben, in the other direction a new office building now houses the political broadcasting battalions from the BBC, ITN (Independent Television News), and Sky.

Another ancient-and-modern feature of British politics is the political parties. Reports of the death of these political parties have been somewhat exaggerated as have reports of the death of the newspaper–party relationship. British newspapers have continued gradually to distance themselves from their preferred parties; loyalty to an individual politician—Margaret Thatcher—was a marked feature of the 1980s (see Chapter 15).

Leading British politicians have indeed become less popular since the 1960s. Table 14.2 shows a steady, but not spectacular decline. Even in the 1960s leading politicians were not super-popular; but these Gallup figures do show that the Prime Ministers of the 1960s—mainly Harold Macmillan and Harold Wilson—were fairly popular. The table also indicates a continuing tendency for the Prime Minister to be more popular than the government. This presumably is partly due to the manipulation of press relations by which less popular policies are blamed on other ministers; the Conservative Party has of course also been adept at dumping

Table 14.2. Declining approval of governments and political leaders (% of UK electorate)

	Approving government record	Approving Prime Minister	Approving Opposition Leader	Average of those three
1960–9	39.2	51.3	41.8	44.1
1970–9	34.8	44.1	42.5	40.5
1980–9	33.7	39.8	29.9	34.5
1990–4	25.4	36.8	40.8	34.3
Average of four periods	33.3	43.0	38.7	

Source: Gallup Poll figures for January each year, as reported in David Butler and Gareth Butler, *British Political Facts, 1990–1994*.

several defeated Prime Ministers as well as one not yet defeated (Thatcher).

Newspapers everywhere have long played an important role in the definition of political crises. In Britain there is a tendency for each level of newspaper to be associated with a different type of negative coverage. The downmarket newspapers specialize in 'scandal', especially sexual or financial. The midmarket papers specialize in 'gossip'; politicians are incorporated into the caste of characters in the gossip columns of papers like the *Daily Mail*. Political 'crises' are primarily defined by the upmarket papers; if the normally Conservative *Daily Telegraph* says that there is a crisis in the Conservative Party, that statement alone gives considerable legitimacy and currency to the notion, which may demand radical measures such as changing the party leader (see Chapter 18).

Britain has indeed seen since the 1960s a huge increase in the number of TV and radio journalists who cover national politics. There has also been an increase in the number of newspaper political journalists; and there has been a big expansion in the numbers of political columnists writing usually once or twice a week (see Chapter 17). Between 1965 and 1995 the number of full-time journalists at Westminster, or covering national politics, probably doubled. The biggest single change was the televising of the House of Commons, which began in 1989. But there has also been a paradoxical element of more means less. As more journalists have descended on Westminster, and as more programmes and columns have been launched, there has also been a trend to smaller audiences. The audience even for fifteen minutes of live Prime Minister's Questions (Westminster's most theatrical offering) is very small. The lengthy newspaper coverage of Commons (and Lords) debates in the 1960s used to summarize not only the main front-bench speeches but also the more interesting back-bench contributions. This was rapidly disappearing around the time that live television became available. The sound-bite tendency has affected not only television and radio but also all of the newspapers, including the upmarkets.

Journalists in the 1960s accused the British government of excessive secrecy, and the accusation survived into the 1990s. There are several historical reasons why the Whitehall British bureaucracy may have been exceptionally secretive. Two of them around 1900 were the increasingly heavy burden of empire and the fear of approaching war. But another reason for putting up secrecy barriers was the aggressive behaviour of the new midmarket newspapers like the *Daily Mail* and *Daily Express*. Certainly since the Boer War period the British governmental machine has tried very hard to keep as much as possible out of the newspapers; in view of the character of much of the press it would be truly astonishing if Whitehall had not reacted defensively. The 'excessive secrecy' accusation has some merit, but only some. The British government is not only exceptionally secretive, but also exceptionally leaky. The Cabinet—and this is a Cabinet system of government—is as leaky as a battered old sieve. Any Cabinet of recent decades (apart from the war period) has included a dozen or more politicians determined to leak stories to their politician and journalist friends. The two biggest leakers are typically the Prime Minister and the Deputy Prime Minister (or number two); the Cabinet includes most of the Prime Minister's political rivals and they 'give guidance' (i.e. leak) in order to protect and to advance their careers, their projects, their departments. Under a Cabinet system of the British type the Prime Minister lacks effective sanctions with which to close the holes in the sieve. All the Prime Minister can do is vigorously use his or her superior leaking mechanism, known as 'the lobby system' (see Chapter 16).

The 'lobby system' includes much else besides the twice-a-day off-the-record briefings by the Prime Minister's press secretary. This press secretary system, however, is perhaps better seen as evidence not of the strength or efficiency but of the weakness and inefficiency of the Prime Minister's staff in Downing Street. This press operation is quite small, but it looms large in the tiny staff which reports direct to the Prime Minister. The Prime Minister exerts his or her extensive powers via several nearby departments and agencies (such as the Treasury and the Cabinet Office). But there is no Prime Ministerial Department. One of the few government functions directly performed by the 10 Downing Street staff is the information and press function. But British government information and press relations have had an accident-prone record in recent years. This appears to be partly because Downing Street's press operation is too small and unsophisticated to handle the demands of today's political journalists.

III

More-journalism-means-less-coverage and the secretive-sieve of government are only two of the paradoxes which abound in British political journalism. Another is that while the number of journalists covering Westminster has doubled in thirty years, it is widely believed among journalists that the importance and significance of the Westminster Parliament has declined. The paradox is partly explained by the fact that the legislature in Britain (as elsewhere) remains the biggest and best listening post from which to cover politics. At Westminster are 650 elected politicians and several hundred unelected but semi-active lordly politicians; this is a very talkative and noisy collection of people. Every week thousands of journalist–politician conversations take place; and every week hundreds of journalist–politician lunches are eaten. A steady breeze of political gossip, anecdote, information, and comment flows through the endless Westminster corridors every day when Parliament is sitting. On more politically exciting days the breeze accelerates to gale force.

Nevertheless, while Westminster is such a good listening post, it is also true that the British Parliament is indeed less important. Much power has floated away into global finance, to the European Union in Brussels, and beyond Whitehall into a privatized, devolved, and decentralized scattering of new agencies. Newspaper executives are well aware of all this. Some subsequent chapters deal with some of these areas. Financial journalism (Chapter 21) is one of these; financial journalism—located in the City of London—is plugged into global finance and also plugs into the Treasury and Downing Street; it largely bypasses Parliament. Foreign news (Chapter 20) is another political area with a paradoxical presence in British newspapers. This is another case of both more and less. Some papers (notably the *Financial Times*) carry more, and more sophisticated, foreign news than ever before. Other papers carry little or no foreign news, but still engage in fierce foreign comment which has considerable political force.

The last of these 'political' chapters (19) deals with royal reporting. In the 1960s royalty received little newspaper coverage; by the 1990s there were huge quantities of press royal coverage, much of it highly negative. This area was also a leading example of news which typically surfaced in the form of downmarket newspaper gossip and then percolated upwards into an upmarket mixture of voyeurism and weighty 'constitutional implications' discussions. In the royal field it was plain for all to see that the newspapers—especially the tabloids—were making the running.

The overall picture presented here, then, is of British national newspapers that are very far indeed from sinking into political oblivion and impotence in the video age. The reverse is the case. The newspapers are engaged in a series of political power plays, especially with the executive, the legislature, and the monarchy.

There is one other political and policy field which attracts the special attention of the newspapers. This is media policy—an area of acute and intimate interest to both politicians and media people. All media policy-making in Britain, it will be argued, involves a significant newspaper input. Public policy for television, for radio, and for newspapers is in effect established by an alliance of politicians and regulators with the national press (see Chapters 22–4).

15 A Partisan and Right-skewed Press

FROM the 1979 General Election onwards the national press was overwhelmingly partisan in supporting the Conservative Party in general and Mrs Thatcher in particular. The right skew continued after Mrs Thatcher's replacement by John Major, and in the 1992 election the national dailies split (in terms of circulation) 70 per cent Conservative and 27 per cent Labour.[1] While the gap between Conservative and Labour voters was 8 percentage points, the national daily newspaper gap was 43 percentage points.

Since 1945 press partisanship has had three main phases. In the immediate post-war period (1945–55) the combined strength of the *Daily Herald* and *Daily Mirror* gave Labour a reasonable share of total press support; the popular papers were extremely partisan and the *Daily Mirror*'s labelling of Winston Churchill in 1951 as a warmonger showed the pro-Labour press engaged in what was negative campaigning by any standard. However, during the two decades from the arrival of Macmillan in 1957 to the departure of Harold Wilson as Prime Minister in 1976, press partisanship continued to be somewhat muted. Macmillan, Heath, and Wilson were all centrist-consensus politicians; and throughout this period Labour had the support of the *Daily Mirror* (the biggest selling daily) plus the Labour-supporting *Daily Herald/Sun*.

It was only in the late 1970s, and especially in the 1979 General Election, that this pattern switched back to a massively right-skewed press. The biggest cause of this was the transformation of the old Labour-supporting *Daily Herald/Sun* into the new Murdoch version of the *Sun* which in 1979 'voted' Conservative for the first time. The *Sun*, as the new circulation leader, also contrib-

---

[1] David Butler and Dennis Kavanagh, *The British General Election of 1992* (London: Macmillan, 1992).

uted to a marked increase in partisan belligerence, which continued through subsequent elections.

The full significance of the rightward skew may even be greater than the 70–27 level of the 1992 election might suggest. The British electoral system since 1945 has featured three main parties running first-past-the-post races. Under these circumstances, small differences in the percentage of votes produce big differences in parliamentary seats. In the ten elections between 1959 and 1992 only 6.05 percentage points on average separated the Conservative and Labour parties. The typical result saw the winning party with 42 per cent and the second party with 36 per cent of the vote. The Conservative party share in four winning elections (1979–92) averaged only 43 per cent of the total vote. When a shift in a few per cent of all votes can determine the electoral outcome, the potential leverage of the newspapers is maximized.

After 1979 Conservative papers dominated at all three market levels. Not only did the Conservatives have the support of the downmarket leader, the *Sun*, but they dominated even more strongly in the upmarket and midmarket. This meant that pro-Conservative papers day after day (as well as during elections) were leading the news agenda for the press, and inevitably, to at least some extent, for television and radio as well.

In recent decades the British national media have turned the two main party leaders into media superstars. The main superstar build-up comes from television and it is television which is especially responsible for the opposition leader normally being the second most widely recognized political personality. But while it is television which builds up British political superstars, it is the newspapers which have the power to denigrate and drag down the political personality seen so frequently on the screen. The partisan support of the Tory press was in the 1980s much less enthusiastic about the Conservative party than about Mrs Thatcher. Moreover, the national newspapers not only supported Mrs Thatcher, they also set out deliberately to emphasize the obvious weaknesses of Michael Foot and Neil Kinnock as Labour leaders. The pro-Conservative papers could more accurately be described as anti-Labour papers; the *Daily Mirror*, rather than being a pro-Labour paper, was really an anti-Conservative paper. One study of newspaper partisanship looked at popular newspapers in April 1993 and found that biased coverage of the Conservative and Labour parties in the *Sun*, *Daily Express*, *Daily Mail*, and *Daily Mirror* outweighed

Table 15.1. Voting preferences of national newspaper readers, 1995 (%)

Readers of	Other	Lib Dem	Conservative	Labour
All	4	13	25	58
Daily Telegraph	3	15	52	30
Daily Express	3	15	47	35
Daily Mail	2	16	45	37
Financial Times	5	7	42	46
Times	3	15	37	45
Sun	5	11	23	61
Today	2	15	19	64
Independent	3	17	18	62
Daily Star	2	11	16	71
Daily Mirror	1	9	6	81
Guardian	3	10	6	81

Source: Mori 1995 (Jan.–July).

'neutral' coverage by nine to one. Of this predominantly biased coverage, negative coverage of the opposing party was twice as extensive as positive coverage of your own party. Of these four dailies the *Mirror* was the most biased and the most negative (against the Conservatives).[2]

The degree of newspaper negative bias has become so great as to seem irrational from a commercial point of view. Voting intentions are always changing but a common pattern is that about half of the readers agree with their daily paper's partisanship, while a quarter support the opposite party. This means that negative or attack journalism as practised by British midmarket and downmarket papers runs counter to the current views of substantial proportions of the readers. Some readers (according to survey data) don't recognize the partisanship; other readers seldom read political stories; and some papers—especially the downmarket dailies—limit their political coverage (or vituperation) to only about one page a day. Even so, it probably remains true that some readers are repelled by the aggressive, negative, and shameless character of the political bias; editors tend to argue that political bias attracts as many

[2] Martin Linton, *Money and Votes* (London: Institute for Public Policy Research, 1994).

readers as it repels. More difficult to deny is that negative political coverage contributes to the strongly negative views which the British public holds about the reliability and honesty both of its newspapers and its journalists.

There does indeed seem to be some element of commercial irrationality here. There is an element of sheer power play in newspaper partisanship. There is also the editorial wish to pick the winner and to be identified with the winner. There is an element of wanting to put one's power in evidence. But there is also distinct anxiety that a demonstration of partisan machismo could have negative commercial consequences. Thus even a friendly party leader with a low poll rating can be in the vulnerable position of a superstar now due for the press hatchet treatment. The key partisan role of the press in current conditions may be the power to withhold the hatchet when the favoured political leader has become unpopular.

I

Winston Churchill was the first British politician to be a media superstar (mainly in radio and press); and during the Churchill–Attlee premiership years (1940–55) the national press was in a highly partisan phase. Churchill himself was the focus of fierce criticism and he was equally fiercely defended by the Conservative papers. This personalized pattern of partisanship indeed involved several Conservative press lords who were long-time political friends of Churchill. He had an especially close connection with Lord Camrose, the *Daily Telegraph* owner, who acquired the serialization rights to Churchill's Second World War memoirs and acted as Churchill's literary agent in selling the US serialization to *Life* magazine and the *New York Times*; generating a total of over a million US dollars, this was probably the world's biggest single literary deal to that date. It was followed by one of the biggest ever peacetime cover-ups. In June 1953 Winston Churchill, when Prime Minister (aged 78), had a stroke. Lords Camrose, Beaverbrook, and Bracken (owners of the *Daily Telegraph*, *Daily Express*, and *Financial Times*) were summoned to Chartwell by Churchill's Private Secretary; an imminent visit to the new US President (Eisenhower) was postponed, and a press statement was released which concealed the seriousness of the Prime Minister's illness.[3]

But soon after Churchill's retirement in 1955 a twenty-year phase of much reduced press partisanship began. One reason was the consensualist politics of the Macmillan, Heath, and Wilson years. Television also showed that its carefully balanced political coverage (required by law) could be popular; it was widely thought that in the age of television the bruising and partisan press coverage of the previous era was now a thing of the past.

Moreover, those newspapers which were most closely linked to political party also seemed by their lack of commercial success to show that rigid partisanship was no longer viable. The *Mail*, *Herald*, and *Chronicle* all lost sales in the 1950s; the *Daily Mail* was fixed into an unchanging Conservative groove; the *News Chronicle* was closely allied with the unsuccessful Liberal party. The *Daily Herald* in the 1950s had the most rapidly falling circulation, while it also had the most rigidly fixed partisan policies; it was commercially run by Odham's while its political and industrial policies were dictated by the Labour party and the Trades Union Congress. The *Daily Herald* also suffered from other problems— it lacked young and female readers and it tacked back and forth between the midmarket and the downmarket. It also failed to pick up significant numbers of *News Chronicle* readers in 1960 and after. But it was widely—and correctly—believed that editorial control by a political party was the *Daily Herald*'s key problem.

Other influential examples suggested that commercially successful newspapers were partisan only in a much more moderate and flexible way. The *Daily Telegraph* combined commercial success with partisanship in the 1950s and 1960s; although it did have a strongly Conservative middle-class readership it still maintained reasonably friendly relationships with senior Labour politicians. The *Sunday Times* was the most successful upmarket newspaper of the period and its approach was centrist. I spent much of the 1966 General Election campaign in the *Sunday Times*; most of the journalists involved in the election coverage seemed to be right-wing Labour in their personal sympathies; the main (Conservative) editorial direction came from William Rees-Mogg. (This combina-

[3] Lord Hartwell, *William Camrose: Giant of Fleet Street* (London: Weidenfeld and Nicolson, 1992), 334–9; Martin Gilbert, *Churchill: A Life* (London: Minerva, 1992), 912–15.

tion was very similar to one which appeared two decades later at the *Independent*).

The *Daily Express* and *Daily Mirror* had the two leading daily circulations. The *Daily Express* was in one of its less partisan phases; in the 1950s Lord Beaverbrook was past his most partisan and was at odds with the Conservative Party over Europe. The *Daily Mirror* was, of course, a Labour-supporting paper; four of its senior journalists (Lords Cudlipp, Beavan, Jacobson, and Castle) received their titles from Harold Wilson. But if these lords were willing, the King himself was less so; Cecil King was the main political force in the *Daily Mirror* and he was a highly maverick supporter of Labour, since he plotted hard against Harold Wilson and made increasingly outlandish plans to get him removed as Prime Minister.[4]

The *Daily Mirror* was also editorially friendly to Edward Heath throughout his leadership (1965–75) of the Conservative Party. To many people, the modest (or half-hearted as Labour politicians thought) partisanship of the *Daily Mirror* seemed to be the pattern to follow.

II

The heightened emphasis on partisanship after 1975 was obviously connected with Margaret Thatcher, but there were also newspaper industry elements. Within the newspaper industry the printing trade unions were regarded with increased hostility by most managers and editors and by many journalists. Hostility towards, and suspicion of, printing trade unions overlapped with hostility towards current developments in the Labour Party. The Labour Party's swing to the left under Michael Foot's leadership (1980–3) was met by a series of 'loony left' stories, which highlighted and exaggerated the excesses of Labour-controlled councils especially in North London (where many journalists live). Michael Foot (although a journalist by background) was not difficult to caricature; he was savagely treated by the newspapers and he did not long survive Labour's defeat in 1983.

[4] *The Cecil King Diary: 1965–1970* (London: Jonathan Cape, 1972); Philip Ziegler, *Wilson* (London: Weidenfeld and Nicolson, 1993), 293–4.

Newspapers and Politics

Newspaper managers and editors not only liked the Conservative government's plans for curbing the trade unions, they also welcomed what came to be known as its privatization measures. Privatization generated substantial extra advertising for newspapers. The newspaper industry also benefited from the deregulation of financial services, the boom in City property values, and the increased value of Fleet Street sites. Finally in 1986 the dramatic events at Wapping made newspaper managements additionally grateful to the government; they were willing and eager to express this gratitude through their partisan support at the 1987 General Election.

Several of the major editorial changes in the industry also contributed to the move towards more partisan pro-Conservative and anti-Labour editorial output. Two such changes were tabloidization and colour. When the midmarket newspapers were large-size broadsheets they still always devoted their front pages to several different stories. But after the *Daily Express* was in 1977 the last daily midmarket to go tabloid, a move was made to political front pages—in the days just before an election—which were more like political advertisements than traditional news pages. By the 1992 General Election, with colour now also available, some midmarkets front pages resembled full colour advertisements, complete with huge cartoons, massive headlines, and a relatively few stirring words of denigration for the Labour Party. The downmarket papers were even less inhibited.

Another relevant change was the greatly increased number of opinionated columnists; on the Conservative papers these columnists were mainly right-inclined and not prone to understatement. So, while in the past anti-Labour arrows were fired mainly from the main news pages and editorial page, now there were further anti-Labour arrows fired from other pages through the paper. Newspapers also received an additional input of partisanship from the new school of dominant entrepreneurial editors. In the *Daily Mail*, for example, the tendency for the editor's point of view to run right through the newspaper also included the political coverage: 'I used to share a room at Westminster with *Daily Mail* political correspondents. They were always on the phone to the office saying "This has happened—what is our line on this?" They would then be told what spin to put on the story.'

III

While Mrs Thatcher was Prime Minister (1979–90) national press partisanship took a markedly personalized form. Earlier in the century partisan press support had focused not on the party but on the person of such Prime Ministers as Lloyd George (1916–22), Ramsay MacDonald (1924 and 1929–35), as well as Winston Churchill (1940–5 and 1951–5). But the case of Margaret Thatcher was nevertheless an extreme example of the press supporting the Prime Minister rather than the party in power. Margaret Thatcher—as her autobiography and numerous other political memoirs recount—considered herself throughout her premiership to be the leader of a minority faction within the Conservative Party. In this eleven-year struggle between radical Thatcherism and more traditional Conservativism, the 'Tory Press' broadly supported the Thatcher faction in preference to the Conservative Cabinet and Parliamentary Party.

Mrs Thatcher probably received more press adulation from more national newspapers than did any other British Prime Minister after Winston Churchill's wartime premiership ended in 1945. It is difficult to believe that Mrs Thatcher could have stayed in office for eleven years and introduced Thatcherism to so many areas of British government and life without this dedicated press support. Even with this dedicated press support she seldom had the approval of half of the British electorate. Her approval rating on the Gallup Poll (Table 14.2) usually hovered around 40 per cent; and for just over one-third of the months she was in office her approval rating stood at 35 per cent or below. But throughout the 1980s Mrs Thatcher's approval rating was six important percentage points better than that of the Conservative party. Tabloid newspaper Maggie-mania certainly played a part in these poll ratings and hence in sustaining Margaret Thatcher in office.

While she was Opposition leader, Margaret Thatcher's advisers worked hard on her image, including her appearance and her voice. She accepted professional public relations advice to focus on television and the tabloid newspapers, while largely ignoring the upmarket newspapers. During the 1978–9 winter run-up to the 1979 General Election, the Conservative tabloids were already strongly committed to 'Maggie' Thatcher, and this continued during the election:

Newspapers which supported the Conservative cause were able to assist the party . . . by portraying Mrs Thatcher as someone with whom ordinary housewives could identify. On her campaign in a casual pose shopping, talking to housewives in the street . . . or having tea with workers in a factory. . . . Of the 57 photographs of politicians appearing on Fleet Street front pages between April 19 and May 3, 24 were of Mrs Thatcher and 9 of the Prime Minister. . . . The strongest impression of Fleet Street's role during the campaign was the extent of bias among the popular dailies. The uncommitted voter could not have relied for informed election coverage upon any of the tabloids. . . . The campaign was more presidential than ever, as the broadcast coverage showed. The secondary political figures had little political impact. . . . Both Conservatives and Labour strategists were aware of something called the 'Thatcher factor'.[5]

The increasingly intransigent behaviour of the printing trade unions gave the newspaper industry and its owners additional reasons for supporting the Conservatives in 1979; Mrs Thatcher's promises of trade union reform were particularly attractive and not only to owners and managers, but also to many journalists and probably to all editors. Moreover, amongst the newly entrepreneurial editors of the 1980s there were several extreme cases of Maggie-mania. In recognition of their support at the 1979 Election, knighthoods were awarded in January 1980 to two editors—Larry Lamb (*Sun*), John Junor (*Sunday Express*)—and in 1982 to David English (*Daily Mail*). Many previous Prime Ministers had set out to flatter and consult editors in the hope of receiving their editorial support. Such flattering treatment—handed out in this case by a physically attractive, female, and unusually dominant Prime Minister—seems to have been part of an exceptionally strong alliance between individual editors and the incumbent Prime Minister. David (now Sir David) English of the *Daily Mail* was generally regarded as the national editor most dedicated to Mrs Thatcher and Thatcherism. There was even a peasants' revolt at the *Daily Mail* in 1983 at the one-sided pro-Thatcher bias of the General Election reporting; no less than fifty-seven *Daily Mail* journalists supported a resolution which asked the editor to modify his stance; David English, of course, did no such thing. While fiercely loyal to Mrs Thatcher, the *Daily Mail* was often equally fierce in attacking

---

[5] David Butler and Dennis Kavanagh, *The British General Election of 1979* (London: Macmillan, 1980), 251, 253, 259, 323.

her current political enemies inside her Cabinet,[6] as well as in the Labour party.

John Junor has described a restaurant lunch he shared with Mrs Thatcher in June 1981, when she was extremely unpopular but was nevertheless getting ready for her first big round of Cabinet sackings:

I had already suspected that the Prime Minister liked me. Now I knew for sure. There was never even one awkward pause in our conversation. Margaret talked about her difficulties in Cabinet and she sought my advice. On almost every single issue and on every single personality I shared her view.

Ian Gilmour really had to go. 'John, he takes every chance to do me down. He is against me on every issue which comes before Cabinet. . . . We then talked about Peter Carrington. . . . We also talked about Fleet Street and about the need to keep support for the government going. . . .

We had talked so much, we had eaten so well that I did not dare look at my watch, but I was well aware that time had slipped past in an extraordinary fashion.[7]

Nicholas Lloyd was another and younger editor (of the *Daily Express*) who was one of Mrs Thatcher's most devoted press supporters in the closing years of her premiership, and he also received his knighthood. He, like Lamb, English, and Junor, shared with Mrs Thatcher a modest middle-class background; this meritocratic bond—and suspicion of upper-class Tory politicians like Gilmour and Carrington—may have been one key to these editor–PM relationships. Here is Nicholas Lloyd discussing his relationship with Mrs Thatcher:

I was very closely involved in the 1986 [in fact 1987] General Election. I enjoyed being part of the power process, to be honest. I enjoyed being kept in the picture as to how things were going. And that night when she won again and came down to the [Conservative] Central Office at three o'clock in the morning, that was a great night. You remember those bits you saw on the television, all the people leaning out of the windows,

[6] Alastair Hetherington gives an interesting account of the *Daily Mail* in action in 1984. While 'fiercely loyal' to Mrs Thatcher, the *Daily Mail* was attacking not only a Conservative enemy such as Sir Edward Heath but a Thatcher-ally such as Cecil Parkinson. Alastair Hetherington, *Newspapers, News and TV* (London: Macmillan, 1985), 128, 148–9

[7] John Junor, *Memoirs: Listening for a Midnight Tram* (London: Chapmans, 1990), 258–9.

Tebbit and Parkinson, and all the others, well, I was actually in that room, I talked to her for about 10 minutes that night. And if you remember that bit where she's making this speech about the inner cities and, as she walked in, her face suddenly lit up and she grinned: at that point she was saying hello to me, she really was. That's the silly bit, you don't talk about it too much, but that's the romantic bit. That's the power bit.[8]

The 1987 Election, to which this last quotation refers, was perhaps the high point of newspaper support for Mrs Thatcher. The 1986 Murdoch-Wapping reforms initially generated a fresh wave of pro-Thatcher feeling which was conveniently timed for the General Election of June 1987. As had happened in 1982–3, so also in 1986–7, Mrs Thatcher's opinion poll rating rose sharply in the year before a General Election, when the government put some attractive goodies before the electorate and as the national press switched back to pro-Tory and anti-Labour battle stations. But paradoxically, after the election win of June 1987, some of the consequences of Murdoch-Wapping tended to reduce the pro-Thatcher slant of the newspapers, especially at the upmarket end. One important development here was the 1986 launch of the *Independent*, which, although vaguely Conservative, was not pro-Thatcher. Secondly, there was a change at the *Daily Telegraph*. Until 1986 the editor was still Bill Deedes, who was a personal friend of the Thatchers and a regular golf partner of Denis Thatcher; this regime was, of course, replaced by Conrad Black and Max Hastings, who believed that the *Telegraph* should be a little more distant from the Conservative party and from Mrs Thatcher. Consequently while after 1986 there was still one firmly non-Tory upmarket newspaper, (the *Guardian*) and four loosely Conservative papers (*The Times, Daily Telegraph, Independent, Financial Times*) all four of these latter papers were now somewhat more sceptical of Mrs Thatcher; most importantly, the BBC and ITV had some much less pro-Thatcher newspapers through which to steer their neutral middle ways. As happened about two years after each of the previous election wins, by 1989 Mrs Thatcher had reached a new low level of poll popularity; this then continued until the leadership challenge and her resignation in November 1990.

[8] Nick Lloyd, in Tony Gray (ed.), *Fleet Street Remembered* (London: Heinemann, 1990), 260–1.

IV

The Murdoch–News International papers did play a very important part in the political skew of British newspapers in the 1980s. Especially important was the fact that three of the six market leaders were Murdoch papers—the *Sun*, *News of the World*, and (after 1981) the *Sunday Times*. Each of these papers in turn had its own unique political characteristics. But apart from the sheer size of the Murdoch stable, these newspapers overall were much more similar to—rather than different from—other newspapers in the *Mail*, *Express*, and *Telegraph* stables.

The only one of the News International papers which completely changed its political complexion was the *Sun*. The *News of the World* had been a right-wing Conservative paper long before Murdoch acquired it in 1979; indeed in 1968 Noyes Thomas, the political editor of the *News of the World*, told me that, although he himself was a Conservative, some of his stories were politically censored in line with the far right political views of the owner, Sir Emsley Carr. Under Murdoch the *News of the World* continued to be Conservative, but perhaps less far right.

After acquiring the *Sun* in 1969, Rupert Murdoch initially continued its previous—pro-Labour—political line. It was not, indeed, until ten years later, at the 1979 General Election, that the *Sun* first 'voted' Conservative. There were several elements to this, and Larry Lamb, the 1970s editor, initially had to persuade Murdoch to support the Conservatives and Mrs Thatcher. One set of factors was assuredly Rupert Murdoch's own switch in political viewpoint, his liking for backing winners, and his hopes of regulatory favours. But very significant also must have been the *Daily Star*, just launched in 1978, as a third downmarket daily; the *Daily Star* created a new three-handed poker game. Of the three the *Daily Mirror* was the only one with a firm partisan (Labour) loyalty. the *Sun* was only just ahead of the *Daily Mirror* in circulation in 1979. Given the *Daily Mirror*'s traditional Labour commitment, the *Sun*'s Conservative vote was in part just commercially competitive differentiation. In 1979 it would have been unwise for the *Sun* to 'vote' Labour, because this would have allowed the *Daily Star* to become the only working-class Conservative newspaper. After 1979 the *Sun*'s executives continued to worry about the *Daily Star*; had the *Sun* in 1983 switched to Labour it would still have risked losing readers to the *Daily Star*. However, by 1983 the *Sun* had been deeply involved, not only in bingo wars against the *Daily Star*, but in the Falklands War against Argentina and the *Daily Mirror*; and (under a new editor, Kelvin MacKenzie) it was madly for Maggie and in ferocious attack mode against the elderly socialist Michael Foot and his walking stick.

The *Sun* did not invent the term 'Winter of Discontent' to describe the strikes of 1978–9, but it did popularize the term. It was also the *Sun* which memorably rephrased what Prime Minister Jim Callaghan said in January 1979 when he returned from arms talks in the West Indies. Asked about strikes and mounting chaos in Britain, Callaghan made a statement which began: 'Please don't run your country down by talking about mounting chaos'; the *Sun* headline abbreviated this statement into 'Crisis? What Crisis?'. Larry Lamb had already established a personal relationship with Mrs Thatcher and her image gurus Gordon Reece and Tim Bell of Saatchi and Saatchi. As part of her charm offensive before the 1979 Election, Mrs Thatcher also visited the *Sun* in Bouverie Street and spent 'several hours', says Larry Lamb, in discussion with senior journalists.[9]

The *Sun*'s support for the Conservative election cause, and for Mrs Thatcher, surely had two important but unquantifiable consequences. It made the Labour party leaders feel that the popular press was biased against them to a grossly unfair degree; this probably contributed to a fatalistic belief among some Labour politicians that any policies which they might put forward would attract press smears and lies. A second consequence of the *Sun*'s political position was a demonstration that anti–Labour political bias could be taken to extremes, while still retaining millions of Labour voters as readers. This was achieved through the use of several techniques—such as rationing overt politics to one page of the paper (where the regular reader could avoid it), and by attacking currently unpopular and unsuccessful Conservative Ministers. In this latter way the *Sun* could both support Mrs Thatcher and demand the resignation of a particular Minister; when Mrs Thatcher duly sacked the Minister, the paper could rejoice both in its own influence and the infinite wisdom of Maggie.

Nevertheless the *Sun* and Rupert Murdoch probably carried on the approach too long, and especially after 1988 when Mrs

[9] Larry Lamb, *Sunrise* (London: Macmillan, 1989), 165.

Thatcher became detached from political reality. Murdoch and *The Times* also had some difficulty in working out a political position in the 1980s. Harold Evans has described at some length his differences with Murdoch over *The Times* in 1981–2.[10] But for most of the remainder of the 1980s the paper broadly supported Mrs Thatcher and the Conservatives.

Overall the Murdoch newspapers showed less than 100 per cent loyalty to Mrs Thatcher and were quite critical of other Conservative politicians. *Today* (after its acquisition in 1987) wandered uncertainly across the political battlefield. The *Sunday Times*, while in some respects the ultimate Thatcherite newspaper, was sufficiently belligerent and critical to earn itself an 'unreliable' label in the Conservative Party. Overall the Murdoch papers were less loyal to Mrs Thatcher than were some other specific newspapers, such as the *Daily Mail*. But it was, of course, the size of the Murdoch stable which was so important when it was placed alongside other pro-Conservative newspapers. The Murdoch papers confirmed the broad pattern of favouring the Conservative party in the run-up to the elections, while favouring Mrs Thatcher most of the time. It was also the Murdoch papers, which when added to the *Mail*, *Express*, and *Telegraph* placed something like 70 per cent of national daily press firepower behind a politician who still often only had a voter approval level of 35 per cent or less.

V

Having succeeded Margaret Thatcher as Prime Minister, John Major had an extended honeymoon period, but then had uniquely bad experiences both in the opinion polls and with the 'Conservative' press. This seemed to underline both the extent to which press partisanship had shaded off into comprehensive savagery, as well as the extent to which press loyalty to Mrs Thatcher as Prime Minister now looked increasingly like the exception rather than the norm. In 1992–3 both John Major and his Conservative government suffered unprecedentedly rapid and steep falls in the opinion polls, and in 1995 the *Daily Mail*, *Sun*, *The Times*, and *Daily Telegraph* all opposed John Major's re-election as Conservative leader.

[10] Harold Evans, *Good Times, Bad Times* (London: Coronet Books, 1984).

Initially John Major was shielded from the wrath of the Conservative press by the proximity of the election. When he became
Prime Minister in November 1990, the Conservative government
was 41 months old and an election could be expected at any time.
Exercising its usual pre-election constraint, the Tory press gave
John Major a long honeymoon period; when he unexpectedly won
the election in April 1992, the honeymoon was extended to an
eventual total of more than twenty months. But in September 1992
the pound sterling fell out of the European ERM (Exchange Rate
Mechanism) and most newspapers concluded that Major's central
economic policy had been shattered.

During 1993 the *Daily Express* was really the only one of Britain's eleven national dailies which was supporting Prime Minister
John Major. There were several overlapping strands within this
unpopularity. Central to these was the exit from the ERM. Further
unpopularity focused on Norman Lamont, whom Major at first
stubbornly kept on as Chancellor of the Exchequer and then
sacked; after another pause, Lamont himself then denounced
Major. There was massive criticism of all this from the Conservative Party's 'friends' in the City of London. There was also the
factor of the opening up of old divisions over Europe within the
Conservative Party. There was continuing bitterness—for example
at the *Daily Mail*—over the way in which the Tory party had
dispatched Mrs Thatcher in 1990; that lady herself delivered adroit
anti-Major messages, for example in her memoirs, published in
1993.

Perhaps there was an element in some newspapers also of thinking that We Were Too Loyal to Maggie. There was undoubtedly a
commercial element of following the opinion polls—of courting
reader popularity by attacking an unpopular government and
Prime Minister. There was certainly an element of social and educational snobbery in the antagonism to John Major; some of this
had existed even in the criticism of Margaret Thatcher—many
journalists (and others) saw her as philistine, uninterested in the
arts and music, too concerned with money and material success.
But Mrs Thatcher was an Oxford (science) graduate and she had
a unique policy vision. Not so John Major, who from late 1992
onwards was subjected to a deluge of press abuse, and snobbery,
plus a good deal of puzzled condescension. While feature writers
complimented him on his nice little wife and told him not to be so
sensitive about his lack of formal education, many of the political

writers were assessing John Major as simply lacking the talent and ability for the job. Paul Johnson was only one of many who wrote in 1993 along these lines.

In my own case, despite my personal loyalty to Margaret Thatcher, I gave her successor the longest possible honeymoon. . . . But I was gradually driven to the conclusion that he was, and is, unfit to govern. . . . My own guess is that Major will go down in history as a substantial comic figure. I cannot wait to include him in my Oxford Book of Political Anecdotes.[11]

Another feature behind these denunciations was the hope and expectation that John Major might be persuaded to depart or that the Conservative Party would be persuaded to vote him out of the leadership. This probably explains some of the savagery, the frequency, and the large total number of these denunciations. Many of the denunciations came from the normally most loyal Conservative papers such as the *Daily Mail* and *Daily Telegraph*.

[11] Paul Johnson, 'How not to handle the press', *Sunday Times*, 25 July 1993.

16 Lobby Journalists, Politicians, and Prime Ministers

THE 'Lobby Correspondents' are the main group of news reporters in British political journalism. Something like 'Cabinet, Prime Minister, and Parliament Correspondent' might be a more accurately descriptive title. These lobby correspondents have sometimes been described as the alert watchdogs of British democracy; but they have been called the tame lapdogs, who merely do the bidding of the Prime Minister's press secretary; however, lobby correspondents have also been seen as fighting dogs whose daily business is to wound and savage the nation's politicians. This chapter will argue that lobby correspondents act in all three ways— tame lapdog, alert watchdog, and fierce fighting dog—at different times in relation to different politicians.

The 'lobby system' is the main channel for the transmission of current political news; the main continuing political story is the relationship between Prime Minister, Cabinet, and House of Commons: how well is the Prime Minister doing at present? How is the new legislation succeeding in its parliamentary passage? What conflicts are there in the Cabinet? Who are the rising and falling stars within the government party and in the opposition? When there is a big political story running—such as the Prime Minister in serious political difficulty—the senior newspaper lobby correspondent may be writing the front-page lead story for days or even weeks in succession; the broadcast equivalents—the political editors of the BBC and ITN—will be leading numerous long and short news offerings per day, and looking in need of a good night's sleep.

The lobby system is a channel down which political news moves quickly between a centralized political apparatus and a centralized media apparatus. A few ambiguous words by the Prime Minister's press secretary at the 11 a.m. briefing in Downing Street may dominate the midday broadcast news and be the lead story in evening newspapers across Britain. A sudden political rumour circulating in the Commons at 11 p.m. can become the lead story in late editions of next morning's national daily papers. But this is also a two-way system. Politicians scan the newspapers each morning to find out what the journalists have to say about their success or failure.

This chapter will look back to the 1960s when—before TV had its main impact—lobby journalism perhaps reached its peak of importance. Since the 1960s both the political system and the media have opened up and expanded. In particular there is now more television, there are more on-the-record press conferences, and also there is much more political column-writing and feature-writing. However, within a more complex political system (including for example the European Union) and within a bigger total quantity of political journalism, the lobby system is still central. The lobby system also contains many oddities, paradoxes, and obscurities, because it has grown up alongside the oddities, paradoxes, and obscurities of the famously 'unwritten' British Constitution. Much of the mystery surrounds the daily 'briefings' given by the Prime Minister's press secretary and the fact that these have been non-attributable; but these 'briefings' are only one of five important types of access available to lobby journalists. These daily briefings probably do not generate more than one-fifth of the stories and take up much less than one-fifth of the working time of a team of lobby journalists. The five types of access are as follows:

1.   The daily briefings by the Prime Minister's press secretary take place at 11 a.m. (in Downing Street) and at 4 p.m. (at Westminster). On many days the press secretary merely lists the Prime Minister's engagements for the following twenty-four hours, which is followed by some desultory questions and answers. Occasionally, however, there are explosive comments about, for example, Ministerial resignations; more frequently the press secretary makes some fairly interesting, but rather ambiguous, comments on current political happenings. There are additional Friday briefings for Sunday journalists, a Thursday briefing by the Leader

of the House of Commons (about next week's business), and traditionally there has been a weekly Opposition briefing as well.

2.   The correspondents have access to the lobby of the Commons debating chamber; this is the origin of the term and it allows lobby journalists to converse with Members of Parliament. Journalists can informally interview one particular MP; but there is also the opportunity to question a number of MPs in quick succession and hence to judge the current views of a particular faction or the strength of a particular trend of opinion.

3.   They have early access to all government publications. Lobby journalists are allowed to see government publications some hours—or a day—before ordinary Members of Parliament see them. This allows the lobby journalists either to have stories ready at the official hour of publication themselves or to hand the documents back to the office to other specialists. This is also one of several ways in which the ordinary lobby journalist tends to be 'ahead' of the ordinary MP in terms of current political information.

4.   Lobby correspondents are given office space at Westminster in very cramped office conditions. This is important because it means that the lobby journalists spend nearly all of their long working week at Westminster. They have their own eating facilities. But they are also allowed into some (but not all) other areas used by MPs. Lobby journalists are typically at Westminster for more hours per day and for more days per year than the average MP.

5.   They also have access to the Commons gallery separate from that available to the public. So a lobby journalist can watch Prime Minister's Questions on Tuesday and Thursday and study live and at close quarters the public performance of any other Minister or MP who is currently in the news.

These five types of formal access mean that the 230 lobby correspondents are near to becoming non-voting or associate members of the parliamentary club, alongside the 651 elected full Members of Parliament. The fifteen or twenty leading lobby journalists—which is mainly the number ones of the national dailies, the BBC, ITN, and the Press Association—are clearly significant players in the national political game. The senior lobby correspondents acquire informal access to the top politicians, including Cabinet Ministers; lunches are common, but so also are interviews with the

Minister either in the Commons, or at the Minister's Department (which is only a few minutes walk away). As insiders to the political game, lobby correspondents also receive many invitations to receptions, launches, and parties. A key point to grasp is that, located at Westminster, these journalists are stationed in the midst of a system which generates huge quantities of paper, statements, speeches, and—above all—gossip. One lobby journalist lists the multiple sources:

> Stories come from the Commons Chamber, from government statements, from numerous reports, from the National Audit Office, from Select Committees, from the Opposition Leader's office, and the Opposition Party, from conversations with MPs, from lunches, from fishing, from other newspapers, from television and of course radio, from putting two and two together and making six. Stories also come from books and opinion polls.

I

All governments and governmental systems combine a concern for publicity with a concern for secrecy. The especially idiosyncratic combination of publicity and secrecy found in the British lobby journalism arrangements is related to central principles of Cabinet and parliamentary government.

The four relevant principles are as follows: first, *collective Cabinet responsibility*—since the British system is not a presidential system, the Cabinet as the executive body can only operate successfully if all Cabinet Ministers loyally accept their collective decisions. Secondly, in order to maintain collective responsibility, there has to be *Cabinet secrecy*—members of the Cabinet cannot reveal disagreements or the details of Cabinet debate. Thirdly, Ministers are individually responsible for their Departments and preside over a *non-partisan civil service*; civil servants also, therefore, cannot dissent from the views and decisions of their presiding Minister and of the Cabinet. Fourthly, Britain has a parliamentary system; the *Cabinet is responsible to Parliament* and only stays in office so long as it can sustain a regular voting majority in the House of Commons. Traditionally Ministers are expected to make significant announcements first to Parliament, not to the media; rather than hold public press conferences, the British Prime Minister answers Prime Minister's Questions twice a week in the

Commons, and each weekday another Minister also answers such questions.

All four of these principles have been greatly modified by the growth of the lobby system since its origins in the late nineteenth century and by the huge growth in government since the early twentieth century. The principles have been severely stretched by developments since the 1960s especially in television, but also in the press, and the recognition by incumbent governments of the need for a more and more activist publicity policy. Parliament has tried to become more active (for example with committees); but the Cabinet, the Prime Minister, and the civil service (both central and decentralized) have become more salient. It is, of course, because of these and other changes that demands for constitutional reform and a written constitution increased during and after the 1980s Thatcher period.

Under the traditional unwritten constitution the most severe stresses and strains appeared to affect the first principle of 'collective Cabinet responsibility'. In practice the complexity and quantity of Cabinet business mean that many decisions are taken by the Prime Minister and other key Ministers in cabinet committees and *ad hoc* meetings and only subsequently reported to the full Cabinet.[1] Considerations of publicity lead the Prime Minister, as the government's chief image and image-maker, to adopt a *fait accompli* approach also to public announcements. Consequently, Cabinet Ministers may only discover by reading the newspapers some significant details of what they have formally agreed to and are collectively responsible for.

The second principle of 'Cabinet secrecy' is, of course, far from fully observed. Cabinet members leak selected items from, and versions of, cabinet business to their friends in Parliament and in the media. But this is done largely on a 'don't mention my name' basis. In recent decades, and especially under Mrs Thatcher, the 'non-partisan' and anonymous civil service rule was increasingly breached. Mrs Thatcher took an active part in trying to promote ideologically correct civil servants into the top jobs. Civil servants also appeared before Commons committees on the record and were increasingly interviewed and quoted in the press.

The fourth principle, that the Cabinet is 'responsible to Parlia-

[1] See the numerous memoirs of Cabinet Ministers. The most acute observations on the complexity of decisions, on the relative passivity of most Cabinet members, and on the publicity dimension, are in Nigel Lawson, *The View from No. 11* (London: Corgi, 1993).

ment'—and thus needs to make policy announcements there—has also wilted in recent decades. British governments do still observe this principle through Parliamentary Questions, through Ministerial statements and speeches in the Commons, in the new select committees, and also in published White Papers and Green (discussion) Papers. But back-bench MPs also know that Parliament does not sit on half the days of the year, while there is an urgent need for a modern government to seek to dominate the news agenda day by day. Back-bench MPs have consequently accepted a huge new outpouring of on-the-record press conferences and sound-bite pronouncements to the TV cameras. Mrs Thatcher introduced a completely new publicity forum to British politics— the brief street statement outside 10 Downing Street.

Until the 1960s the British system was internationally unusual in that the Prime Minister did not give on-the-record press conferences either in person or via a press secretary. That has changed. The Prime Minister now operates a much wider portfolio of different types of public pronouncement: the Prime Minister speaks in the Commons and answers Questions about seventy times per year; there are numerous on-the-record press conferences, especially at Party Headquarters and at European and other foreign gatherings; there are sound-bites in Downing Street and at other visits and meetings. The Prime Minister also each month does a number of interviews (both on and off the record) with individual journalists. Finally there is the press secretary, who briefs on behalf of the Prime Minister twice per weekday and who, with his staff, is also available for face-to-face and telephone consultations. These press secretary briefings now occupy an odd grey area. The briefings are formally 'off-the-record' and can thus be denied. However, these stories are no longer attributed to 'Whitehall' but to 'Downing Street' and anyone who cares to know—such as the international money markets—knows that this is the Prime Minister's spokesman speaking. A denial will not alter the financial market reaction, although it still, just about, satisfies constitutional propriety.

The lobby arrangements obviously now inhabit a very peculiar constitutional limbo land. They have been driven into that limbo land because, first, the media have 'become bigger', quicker, and more insistent; and, secondly, because the Cabinet in general, and the Prime Minister in particular, have also 'become bigger', potentially in power and certainly in terms of publicity image.

Another, less noticed, point is that while the reduced reality of 'collective responsibility' creates problems for lobby journalism, it is also true that lobby journalism (quite apart from the wider media explosion) poses special problems for 'collective responsibility'. Cabinet splits and Cabinet leaks were common in the 1960s, but have become still more prevalent. The supposedly 'dominant' Mrs Thatcher suffered both in epidemic proportions. Perhaps the old doctrine of 'Cabinet collective responsibility' needs to be rephrased as 'Cabinet responsibility-split-and-leak'. The lobby arrangements are intimately connected with all this. They can, indeed, be used as an instrument of government domination; but the lobby arrangements are also not only a threat to collective responsibility, they are a continuing element of government weakness.

II

It was only in the 1960s that the first published accounts of lobby journalism appeared. It was not easy to generalize, because lobby journalism went through several quite distinct political phases in the 1960s. A key event in the later part of Harold Macmillan's premiership was his sacking of one-third of his Cabinet in July 1962. The main changes—including the departure of Selwyn Lloyd as Chancellor of the Exchequer—had been accurately predicted in the *Daily Mail* by Walter Terry. Macmillan admits in his memoirs that press leaks caused him to rush the changes.[2] Of these panic changes one of the sacked Ministers (Charles Hill) later wrote: 'There are times when the way a thing is done is so much more important than what is actually done.'[3] Macmillan's premiership continued for another full year of unpopularity—including the Profumo crisis of 1963.

There then followed a lengthy electioneering phase from October 1963 (when Sir Alec Douglas-Home became Prime Minister) which included the General Elections of 1964 and 1966. This thirty-month period was one of continuing political excitement in which Harold Wilson was the dominant political personality. Wilson received largely favourable coverage from the lobby journalists both before and after he became Prime Minister in

---

[2] Harold Macmillan, *At the End of the Day* (London: Macmillan, 1973), 91–8.
[3] Charles Hill, *Both Sides of the Hill* (London: Heinemann, 1964), 247.

October 1964. Throughout this period Wilson was around 20 percentage points ahead of the Conservative leaders (Home and
Heath) on the Gallup Poll.

After 1966 Wilson's popularity declined steeply. A key event was
the devaluation of sterling on 18 November 1967. In early and mid-
1968 most of the national lobby journalists agreed both to be interviewed by me and to complete a lengthy written questionnaire. By
now the Wilson government was getting the critical press coverage
which was to continue up to the Labour electoral defeat of 1970.
This was not simply a case of lobby journalists dutifully obeying
newspaper-owner demands for anti-Wilson coverage. The newspapers during the November 1967 devaluation were certainly hostile to Wilson; but when interviewing the lobby journalists two
months later I was nevertheless surprised at the strength of anti-
Wilson sentiment. A sizeable number of lobby journalists thought
that they had believed Wilson too easily in his early days; that they
had allowed him to manipulate the press; that he had made many
factual claims which had been shown to be untrue or worthless; and
that he now deserved the criticism he was receiving.

During the early Wilson years (1964–7) the senior lobby journalists were probably at a high point in terms of political independence
and significance. The national press itself at this time was relatively
balanced politically. In the lobby were some extremely experienced
people and their prestige was high. Some senior lobby journalists
said that their night desk often had little idea what a big political
story was about until it arrived in the office very near to first edition
time. Several senior lobby journalists wrote down the first paragraph or two and then dictated the rest straight down the telephone
and onto the front page. Like most journalists, these lobby correspondents had mainly centrist views. They were split three ways—
one-third being Conservative, one-third Labour, with one-third
being Liberal or other (including not voting). Overall they were a
little to the left of their employing news organization. They also
said that they (not the news desk) usually decided what stories to
cover.[4]

News desk executives—like the readers—were largely dependent on the press for their political information. This meant that if
two, three, or four prominent newspapers carried a story, the other

[4] Jeremy Tunstall, *The Westminster Lobby Correspondents* (London: Routledge, 1970), 35–
6, 69–70.

papers might feel forced to follow. Much political journalism is a search for political conflict and rows; in Britain's case this usually means a conflict, clash, or row in the Cabinet. But when does discussion and argument become a row, conflict, or clash? The answer in practice may be: when several newspapers say it is.

In the lobby, as in other fields, some competitors actually co-operated with each other. There was co-operation between *The Times*'s chief lobby man, David Wood, and the BBC TV number one, Peter Hardiman-Scott. There were other groupings, such as one involving the *Daily Telegraph* with the *Daily Mail* and the *Sun* (IPC). The *Guardian* also co-operated with the *Financial Times*, the *Sunday Times* with the *Sunday Mirror* and the *People*. Such groupings strengthen the hand of specialist journalists in relation both to their sources and their employers. The co-operative arrangements were certainly in part a defence against excessive competition. But the 1960s lobby was less competitive and less polarized than it later became. There was a marked hierarchy between the heavier and lighter newspapers. In the lobby there were then a bigger number—and a much bigger proportion—of provincial newspaper correspondents than is the case today.

At the top of the system were the highly experienced men of *The Times*, *Daily Telegraph*, and *Sunday Times*. (There were only two women out of forty-six national lobby journalists.) *The Times* and the *Daily Telegraph* had much better office space and much bigger total Westminster teams than the others; both of these dailies had their own teams of shorthand notetakers who took down the debates in full.

David Wood of *The Times* was seen by himself and others as the senior lobby journalist. His personal views were Conservative but he was giving the Labour government extensive and 'balanced' coverage. He stressed that he was absolutely free to choose his own stories and that he could and did telephone late stories into the paper without sub-editing. He emphasized to me the need for 'theoretic' pieces, by which he meant a lengthy discussion as to the implications of current events. He favoured polite but vigorous newsgathering. For example, he would 'blackmail' (his word) a Cabinet Minister by indicating what he knew so far and was about to print. He was confident that he could find out most of what had happened at a midday Cabinet meeting in time for the same evening's first edition. David Wood was known to have been a favourite of *The Times*'s editor, William Haley, and he stressed to me that he continued to report, not to the news desk or night desk but to the editor. The current editor (William Rees-Mogg) in another interview broadly confirmed this position. David Wood claimed that there was no serious competition. He scoffed at the then struggling *Guardian*. His confidence—which bordered on arrogance—must partly have depended on his exchange partnership with the BBC, which Peter Hardiman-Scott described to me.

Next in the 1960s lobby hierarchy was Harry Boyne of the *Daily Telegraph*. He had worked for the *Glasgow Herald* when he entered the lobby seventeen years earlier. The *Telegraph* was the only other well-established prestige daily and it was regarded by all the lobby people as carrying the widest collection of separate political stories. It had what looked like the one and only really efficient newspaper filing system at Westminster. The number three man, David Harris, specialized in covering government publications. The number two, Roland Summerscales, had mainly specialized on the Labour Party over the previous decade. Harry Boyne, the number one, dealt mainly with the Conservative Party; MPs, he said, all assumed (incorrectly) that he himself held Conservative views.

James Margach was the most senior (in several senses) of the Sunday lobby journalists. Like Wood and Boyne he was not a university graduate. He had already been in the lobby for thirty-five years, starting at age 23 for the Aberdeen morning paper. Between 1935 and 1955 he was a lobby journalist for the (Conservative) Kemsley regional group. James Margach was diffident and charming. The young turk *Sunday Times* 'Insight' feature journalists of this period regarded Margach as exemplifying the 'corruption' of the lobby. But Margach fitted well into Denis Hamilton's centrist *Sunday Times*. Margach had long-standing political connections with both main parties. He told me he had especially cultivated the 1950 intake of Conservative MPs which included Macleod, Maudling, and Heath. Margach also had excellent contacts in the 1960s Labour Cabinet. He would normally make phone calls on Monday and Tuesday, aimed at appointments with Ministers later in the week. The memoirs of Richard Crossman and others indicate that Margach did indeed see Labour Ministers with some frequency. When he talked to me, Margach regretted that the *Sunday Times* now carried more features and fewer political stories. He did admit, however, that he had still had the front-page 'splash' on all four previous Sundays.

On the non-Tory papers was another collection of able individuals. Harold Hutchinson on the *Sun* (IPC) had been a war correspondent and labour correspondent. His energetic number two was Joe Haines, notable as one of the few lobby journalists still in early 1968 strongly committed to Harold Wilson. The *Daily Mirror*'s number one was Victor Knight, who confirmed to me that he got on better with Conservative politicians. Terence Lancaster described his job at the *People* as wonderfully easy and relaxing; he had previously been Beaverbrook's choice for *Daily Express* man in New York. Lancaster had recently done a long interview with Edward Heath, which he said was too boring to publish. The *Guardian* was represented by one of its grand older men, Francis Boyd, who tended to focus on briefings, documents, and gallery. His energetic number two was Ian Aitken, another Beaverbrook protégé who had been the *Daily Express* number one lobby man. Aitken said that his left-wing Labour views had made him dread the prospect of working for the Tory *Express* in the 1964 election. He had jumped ship to the *Guardian* and described his three newsgathering methods as standing in the lobby, drinking with MPs, and lunching with MPs. Aitken was an expert on the Labour left, who were a big story in this devaluation era. He said that Labour Cabinet members (some of whom he knew from Oxford) consulted him about the rebellious left.

The two important remaining dailies were the *Mail* and *Express*. The chief *Daily Mail* lobby correspondent was Walter Terry, who was regarded as the lobby's leading provider of major 'exclusive' stories. It was widely believed that his already legendary 1962 Cabinet reshuffle exclusive had come from the Cabinet number two, Rab Butler. Terry told me that the *Daily Mail* gave him no directions at all apart from advising him to concentrate on exclusives. Terry said that when he first entered the lobby he was much too shy to talk to anyone. He said that 'if you're not talking to Heath, make sure you are talking to Maudling'. My own guess was that he cultivated the very top people in each party and their entourages. Walter Terry took me to lunch at the Reform Club, where he introduced me to Richard Crossman, then a senior Cabinet Minister. This was on 24 January 1968, two months after sterling devaluation and in the middle of public expenditure cuts and a Labour left revolt. Terry suggested that surely things couldn't get any worse. Richard Crossman replied that things could indeed get still worse; he was thinking (he said) of going back to writing and/or journalism, his only real skill. His sole cheerful point was that under his contract with the *Sunday Times* for his political diary and memoirs, the newspaper had agreed to start paying him five years in advance of delivery. Terry commented to me that he would not directly report this conversation or Crossman's remarkable pessimism. That, said Terry, was how the lobby system worked.

The critical onslaught on the Labour government in 1968 was being led by the *Daily Express*, whose chief lobby man and fighting dog journalist was Wilfred Sendall. He had been in the lobby for twenty years, first on the *Daily Telegraph* then the *Express*. He had finished the Second World War as a Marine Captain. And his stories in 1967 and 1968 were belligerently anti-Wilson and anti-Labour. He liked working for the *Daily Express*, he said, because of all the Fleet Street papers its politics most closely matched his own. Previous Prime Ministers, said Sendall, had provided true facts with a partisan gloss. Harold Wilson, he said, was 'a creep and a liar' who insulted you by putting out fabricated information.

This was a collection of very individual individuals, most of whom felt few partisan constraints. They sensed they were in a powerful position because the Labour government badly needed press support. They were a hard-working group of people; David Wood said that he had last been to a London theatre about ten years previously. Walter Terry spoke for most of the 1960s lobby journalists when in describing the strong attractions of the job he said: 'Where is there a better play showing?'

III

While British government in general favours secrecy, the Cabinet—the core of both politics and government—is leaky. The Cabinet is leaky for the very simple reason that it is a political body, full of professional politicians who are therefore also professional publicists. As the lobby journalists say, 'it's a market'. From the politicians the journalists acquire gossip and information; from the journalists the politicians may acquire relevant gossip, but they also acquire publicity for their causes, departments, and factions, and for themselves as individual politicians.

In this market some politicians are much more in demand than others. The Prime Minister is the most in demand and consequently strictly rations his or her personal contacts, while speaking primarily via a press secretary. Next in demand are the twenty plus members of the Cabinet; then come junior Ministers and Opposition leaders. There is a similar market hierarchy on the journalism side. Senior lobby journalists regard themselves as in a stronger market position than new back-bench MPs. A Cabinet Minister typically wants to obtain favourable publicity on TV and radio and in the broadsheet newspapers. The tabloid papers are less attractive because of their unpredictable and sensational nature; a tabloid will seldom devote long stories to details of policy. But for a Treasury Minister lunch with one journalist from the *Financial Times* and another from the *Daily Telegraph* might be an ideal way of 'flying a kite' about some possible taxation changes. Or for the Social Minister an hour with one *Observer* journalist and one *Times* journalist could be a useful chance to swap thoughts on currently important social policy issues. Or if a Minister is phoned on Sunday by a *Guardian* journalist to whom he has previously given his weekend home number, this is a chance to insert one or two friendly paragraphs in a longer story.

Political journalists strive hard to establish friendly relationships with well-placed politicians. But well-placed politicians also have previously invested time and energy in developing relationships of trust with selected individual journalists. The British Cabinet is not merely a committee of politicians; the Cabinet is a broad spectrum body which typically includes representatives of the main factions and groupings within the governing party. Each Cabinet has its right-wing and left-wing members. When a new Prime Minister chooses his or her Cabinet, typically most of the new PM's chief political rivals (within the party) are included. The Prime Minister has few sanctions against talkative senior Ministers; the normal perception is that it is preferable to have major political rivals inside the Cabinet and whispering to journalists rather than outside the Cabinet and shouting denunciations of the government. Nor are there effective sanctions even against lesser Cabinet Ministers; there is, for example, no way to prevent a Minister loyally selling government policies to journalists while also adding on a personal reservation here and a strong criticism there.

Typically amongst the Prime Minister's three or four top Ministers there is at least one extremely active talker-to-the-journalists. Especially talkative in the past have been Deputy Prime Ministers (who are typically defeated political opponents). Economic Ministers outside the Treasury often disagree with major aspects of Treasury policy. Social and Defence Ministers typically are fighting against expenditure constraints. Also highly talkative are current Leaders of the House of Commons; it is this Minister's job to brief the lobby journalists on Thursday about next week's business, but that activity can extend into wider speculation and fewer loyal opinions.

Under the British system some of the most talkative people are the three or four non-Cabinet Ministers found in the typical Department. They are part of the hundred-plus members of the administration, but they are not part of the twenty-plus Cabinet. Typically a junior Minister is required to specialize in certain sub-areas of the Department's activities. This involves seeing selected Cabinet and Cabinet committee documents and being aware of civil service, Cabinet, and back-bench views on the relevant issues. Included in this second tier of junior Ministers are some older politicians (who have reached their ceiling) as well as the most talented, most ambitious, and most publicity-seeking younger members of the parliamentary party in power. In using their talents and pursuing their ambitions, junior Ministers develop friendly relationships with lobby journalists—often journalists of about their own age who arrived in Westminster at about the same time.

Any new Prime Minister will have been an ambitious politician in the past and will have a record stretching back years or decades of talking to journalists. A new Prime Minister will probably have a number of long-established relationships with journalists. Ministers are also invited by editors to lunch or other meetings in newspaper offices. So a new Prime Minister will also already be acquainted with some editors. And Prime Ministers tend to cultivate their relationships with particular friendly editors.

But Prime Ministers and Cabinet Ministers under the British system are exceptionally busy people. A Cabinet Minister must run a large Department; must attend perhaps 150 Cabinet and Cabinet Committee meetings per year; must attend, vote, answer Questions, and make speeches in the House of Commons; and must continue to visit his or her constituency and to answer constituency mail. In recent years Ministers have become increasingly active in the European Community, which means more flying visits, more meetings, more speeches. During her first eleven years as Prime

Minister Mrs Thatcher attended 32 European Councils (EC Summits), visited France 23 times, Germany 16 times, Belgium 14 times, and the USA 14 times. She visited 54 different countries.[5] This continuing level of activity is, of course, one reason why successive Prime Ministers have tended to rely ever more heavily on their press secretaries to talk to journalists. In the mid-1960s Harold Wilson himself used occasionally to speak to lobby meetings. Mrs Thatcher almost never did this, except when travelling abroad.

IV

Since the 1960s the professionalism and career prospects of both lobby journalists and Members of Parliament have been enhanced. The total number of accredited lobby correspondents has increased from just over 100 in 1968 to about 230 in 1995. There has been a big increase especially in television and radio (including local radio) lobby journalists; meanwhile national daily newspapers which in the 1960s had two or three lobby journalists by the 1990s had between three and five.

This increase in numbers has created a larger career ladder within lobby journalism. There are more young lobby journalists, who have often had only fairly brief experience in journalism between leaving university and entering the lobby. Experience of economic and financial journalism, rare in the 1960s, is now more common. Several senior lobby journalists have served as foreign correspondents, especially in Washington. While lobby correspondents tend to reach the top jobs at a younger age, there are also better prospects further ahead. The 1968 lobby journalists were asked about their career prospects but most wanted to stay where they were until retirement. Today additional career vistas have opened up with the expansion of political journalism—not only in TV and radio, but in political column-writing.

British politicians have also followed the international trend in becoming 'professional politicians'. For the party in power there are over 100 MPs 'involved in the government' from Cabinet Ministers down to the (most junior) Parliamentary Private Secretaries.

[5] Robin Oakley, 'Good housekeeping on Thatcher's away-days', *The Times*, 23 June 1990.

However, there are only about twenty-two Cabinet positions to aim for. Back-benchers' salaries are below those of national lobby correspondents; the MP's seat may also be insecure and he or she has a tiny full-time staff (one secretary, one researcher). Not surprisingly, then, many MPs use their secretarial and/or researcher allowance to employ their spouse and/or children; many MPs become paid consultants and advisers, while a smaller number have become directors of, or consultants to, lobbying and public relations companies.

These parallel developments in the careers of politicians and political journalists generate considerable suspicion and enmity as well as much mutual understanding. Undoubtedly there are plenty of examples of new boy MPs going into partnership with new boy lobby correspondents; this is most common between the MP and the lobby correspondent of the local constituency media. It can be, and has been, said that newly professional politicians have narrow backgrounds—unlike their equivalents of previous decades, who had extensive war service and other extra-political work experience. The same can be said of the political journalists. Both occupational strands can be said to suffer from the British disease of 'short-termism'. These two somewhat inward-looking occupations can be said to dominate political debate in Britain, to focus too much on short-term issues of political tactics, fashion, and gossip at the expense of longer-term issues such as Europe, British industry, the constitution.

Antagonisms are expressed every day in journalists' stories about politicians, and in politicians' references in their speeches to journalists and unreliable newspaper stories. Increasingly it is not the long speech, but the few hundred words which is expected of the politician. Thus both journalists and politicians specialize in the sprint events.

The political culture of Westminster—shared by politicians and lobby journalists—involves a big element of the spoken word in general and the humorous anecdote in particular. Within this gregarious, noisy, predominantly male, anecdotes-and-alcohol, spoken culture there is also an important place for the unspoken word. The normal formula of 'lobby terms' translates loosely as 'not for direct attribution'. But in practice the politician waxing talkative over lunch is implicitly trusting the journalist to know how much of what is said can, and cannot, be used. 'They almost never tell you how much of what they say you can use; they trust you to know', say the journalists. This usually works reasonably happily, especially with a lobby correspondent who wants to retain the source for the future. But 'misunderstandings' and bitter recriminations are not unknown.

V

Much interest has focused on Prime Ministers' press secretaries in general and on Mrs Thatcher's press secretary, Bernard Ingham, in particular. In three books—one of them by the man himself—Bernard Ingham has been portrayed as the uniquely dominant press secretary of a uniquely dominant Prime Minister.[6] But while there is clearly considerable substance in the dominance argument, I believe that the dominance largely consisted of an effective pact between the Conservative press and Mrs Thatcher. Especially after 1987 the Conservative press 'withdrew its affection' from Mrs Thatcher, and the 'dominant' press secretary pattern not only revealed weakness, but actually contributed to Mrs Thatcher's downfall. This view depends in part upon Nigel Lawson, who was, of course, the Chancellor of the Exchequer (1983–9)—and more Thatcherite than the lady herself during Mrs Thatcher's middle, and most successful, years as Prime Minister. Lawson writes:

A blunt, sometimes thug-like, xenophobic Yorkshireman, and inordinately proud of it, Ingham became a tremendous admirer and promoter of the Prime Minister. . . . He was only really at home with the tabloids—above all the *Sun*. . . . It was also the paper whose contents he could most readily influence. This led to a marked circularity. Margaret would sound off about something, Ingham would then translate the line into *Sun*-ese and feed it to that newspaper, which would normally use it. This would then take pride of place in the news summary he provided for Margaret, who marvelled at the unique rapport she evidently enjoyed with the British people. . . . Moreover his concept of promoting her included denigrating her Cabinet colleagues. This not only irked the colleagues, but was plainly unhelpful to the Government as a whole.[7]

---

[6] Michael Cockerell, Peter Hennessy, and David Walker, *Sources Close to the Prime Minister* (London: Macmillan, 1984). Robert Harris, *Good and Faithful Servant* (London: Faber and Faber, 1990). Bernard Ingham, *Kill The Messenger* (London: Harper, Collins, 1991).

[7] Lawson, *The View from No. 11*, 467.

Mrs Thatcher clearly valued Bernard Ingham's devoted loyalty, but she actually chose him without a preliminary interview. Previous Prime Ministers had usually brought in as press secretary someone they already knew. Harold Wilson initially used the lobby correspondent of his Liverpool constituency daily (Trevor Lloyd-Hughes) and later switched to Joe Haines (previously the *Sun*'s lobby number two). In the eyes of senior lobby journalists, both of these were rather junior appointments. But Harold Wilson was fascinated by the media in general and the press in particular. He personally master-minded government publicity and he had a flair for neat phrases and colourful details which journalists initially found irresistible. Wilson was also famous among journalists not only for his careful reading of the newspapers, but for his habit of reading late at night the early editions of next morning's newspapers.

Other Prime Ministers (Heath, Callaghan, and Major) preferred press secretaries with civil service backgrounds (such as the Foreign Office and the Treasury). Mrs Thatcher tried a civil servant before switching to Bernard Ingham, who was a hardened newspaper hack first, and a civil servant only second. Mrs Thatcher apparently favoured the notion of a strong press secretary who would even read the newspapers for her early each morning (he then typed out a 1,200-word summary). Bernard Ingham was encouraged to establish a dominance of government media relations which had not previously been attempted in peacetime. Although Bernard Ingham did personally conduct the daily lobby briefings, his influence went much further. One of Bernard Ingham's tasks was to indicate the forthcoming dismissal of Cabinet Ministers of whom Mrs Thatcher had tired. In some cases Mrs Thatcher continued—like a medieval monarch—to praise the relevant Minister in public while Bernard Ingham, behind the lobby curtain, signified the forthcoming political death of the Minister in question. The most remarkable case was that of John Biffen, who in 1986 was Leader of the House. Late in the afternoon of 12 May John Biffen was asked by lobby journalists whether he had heard Bernard Ingham's description of him (at the afternoon briefing) as a 'semi-detached' member of the Cabinet. He had not. But next morning (13 May) all of the newspapers carried similar stories. The *Sun*, as usual, could not resist a pun: 'Axe threat as Biffen gets biffing'. The axe was in fact suspended over John Biffen for another year until Mrs Thatcher sacked him immediately after the 1987 election.

John Biffen himself neatly described Bernard Ingham as 'the sewer rather than the sewage'. Such former senior Conservative politicians as Sir Edward Heath and Sir John Nott publicly denounced these tactics as distasteful, corrupt, and Machiavellian. And it was at this time that the *Independent* and *Guardian* decided not to attend Ingham's lobby briefings. Many journalists outside the lobby wondered why senior political correspondents would allow themselves to be manipulated into reporting such political terror tactics. Perhaps a more pertinent question is why two other groups accepted this—namely the members of the Cabinet and the owners and editors of the press. One obvious reason why other Cabinet ministers did not rush to John Biffen's defence was their recognition that they also could also face the political death-row experience; they feared also the active working alliance between the Prime Minister, the press secretary, and the Conservative press owners and editors. For Mrs Thatcher's support of Bernard Ingham's unprecedentedly belligerent and uncouth behaviour depended upon the acquiescence of the bulk of the national newspapers.

Bernard Ingham's 'dominance' began to weaken from 1986–7. He was extremely upset when both the *Independent* and the *Guardian* boycotted his briefings from late 1986 onwards; in his autobiography he tediously and repeatedly abuses both papers. From here on his story begins to acquire a bunker mentality. With Mrs Thatcher's help, he was now extending his reach to encompass the entire government information machine. But the voices of other senior Conservatives were becoming increasingly insistent, not least because of the ever-increasing number of sacked Ministers—who knew all too much about Mrs Thatcher's now domineering style—and because of the ever more ferocious sounds coming from her doggedly faithful press secretary. Michael Heseltine, having left the Cabinet in January 1986, was preparing for his eventual leadership challenge with a marathon speaking tour. Nigel Lawson—as an ex-journalist Chancellor—briefed the upmarket papers increasingly vigorously up to his departure in 1989.

The disastrous poll tax policy of the late Thatcher period illustrates the weaknesses of this style of Prime Ministerial press secretaryship. More than any other issue, it was the poll tax which destroyed Mrs Thatcher as Prime Minister.[8] There was no effec-

[8] David Butler, Andrew Adonis, and Tony Travers, *Failure in British Government* (Oxford: Oxford University Press, 1994).

tive resistance to the dictatorial Prime Minister. The newspapers were broadly hostile but Mrs Thatcher's eyes-on-the-press—Bernard Ingham—seems to have failed to notice this. Nigel Lawson, the ex-journalist chancellor saw and argued the folly of the poll tax from the beginning (as did Michael Heseltine), but he was ignored. Mrs Thatcher did not herself read either the newspapers or a full stack of photocopies; she read only Bernard Ingham's summary, which, from the minimal mentions of poll tax in his book, we can assume to have been unsatisfactory on this issue.

In retrospect it is easy to look back at the limitations of Sir Bernard Ingham, his lack of either economic or foreign affairs knowledge, his excessive belligerence, and his attacks on all but the most obsequious journalism. This is true but irrelevant, because the publicity problem was not the inadequacy of an individual press secretary, or even an individual Prime Minister, but the weakness of Downing Street itself.

VI

The Prime Minister's press secretary runs one of four main sections within 10 Downing Street, which itself is a small operation employing only about 100 people (including secretaries, cleaners, and messengers). When I visited 10 Downing Street in 1968 the impression was something between a rather grand London home and an old-fashioned family-owned book publisher. Although in the 1990s security arrangements are more severe, there has been no expansion of the office size or of the tiny staff. This is neither a Washington White House (actually occupying three sizeable buildings) nor a French Presidential Palace, nor is it the sizeable Prime Minister's Department found in the historically related systems of Canada and Australia.

In order to lead or to dominate the British government, the Prime Minister has to use not only the tiny Downing Street staff (of about twenty seniorish people) but the Cabinet Office. The textbooks (and the memoirs) suggest that effective Prime Ministers achieve their success by adroit use of the highly complex web of Cabinet committees, subcommittees, and *ad hoc* groups. Also important are bilateral meetings with individual Ministers and especially with the Chancellor of the Exchequer (whose office is next door in No. 11 Downing Street). The Prime Minister needs to perform well in the Commons and to keep in touch with the Chief Whip, another neighbour in Downing Street. Finally, a modern Prime Minister has two key media requirements: he or she needs to be an accomplished performer on TV and talker to key print journalists, and needs an effective press secretary and press office. Between 1955 and 1995 such success was achieved by only four out of nine Prime Ministers and even then for only part of their term—early Macmillan, early Wilson, early Callaghan, and mid-phase Thatcher. Each of these successful phases averaged only between three and four years. For more than half of these forty years the Prime Minister was doing badly on the opinion polls and also with the press.

The exceptionally friendly attitude of the newspaper owners and editors in Mrs Thatcher's middle years (1982–7) may have obscured the longer-term trend towards a predominance of unsuccessful years on the part of both the Prime Minister and the press office. John Major, succeeding Mrs Thatcher in November 1990, had an eighteen-month honeymoon up to the April 1992 election and then soon plunged into publicity disaster. He chose as his press secretaries, not hard-working non-graduate journalists in the Haines and Ingham mould, but high-flying mandarins from the Treasury and Foreign Office. These mandarin press secretaries did no better—possibly even worse.

The Downing Street press operation is only fully capable of smoothly functioning in politically quiet times; immediately there is some kind of political excitement, or crisis, the press operation itself is in crisis. This is at least partly due to its small size, its lack of expertise, and the lack of continuity in personnel. During Bernard Ingham's time (1979–90) there were only two senior people—Ingham and a deputy press secretary; there were also several middle-level 'press officers' who typically only stayed for two years. There were twelve press secretaries in forty years (1955–95), with an average stay of about three-and-a-half years.

Two senior press secretary personnel is simply an inadequate team with which to confront 230 lobby correspondents plus other political journalists. These two senior people face, even within a single major newspaper, lobby teams of four or five journalists who combine greater supplies of talent, knowledge, and experience than do the press secretaries. Ideally the press secretaries need experience of both national and regional journalism, of TV and radio, as well as of the press (upmarket and downmarket); they badly need economic and foreign affairs experience; and they should also have good political insight and judgement. In addition they require committee and speech-writing (for the Prime Minister) skills. This demanding range of competences was simply not present in the Ingham operation with its rather tabloid headline style. The range was also not available in the John Major era from either Gus O'Donnell (Treasury) or Christopher Meyer (Foreign Office).

Several Prime Ministers have recognized the need for additional heavyweight media expertise. Harold Wilson's political intimates, for example, included such Cabinet Ministers as Richard Crossman and Barbara Castle, both of whom had experience at, and connections with, the *Daily Mirror*. Margaret Thatcher's most successful middle phase involved her partnership with the experienced financial journalist, Nigel Lawson. John Major's political intimates also included former journalists such as Sir Norman Fowler, Sarah Hogg, and Richard Ryder.[9]

One of the dangerous consequences of the inadequacies of the Downing Street operation is that the lobby correspondents spend more time talking to other Ministers and to those potentially dangerous people, ex-Ministers. There is certainly now—compared with the 1960s—more interaction between lobby correspondents and back-bench MPs on both sides and this is beyond the reach of press secretaries who, as civil servants, do not get involved in party relationships. The big increase in the numbers of political journalists has included the arrival, for example, of local radio lobby journalists, often working for several stations in one region of the country. This now makes it more possible for a group of MPs—perhaps allied to a particular regional industry—to attract more media attention than previously. But the expanded numbers of journalists, and the expanded amount of media space and time needing to be filled, has also played into the hands of publicity-seeking national factions. The Major governments were continually plagued by 'rebellions' of quite small groups of Conservative MPs; these rebellions received what from a Downing Street viewpoint was excessive and grossly exaggerated publicity. But with 230 lobby correspondents seeking new political angles and

---

[9] Respectively Conservative party chairman (1992–4); head of 10 Downing Street Policy Unit (1990–4), and Conservative Chief Whip (1990–5).

Graham Bright The PM's Parliamentary Private Secretary	**John Deans** Political Correspondent, *Daily Mail*
Eleanor Goodman Political Editor Channel 4	**Andrew Turnbull** Second Permanent Secretary to the Treasury
Robin Oakley Political Editor, BBC	**George Jones** Political Editor, *Daily Telegraph*
Stephen Wall Ambassador to Lisbon	**Tony Newton** Leader of the Commons
Helen O'Donnell Gus O'Donnell's mother	**Sir Nicholas Lloyd** Editor, *Daily Express*
John Major Prime Minister	**Gus O'Donnell** PM's Chief Press Secretary
Melanie O'Donnell Gus O'Donnell's wife	**Norma Major** Prime Minister's wife
Sir Charles Powell Mrs Thatcher's former private secretary	**James O'Donnell** Gus O'Donnell's father
Donald Macintyre Political Editor, *Independent*	**Dame Sue Timpson** Associate Editor, ITN
Alex Allan PM's Private Secretary	**Lord Wakeham** Leader of the Lords
Peter Riddell Political Editor, *The Times*	**Stewart Steven** Editor, *Evening Standard*
Roderic Lyne PM's Foreign Affairs Secretary	**Sarah Hogg** Head of No 10's Central Policy Unit
Chris Moncrieff Political Editor, Press Association	**Michael Brunson** Political Editor, ITN

Fig. 16.1. Prime Minister John Major hosts a dinner for his departing press secretary, 13 January 1994

happenings for numerous deadlines through each day of the week, a lively little 'back-bench rebellion' story is often the most colourful political story available. For Downing Street such 'excessive' coverage of the government's own rebels is especially threatening; such stories run and run partly because they do indeed affect important internal party splits over European or other sensitive issues.

Another characteristic of Major-era press relations was the tendency for a succession of minor 'sleaze' stories to escalate into a public impression of a confused Prime Minister and a chaotic Downing Street. One such succession of stories included an incident on Thursday 13 January 1994 at a 10 Downing Street farewell dinner for Gus O'Donnell who was departing his job as John Major's press secretary. At the dinner were six newspaper journalists, plus four from television, and one agency man; but it was two other lobby correspondents—the political editors of the *Sun* and *Daily Mail*—who next day reported John Major as having said (before the dinner), 'I am going to fucking crucify the right for what they have done and this time I will have the party behind me.' This story—with its apparent acknowledgement by a rattled Prime Minister of serious splits in his Cabinet—received massive media coverage over the ensuing weekend.[10] This particular week had featured a succession of other scandals, crises, and excitements: there had during the week been revelations about the sexual and extra-marital activities of no less than three Conservative politicians; there had also been stories about three separate examples of Conservative politicians involved in possible local government and housing scandals; and Lord Howe (ex-Foreign Secretary) had been giving evidence to the Scott arms-for-Iraq inquiry.

Like many stories this one contained subtle ambiguities and undertones; but the simple public impression was clearly highly negative and highly damaging. There was an impression of a Downing Street press operation which was overwhelmed by multiple minor political crises during the week, and which by Thursday was turning a quiet farewell dinner into a noisy publicity disaster.

The chief responsibility for such disasters must lie not with the press secretaryship but with the Prime Ministership. The Prime Ministerial apparatus was archaic and inadequate in the 1960s and

---

[10] For example the *Sunday Times* (16 Jan. 1994) carried a 'Three Page Special' headlined in massive red type: 'NEVER HAD IT SO BAD (. . . and it could get worse)'. It was written by Michael Jones, Andrew Grice, and Michael Prescott.

has changed little since. Lobby journalism in the 1960s was also archaic and inadequate; but both wider political journalism and narrow lobby correspondence have become much bigger and more formidable. There are not only fewer lapdogs, but there are also many more watchdogs and fighting dogs.

17 Columnists and Wider Political Journalism

A SMALL number of political columnists are Britain's leading independent political commentators. The key group number only about twelve or fifteen (all of them men) and they write mainly in the upmarket daily newspapers; they mostly write on two set days of the week; they appear in a fixed position—usually on or opposite the main anonymous editorial page; they are autonomous exceptions to the normal discipline of editorial approval and sub-editing cuts. They are the most weighty and most individual part of the newspaper's political output. Most are of advanced years by the general standards of journalism. They tend to write in the first person and express their cantankerous opinions on half-a-dozen or so favourite themes—of which the political misfortunes of the Prime Minister tends to be number one. Beyond this small inner group there is a somewhat larger category of another forty or so commentators, who may write only once a week on politics, but who may also write columns on non-political topics, or may also write anonymous editorial leaders. Some of these people write for several different publications. This total group of perhaps fifty or sixty political columnists shades off into columnists in general. But the political columnists are especially notable for the strength of their opinions; most of them have decided that understatement is a columnist's vice, while robust opinions are a virtue. The majority leans towards the political right; but the columnists' views are also maverick, and eccentric—not the same as the current policies of the Conservative party. In this respect the political columnists are quite traditional.

But they are new and untraditional in two important ways—they are part of bigger political teams than those of the past; and the columnists personify a broader personalization and fragmentation of opinion. All of this can be illustrated by what happened at *The Times* between 1965 and 1995. In 1965 the main thrust of its political coverage was the reporting—or summarizing—of debates in both Commons and Lords. It had a political reporting and commenting team of about ten—three lobby correspondents, plus a sketch writer and leader writers—all of them anonymous. By the 1990s *The Times*'s effort had switched almost entirely to news reporting and comment; this was now done in a mainly highly personalized way by a team of about double the size. There were now five political columnists and five lobby correspondents, a high-profile sketch writer and columnist, plus the usual anonymous leader writers, and also a new breed of feature writers and big interviewers who write lengthy feature pieces (up to 5,000 words) on, for example, the biographical background of a politician currently in the news.

These trends were exemplified around 1994–5 by two individual journalists—Lord William Rees-Mogg and Simon Jenkins. Both had previously been the editor of *The Times* and specialized in the paper's traditional offering, the anonymous editorial 'leading article'. But in the 1990s these two ex-editors were appearing in *The Times* across the page—on the Op Ed page—where they now thundered forth under their own names, in the first person singular, as high-profile, high-prestige, and very highly opinionated columnists. Jenkins and Rees-Mogg were two highly individual individuals (see Boxes 17.1, 17.2); but they had several other things in common besides having previously edited *The Times*. Both wrote twice a week in *The Times*, but they also wrote elsewhere as well. Jenkins had a regular column in the *Spectator*, while upmarket Lord Rees-Mogg also wrote once a month in the midmarket *Daily Mail*; each man was writing over 3,000 words of columns per week. Each also appeared frequently on television and radio and had already published a number of books. Both specialized in politics, but also wrote on other topics; Rees-Mogg's second topic was economics and finance, and predictions about the economic decline of Europe and the United States, but he also wrote about history and literature. In Simon Jenkins's case only one of his weekly columns was on politics; the Saturday column was on something else such as architecture or the preservation of London. Both, then, were Renaissance Men, offering their opinionated views on a wide range of topics. Both were also active committee operators, mem-

---

BOX 17.1. LORD (WILLIAM) REES-MOGG

Born: 1928
Educated: Charterhouse and Oxford, where he read the *Financial Times* every morning in bed
Began Journalism: *Financial Times* 1952; promoted to
  leader writer
  then lobby correspondent (he co-operated with Ian Trethowan of the *Yorkshire Post*, later Director-General of the BBC)
Briefly in 1956 a member of the speech-writing team of Prime Minister Sir Anthony Eden, during the Suez crisis
Sunday Times business editor from 1960,
  then political and economic editor
  later deputy editor (effectively editor) *Sunday Times*
  in 1964 he wrote signed article describing the then Prime Minister (Douglas-Home) as inadequate for the job
Editor of *The Times*, 1967–81
Deputy chairman of BBC Governors, 1981–6
Chairman of the Arts Council, 1982–9
Chairman of the Broadcasting Standards Council, 1988–92.
Columnist (weekly) *Independent*, 1986–92
Columnist (twice weekly) *The Times* 1993–
In 1993 he wrote a column describing the then Prime Minister (Major) as inadequate for the job
Books:
  Reigning Error: The Crisis of World Inflation 1974
  An Humbler Heaven 1977
  How to Buy Rare Books 1985
  (with James D. Davidson) *Blood in the Streets* 1988
  and *The Great Reckoning* 1991
  Picnics on Vesuvius 1992

---

bers of Britain's 'Great and Good'. William Rees-Mogg had been a powerful figure in the BBC and the Arts Council—London's two most potent cultural bureaucracies. Simon Jenkins had also been an active committee man, and in 1995 began work as one of the committee which awarded Millennium grants from the national lottery.

In addition to the two columns each per week by Rees-Mogg and Jenkins, *The Times* had several other sorts of political columnists; the two most prominent in 1994–5 were Matthew Parris and Peter

---

BOX 17.2. SIMON JENKINS

Born: 1943
Educated: Mill Hill and Oxford
Begin Journalism: *Country Life*
                  Times Educational Supplement
                  Evening Standard
Editor of 'Insight' page, *Sunday Times*
Editor of *Evening Standard*, 1976–8
Political editor of *The Economist*, 1979–86
Weekly columnist and Books section editor, the *Sunday Times*
Editor of *The Times*, 1990–2
Member of: Board of British Rail, 1979–90
               Board of London Transport, 1984–6
              The South Bank Centre
              The Museum of London
Deputy Chairman of English Heritage, 1985–90
Member of the Millennium Commission, 1995–
Married to Gayle Hunnicutt, actress
Columnist (twice weekly) *The Times*, 1992–
Columnist (weekly) *Spectator*, 1992–
    (combined column output: 3,900 words per week)
Books:
    A City At Risk, 1971, was the first of four books about London
    The Battle for the Falklands (with Max Hastings), 1983
    The Market for Glory, 1986
    More books in progress

Riddell. Matthew Parris was the daily writer of the 'political sketch'—the amusing account of the day's activity usually in the Commons; Parris also wrote a once-a-week column. He was original in having been not only an elected Conservative Member of Parliament, but the first one to reveal his homosexuality. He was also an active TV and radio broadcaster. Parris sketches often focused on one minute incident or sentence from a particular politician; he then wove around it a combination of visual description, outlandish humour, and political insight. Parris's columns were a little weightier but his was still a unique and idiosyncratic voice.

Peter Riddell was yet another political journalist on *The Times* who evolved his own distinctive version of the column. Riddell specialized in a daily version of the column, which fell half-way between the conventional column and the normal lobby columnist's daily pursuit of political news and gossip. Peter Riddell had been a precocious star at the *Financial Times*, where he became Economics Correspondent at age 27. He next did a long spell as *Financial Times* political editor (chief lobby correspondent) and a shorter spell as Washington correspondent. He was then headhunted by *The Times* (Peter Stothard) and became their Assistant Editor (Politics). In some papers this is a senior co-ordinating role back in the office, but Peter Riddell based himself at Westminster with one foot in the lobby and the other foot in his column. His daily 'commentaries' were about 600 words and were usually thoughts off the back of the day's news. He also wrote a longer regular piece once a week. Peter Riddell was known as an exceptionally thorough reader of long documents; but he also lunched with Cabinet Ministers or other senior politicians two or three times a week, attended press conferences, and talked to MPs in the lobby. Then around 6 p.m. he would make his final choice of topic and write his 600 words. These columns probably offered the most respected combination in British journalism of independent judgement, deep background knowledge, and simple speed of reaction. Riddell's seniority and prestige allowed him 600 autonomous words each day; but he was free not to write on a particular day. He was also the regular commentator for *The Times* on its political poll (MORI) and he did occasional longer pieces such as an on-the-record interview with a senior politician.

Although *The Times* had the most stellar collection of political columnists, a number of other newspapers—especially the upmarket dailies and Sundays—had their own distinctive teams of columnists. The *Sunday Times* and *Guardian* each had a sizeable team of political and *semi*-political columnists. The *Guardian*, because of its left-of-centre low-pay tradition, had lost several columnists in the column explosion of the late 1980s onwards. But it also gained in 1994 the unique services of Paul Foot. Like most other prominent British newspaper columnists, Paul Foot was an Oxford graduate (and a member of the Foot political family). Over three decades he became Britain's most admired (and hated) investigative journalist: for many years he wrote for *Private Eye*, where he played a leading role in investigating national political scandals and also miscarriages of justice (especially in murder cases). Despite his far left political views and his leading role in the National

Union of Journalists, Paul Foot joined the *Daily Mirror* in 1979 to write a weekly multi-item column. Unusually for a British columnist he had a support team; he continued to pursue his numerous investigations with unsurpassed dedication and a number of successful outcomes. He finally fell out with the new *Daily Mirror* management in 1993; it was only then that he began a regular column in the *Guardian*.

The *Guardian*'s leading political columnist in the late 1980s and early 1990s was Hugo Young. He had been for a lengthy period at the *Sunday Times* and was political editor for much of the Harry Evans period up to 1981; soon after Rupert Murdoch's appointment of Andrew Neil as *Sunday Times* editor in 1983, Hugo Young's departure precipitated a huge additional exodus of Harry's people. Young initially wrote one column a week at the *Guardian*, but in 1988 became the paper's senior columnist (in succession to Peter Jenkins). Hugo Young used his lower profile during the mid-1980s to study Margaret Thatcher at close quarters and in 1989 published *One of Us: A Biography of Margaret Thatcher*; he also became chairman of the Scott Trust, and thus the official keeper of the *Guardian*'s nonconformist conscience.

The *Guardian* was, of course, the only overtly left-of-centre upmarket daily paper and thus it was the leader of daily newspaper opposition during the Thatcher and Major premierships. Over these post-1979 years a common *Guardian* pattern was of senior journalists who wrote a once-a-week political column in addition to other duties such as being a senior editorial leader writer. The *Guardian* (along with the *Sunday Times*) was the main pursuer of the 'sleaze' stories of the John Major period. Especially active in these endeavours were one of the lobby journalists, David Hencke, and also the chief lobby correspondent (and former Washington correspondent), Michael White; both frequently wrote lengthy political features, but not designated regular columns.

These loosely organized broad political teams of up to twenty journalists constitute formidable machines for political information gathering, analysis, and critical comment. They include weighty expertise and wide experience together with the high speed at which journalists are used to working. Each of these political teams is more than a match for the quite small operation in 10 Downing Street. Moreover, the newspaper political team is not inhibited by the government/party divide, which means that the Downing

Street press secretary tends to be out of touch with the latest twists and turns in government back-bench opinion at Westminster.

The significance of the senior columnists is that they are the most prominent individual commentating voices in British politics. While they do indeed work quite independently, their thundering columns are available to the editor in the early evening along with the lobby correspondents' investigations, the leader writers' 'house' opinions, and the offerings of political feature writers. This adds up to a formidable orchestra for the editor to deploy each evening.

I

The modern history of political columning in Britain includes some extremely colourful characters; but their total number previous to the 1980s was quite small and the entire history is quite brief. In the 1930s the standard anonymity of upmarket journalism discouraged both general and political columnists. One rare exception to this rule was A. J. Cummings, whose 'Spotlight on Politics' column in the *News Chronicle*[1] was probably the model for the *Daily Mirror*'s Cassandra offering.

After 1945 two sorts of political column emerged. One was the kind of hard-hitting offering of John Gordon in the *Sunday Express*, which was continued by John Junor and transferred to the *Mail on Sunday*. While John Junor certainly saw himself as a political animal and a political columnist, he continued into the 1990s the old Beaverbrook notion that the reader should be fed a multi-item meal in which the political meat was surrounded by other tempting helpings of entertainment. This combination points to a continuing dilemma for political columnists; most readers—even the more serious readers among the readerships of the more serious papers—find most politics boring. Simon Jenkins, for example, observed that his own friends preferred his non-political columns to the political ones.

Several columnists in upmarket—especially Sunday—papers after 1945 confronted this dilemma through the device of the Amusing Political Essay. Its leading practitioner in the 1950s was

---

[1] Linton Andrews and H. A. Taylor, *Lords and Laborers of the Press* (Carbondale, Ill.: Southern Illinois University, 1970), 229–41.

Hugh Massingham at the *Observer*. Another pioneer was Henry
Fairlie, who worked and drank his way through numerous short-
stay jobs, first in London and later in Washington. Two political
columnists who continued to write amusing political essays into the
1990s were Alan Watkins (mainly at the *Observer*) and Peregrine
Worsthorne of the *Sunday Telegraph*.[2] These columnists believed
in retaining an element of the amusing daily 'Political Sketch'; they
assumed that their readers were mainly interested in the political
scene and the interplay of political personalities, but not in the
heavy matter of policy, let alone the implementation and financing
of policy.

The amusing political essay will doubtless have a long life, but
the 1960s saw a trend to some more weighty columns which did
focus on policy, as well as personalities; which did discuss economics as well as entertainment; and which encompassed international politics as well as Westminster in-fighting. Two pioneers
here were David Watt and Peter Jenkins, both of whom died relatively young. Their more weighty version of the column was probably only made possible by the greatly expanding numbers of
university graduates.

David Watt worked on the *Spectator* (under the editorship of the
politician-editor Iain Macleod) and was the *Financial Times*'s first
ever correspondent based in Washington (1964–7). I interviewed
him there in 1965 when he was (successfully) struggling to establish
his paper's reputation. In 1967 Watt became *Financial Times* political correspondent and for a decade wrote an influential Friday
column called 'Politics Today'.[3] In 1977 he became Director of the
Royal Institute of International Affairs and also wrote a weekly
column in *The Times*.

The other British pioneer of the weighty, policy-oriented, political column was Peter Jenkins, who mainly worked for the *Guardian*. Interviewed by me in 1971, Jenkins said that he wanted to
follow Joseph Alsop's American conception, which required the
column to offer some new information as well as discussion and
criticism. Like David Watt, Peter Jenkins had worked outside narrow political journalism; he began on the *Financial Times* and was
the *Guardian*'s labour correspondent during the early years of
Harold Wilson's premiership. He was the chief political columnist

[2] Peregrine Worsthorne, *Peregrinations* (London: Weidenfeld and Nicolson, 1980).
[3] David Kynaston, *The Financial Times: A Centenary History* (London: Viking, 1988), 322–3, 353.

of the *Guardian* for nearly two decades (1967–85), with a two–year stint in Washington, during which he percipiently and ferociously denounced Richard Nixon at the time of his November 1972 re-election.[4] In 1985 Jenkins was head-hunted to the *Sunday Times* and moved to the *Independent*, where he died in harness in 1992. For twenty-five years he wrote usually two or three columns a week; he was close to numerous Ministers in all Cabinets from those of Wilson to Major. He specialized in analyses of current government policy, domestic, economic, and international; Jenkins was a committed European with an especially close interest in Germany. He also wrote frequently on international financial and military issues. He was widely admired in Fleet Street as a champion of the expensive political lunch and the frequent political dinner. He was a virtuoso performer in the role of renaissance man with a semi-professional involvement in the West End stage and in gambling on horses.[5]

The policy columnist mould was, of course, especially unsuitable for the downmarket newspapers. Their main solution over several decades has been to employ the general columnist who also writes on politics. This approach by the *Daily Mirror* was illustrated from the 1930s to the 1980s especially by Bill O'Connor (Cassandra) and Keith Waterhouse. But the *Daily Mirror* did make other attempts; one was to use the Labour academic-turned-politician, Richard Crossman—who after an initiation at the *Sunday Pictorial* was a *Daily Mirror* regular columnist during 1955–9. Crossman suffered the disapproval of two party leaders (Attlee and Gaitskell) and like most politicians who are seriously ambitious for office he gave up political columning;[6] politician-columnists, of course, have become more, not less numerous, but they were mainly non-office seeking mavericks (like Eric Heffer and Julian Critchley) or the ever-growing chorus of ex-Ministers whose columns criticized Thatcher and Major.

The *Daily Mirror* did during the 1980s manage to maintain some remarkable political columnists. One already mentioned was Paul Foot, the leading British investigative journalist. The *Mirror* also found a home for John Pilger who (as a star feature writer) sustained double-barrelled (*Mirror* and ITV) campaigns against

[4] Peter Jenkins, 'Stink of Success', *Guardian*, 2 Nov. 1972.
[5] Obituaries in the *Guardian* and *Independent*, both 28 May 1992.
[6] Tom Dalyell, *Dick Crossman: A Portrait* (London: Weidenfeld and Nicolson, 1989), 89–94. Anthony Howard, *Crossman: The Pursuit of Power* (London: Jonathan Cape, 1990).

American policy in Vietnam and Cambodia over three decades, against the Indonesian government's treatment of its minorities, and in support of British coalminers. The *Daily Mirror* also made intelligent use of Joe Haines, after he concluded his long service as press secretary in government and opposition to Harold Wilson; Haines wrote a *Mirror* column for some fifteen years (1976–91). The Haines torch passed to the *Mirror*'s youthful lobby editor, Alastair Campbell, who was the most articulate, belligerent, and effective press opponent of John Major in his early (1990–2) pre-election honeymoon with the Conservative press. Alastair Campbell fell out (like Paul Foot) with the new *Mirror* management in 1993, immediately moving across to Richard Stott's *Today*. But he was soon persuaded to become the press spokesman for the new Labour party leader, Tony Blair.

Daily Mirror recent history illustrates the difficulty which downmarket papers have in hanging on to top political column talent. The normal columnist's prerogative of set space and no sub-editing does not fit easily into the downmarket tabloid way of life. Meanwhile the successful downmarket political columnist is worth his weight in gold in terms of prestige with the political and advertising worlds; inevitably such a columnist receives numerous tempting offers to move upmarket and also across into radio and TV. A leading example of these tendencies was Richard Littlejohn, whose twice-a-week column appeared in the *Sun* for over five years (1989–95). His most important previous experience was as industrial correspondent on the Birmingham *Evening Mail*. Richard Littlejohn at first glance seemed the perfect working-class voice of Thatcherism; but he subsequently became the most ferocious of all the numerous critics of John Major and his Conservative government. Norman Lamont (December 1992) was 'the third rate Chancellor in a fourth rate government'. John Major was repeatedly denounced as a man in a dream: 'When you open your eyes you will find you are Prime Minister' (December 1994). Richard Littlejohn also became a star of London (LBC) radio, and at one time he hosted fifteen hours of radio talk each week in addition to his two columns in the *Sun*; the radio show consisted of Littlejohn and fellow journalists taking phone calls and denouncing their favourite enemies in showbiz and politics. Amongst those denounced were the good people at the Radio Authority (both before and after they removed LBC's licence).

Richard Littlejohn was not really the working-class Thatcherite.

He was a latter-day example of the cynical I've-seen-it-all hack, now redefined as journo. Littlejohn's attitudinizing resembled that of thousands of journalists down the years—large amounts of cynicism about public figures, officials, Cabinet Ministers, and foreigners, but also substantial offerings of sentimental regard for famous-footballers-of-my-youth, the genuinely unemployed, decent women, and the poor. Littlejohn added to these familiar tunes a wonderful facility with words and a truly original surrealist sense of humour ('My years of hell with the stars, by boozy the bottle'). He took humorous political abuse to new extremes even for the *Sun*; and he demonstrated how, with the use of savage abuse and brilliant humour, politics could win a premier position in a paper read by a quarter of all British adults. But Littlejohn was now a big star; and in 1995 the *Sun* and radio lost him to a new combination of the midmarket *Daily Mail* and assorted television shows.

II

Most of the established political columnists have had an élite career involving heavyweight reporting experience; apart from lobby reporting, the most common previous career elements seem to be labour reporting (in the 1980s or before), economic and financial journalism, and foreign correspondence (especially in Washington). The other common journalism pre-experience is the writing of anonymous editorial leaders. This latter is often combined initially with column-writing. Even after getting into column-writing the columnist typically continues to evolve and to discover the pattern of weekly output which he prefers. Quite common is a pattern of primary output, plus a lesser amount of output in a different publication, or a TV or radio show. This enables the columnist to reach a wider audience and avoids total dependence on a single editor.

Several of these characteristics are illustrated by the career of Woodrow (later Sir and then Lord) Wyatt, who in the 1990s—and in his seventies—was writing weekly columns in both *The Times* and the *News of the World*. Born in 1918, Wyatt had had a lengthy career as politician, printer, and both TV and print journalist. His autobiography[7] describes an exceptionally varied personal,

---

[7] Woodrow Wyatt, *The Confessions of an Optimist* (London: Collins, 1985).

political, and professional life. Like many columnists he moved to the political right, starting as a Labour MP (at age 27) in 1945, and eventually becoming a political intimate of Mrs Thatcher and Rupert Murdoch. His international experience included involvement in the birth of India and travelling the world for the *Panorama* TV programme in the 1950s. In his later years Wyatt remained an active collector of gossip and anecdotes as a member of the House of Lords and the lord high regulator of British horse-racing (chairman of the Totalizator Board) with a rather generous salary.

The number of suitable locations for even the most prestigious British columnist is quite limited. This point is illustrated by the case of William Rees-Mogg, who in the mid-1990s wrote twice a week for *The Times* as its most weighty political columnist. But he did leave journalism for five years (1981–6) between retiring as editor of *The Times* and being talent-spotted to write one political column a week in the *Independent*.[8] This column was widely adjudged a success, and Simon Jenkins, while editor at *The Times*, set out to lure Rees-Mogg back to his old paper. He was offered two columns a week (at £120,000 a year) in place of one a week (at £60,000) and various other minor trimmings, including a rather grand location on the Op Ed page. There was a problem because Rees-Mogg was currently chairman of the Broadcasting Complaints Commission and (because of Murdoch's joint ownership of *The Times* and BSkyB TV) he had to wait until retiring from this Great and Good post. Simon Jenkins proudly regarded this transfer as a classic of the columnist market. He described the seduction process: 'First you see if he'll accept an invitation to lunch . . .'.

III

Political column-writers inevitably have a repertoire of favourite subjects to which they frequently return. Their critics say that they keep repeating themselves; the columnists claim that they return to the same topics, perhaps with similar arguments, but with different examples and fresh information. Nearly all political columnists write regularly on the government's current problems. Several

[8] Some of the columns are reprinted in William Rees-Mogg, *Picnics on Vesuvius: Steps towards the Millenium* (London: Sidgwick and Jackson, 1992).

write on the politics of crime in Britain; Simon Jenkins argues that the media sensationalize crime and deliberately focus on the police's melodramatic account of crime rather than the public's more relaxed view of crime as reported in the British Crime Survey. Paul Johnson, however, argues that crime in Britain has reached epidemic proportions and that a return to the death penalty would be both wise and popular.

The political columnists write books; indeed between them they have written some of the best books on contemporary and recent British politics. For most book-writing is an important secondary activity, but for some it is the other way around. Paul Johnson, for example, has a track record of nearly one book per year, but also writes political columns in amusing and abusive essay style.

Some political columnists have one foot in the lobby, while most do not. The majority scan the newspapers carefully, read documents, and talk to politicians. Lunch seems to be an especially well-used method of keeping up with long-standing political friends and contacts. The political columnist has a well-refined stock of political phone numbers; press relations people can be triggered to look for details; the electronic archive can be activated. Columnists review new books and quote old ones.

The political columnist typically has a 6 p.m. deadline for tomorrow morning and starts writing only two or three hours before this. Such timing allows for the latest information to be used and accords with ingrained habits. Usually there is a phone call in the morning to tell the relevant page editor what today's column will be about. The 'intro' sentence is crucial; William Rees-Mogg likes to start with something gentle and easy—perhaps something his mother told him—as a means of easing the reader into the more difficult material which lies ahead. Most political columnists agree that strong opinions are vital. They also use the first person as another device for humanizing the weighty material and as a means of hammering out the argument. They like a logical progression towards a sharp sting in the final paragraph (the Minister must be sacked or the troops should be withdrawn). These columnists write to precise lengths such as 1,250 words, and the column disappears via modem into the newspaper computer. They are quick workers:

Having written editorials for most of my life I have a bit of spurious adeptness. . . . The key to high productivity in writing is not wasting any research, or any time, not wasting any reading or any writing. I seldom take notes. Just simply do the reading and put it straight into the screen. (Simon Jenkins)

They can also be slightly lonely workers. They are one-man bands; most do not work from the newspaper office, and so they lack the daily response from colleagues which most journalists receive. They rely quite heavily upon their steady trickle of letters to the columnist. They also rely upon the response of politicians.

IV

Political columnists are so relentlessly self-confident, opinionated, and critical in their columns that they may seem to have an exaggerated conception of their own political influence and significance. However, the reverse could also be the case.

When asked about their political influence they tend to make quite modest statements. Simon Jenkins did not claim single-handedly to have saved any of London's Victorian buildings, and William Rees-Mogg did not claim to have been instrumental in sinking Sir Alec Douglas-Home as Prime Minister; but many other people have made such claims on behalf of these two journalists. These columnists do claim for themselves some quite modest forms of influence. The most common claim is that the columnist—by reading, by talking, and by sniffing the political wind—can be the first to distil a trend in political opinion: 'I was the first to write about the switch in opinion on . . .'; Rees-Mogg talked about sometimes being the first to 'break the ice', when the ice of opinion was already wearing thin and almost ready to break. A somewhat similar type of influence was claimed by Andrew Marr (of the *Independent*): 'Sometimes you can be the bird carrying the seed between one Minister and another; most Ministers are too busy to notice much outside their own departments. You may point out a policy connection which two Ministers had not previously noticed.'

The political columnists says that individual MPs admit to having had their opinion changed by a particular column. Ministers and senior civil servants sometimes tell the columnist: 'What you said was what we did', or 'What you said could not change the policy, but it did reinforce the case which some of us are making against the policy.'

BOX 17.3. POLITICAL COLUMNISTS AND A PRIME MINISTER

'The biggest aftershock that I've had for a column in *The Times* was when I wrote a column saying I didn't think John Major was any good.[a] The John Major leadership question—is he up to the job?—has been going on ever since . . . presumably the John Major ice had got very thin and I just happened to be the first person to go through it.'

William Rees-Mogg, June 1994

'In John Major you've got a man who's obsessed with what the papers say about him. . . . Mr Major is so sensitive that it's producing all kinds of brittleness. I see him quite often . . . usually talking about things he knows I'm interested in . . . Sometimes we talk about his problems with the press. . . . I always tell him the same thing—to stop reading the bloody things.'

Simon Jenkins, June 1994

'I've seen John Major twice in the last four months. . . . The second time was a set-piece on-the-record interview, and after that I had an additional hour with him. After a couple of sips of gin and tonic he said to me: "Well you're a very reasonable person—that's not what I read in your column—but you seem a reasonable person." The implication was why couldn't I write nice stuff.'

Hugo Young (*Guardian*), June 1994

[a] *The Times*, 10 May 1993.

However, the basic significance of political columnists probably resides more firmly within the simple description of what they, and they alone, do within the political system. These political columnists differ from most political journalists in that they write about policy. They are unique in that their serious writing about weighty policy issues is brief, entertaining, and personalized (my mother used to tell me; these facts are relevant; I now think the government must do the following). Because the columnist has two autonomous and permanent slots in the paper per week he can control the timing of his intervention—either moving quickly or delaying until the ice gets a little thinner.

A final factual point is that these serious-but-readable and brief-but-timely columns are high-profile summaries of current debates.

Newspapers and Politics

Here is an independent commentator saying This Is Where The Argument Has Now Reached. In no other area of British policy-making are such brief summaries so readily available. Moreover, the tendency of columnists to return frequently to their favourite subjects also provides a unique service to politicians and to the relevant policy community. The columnist is in effect saying: 'It's now six weeks since I told you what was wrong with the government's policy on Northern Ireland (or Scotland, or Crime, or Bosnia, or the pound sterling); so here is a 1,000-word update on what's happened in the last few weeks.' Nobody else provides this service and makes it so widely, cheaply, and quickly available (and suitable for photocopying) on a single sheet of paper.

The total output of all political coverage in Britain's national newspapers is, of course, quite large—perhaps 300,000 words, or the equivalent of three full-length books—per week. The leading political columnists write between them perhaps 30,000 words per week. This is the most policy-oriented and most visible one-tenth of the much larger political journalism output.

18 Newspapers and Crisis Definition

NEWSPAPERS play a leading role in deciding whether or not the current national government is in a state of 'crisis'; this also involves defining the timing and character of the 'crisis'. Of course newspapers do not perform this function entirely unaided. 'Crisis' is a favourite word of (especially opposition) politicians. Moreover, some events such as war or earthquakes are so big as to have a voice of their own; but even here the media play a major part in defining significance. Many governmental and political events also carry with them their own measures—election results, unemployment figures, foreign exchange numbers, and stock market prices.

But it is the media which provide public summaries and explanations; and since 'crisis' is a critical label it is one which television and radio hesitate to be the first to use. The newspapers have no such inhibitions; they have a daily need for short snappy words and phrases to fit into front-page headlines. In potential headlines 'crisis' fits neatly with the name of the Prime Minister, or another politician or a current issue, as in 'Tax Crisis', or 'Prisons Crisis', or 'Meat Crisis'. Other shock, storm, and clash terms convey related meanings.

The press typically creates the image and framework of the crisis; the newspapers compete not only to be first with the news, but also first with the crisis. Individual newspapers compete with each other for the exclusive crisis angle. But newspapers also collectively confront the government, which typically denies that its present minor difficulties justify the 'crisis' definition; the newspapers, however, often succeed in imposing their definition. At the very least the politicians in office will have to deny that there is a crisis.

'Crises' can involve particular government departments or lesser

members of the government team; they can affect major departments, key policies, or leading politicians; or the crisis can concern
the survival of the government or the Prime Minister (or President). 'Crises' also affect for example the monarchy (see next chapter), or companies, or football teams. In each of these cases the
perceptions of the relevant public are crucial. In the case of a
national 'political crisis' politicians in office will naturally be worried about how the voting public will respond to what the media are
saying. This information becomes available on a monthly basis
from polls, and most of these polls appear in newspapers. The
polls in any particular month tend to be ambiguous; there are
ratings for the government, the Prime Minister, the Opposition
leader, and perhaps for particular policies and other politicians.
There is normally some movement, and month-to-month changes
of 5 or 6 per cent are not unusual. Different newspapers and
journalists may draw different conclusions from the somewhat ambiguous and conflicting evidence available from these polls. But
sometimes several newspapers will conclude that the trend of several polls over the last few months now indicates a serious government 'crisis'.

If several or most newspapers (and perhaps TV programmes
which share some of the polls' costs) reach these 'crisis' conclusions, the issue of 'government crisis' is firmly placed by the media
on the national agenda. Members of the government will now
increasingly be requested to comment on the current 'government
crisis'. They face a dilemma as does the Prime Minister (and related press relations staff). If the Prime Minister denies on the
record that there is a crisis this may successfully dampen the media
excitement; perhaps some other mini-crisis or scandal will be discovered elsewhere, or perhaps some foreign disaster will distract
media attention. But sometimes the denial of a crisis only makes a
bad government situation worse; it can lead to 'Crisis? What Crisis?' headlines followed by the accusation that while all readers of
the *Sun* know that there is a crisis, the government is so out of
touch that it hasn't yet recognized its existence, let alone decided
how best to solve it.

At this point the perceived crisis is perhaps escalating from a
fresh breeze towards the gale range; the government will be anxious
to prevent further escalation up the scale past gale force to hurri-
cane or storm. Often at this point the Prime Minister, in consultation with colleagues and press personnel, will decide to make some

kind of fresh pre-emptive move: 'Yes, the public debate and anxiety are at least partly justified, and I have therefore decided . . .'. This may involve the Prime Minister announcing in the Commons the setting up of some kind of neutral committee or inquiry. Or certain elements in the current scandal or crisis may be unreservedly denounced. In Britain a favourite device is to sack the relevant Minister or to find a suitable scapegoat in the form of some nearby Minister who was already expendable; this often involves the Prime Ministerial 'reshuffle'—one or two Ministers are sacked, others promoted, and others moved sideways. This may silence much of the crisis talk at least for some months. It can, of course, have the opposite reception—this is a panic reshuffle; it doesn't address the real crisis; it amounts to rearranging the deckchairs on the sinking *Titanic*.

Political crises tend to have media sub-plots.[1] As perceived by politicians, anything which seriously threatens their electoral support must be taken very seriously. Since the electors rely mainly on their own immediate experience heavily topped up with media stories and images, the politicians are often inclined to see a loss of political support as caused by media coverage. Like normal human beings, politicians tend to accept media praise while resenting media criticism. Consequently there is seldom a shortage of politicians who believe that at least some of their present difficulties are media created. From this it is only a very small step to attribute public blame to the media. This is what journalists slightly simplistically call 'Killing the Messenger', as if the media were merely a two-footed, or two-wheeler, message delivery service.

In Britain blaming the media often involves attacking the BBC, or particular small elements of the BBC. However, the media sub-plots, which enliven virtually all political dramas, tend to focus on the newspapers. Often newspapers are accused of having broken the rules of correct journalism; most common of all is the accusation that something which was said off the record has been reported on the record—or 'inaccurately', 'out of context', or from an 'inaccurate shorthand note'. Another criticism is that several journalists from different papers 'ganged up' on the innocent politician, by 'agreeing a version' of what was to be reported.

The more serious the crisis the more serious the anti-media

---

[1] Jeremy Tunstall, *The Westminster Lobby Correspondents* (London: Routledge, 1970), 98–108.

accusations, and the more complex the media sub-plot. The politicians also seek to accuse the journalists of not merely breaking the rules of journalism, but of breaking the rules of Parliament or the law of the land. Journalists are accused of having 'stolen' public documents, rather than merely having listened to leaked gossip. Sometimes there is a military or security aspect which allows accusations in that direction. The Official Secrets Act is often referred to, but seldom fells a journalist. Also quoted are the laws of libel and defamation.

Some media sub-plots quickly fade, but others run and run. For an editor or a journalist to be accused by a senior politician of having broken the vague rules of politics and journalism, or having broken the often equally vague law of the land, can be a little frightening; but it is also flattering. There is, moreover, a marked tendency for the media to support each other. Newspapers which normally are competitors, or even enemies, can praise each other for their brave pursuit of the truth in the face of government lies, scandal, and corruption. In the press campaign against 'government sleaze' in 1992–5 the *Sunday Times* and the *Guardian*—not usually the best of friends—were the leaders which encouraged each other (as both sailed close to the legal winds) and were in turn encouraged by a range of other newspapers. With further support coming from certain co-operative television producers, the combination of media forces was inevitably seen from within the government as threatening.

Partisanship is another obvious ingredient of the media sub-plot to the political crisis. Quite often the media sub-plot involves a partisan newspaper opposing its 'own' government. Conservative governments in the past have suffered from the doubts of the normally loyal *Daily Telegraph*, just as Labour governments have been badly shaken by the doubts of the normally loyal *Daily Mirror*. Such criticism by one's own side seems to be especially punishing because it works at all political levels; it impinges on our most loyal voters, and our local party activists; it increases the restlessness of the parliamentary party; and it seems in the past to have increased, or inflamed, the Prime Minister's difficulties in the Cabinet. Such newspaper criticism from within the family may make the Prime Minister over-eager to do something new, dramatic, and impressive. In this frame of mind, and in a hurry to pre-empt a continuing sequence of hostile headlines, the Prime Minister may do something which is indeed dramatic, but which is also ill considered and leads to additional unforeseen complications and disasters. A newspaper-proclaimed 'crisis' can become a self-fulfilling prophecy.

I

Waiting for a British political crisis can be like waiting for a London bus; there's a long wait, before three arrive all close together. This was the experience of John Major in 1993–4, of Harold Wilson in 1967–8, and of Harold Macmillan in 1963. The arrival of three crises in a row is probably partly accidental, but partly the deliberate work of the press; one crisis whets the newspaper appetite for the next.

Harold Macmillan's most famous crisis was the Profumo Crisis of 1963; but the emergence and definition of this crisis was partly shaped by its immediate predecessor, the Vassall Crisis; Profumo was quickly followed by the crisis in Macmillan's own health, which led to his precipitate retirement. Both the Vassall and Profumo crises involved sexual revelations and supposed security implications; both stories had overtones of the sexy cold-war spy thriller. The truth of these stories was more enticing than the respectable fantasies supplied in the gossip columns of the early 1960s. The leading gossip column was William Hickey in the *Daily Express*; as recently as 1959 Hickey had been daringly providing some spicy details of private lives. However, 1959 saw a falling out between the gossip columns and the Angry Young Men; the leading AYM, John Osborne, wrote a musical which satirized Hickey, *The World of Paul Slickey*. Hickey and the gossip columns then criticized Osborne; in 1960 Penelope Gilliatt attacked Fleet Street standards in general and its gossip in particular. The Press Council and several newspaper owners agreed to outlaw spicy gossip, and when I talked to Fleet Street gossip journalists in 1965–6 they referred to the 'Gilliatt Axe'—orders from on high to quieten down. The gossip staffs were large—Hickey in the *Express* had twelve journalists; but the material mainly consisted of bland and trivial details in the life of a fantasy gracious upper class, quietly going about its wealthy, servant-supported life-style. Between 1954 and 1967 the *Daily Express* William Hickey column focused first on 'aristocracy'; second equal were money and big business, royalty, and government and parliament. The most common events reported were property transactions/house moves; births, weddings, and other rites of passage; and finally first nights/book launches and the like;[2] all of these were doubtless chosen because they maximized ease of reporting and minimized offence.

Gossip/diary columns, then as now, were especially prominent in the midmarket papers—like the *Daily Express, Daily Mail,* and *Evening Standard.* Upmarket newspaper gossip was even blander; Auberon Waugh describes his work on the *Daily Telegraph*'s Peterborough column as writing pieces on the birthdays of 'octogenarian generals'.[3] This was, of course, when all of Fleet Street was on its 1960s best behaviour, with some partial exceptions like the *News of the World.*

It was out of this clear blue sky of bland gossip and respectable behaviour that the Vassall Affair fell to earth. The Vassall case followed several spy scandals and Committee investigations (starring Lord Radcliffe), but these were bureaucratic, rather than political, bungles. The Vassall case involved a British government white-collar employee who was homosexual and while employed in the British Embassy in Moscow had been blackmailed into spying when he returned to London. The political Minister, Tom Galbraith, was at the relevant time a non-Cabinet, junior Minister at the Admiralty, and Vassall was Galbraith's Assistant Private Secretary. There were newspaper suggestions that Vassall and Galbraith had been involved in a homosexual relationship, with obvious security implications. But Harold Macmillan as Prime Minister set up two inquiries; the second was the Vassall Tribunal, chaired by Lord Radcliffe. It concluded that personal letters which passed between Vassall and Galbraith were innocent, with Vassall in effect attempting (but failing) to expand the correspondence much beyond superficial Christmas card level.[4] Vassall was duly dispatched to a long prison term and Galbraith was declared totally innocent. However, two journalists went briefly to jail for refusing to reveal their sources. Harold Macmillan as Prime Minister was heavily criticized in the press for his initially over-relaxed (but justified) attitude to the Vassall case as of little real significance, even in cold war terms. However, he says in his memoirs, he was

---

[2] 'William Hickey: The Charmed Circle', in A. C. H. Smith, *Paper Voices* (London: Chatto and Windus, 1975), 205–31.

[3] Auberon Waugh, *Will This Do?* (London: Century, 1991), 145.

[4] *Report of the Tribunal Appointed to Inquire into the Vassall Case and Related Matters* (London: HMSO, 1963).

aware that the incident overall had created newspaper 'martyrs' and angered journalists.

The Profumo case also had a pre-history, but it followed Vassall onto the public agenda early in 1963. The essence of the story was that a very attractive young woman, Christine Keeler, had had sexual relationships with both John Profumo (who as Minister of War was an important Minister, but outside the Cabinet) and (simultaneously) Eugene Ivanov, assistant naval attaché at the Soviet Embassy in London. The story had numerous other enticing sub-plots; one of the settings was the Astor family's grandiose Cliveden country house; John Profumo's wife was a famous actress (Valerie Hobson); the fall guy was a mysterious high-society osteopath, Stephen Ward, who later committed suicide. The *News of the World* bought Christine Keeler's story for the large sum of £23,000, and its editor later wrote: 'The Christine Keeler story was the greatest of my time. It had everything—sex, intrigue, espionage, politics, high society, crime, passion, the law. You name it.'[5] Profumo finally resigned on 6 June 1963, but journalists had been aware of the three-sided relationship at least since the beginning of the year. However, the only stories which initially appeared in the newspapers were indirect and required reading between the lines. Profumo told his senior Conservative colleagues that there was no truth in the rumours about an affair with Christine Keeler; he also made a formal denial in the Commons. Macmillan accepted the word of a fellow Conservative politician. When Profumo finally admitted the affair and—what was politically serious—that he had lied to the Commons in a personal statement—Harold Macmillan was made to seem out of touch with the realities of modern life. On the day (22 March) of Profumo's personal statement Macmillan had noted: 'His statement was clear and pretty convincing . . . of course, all these people move in a raffish, theatrical, bohemian society, where no-one really knows anyone and everyone is "darling".'[6] Profumo resigned on 5 June and the *News of the World* began the Christine Keeler serialization on the following Sunday, 9 June. As the public's curiosity was satisfied, and as more and more of the lurid details were revealed in the newspapers, the fact that only a few months earlier Harold Macmillan had trusted someone like Profumo made the Prime Minister seem all the more out of

---

[5] Stafford Somerfield, *Banner Headlines* (London: Scan Books, 1979), 139.
[6] Harold Macmillan, *At the End of the Day, 1961–63* (London: Macmillan, 1973), 439.

touch. Compared with the new Labour party leader Harold Wilson (who was 22 years younger), Harold Macmillan was easily portrayed as a figure from a now bygone age of old Etonian politicians who were happy to accept the word of a fellow officer and gentleman, who was also an old Harrovian. In June and July 1993—immediately after the Profumo revelations—Macmillan was 20 percentage points behind Wilson on the Gallup Poll.

The third crisis in a row which hit Macmillan was his own illness in the autumn of this fateful year of 1963. Macmillan has recorded that—on the eve of the annual Conservative party conference (7 October 1963)—he had just decided to continue as Prime Minister through the election due in 1964; but he was taken ill and required prostate surgery. He stayed in hospital for nineteen days and during that time he resigned as Prime Minister (in the middle of the party conference proceeding in Blackpool) and also effectively designated his successor, Lord Douglas-Home. With hindsight Harold Macmillan regretted his resignation from the hospital bed.

This third crisis and the choice of Home certainly played into the hands of the Labour party; it also gave the national newspapers another wonderfully colourful story in the later part of 1963. If Macmillan was somewhat Edwardian, Home was even more so. His very name was like something out of Oscar Wilde and it was pronounced Hume, not Home. Then there was the equally comic spectacle of Home renouncing his title, followed by the Prime Minister fighting a by-election in the perfect Victorian setting of Kinross and West Perthshire. Home was damaged also by the refusal of two prominent former Ministers—Iain Macleod and Enoch Powell—to serve in his administration. It was Iain Macleod who used the term 'charmed circle' to refer to the group of top Tories who had passed the premiership from one old Etonian to another.

In Macmillan's three crises of 1963 the newspapers certainly played a very prominent part. Macmillan certainly believed that during the Profumo and prostate crises the newspapers were seeking vengeance for the way in which they had been punished during the Vassall crisis: 'It [Vassall] infuriated Fleet Street, at every level of activity, and made the newspapers anxious to seek and exploit any possibility of a counter-attack.'[7] Macmillan himself had a

[7] Macmillan, *At the End of the Day*, 436–8.

somewhat unorthodox personal life. His wife, Lady Dorothy Macmillan, had been involved in a long-lasting affair (almost a second marriage) with Bob Boothby. But Macmillan refused her a divorce and the three continued for many years in a sort of *ménage à trois*.[8] Although this three-way relationship was well known to senior politicians and people in the press, no word of it appeared in the newspapers. Having this secret but uncomfortable personal life perhaps made it more difficult for Macmillan to evaluate someone like John Profumo.

The media clearly played a big part in defining the three crises of 1963. For the first time television, as well as the press, covered unscripted political crisis events—such as the chaos and excitement at the Conservative Conference, when Macmillan resigned the premiership. Another pointer to the future was the way in which the Profumo crisis was tackled at different levels by different media. A downmarket Sunday, the *News of the World*, serialized the call-girl memoirs; the midmarket papers were presented with an ideal mix of politics, high society, and showbusiness; the upmarket papers could savour the weighty details of the security threat, the legal implications, and the political fall-out.

II

Harold Wilson's year of three crises in succession occurred in 1967–8 and in each case the newspapers played an active role in defining the character of the crisis. The central crisis was the devaluation of the pound sterling on 18 November 1967; this was followed by a Wilson Must Go campaign within the Cabinet and especially in the *Daily Mirror*, the main newspaper supposedly friendly to Labour. But the first of this sequence of three crises was the 'D-Notice' crisis of summer 1967.

The 'D-Notice' crisis antagonized a newspaper press which, since Labour's October 1964 Election win, had been less hostile than Labour might have expected. The newspapers collectively saw Harold Wilson's handling of the 'D-Notice' issue as a deliberate and unjustified attack on the press. Harold Wilson himself subsequently accepted much of this interpretation; he later stated

---

[8] Robert Rhodes James, *Bob Boothby: A Portrait* (London: Hodder and Stoughton, 1991), 111–29.

that it was his biggest single political mistake. The 'D-Notice' system was a typically British device—it was a vague and voluntary system of self-restraint which had by 1967 become largely inactive. 'D-Notices' were government requests to editors not to mention certain facts and issues because of security/military sensitivity. Many journalists, especially left-wing ones, at the time mistakenly believed that via the D-Notice system the government of the day could impose military type censorship over selected categories of stories. Harold Wilson seemed to believe that the government had this power. There was much advice from editors and others at the time that this view was incorrect. The D-Notice system was indeed voluntary and (with the cooling of the cold war) largely ineffective.

This D-Notice sequence of events began with a story in the *Daily Express* by Chapman Pincher on 21 February 1967. Under the front-page heading 'Cable Vetting Sensation', Pincher 're-vealed' that many thousands of 'cables and telegrams, sent out of Britain from the Post Office or from commercial cable companies are regularly being made available to the security authorities for scrutiny'. Given that in 1967 the cold war was still not over, and the Post Office was still a government department, this was the kind of 'secret' which was not known to the general public but which would have been known to—or assumed by—foreign security and diplomatic services in general and by the Soviet Embassy in particular. In journalism terms it would have been one of those 'exclusive revelations' which genuinely told the readers something new, and would have rumbled on for a week or two at most. After one week Harold Wilson announced the setting up of a (multi-party) Committee of Privy Counsellors to look into the issue. This committee reported back four months later;[9] the report contained plenty of fascinating detail for students of the press and it remains one of the best documents on Fleet Street journalism of the period. But the committee had very little to say about anything new that the government could or should do. As described by the committee, the D-Notice system had very little substance. It primarily consisted of one person—a typically British, mildly eccentric, (retired) Colonel Lohan, who was respected in Fleet Street and exerted such influence as he had through personal discussions, often

[9] *Report of the Committee of Privy Counsellors Appointed to Inquire into 'D' Notice Matters* (London: HMSO, June 1967).

over lunch. Chapman Pincher was well acquainted with Colonel Lohan and had told him of his forthcoming 'Cable Vetting Sensation' story; Lohan asked Pincher not to publish, but Pincher politely refused. So did the *Daily Express* editor (Derek Marks). The committee report revealed a good deal of uncertainty as to how D-Notices worked—reflecting, of course, the decline and increasing disuse of a basically wartime system. The then editor of the *Spectator*, Nigel Lawson, for example had actually published the texts of some D-Notices on the assumption that his publication was not part of the system; apparently the *Spectator* was supposed to be in the system but the Privy Counsellors accepted Lawson's word that this was an honest misunderstanding. This was low-key, relaxed, and gentlemanly stuff.

That is, until Harold Wilson's reaction. The Prime Minister angrily rejected the unanimous advice of his own committee (which included Emanuel Shinwell, a former Labour Defence Secretary). He even put out a White Paper on the subject. By July 1967 Harold Wilson was already beginning to recognize that he had mishandled this issue.[10] But especially during June and July of 1967 he had, in a confrontation with all the national newspapers, shown startling signs of antagonism, political ineptness, and paranoia. By early 1968 I noticed very strong signs of journalists' personal opinions having swung strongly and decisively against Wilson. It was a media perception from which Wilson never fully recovered right up to his final retirement as Prime Minister in 1976.

The next big crisis for Harold Wilson was the sterling devaluation of November 1967, but the D-Notice confrontation—and the related disillusion of the newspapers—meant that even before devaluation Wilson's approval rating fell between February and October from 57 to 38 per cent. Previous to November there was very little newspaper discussion that devaluation was a possibility. But, of course, the City and financial journalists were fully aware; the financial journalists broadly held back from discussing devaluation as a policy option (see Chapter 21). However, once the sterling devaluation (from $2.80 to $2.40) had happened, these constraints were removed. James Callaghan, the Chancellor, did the honourable thing and resigned later in November; this prob-

---

[10] Richard Crossman, *The Diaries of a Cabinet Minister*, ii (London: Hamish Hamilton and Jonathan Cape, 1976), 419.

ably had the result of focusing the newspaper criticism on Harold Wilson. The crisis led to the press accepting the Edward Heath argument that the devaluation of sterling was also 'the devaluation of Mr Wilson'.

The devaluation crisis merged into a third, 'Wilson Must Go', crisis which ran through the winter of 1967–8. The Conservative press was, of course, hostile; but it was the *Daily Mirror*'s anti-Wilson views, which grew increasingly fierce from November 1967 to June 1968, which heightened the sense of crisis within the already badly battered Labour Cabinet. For the antagonism of the *Daily Mirror* meant that the Cabinet really had no remaining friends in the press. This period is very fully covered in the writings of Wilson, Crossman, Benn, Castle, Healey, and also Cecil King (of the Mirror Group) himself. The Defence Secretary, Denis Healey, says:

> The crisis from December 1967 . . . was about Harold Wilson's style of government. . . . Inevitably, his persecution mania finally turned his nightmares into reality. There was increasing talk both inside the Labour Party and outside about trying to find a new leader. . . . Much of this talk was reflected and magnified in the changing attitudes of Cecil King, the chairman of . . . the only part of Fleet Street to support the Labour Party.[11]

Philip Ziegler, Wilson's authorized biographer, writes: 'Cecil King, the *Daily Mirror* chairman, had been waging an unrelenting campaign against Wilson for the best part of two years, inciting Callaghan, Jenkins and Healey in particular into a revolt against their leader.'[12] Cecil King himself reports in remarkable detail how he invited a succession of Labour Cabinet Ministers and senior civil servants to lunch and tried to persuade them to join his and the *Daily Mirror*'s campaign to unseat Wilson.[13] The high (or low) point of this campaign was a front-page attack on Wilson in the *Daily Mirror*, headlined 'Enough is Enough' (10 May 1968). Despite all of this Harold Wilson survived. One key reason was that his senior colleagues were unable or unwilling to unite behind a single agreed successor. The political assassination of the incumbent Prime Minister would obviously have exacerbated the already high levels of unhappiness within the Cabinet. Moreover, any

---

[11] Denis Healey, *The Time of My Life* (Harmondsworth: Penguin, 1990), 336.
[12] Philip Ziegler, *Wilson* (London: Weidenfeld and Nicolson, 1993), 293–4.
[13] *The Cecil King Diary, 1965–70* (London: Jonathan Cape, 1972).

would-be successor could also presumably anticipate further hostile newspaper campaigns.

Harold Wilson's experiences of 1987–8 again showed how the
press could play a significant part in defining the current 'crises'
facing the Prime Minister. A press campaign to remove the same
Prime Minister did not work—and may even have helped Wilson
to attract party sympathy; but continuing press hostility to Wilson
up to his 1970 electoral defeat coincided with low opinion poll
ratings. Some of the negative 'crisis' images of 1967–8 seemed to
stay in the electorate's minds right up to the 1970 defeat.

III

John Major was another Prime Minister who suffered three crises
in a year (1993–4)—crises of which the newspapers were primary
definers. This was another example of a Prime Minister facing a
hostile press combined with some plain old bad political luck and
bad political management. A key factor was that after John Major's
election win of April 1992, the Conservative press felt few political
inhibitions. Major also found that many of Mrs Thatcher's friends,
both in politics and in the press, were against him. He had to handle
a Conservative party which was increasingly severely split over
Europe. He may even have been unlucky with the impact of a
televised House of Commons; when this began in late 1989 it was a
novelty, but increasingly during the 1990s the reputation of Parliament and MPs declined. This may well have been partly due to
public uncertainty as to what MPs did—after all television suggested that the typical debate was attended by less than 10 per cent
of the 651 members. On the other hand the voters had a higher
opinion of their own MP—possibly because their local media presented the MP positively in the constituency advocate and social
worker roles.

Within a period of fourteen months in 1993–4 John Major's
government faced three crises. First, in May 1993 Norman Lamont
was sacked from the Chancellorship of the Exchequer; this was a
resignation demanded increasingly loudly by the newspapers ever
since eight months earlier Britain had left the Exchange Rate
Mechanism, membership of which was the main plank of Major–
Lamont economic policy. Having pursued Norman Lamont personally and politically until his sacking, the newspapers then joined

with the sacked Lamont in a combined attack on John Major. Secondly in October 1993 John Major announced his 'Back to Basics' policy; these 'Basics' explicitly included family values and the importance of children being born within wedlock, which fitted badly with an ensuing series of newspaper revelations about Conservative MPs having extra-marital affairs and fathering children out of wedlock. Thirdly, in July 1994 came the 'Cash for Questions' crisis; this one was very distinctly newspaper led and revealed that some Conservative MPs were willing to ask Parliamentary Questions to Ministers on behalf of commercial interests and in return for money.

These three were by no means all of the crises and scandals of John Major's administrations. They do not include the Scott Inquiry on the long-running saga of Arms-for-Iraq. Indeed the period seems to be unusual in British political history. David Butler's list of 'Political Scandals' includes four political scandals in the years 1992–4 against, for example, only two in the whole of the 1960s decade (Vassall and Profumo).[14] There was also an unprecedented number of political resignations; in the three years after John Major's election victory of 1992 there were fourteen resignations on grounds of scandal[15] (not including political resignations/sackings like that of Norman Lamont); this was out of a total government list (Commons and Lords) of about 130. To lose 11 per cent of an entire administration in three years was unprecedented. About half of the cases involved sexual activities and about half financial irregularities. The *Independent on Sunday* claimed that a five-year period (1990–5) saw thirty-four Conservative, one Liberal Democrat, and four Labour scandals; of these thirty-nine at least a quarter involved sex.[16]

A prominent feature was the way in which each main category of the media in practice focused upon a specific aspect of crisis and scandal, or what the newspapers increasingly described as 'sleaze'. Sexual revelation was the main approach of the downmarket newspapers in general and of the Sundays in particular. The *News of the World* and the other downmarket Sundays had long specialized in sexual revelations; but whereas in the past they had only occasion-

[14] David Butler and Gareth Butler, *British Political Facts, 1900–1994* (London: Macmillan, 1994), 276–7.

[15] Tim Butcher, 'Spring joins roll-call of Tories who had to go', *Daily Telegraph*, 10 Apr. 1995.

[16] 'Sleaze: a guide to the scandals of the Major years', *Independent on Sunday*, 23 July 1995.

ally focused on politicians, now they had a steady stream of politician scandal stories. There was even a publicist, Max Clifford,
who seemed to specialize in such stories. If you were a woman
wronged by a Tory MP you could pay Mr Clifford 20 per cent and
he would not only sell your story to a Sunday tabloid but also
dispose of appropriate magazine and foreign rights. In addition he
advised on television appearances.

The midmarket newspapers had a different approach to politicians. By the 1990s the Nigel Dempster offering in the *Daily Mail*
was the leading gossip diary. While Dempster (and team) only did
one page (seven days a week), that page's approach rippled out
across all of the *Daily Mail*, all of the *Mail on Sunday*, and beyond.
The Dempster approach was to write not from the outside, but
from the inside of the world portrayed. In several respects it had
not changed from the 1960s Hickey column—it was still the
wealthy and the titled mixing with entertainers and some politicians. The politician stories were mainly focused on their young
adult children. In 1990s Dempster-land people were adult and
worldly, and were now buying and selling million-pound flats and
houses; they had affairs (or 'flings'), lived with people they were not
married to, and had children who got into trouble with drugs, went
to prison, and married unsuitable people. The focus both
in Dempster and in the *Daily Mail* was on personalities and
families.

The *Mail on Sunday* was the ideal setting for serializing in May
1993 the amusing political diaries of Alan Clark,[17] a former Tory
MP and junior Minister in Mrs Thatcher's government. Alan
Clark (son of Lord Clark of BBC TV's *Civilisation*) was a splendidly entertaining diarist, wonderfully rich, arrogant, and ob-
noxious, and obsessively interested in numerous women. If
someone as magnificently unreliable as this could actually have
been a junior Defence Minister, *Mail on Sunday* readers could be
forgiven for guessing that some ordinary Conservative MPs might
be leading quite feverish private lives. Midmarket newspapers like
the *Daily Mail*—which also chronicled in loving detail the sexual
infidelities of various royals—were telling the great British middle
class that many people in public life were not exactly angels.

It was the upmarket newspapers which focused upon what
they saw as the weightier issues, but even here there was some

---

[17] Alan Clark, *Diaries* (London: Weidenfeld and Nicolson, 1993).

specialization between newspapers. The *Guardian* and *Sunday Times* were the two leaders in generating scandal stories about Members of Parliament. The main accusation was that MPs were using their elected status for commercial gain, as consultants, as advisers to lobbying companies, and in taking cash for questions and cash for amendments. The *Independent* focused especially on what it called 'the sleazy state'—the argument was that various kinds of corruption had arisen in unelected quangos, in government, and in the Conservative party machinery, in the arms business, and in foreign aid. The *Financial Times* ran stories about links between the Conservative party, British business, and the non-British contributors of undisclosed amounts of money to Tory funds.

Finally, of course, television played its part. It summarized most of what the newspapers said—including the sex-scandal-and-resignation stories. Television presented Parliament looking either like an overfull 300, or an empty 300 with the human animals apparently engaged elsewhere. Meanwhile television current affairs programmes presented their usual combination of actual documents with background film and interviews.

All of this coverage left John Major as Prime Minister engaged in literally hundreds of denials; what the newspapers said was exaggerated; the Minister would not be resigning; the scandal stories were unreliable; there was no crisis; the government was not corrupt; nothing needed to be done. But Major nevertheless did have to sack Ministers and he did have to set up various inquiries, including Scott and Nolan.

Prime Ministers had faced scandals and crises before. These had often been driven and defined by the press. What was perhaps different in the 1990s was the vigour of the newspaper anti-government campaign. Also unusual was the way in which each segment of the media operated almost as if part of a co-ordinated plan. While they were not in fact co-ordinated, the newspapers did indeed have a common urge to sustain their definition of the government as in a state of continuing crisis.

19 Hacking down the Monarchy

FOR the British Monarchy, 1992 was a crisis year and the primary definers of this crisis were the newspapers. 'During the 1980s the tabloids discovered they could sell more copies by attacking, rather than defending, the monarchy,' said one royal correspondent. Most royal correspondents would deny that they were attacking the monarchy; they would claim to have been reporting 'the facts' rather than the lies put out by Buckingham Palace. But the press—and mainly the tabloid newspapers—did increasingly see the royals as a good (or the best) human interest story. In doing so they helped to put on the national agenda not merely the behaviour of some young members of the royal family, but the broader issue of the monarchy as an institution. There was also the common phenomenon of a tabloid lead being followed by the upmarket broadsheets; here the royal question was added to, and gave sex appeal to, the normally boring question of general constitutional reform.

The requirements of the Northcliffe era popular press had been central to the redefinition of the British monarchy, and the invention of new traditions, which occurred around 1890–1914. To suit the requirements of these new readers (who were also new voters) the monarchy went public with lavish new ceremonies especially in Westminster Abbey; the turn-of-the-century changes redefined the monarchy as the Imperial Monarchy, itself supposedly a culmination of centuries of tradition.[1] In the mid-century, during the reign of George VI, a quiescent, deferential, and war-focused

---

[1] David Cannadine, 'The Context, Performance, and Meaning of Ritual: The British Monarchy and the "Invention of Tradition", c.1820–1977', in Eric Hobsbawm and Terence Ranger (eds.), *The Invention of Tradition* (Cambridge: Cambridge University Press, 1983), 101–64.

media accepted another redefinition; George VI's redefinition (1936–52) involved a family monarchy still presiding over an empire. This model prevailed under George VI's daughter, Queen Elizabeth; it was against this definition that the newspapers in the years 1977–92 increasingly redefined the monarchy as 'Our Royal Soap Opera' (in the words to me of one tabloid daily editor).

Early in 1992 Queen Elizabeth II celebrated the fortieth anniversary of her reign; but later in the year she described 1992 as her *Annus Horribilis*. 1992 marked the public breakdown of the marriages of all three of her married children; all three breakdowns involved messy extra-marital relationships which had long been indicated in the press and denied by the Palace. Also in 1992 part of Windsor Castle burned down and the press revealed inadequacies in its general management and fire prevention regime. The financial implications of the fire further fuelled the debate on royal family finances in general and why the royals were exempt from income tax.

Queen Elizabeth's term *Annus Horribilis* was perhaps indicative of some of the relevant issues. Certainly, the use of a Latin phrase showed a continuing inability to predict tabloid newspaper responses; the *Sun*, following its naughty punning ways, translated the Latin phrase as 'One's Bum Year'.

1992 marked a crescendo in royal disaster and media fascination; but broader changes in the press and public opinion, especially over the previous decade, lay behind this. After Prince Charles was invested as Prince of Wales in 1969, the bulk of media attention gradually switched away from the Queen and her husband to her children. But Charles initially spent much of his time afloat in the Royal Navy and only in 1977 did the main media focus switch to the Prince of Wales. His 1981 marriage was the biggest royal media event to date and launched the continuing Charles and Diana saga. Princess Diana after 1981 became the leading celebrity figure for the national tabloid newspapers. She filled a gap opened up by the big expansion in soft features, personality coverage, and showbusiness material; especially after 1986 there was the explosion of extra sections focusing on lifestyles and consumerism. Diana and Duchess 'Fergie' (Sarah Ferguson) of York—with their rapid clothes changes and public appearances, their frequent holidays and travels, as well as their marital, parental, and weight problems—royally satisfied the newspapers' needs.

Increasingly in the late 1980s the broadsheet newspapers, which had largely ignored the royals, now began to increase their coverage. One broadsheet approach was to describe the antics of the popular press—for example the 200 photographers and the camera people who waited outside a London hospital while the Duchess of York gave birth in 1988. One estimate was that this photographic battalion—complete with step-ladders, locks and chains, golf umbrellas, and mobile telephones—had during one week's activity used over 7,000 rolls of film.[2] The broadsheets also focused on the serious issues discussed by the Prince of Wales, and used the Princess of Wales to adorn their front pages. As the royal crisis deepened after 1990 the broadsheets increasingly used the 'constitutional implications' as an excuse for running royal stories. A content count in 1991 (a quietish royal year) found that in a sample of mainly broadsheet national newspapers Prince Charles was the fifth most frequently mentioned Briton (after four leading politicians).[3]

Opinion polls did show a gradual decline in uncritical public support for the monarchy; there was a big range from a still very popular Queen to some of her less appealing relatives. And the press coverage both influenced, and was influenced by, these poll findings. The Queen continued to get favourable—if somewhat less reverential—treatment. The Queen's children and other relatives received more mixed treatment. While in 1980 marital problems would only be alluded to rather gently, by 1990 royal marital difficulties were being described with routine enthusiasm, while outright savagery was increasingly common.

This loss of reverence was shown by the polls to be fairly widespread in the British population, but especially strong amongst the young. Within the newspaper world the change of mood was also quite widespread. In contrast with the deferential 'court correspondents' of previous decades the new royal specialists saw themselves as no-nonsense, aggressive, 'professional' journalists. They—and the specialist royal photographers—were in demand not only from newspapers but also from magazine and book editors. While the monarchy came badly out of 1992, the reputation of the journalist royal-watchers was enhanced.

[2] John Downing, 'Fergie Fever', *UK Press Gazette*, 22 Aug. 1988.
[3] *Sunday Times*, 5 Jan. 1992.

I

The 'family monarchy' redefinition of the mid-century initially seemed to be viable and successful. It was, however, fundamentally flawed because neither the parents nor the children could match the unrealistic standards of behaviour which the definition required, but also because the required levels of media deference could not be maintained.

The 1936 abdication of Edward VIII was the key event in the twentieth-century histories both of the British monarchy and the reporting of the monarchy by the media. Previous to the abdication 'crisis' both the politicians and the newspapers initially kept their silence; the newspaper owners and editors then played a key part in the negotiations with the King. Politicians and press were nearly (but not completely) unanimous in announcing the crisis and then demanding that, if Edward VIII insisted on marrying the divorced Mrs Simpson, he would have to go. It was against this background that the George VI (1936–52) redefinition of the monarchy took place.

The abdication was a monarchical earthquake and the after-shocks continued for decades to come. There ensued an overwhelming urge to ensure that there would be no repetition. The family monarchy was to incorporate the happy family elements of George V and to be the opposite of Edward VIII, who had been a bachelor playboy with a strong interest in married women. George VI, however, seemed to be perfectly equipped—with a splendidly suitable wife and two lovely daughters—for a happy family monarchy. He himself was shy and his perceptive wife was reluctant; but the family monarchy was a success in the late 1930s. Then, during the 1939–45 war, the family monarchy was a symbol of British resistance to Hitler; after 1945 the wartime glow lingered on, right up to George's death in 1952.

But the family monarchy definition created immense problems, because it was a definition which did not fit with continuing realities. One of these was the 'Prince of Wales' problem. The family monarchy definition implicitly assumed that Edward VIII in 1936 had been an exception; but he had not—he was following in the footsteps of Edward VII. The next Prince of Wales, Charles, was to follow broadly the same pattern in the 1980s. The exceptions were George V and VI. The 'Prince of Wales' problem is not just one of women, wives, and divorces—although that problem was exacerbated by the unrealistic ideal of the family monarchy. The problem was part of the larger question of what junior members of a family monarchy should do with their time. A prevailing assumption seemed to be that young male royals should serve some years in the armed forces and then retire. But should they retire to being 'Gentlemen of Leisure' in the Victorian/Edwardian mode? Or should they get a 'proper job'?

The Prince of Wales question did not seem an urgent one in mid-century because George VI's two children were both daughters; but daughters also were to cause problems in the future. Another weakness in the family monarchy was its unrealistic expectations, not just of children, but of parents. The British royal family during the twentieth century have not been brilliantly adept and loving parents. A number of British royals and heirs to the throne seem to have had unhappy childhoods, a tradition which, sadly, has continued into the late twentieth century.

The family monarchy definition involved unrealistic expectations about not only the royal children and royal parents but also about the media. The media during 1936–52 were extremely deferential and uncritical. But what was not noticed at the time was that these conditions were atypical. After the abdication the new royal family was immensely popular. Princess Elizabeth (born 1926) and Princess Margaret Rose (born 1930) were appealing and photogenic children. Access to them was restricted largely to carefully selected photographers such as Cecil Beaton and to newsreel camera crews. The princesses glowed serenely—if distantly—through the fog of war and the smogs of post-war Britain.

During these atypical war and post-war years the family monarchy did not rethink its strategy for handling the media. But reliance was placed on what had been successful in the interwar and war periods—this was a carefully controlled visual presentation of the monarchy. Back in the 1920s the then Prince of Wales (Edward VIII) had been a star of the silent newsreels, and as such immensely popular right up to 1936. He had also been (like his father George VI) an occasional talker on radio; indeed he made his 1936 resignation speech live on radio. These 'new media' successes may have lulled the royal family into thinking it could project itself through careful management of the audio-visual media.

There were several other possible reasons why the newspapers were largely ignored. Under the newsprint rationing conditions of the 1940s the newspapers looked thin, unthreatening, and comfortably deferential. There was probably also an underlying fear that the press could one day unite with the politicians to discipline the monarchy. George VI at the very least was aware that his cousin and close friend Earl Mountbatten had been attacked by Lord Beaverbrook's *Daily Express*.[4] Perhaps it was best to leave such an unpredictable medium well alone and stick with the more predictable BBC, cinema newsreels, still photographers, and women's magazines.

II

At least five public characteristics of the family monarchy caused difficulties in the fourth quarter of the twentieth century, but seemed relatively trouble free in the third quarter. These characteristics were the greatly extended family, the thousands of separate public engagements, the multi-palace operation of the monarchy, the focus on wedding and other rituals, and finally the reliance upon television.

First, the initial family monarchy concept of George VI after 1936 was a two generation family of four people; all three of his brothers kept a low profile (one was in exile and another was killed in 1942). Subsequently, however, the Queen Elizabeth–Duke of Edinburgh concept grew into an extended family monarchy composed of all of the direct descendants of George V and their spouses; in the early 1990s the membership of this royal family reached a total of sixty living people.

Secondly, the answer to what the royals should do with their time was the programme of multiple public engagements. For example, in the twelve months beginning 1 May 1992 (*Annus Horribilis*) the nine leading royal players performed 3,216 public engagements, according to the annual *Illustrated London News* league table. Anne, the Princess Royal, topped the 1992–3 chart with 638 public appearances. Most common was the category of 'Engagements, opening ceremonies, prizegivings, church services and military parades'. Next most common were 'official engagements overseas'; eight royals spent between them 202 days outside the UK, with 859 engagements or 4.4 engagements per day abroad.

---

[4] '...his most striking vendetta...was against Mountbatten,' Anne Chisholm and Michael Davie, *Beaverbrook: A Life* (London: Hutchinson, 1992), 493.

Most of the remainder of these public engagements consisted of 'receptions, garden parties, lunches, banquets and dinners'.[5] Obviously this was a big change from a previous pattern of royal appearances focused much more on a few state occasions. These hundreds and thousands of engagements involved a huge increase in charitable activities, which often in turn involved the main fund-raising event of the year for the relevant charity or cause.

Thirdly, the greatly inflated monarchy involved the continuation into the late twentieth century of very large-scale landowning, big staffs of courtiers, and elaborate travel provision (including a huge yacht, and several aircraft and helicopters). The royal family continued to control four major buildings in central London, plus palaces in Windsor, Norfolk, and Scotland.

Fourthly—and perhaps appropriately for a family monarchy—the biggest public occasions were royal weddings in particular, but also funerals, christenings, and other anniversaries. Following from this, television became the final public dimension of the British family monarchy; the British people came to pride themselves that they retained world leadership in ceremonies and traditional rituals. This meant royal spectaculars on television.

In the final quarter of the century, and especially in the 1980s, all five of these public dimensions of family monarchy generated difficulties. The extended family version of the monarchy was an over-extended family in terms of media coverage; there were too many characters on stage who lacked clearly defined roles; as the media became increasingly critical it was relatively easy for journalists to find amongst such a huge team members of the extended family who were in some kind of newsy difficulties.

The thousands of public appearances gave many hostages to media misfortune. At busy times of the year 'major royals' would be doing between fifty and a hundred appearances per week. The media could ignore the boring majority while focusing on those few public appearances most capable of generating 'good'—often negative—stories. Because these numerous appearances were booked well in advance, the royal person in question could never withdraw without generating 'Princess cancels engagements' headlines. The public appearances—for example at the big annual event of a particular charity—often directly or indirectly involved fund-raising. By getting a high-profile royal to attend the annual event, the

[5] *The Illustrated London News* (Royal Issue, 1993), 58.

charity hoped to attract more money. Each major royal family member has his or her one hundred or more charities and there are negotiations over dates, appearances, and commitments. Some charities are also involved with commercial sponsors and professional fund-raisers, which adds to the commercial character of the activity. These charities also become sources through which journalists pick up information about royal family members; some charities undoubtedly leak items of royal gossip to the press in order to attract publicity for the good cause.

The number of palaces and the hundreds of employees left the royal family vulnerable to accusations of excessive wealth and ostentation. After 1977 there was a continuing flow of news stories, features, and books about these royal servants and possessions. The massive royal yacht and its 200-plus crew were one favourite focus. Numerous news stories complained about public subsidies—via several different Ministers' budgets—plus the fact that the Queen did not pay tax.[6] The unclear dividing line between what belonged to the Queen and what to the British state enabled journalists to claim that the Queen was a billionaire while Palace sources claimed relative poverty. On the one hand there were the upper-class courtiers—a quaint sort of private hereditary civil service—with their grand subsidized apartments in Central London; journalists could then make an easy contrast with the numerous cleaners, dressers, messengers, valets, and chauffeurs being employed on minimal rates of pay. These low rates of pay also encouraged the palace servants to leak stories to the tabloids for a few hundred pounds.

The special royal occasions remained the marriages, births, deaths, and anniversaries. These were, of course, extremely carefully rehearsed and scripted and were watched, in whole or in part, by large television audiences. However, while the royal weddings in particular were great popular successes, the fairy-tale marriage looked somewhat different in retrospect if the couple subsequently separated or divorced.

The royal linkage with television was especially evident at these royal ceremonies. For example, the preferred venue switched from the medieval Westminster Abbey to Saint Paul's, which is a more open plan building and therefore much more suitable for a televi-

---

[6] Philip Hall, *Royal Fortunes: Tax, Money and the Monarchy* (London: Bloomsbury, 1992).

sion spectacular. These connections with television also led the royal family into a number of other television specials; because television needed pictures and access, the Palace could easily control the content and the filming arrangements.

In 1968 a new press secretary had taken over; this was the Australian William Heseltine, who persuaded the Queen to adopt a slightly more open approach. Evidence of the new approach included the 1969 BBC TV film *Royal Family*, which portrayed the Queen as a hard-working woman at the centre of a warm human family. BBC research indicated a very positive public response. A new special royal series was planned for 1977, the twenty-fifth anniversary of Queen Elizabeth's accession to the throne. This series, called *Royal Heritage*, involved the Queen but focused on the royal palaces and old master paintings; the negotiations and filming together occupied over four years.[7] The TV series was indeed of high quality and high interest, but its success was misread. These television successes encouraged the royal family to stick with television and to ignore the press. After 1977 there were increasing numbers of royal TV specials and many short sycophantic interviews often featuring royal newly-weds. ITN competed with the BBC to run soft uncritical royal interviews and features on such topics as the royal racehorses.

Prince Charles was involved in 1988–90 in three major television performances—two on the environment and the 1988 BBC *Omnibus* epic in which he sailed serenely down the Thames delivering his controversially conservative views on architecture.

But it was the *Annus Horribilis* of 1992 which illustrated the previously hidden dangers of grandiose and obsequious television coverage. In celebration of Elizabeth's forty years as Queen, the BBC screened a television spectacular called simply *Elizabeth R*. Once more the approach was by normal BBC standards markedly sycophantic; it focused again on the Queen as a hard-working professional, but the film also showed something of the rather grand life-style, including a massively opulent formal dinner at Windsor. This television spectacular was transmitted in February. Within the next few months the British public was told of major problems in the marriages of all three of the Queen's married children—one separation (Andrew), one divorce (Anne), and, in

[7] Paul Ferris, *Sir Huge: The Life of Huw Wheldon* (London: Michael Joseph, 1990), 257–67.

the case of Charles's marriage, there was the explosive *Diana: Her True Story*, the Andrew Morton book serialized in the *Sunday Times*. That all three of these marriages were in trouble had been fully documented by the newspapers for many months previously. So what did this combination of royal coverage by television and press tell the British public? It certainly showed that the newspapers—while sometimes messy and intrusive—were first with the truth. The television spectaculars were shown to be focusing on the surface gloss of a picture postcard family monarchy. Put alongside the messy-but-true press coverage, royal television seemed to be more concerned with concealing, than revealing, the truth.

III

1977 was the peak of royal popularity and the next fifteen years— down to 1992—were to be ones of decline in public esteem. In some respects the royal family were plain unlucky. Partly it was simply the timing of the generations; in the 1960s the Queen's children were still young, but by the 1980s their marriages were starting to go wrong—the worst possible train of events for a family monarchy. During most of 1977–92, Margaret Thatcher was the Prime Minister; 'Thatcherism' involved a questioning of many established British traditions, institutions, and professions, with marked emphasis on value for money, personal achievement, competition, and no more jobs for life. Mrs Thatcher herself, of course, made no attempt to apply any of these favourite criteria to the monarchy. But inevitably others—especially the press and young people—did ask these Thatcherite questions of the monarchy.

The royal family were unwise in their overwhelming preference for television; they were also unwise to treat the tabloid press as if it were a latter-day version of the revolutionary mob. But they were unlucky that the industrial development of the press in the 1980s favoured more aggressive reporting and also required more human interest feature coverage.

The royal family firm had experience of media stardom. But up until about 1977 superstardom was outside its experience. When superstardom came—first to Charles and then to Diana—it created entirely fresh problems, which were not adequately addressed. Prince Charles became a media superstar in the four years between his emergence from the Navy in December 1976 and his wedding to Diana in 1981; the story which made him a superstar was his search for a wife. Diana became a superstar more quickly—in the six months between the engagement announcement of 24 February and the wedding of 29 July 1981. Both Charles and Diana played the superstar game; after some initial shock at the tidal waves of publicity and media attention, Charles used the media to attract massive publicity to a range of his causes in such fields as the environment, architecture, and the inner cities. Diana apparently rose to the superstar challenge with even greater speed and success; she rapidly became the Model Princess, the face and the body which adorned thousands of magazine covers, newspaper front pages, and television shows around the world.

The royal family firm and its publicity advisers had some previous experience of huge audiences for special occasions and large amounts of press coverage. But they had no previous experience of the 1980s scale of continuing publicity. Had they consulted publicity specialists with experience of superstardom they would certainly have been told that media superstars ration their public appearances and focus them on publicizing selected new products or events. It would have been difficult, if not impossible, to ration Charles and Diana appearances by the mid-1980s. By this time both superstars had become accustomed to the new status. A radical reduction in the number of appearances would have become a massive new story-line in itself. By 1986 there was ample evidence of marital conflict; there had already been heavy media emphasis on the fact that Diana attracted more media attention—especially from the photographers[8]—than did Charles; there was already fairly overt publicity rivalry between the two. By 1986 many journalists had hitched their careers to either Charles or Diana (but not to both).

Precedents set by Princess Anne in the 1970s may have had some unanticipated consequences. Princess Anne (born 1950) married Captain Mark Phillips (in 1973) at a sufficiently young age as largely to avoid the unattached youth phase. Anne was also an outstanding success as a horsewoman (one of the royal family's traditional fields of endeavour); she won a place in the British Three Day Event team for the Montreal Olympic Games of 1976. Anne also associated herself with the Save The Children charity

---

[8] A revealing book by a royal photographer is: Arthur Edwards, *I'll Tell the Jokes, Arthur* (London: Blake, 1993).

from 1969 onwards and pursued this particular line of good works with remarkable vigour and stamina. She did not cultivate media superstardom, but she did cultivate a long-term relationship with—appropriately—a children's TV programme (*Blue Peter*); she also became infamous for shouting abuse and obscenities at journalists. But in the long run the media excused both her bad language and her broken marriage. Both the journalists and public came to admire Anne for her genuine dedication to good works; the tabloids also became bored with her scandal-free and punishing trips around Africa. Anne survived—not as a carefully confected superstar—but at a lower level of media stardom and public respect.

The Charles–Diana wedding of July 1981 was welcomed by the tabloids—with typical British modesty—as 'the wedding of the century'. Both the Palace and Charles wanted the maximum publicity. The Palace conferred with the BBC—in the person of Cliff Morgan, who as 'Head of Outside Broadcasts Group, Television' was in charge of major sporting as well as non-sporting events. The Palace and Cliff Morgan slotted the wedding into the BBC's busy summer sports schedule; this enabled the BBC to use some sixty cameras along the route and in Saint Paul's. Each of three US TV networks carried seven or eight hours of London wedding coverage on the great day. The total live audience around the world was said, at about 600 million, to be the largest ever to that date.

Until the age of 28 Charles's image was primarily that of the military man. He learned to pilot aircraft as well as helicopters; he also commanded a Royal Navy minehunter during the year 1976. After this 'action man' phase he made a gradual transition to the 'issues man' of the 1980s. Throughout the transition he continued with some of his old pursuits such as polo. Nevertheless it became especially evident in the early 1980s that Charles was entering into a number of sensitive public issues and debates on a scale not attempted by his parents. In each of these fields Charles was advised by groups of specialists—usually relevant professionals, business people, academics, and media people. He gave enormous emphasis to media imagery and media publicity. His occasional television specials were often accompanied by a book; he funded various pilot projects which were intended to generate publicity and to attract additional funds. Charles also adopted the professional politician's habit of making speeches in which sober argument is mixed with sensational phrases aimed at television sound-bites and newspaper headlines.

His environmental and architectural campaigning had perhaps the biggest impact. Prince Charles also became a leading Green campaigner in Britain. His criticism of a planned National Gallery extension led to its cancellation. His architectural criticisms, it was said, effectively blighted the careers of several outstanding British architects and forced them to seek patronage abroad. His arguments were broadly conservative; classical architecture was better than modern; all children should study Shakespeare, and so on. Charles's ideas were discussed at length in the broadsheet newspapers and on TV, but the tabloid newspapers tended to portray him as at best a harmless eccentric with romantic views about nature, and at worst a pompous and snobbish bore. One obvious problem was Charles's need to remain royally neutral on these sensitive political areas; but in image terms he came out sounding like an upper-class wet (in Thatcher terminology) or One Nation (moderate) Tory.

Another problem for Charles was that while Diana enhanced his superstar qualities, she herself matched the required superstar profile better than he did. The model Princess Diana was a superstar without uttering a word. She could make the TV news and the tabloid front page by walking (without talking), by wearing yet another new designer costume, and by pausing to smile carefully at the cameras. Diana quickly became the darling of the cameramen and photographers in general and of the tabloid headline writers in particular. Diana recognized the cameras and the people behind them as her friends. She became known as the only royal who routinely talked to camera people. She was also willing to spend hours—and in some cases days—posing for special picture stories which subsequently adorned magazine covers around the world.

By 1986—with two children born and the fifth wedding anniversary—there were already signs of marital conflict. Given that the two people were so different in background, age, and outlook, such conflict was perhaps not too surprising. But the strains and conflicts of superstardom surely contributed. Diana—as Andrew Morton subsequently explained—was suffering from the eating disorder bulimia nervosa. She was also suffering from the common star affliction of believing one's own publicity. Charles and Diana's media superstardom was following patterns familiar from showbusiness. Private anger, frustration, and rivalry began to spill over into the public sphere. In 1987 the upward superstar trajectory ended and the descent began, with several publicity mistakes and semi-public fits of temper. But overshadowing these was the public revelation that Diana and Charles were leading increasingly separate lives. For at least one summer month Charles was in Balmoral while Diana was in London with the two boys and leading an active evening social life. Nevertheless the 'separate lives' situation allowed the marriage to continue.

1987 was a really bad year; in addition to the Charles and Diana 'separate lives' story the *Sunday Times* claimed that major tensions existed between the Queen and the Prime Minister, Mrs Thatcher. Also in this year the youngest of the Queen's children—Prince Edward—gave up his attempt to become an officer in the élite Royal Marines; instead he went to work for Andrew Lloyd Webber's Really Useful theatre company. 1989 was another bad year; after the Lockerbie airliner crash in January no royal family member visited the disaster site. During 1989 the press focused on a new royal target—Sarah Ferguson, who had married the Queen's third child, Andrew, in 1986 and became the Duchess of York; the new sport of 'Fergie-bashing' portrayed the princess as gauche, greedy, and more concerned with holidays than looking after her two small children. In 1991 the criticism became still louder. In February the young royals were accused of too much noisy eating and drinking in expensive restaurants while British forces were preparing to play their part in retaking Kuwait from Iraq. The popular dailies found a new angle on Charles, the eccentric Green prince; the *Daily Star* (2 May 1991) under the headline 'ON YOUR BIKE CHARLIE!' called him a hypocrite for campaigning against pollution while he owned five cars, all five of them at the gas-guzzling and dirty end of the spectrum.

1991 was a year in which the newspapers—having built up unrealistic expectations of a whole large family of royal superstars—turned against one lesser royal after another; each lesser royal was savaged for leading a muddled and messy life and for failing the test of superstardom. An instructive case was that of Mark Phillips, who had married Princess Anne back in 1973. It could be argued that he had solved the key royal problem by refusing to become a superstar. Like Lord Snowdon before him, he had insisted on having a real job and doing something in which he had genuine expertise. On leaving the Army he carried his junior officer rank with him; 'Captain Mark Phillips' was perhaps a way of indicating his modest ambitions. Having met and married Princes Anne via their common success in horse-riding events, Phillips developed his horse expertise into a successful small business; he was not dependent on royal financial support. He thus cleared two of the hurdles confronting those who marry into the royal family; first, he had a proper job and, secondly, he did not adopt an extravagant life-style but lived according to his own earnings. However, having cleared these two, Mark Phillips did less well at clearing three other hurdles. He developed some showbusiness and media connections; he signed with International Management (IMG), the American company which manages golf and tennis stars. He may have needed IMG to handle not only his competitive horseback commitments but also articles which he wrote (or had ghosted) for horse publications and women's magazines. He, also like some other royals-in-law, was eventually accused by the tabloid press of a secret extra-marital affair. The *Daily Express* (21 March 1991) revealed that a New Zealand woman, Heather Tonkin, claimed that Mark Phillips was the father of her 5-year-old child. Her story was lavishly serialized in the *Daily Express*; Heather Tonkin revealed that she was being paid a regular monthly fee by IMG for consultancy on 'equestrian matters'. Other London newspapers pounced on the *Express* story; their language and denunciations of Mark Phillips were remarkably fierce:

He is not a fellah comfortable in his own riding boots . . . a man ill at ease with his emotions and unable to express who he is. . . . one observes his body language: hunched shoulders, body tensed and rarely relaxed, overstressed and uptight. (Caroline Phillips, *Evening Standard*, 21 March 1991)
. . . a pea-brained, pea-souper of a character. . . . Now at last, the unlikely stud is the subject of speculation that there is indeed more between his legs than half a ton of perspiring horse meat. (Judy Rumbold, *The Guardian*, 23 March 1991)

Captain Mark Phillips seemed to have crashed into all three of the last hurdles; he had become involved with the media/showbiz circus, he had kept secret a messy extra-marital affair, and finally he was denounced as an inadequate human being who had failed to live up to his star billing.

The year 1991 saw somewhat similar treatment handed out to other lesser royals. When Prince Andrew was a bachelor Royal

Navy officer, his amorous adventures led to an inevitable rhyming tabloid nickname, Randy Andy. Andrew had at least cleared the first hurdle by having a proper job as a naval helicopter pilot; his wife, Sarah Ferguson, however, had difficulty with this first hurdle, because she seemed unable to carve out for herself a portfolio of causes (and related appearances) which were consistent with her married title, Duchess of York. There was trouble also with the second test; the Duchess especially was found guilty by the tabloids on the extravagant life-style charge. With a husband often away at sea, she was guilty of having a jolly time in mixed company; and when she went to Australia, to be with her seafaring husband, she was accused of neglecting her newborn baby. The couple's newly built home was criticized as a fifty-room mansion of unparalleled vulgarity and ostentation. A neat link was drawn between Fergie's acquisitiveness, frantic shopping, and expanding waistline with newspaper nicknames such as Duchess of Pork and Freebie Fergie. The Yorks also hit the third hurdle by becoming unwisely involved in showbiz and the media. There were accusations that they failed to hand over to charity all of the money involved in some media appearances. Fergie wrote children's books and the couple posed endlessly for *Hello*, the celebrity-obsequious magazine. By 1991 Duchess Fergie was increasingly being linked with the names of various men other than the Duke. Finally, both Andy and Fergie had by 1991 hit the fifth hurdle fairly hard. She was portrayed as interested in food, shopping, holidays, and men; he was portrayed as—when away from the sea—mainly devoted to watching television. Fergie and Andy were judged by the popular press as not living up to expectations and clearly failing the superstar test.

Compared to the dazzle of Diana and the barrage of weighty speeches from Charles, the Queen's fourth child, Prince Edward had serious difficulties with the first hurdle; having decided to leave the Marines in 1987, Edward failed—as seen by the newspapers—to get himself a proper job. When the tabloids had difficulty discovering much about his personal life, they forced Andrew to announce in public that he was not homosexual.

1992 may have been a horrible year for the Queen, but it was a good year for certain newspapers. The two big stories—the Andrew–Fergie separation in March and the Charles–Diana separation in December—significantly boosted circulation figures. It was also a good year for the *Sun*, *Daily Mirror*, and *Daily Mail*, and the *Sunday Times*, which led the charge. They could—and they did—claim that they had been right all along; they had had the confidence specifically to predict both separations shortly before each occurred. On 18 March 1992 the *Daily Mail* and the *Sun* predicted the Andrew–Fergie separation, which was officially announced less than forty-eight hours later. One of the two authors of the *Daily Mail* story was Andrew Morton, who had written some of the most sensational (and accurate) royal stories of 1991.

The Murdoch stable, the *Sun* and the *Sunday Times*, combined against the *Daily Mail* in the days leading up to the first serialization of Andrew Morton's book, *Diana: Her True Story*. The first lengthy excerpt was to be published in the *Sunday Times* of 7 June. The *Mail* ran one of its expert 'spoiling' operations, using a book written by Nicholas Davies. The Friday headline read:

PRINCESS DIANA 'TRIED TO TAKE HER OWN LIFE'

The Saturday front page revealed that Diana had suffered from bulimia nervosa. Starting five days before the *Sunday Times* bombshell, the *Sun* served up the following front-page headlines:

SEPARATE BEDS AT HIGHGROVE: First Photos that prove Royal rift (Tuesday, 2 June)

THE HEAT'S ON DIANA: Palace puts the pressure on her over tell-all book (4 June)

DIANA HAS BETRAYED ME: Charles 'hurt' over book (5 June)

QUEEN MUM SAW DI SUICIDE ATTEMPT (6 June)

In August another sequence of revelations began in the *Sun*:

MY LIFE IS TORTURE: Dianagate tape of love call reveals marriage misery (24 August)

I TAPED DI: Ex-banker heard her by chance as he scanned airwaves (25 August)

THE SUN NAMES MAN ON THE TAPE (26 August)

The man on the taped telephone call was James Gilbey; this was the famous 'Squidgy' tape, which had already been published in Australia, where it was pointed out that the conversation implied an ongoing sexual relationship. The *Sun* was extremely hesitant in drawing any conclusions but it did return to the story with this front page:

DEAR DIANA: First came the book. Next came the tapes. Now you're accused of visiting a deserted house with Gilbey. The Sun humbly asks: What on earth's going on? (3 September)

In November the focus switched to Charles and his 'friend' Camilla Parker-Bowles:

DIANA CALLS CAMILLA THE ROTTWEILER (9 November)

I LOVE YOU: Sensational tape of Camilla and Charles talking of their romance. (13 November)

On 9 December John Major, the Prime Minister, officially announced the separation and the *Sun*'s headline read:

THRONE ALONE: MPs say Charles won't be King, Di won't be Queen. It's down to Wills. (10 December)

On 25 December the Queen made her annual Christmas day TV broadcast, describing the year as her *Annus Horribilis*. The text had already been published (against the normal embargo) by the *Sun* newspaper.

IV

Royal reporting in the 1980s became an established specialist field of journalism. New specialist fields require a 'precipitating event', which in this case was the 1981 Charles–Diana marriage. But royal reporting also had some previous history. One historical origin was the news agency and BBC court reporters who were deliberately conceived of as 'captured'—semi-official—voices of Buckingham Palace. The second historical origin is gossip/diary reporting; royal reporting broke away from gossip columns especially on the *Daily Mail*, *Daily Express* (Hickey), and *Sunday Times* (Atticus). James Whitaker, who is widely regarded as the father of aggressive royal reporting, joined the *Daily Mail* gossip diary in 1967 and immediately began to do some royal stories; he moved to William Hickey (*Daily Express*) in 1971 and 'did more and more royal stuff' especially about Charles (who was still in the Navy) and his girl-friends. In 1975 Whitaker joined the *Sun* and teamed up with the photographer Arthur Edwards. Upmarket royal journalism developed on the *Sunday Times* in the persons of Robert Lacey and Anthony Holden, both of whom wrote original and successful books.[9] Holden was in charge of the Atticus gossip column when he accompanied Prince Charles on a South American trip in 1977; he was the only writing journalist, with three photographers, on the trip.

The so-called 'royal rat pack' of the 1980s and 1990s were only the hard news advance guard of a much larger number of journalists who sometimes wrote on the royals. These sometimes royal writers included general reporters, gossip/diary journalists, feature-writers, book authors, and freelance journalists. In addition, journalists who occasionally wrote about royal topics were the newspaper's Big Interviewers, fashion correspondents, and regional reporters (in relevant royal locations) as well as the newspaper's regular columnists. On just 23 days in late 1993 and early 1994 the *Sun* used no less than 38 separate named journalists (staff and non-staff) to write 66 royal stories. More surprisingly perhaps, the *Guardian* on 20 days ran 38 royal stories and used no less than 21 different journalists. A wide spread of this kind happens in any broad field, but the royal story may have been unusually broad— stretching as it did from politics to fashion and from architecture to zoos (royal children visiting).

It has been stated that the royal rat pack are republicans, seeking to terminate the monarchy in the shortest possible time. My impression after talking with some of its leading members in 1994 was that few, if any, royal correspondents had republican sympathies. Their views were quite similar to those of the British public as revealed in current opinion polls—critical of several members of the royal family but still in favour of retaining the monarchy. My impression in 1994 was that most newspaper editors also had similar middling royal views. Amongst the wider range of sometime-writers-on-the-royals there also was a wider range of views. Most critical were some successful younger feature-writers, columnists, and section heads. One young *Sunday Times* section head said, 'What you think of the royals—and personally I could do without them—is obviously going to guide how you write about them. People tend to lay off the Queen, but the rest of them are fair game. I don't think you'll find any royalists on the paper.' But some of the most enthusiastic supporters and friends of royalty are to be found amongst the most established and cantankerous male columnists

[9] Robert Lacey, *Majesty: Elizabeth II and the House of Windsor* (London: Hutchinson, 1977). Anthony Holden, *Charles, Prince of Wales* (London: Weidenfeld and Nicolson, 1979).

such as Lord William Rees-Mogg, Lord Woodrow Wyatt, and Simon Jenkins.

Recently appointed royal correspondents seem to be among some of the most enthusiastic journalistic supporters of royalty:

Contrary to what is said, now that I've got to know Fergie a bit, I think she's a really nice lady.

When I began the job I thought the monarchy was a bit outdated. In a short time, my views have changed. Now I'm quite impressed with Charles. He should lighten up; he was a prankster when he was younger, he was more human. He feels trapped by his destiny. But he has amazing dedication.

Charles appeared to have impressed some journalists with the very wide range of things he had already been involved in by his mid-forties. Journalists knew about Charles's portfolio of difficult topics, and how he could fly aircraft and helicopters, how he could make speeches in Welsh, French, or German, and how he had time to be married to—and unfaithful to—the 'most photographed woman in the world'. Royal journalists were also impressed by their first royal tours with Charles (and other royals). The tours are complex operations which the courtiers seem to organize with considerable efficiency. The performance of the principal royal player—a hectic round of visits, dinners, speeches, clothes changes, and time-zone changes—can be impressive. The journalists know that the royals have been doing these trips for decades past. There is also an established tradition that the royals are more approachable on foreign tours. On a 1925 royal tour of South Africa, the future Edward VIII (then aged 31) 'delighted the press correspondents travelling on the royal train by regularly inviting them in for drinks and a sing-song; he would play the ukulele and Thomas a small harmonium.'[10] The 1920s royal tours were physically demanding and crowd control was often minimal. But the visiting royal star did have rest-stops on farms and ranches; he travelled across Australia and Canada by train. And the trip to and from Britain was by naval warship. In the 1980s travel was by jet aircraft (sometimes with Charles at the controls). The speed and the stress and strain were much greater.

Some royal correspondents newly arriving on the royal scene appeared to be humbled by the performance of a key royal player

[10] Philip Ziegler, *King Edward VIII* (London: Fontana, 1990), 159.

chosen only by an accident of birth, but yet expected to play the superstar. These journalists recognized that they could not do what Charles found himself doing; many politicians or entertainers—trained and selected as public performers—would also find the royal superstar role a hard one to play. The journalists could understand how the pent-up strains of royal superstardom led to aggressive behaviour, not only on the polo field but towards servants, friends, and journalists.

There was, however, a tendency for this admiration or respect to cool with time. Anthony Holden's changes of view are documented in his sequence of three books. His initial view (in 1979) was warm and uncritical; this was the first book to point out the disadvantages of being Prince of Wales. The second Holden book (in 1988), which marked Charles's fortieth birthday, balanced a broadly positive portrayal with some criticisms, including the observation that the marriage was in difficulty.[11] The third Holden book, *The Tarnished Crown* (1993) was a comprehensive critique of the British royal family up to and including the horrible happenings of 1992. But Holden was not alone. Andrew Morton and James Whitaker were two other respected royal specialists who had over the years, and through their numerous books, developed a very critical view of the royal family.

It was widely believed among the royal correspondents that the press relations personnel at Buckingham Palace had been ineffective, largely because they were not properly trusted or informed by their royal masters. The journalists claimed that they frequently knew things ahead of these press relations personnel. Of the royal courtiers one journalist noted that many of the names had not changed since Queen Victoria's time; courtiers were appointed on the basis of family tradition. The royal family were accused of being unable to accept outsiders—those who were transplanted by marriage into the royal family were later rejected as unacceptable alien tissue. The royal family were seen as belonging to a very restricted world whose main social connections were Eton, old wealth, large landowning, polo and horse-racing, the armed forces, the City of London, and the Conservative Party. The royals were also seen as politically insensitive in other ways. Charles tended to make some speeches which sounded like British

[11] Anthony Holden, *Charles: A Biography* (London: Weidenfeld and Nicolson, 1988), 134–40, 179–83, 199–200.

Conservative social policy and other speeches which conformed to French government agriculture policy. Most royal journalists said that as a description of the Windsor family manner 'arrogance' was an understatement.

'Windsor Arrogance' was a key reason for most of the royal journalists saying they preferred Diana to Charles. Diana was a better tabloid story; she was helpful to photographers, while Charles was often deliberately as unhelpful as possible. Diana's obvious difficulty with words and her general vulnerability also seemed to bring her sympathy—and again to make her a better story. When I asked them whether Diana might have selected a cause such as children-with-AIDS because of its visual as well as emotional appeal, these hardened hacks answered that Diana was less cynical and calculating than this question implied.

A key reason for favouring Diana was that she was more popular. These journalists said that both they themselves and their editors were impressed with Diana's poll popularity. But they were even more impressed with her rare ability to attract crowds in the street.

V

From 1991 onwards Charles and Diana engaged in increasingly active competitive briefing of the newspapers with their separate versions of a marriage in difficulties. They were behaving somewhat like different warring factions within a single political party. This was very different from what had happened a few decades earlier. Especially after the 1936 abdication crisis, Buckingham Palace effectively adopted the naval motto—the Silent Service—in its press relations. Richard Colville, who was the Palace press secretary for two decades (1947–68) offered a 'No Comment' response to most press enquiries. Under the prevailing conditions, it was a largely successful strategy; and the main problem royal of the 1960s—Princess Margaret—received relatively little coverage. The fact that Margaret's husband (Lord Snowdon) worked for the *Sunday Times* may have helped the tacit press agreement to play down the well-known difficulties of the marriage. In 1968 a new press secretary, William Heseltine, took over and his more media-friendly policy initially worked well.

Even in the superstar period (1981 and after) the royal family initially managed to maintain a more or less coherent approach to the media. Charles and Diana had their own press secretary, who was officially subordinate to the senior Palace press secretary. Despite Diana's media success and Charles's less rapturous response, this approach held together even past 1986 (when Charles later admitted the marriage had effectively broken down). The first really big divergence occurred in 1991, as one royal journalist said:

It all started with a story about Diana's 30th birthday in 1991—that Charles wasn't giving her a party and they were going to be apart on the day. Apparently he'd offered her a party down at Highgrove with the local parish council. You know, really dreary. And she'd said No Thanks. Friends of Prince Charles then phoned the papers to say that he had offered her a party, but she turned him down. Charles used the technique of leaking to newspapers to contradict her leak. And the next thing was that friends of hers started talking to Andrew Morton. . . . It was a leak from his camp that started that massive ball rolling. . . . It's very tit-for-tat. But the newspapers go along with it and are used happily because they get very good stories out of it. . . . Charles and Diana were conducting their marital spats via the tabloid press—rather than talking to each other across the room.

It was, then, this competitive press briefing which led to Andrew Morton's 1992 book *Diana: Her True Story*.

The competitive briefing of journalists continued to generate huge trails of 'his' and 'hers' newspaper stories and also 'his' and 'hers' books. In late 1993 Diana announced her retirement from public life; but the retirement generated yet bigger press coverage—for example, without any security back-up, Diana attended the Royal Opera House in January 1994. In May 1994 a story, which obviously came from the Charles camp, revealed that Diana's clothes and grooming cost £160,000 per year of £3,000 per week. Also in May Charles made a trip to St Petersburg—the first British royal to visit Russia since 1917. But while most of the royal correspondents were in St Petersburg, Diana's friends in London managed to inflate her somewhat peripheral involvement in a near-drowning into 'Diana Saves Man from Drowning' headlines. On the day in June 1994 when Charles confessed all to Jonathan Dimbleby in a 150-minute television epic, Diana wore her—according to the tabloids—most dazzling dress of the year to a gala dinner at the Serpentine Gallery in London.

In October 1994 the Dimbleby book was published. As his reply to her 1992 cries of pain to Andrew Morton, the 620-page *The Prince of Wales: A Biography* included many cries of pain from his own upbringing; the book takes 100,000 words to record Charles's childhood, education, and time in the armed forces. One month after the Charles (and Dimbleby) book, came the next Diana broadside—the second volume about Diana by Andrew Morton.

VI

During the 1980s the press and the other media executed the third reinvention and redefinition of the British monarchy within a hundred years. No longer the turn-of-the-century popular imperial jingoistic monarchy; no longer the buttoned-down family monarchy of the mid-century; in the 1980s the initiative was seized by the tabloid press, which redefined the monarchy as a soap opera. Quite accidentally the soap opera was created by the royal family firm's lack of a business plan and the newspapers' lack of other sufficiently succulent human interest running stories.

A key appeal of television soap operas is that they happen in real time. So it is with the royal soap. The same London rain falls at the same time on them and us. The press tells us whether the princess will spend Christmas with the in-laws at the very moment we are considering the same question. Soaps need strong women's parts and the royal family has a formidable detachment of such parts. Soaps need to have several families with interlinked plot lines; the British royals provide these linkages—one tends to marry one's second cousin. Soap operas need a central place—a pub, a street, a small town. The royal soap's central focus is Harrod's (the expensive department store); their location stretches one mile east to Buckingham Palace and the Mall, and one mile west to Kensington Palace, the *Daily Mail* building and the nearby streets and restaurants.

Along with the strong women characters, a soap opera needs some errant males and some outright bad guys; the British royals field an impressive team of such males—the leading rogue males are the royal princes, but there is strong minor character support often in the form of ex-Army majors; given such tabloid tags as 'Love Rat' and 'The Galloping Major', these minor Majors generate valuable sub-plots. Other sub-plots abound; there is one rather sombre political connection with the Douglas-Home family.[12] Another more cheerful political sub-plot focuses on Nicholas Soames, chief 'source close to Charles' and in fact a friend since age 12. Known apparently to his friends (not enemies) as Nickers and to the tabloids as Fatty, Nicholas Soames is a grandson of Winston Churchill and a member of the Tory grandee Soames family.

Other sub-plots have overtones of mystery, spies, and alleged routine tapping of royal phone lines by secret service personnel anxious about the security implications of some untidy royal personal lives. The media also make claims for additional elements of real-life melodrama on the fringes of the royal story—elements which include suicide and AIDS. Yet other sub-plots focus on long-past skeletons in the royal family cupboard: was George V guilty of refusing asylum to his cousin Tsar Nicholas and thus leaving him and his family to their fate? And then there is the royal family's favourite uncle, Lord Louis Mountbatten, and continuing publication of stories about his and his wife's extraordinary private lives.[13]

Soaps also need to write in fresh characters and to write out old characters. There is a strong supply of new royal characters, some of whom partner major players, only later to be discarded from the royal family and the soap script. One unusual soap feature is that senior royal players cannot be sacked, although they can be moved down to sub-plot status. The royal soap is strong in The Next Generation; a virtue of the highly extended family is that as soon as one generation of young royals starts to get boring the first members of the next generation are well onto the scene. Thus while Princess Diana was still in her mid-thirties the newspapers had already begun to speculate on the marital prospects of her son, William, not yet thirteen years old.[14]

Soap operas require a team of plot-line strategists and scriptwriters, as well as a bible of character and plot details to date. The chief scriptwriters are of course the journalists at the *Daily Mail*, *Daily Express*, *Sun*, *Daily Mirror*, and *Sunday Times*. A number of senior scribes (Dempster, Benson, Whitaker, Morton,

[12] One of several connections was the Charles–Charles friendship between Charles, Prince of Wales, and Charles Douglas-Home, when the latter was editor of *The Times*, until his death in 1985.

[13] Victor Davis, 'Yola, the French model Mountbatten loved secretly all his life. Lord Louis' daughters reveal their parents' sexual passions.' *Mail on Sunday*, 5 Mar. 1995, 37, 39.

[14] e.g. Alice Fowler, 'William and his ladies-in-waiting'. *Daily Mail*, Weekend, 18 Feb. 1995, pp. 12–13.

Holden) have also in their books compiled a multi-volume bible for the ongoing soap. Most biblical of all is Jonathan Dimbleby's biography of Charles; there is much background material here for many skeleton-in-the-cupboard tales and docudrama TV shows yet to come.

This royal soap has some unique features which also seem likely to ensure its longevity. It is an interactive soap, which allows the public to vote—via telephone hotlines and opinion polls—on which characters should be portrayed as goodies and which as baddies. The scriptwriters are eager for such guidance. This is a multi-media soap, with fresh material appearing in newspapers, magazines, and books as well as on television and radio. But this soap is unusual in that it is mainly newspaper driven. In this particular soap the newspapers hold all the cards; they have the space, the daily frequency, the lack of deference, the specialist correspondents, the team backup, and the general tabloid approach—all characteristics which British TV and radio lack. Television and radio, of course, do their specials, but television follows several steps behind the tabloid press. This is a perfect relationship for the newspapers, where sales are generously boosted by the big television royal special shows. The newspapers do not only dominate the tabloid coverage of the monarchy. The upmarket newspapers dominate the high ground, the-monarchy-and stories: the monarchy and Europe, and the Church of England, and the Constitution, and taxation, and all other serious issues.

The newspapers have a significant investment in their soap opera definition of the monarchy; it is this à-la-soap definition of royalty which sells newspapers in Britain. There is also a group of highly competent journalists who have used the royal story to build their careers, to boost their salaries, and to earn sizeable sums in book advances and royalties. One successful royal journalist-author told me that back in the early 1980s he recognized the royals as Britain's only story of truly global appeal. He and others will not easily let it go.

The newspapers have not reformed the monarchy, but they have redefined and reinvented it in terms of public image and reputation. The royals, the politicians, or anyone else who wishes to reform, redefine, or reinstate the monarchy must start with the monarchy as super soap. To take the script away from the newspapers will not be easy.

20 Shrinking Foreign News

> Traditionally . . . foreign news is considered to be rather 'difficult'. The Englishman's knowledge of geography has always been hazy and he dislikes having to remember the difference between Bucharest and Budapest. He is not interested in even the simplest political facts about countries which are not at war with him.
>
> Ian Fleming, 1950

IAN FLEMING, the James Bond author, was 'foreign manager' at the *Sunday Times*; since he wrote these words much has changed both in the world and in media representation of the world, but the basically insular character of the British population (and many others) has continued.

Television's foreign news impact has steadily increased down the decades; its colour pictures and its speed give television the ability to dramatize one or two stories per evening and to demand that 'Something Must Be Done' about a current crisis, coup, earthquake, famine, or civil war. Television foreign news has competed especially with midmarket and downmarket newspapers. Since 1965 these popular newspapers—now all tabloids—have largely given up employing staff correspondents permanently stationed in foreign cities.

Table 20.1 shows that the upmarket dailies have increased their numbers of foreign correspondents. These five dailies now have between them about 100 staff correspondents. This is an extremely expensive field of coverage, but having a team of staff foreign correspondents is part of the basic definition of being an upmarket or prestige London daily.

The widening of the gap between the upmarket newspapers,

Table 20.1. Staff foreign correspondents of British national daily newspapers, 1965–1991

Daily newspaper category	1965	1974	1976	1990–1
Upmarket	70	73	55	101
Midmarket	30	19	11	6
Downmarket	11	11	7	0
TOTAL	111	103	73	107

Sources: 1965: The Economist Intelligence Unit, *The National Newspaper Industry* (London: EIU, 1966), 65. 1974–76: Oliver Boyd-Barrett, 'The Collection of Foreign News in the National Press', in *Studies on the Press* (London: HMSO for Royal Commission on the Press, 1977), 18. 1990–91: author interviews.

which contain a lot of foreign news, and the tabloids, which contain almost none, has taken place against the background of Britain's reduced importance in the world. But London's status as a news centre has continued and perhaps even increased. Reuters, the old British Empire news agency, has hugely expanded its importance and is arguably the world's leading news agency (or at least first equal with the Associated Press of New York). But London has also seen a big expansion in the importance of the *Financial Times* and *The Economist*. Foreign news has acquired an increasingly financial flavour. The upmarket daily newspaper may devote the equivalent of three full pages (without advertising) to foreign news; but if one includes front-page foreign stories, editorials, columns, and features—and then adds this to foreign stories on the financial pages—the upmarket daily is carrying up to six full pages of foreign news (broadly defined). In the case of the *Financial Times* (even the domestic UK edition) a broad definition of foreign news would produce a much higher total number of foreign pages.

It can now be argued that the *Financial Times* has taken over from *The Times* as Britain's leading prestige newspaper. For most of its life *The Times* was the newspaper Voice of Britain and until the 1950s it had the most foreign correspondents. The *Daily Telegraph* was ahead of *The Times* in the 1960s, until the *Financial Times* took the lead around 1974–5. Incidentally, 1975 was a particularly bad year for Fleet Street (rising paper prices, falling advertising) and there were big cuts between 1974 and 1976 in foreign staff numbers.

Foreign coverage is subject to such short-term financial problems on the London newspaper scene. Foreign news coverage also changes in line with the changing international scene; at any time the media select from the numerous world conflicts and available crises one or two 'top world trouble spots' for crisis and 'war correspondent' style coverage. 'World trouble spots' often come in two forms. Some are recognized by the whole world (the Korean or Vietnam wars, the break-up of the Soviet Union) while others are world trouble spots which are especially significant for Britain (Biafra and the Nigerian Civil War, the Falklands campaign, Bosnia and the presence of British soldiers). But while trouble spots often change, the overall world pattern remains very similar. Since the 1930s the great majority of British staff correspondents have been based first in Europe and secondly in the USA. There remains a scattering along the grand imperial route—Cairo, Delhi, Hong Kong, Australia. Latin America has long been largely unreported in Britain. For decades London foreign editors have worried about the vast continent of Africa: 'ideally we'd like to have a staff man in Nigeria . . . but we haven't managed to so far.' Africa is still covered by the British media from Johannesburg with a few part-time stringers scattered across forty countries and 4,000 miles to the north.

I

While a single foreign news desk in a single daily newspaper is unlikely to rewrite the world international order, the long-term drip-drip-drip of newspaper foreign coverage may gradually wear away some prevailing assumptions while encouraging others. The basis of newspaper foreign influence lies in Ian Fleming's observation; Fleming was working for an upmarket newspaper, the *Sunday Times*, and recognized that even its readers were confused as to the capital cities of Hungary and Romania. It was, and still is, therefore incumbent on the foreign editor to make the foreign world interesting. This was, and is, done especially by conflict in general and the clash of personalities, in which and in whom the readers' interest can be aroused. A nation's foreign news—like its definition of history—reflects its prejudices and sentiments; it ignores the events and places we want to forget and it emphasizes the events, places, and faces we prefer and admire.

Only 200 miles away from London, Brussels has been the focus of a new Europe-wide arrangement of nations. But the British public have always been rather bored by Brussels. Newspaper foreign coverage has accepted this attitude and has looked elsewhere for international conflict, personalities, and excitement. Suspended between its European neighbours, its Empire and Commonwealth history, and its cultural and language proximity to the USA, British foreign news coverage has attempted to focus on the most enticing dishes from all three menus. This news approach has been enticing and flattering not only to newspaper readers but also to newspaper foreign editors and correspondents.

The 1960s offered a particularly strong list of foreign cities with more exciting and appealing news than Brussels. The senior foreign correspondents of the 1960s covered more numerous exciting stories in more different places than did any other generation of correspondents before or since. The period 1940–70 offered a unique collection of big stories—the Second World War, the cold war, the hot wars of Korea and Vietnam, the end of empire, and the rise of new nations. Air travel enabled foreign editors to switch correspondents huge distances at high speed and relatively low cost. Young correspondents had extraordinary experiences. Frank Robertson, who was the *Daily Telegraph* Hong Kong correspondent and also spent time in Vietnam, had earlier been a war correspondent. At age 27 he

arrived in Tokyo in 1945 ahead of General Douglas MacArthur's forces and filed the first news story of their arrival. Robertson . . . left the American troops gathering at Yokohama and with a colleague boarded an electric train for the capital. The pair were regarded with polite bewilderment by the Japanese passengers, who included some soldiers, and at the Imperial Hotel had no difficulty charging a five-course meal to the Japanese government.[1]

Over two decades later, a youthful Godfrey Hodgson covered three big stories in the single year of 1968—the Prague Spring and the Soviet tanks; the Paris 'events' of May 1968; and the US Presidential Election. These were precisely the kind of stories the readers seemed to like. The *Daily Telegraph* in 1968 had one corre-

---

[1] 'Frank Robertson' (obituary), *Daily Telegraph*, 25 Jan. 1995.

spondent in Brussels, but Britain was not yet in the Common Market and the *Telegraph* had three correspondents in Paris and three in Bonn. The Paris correspondents also covered not only the 1968 Parisian riots but the explosive happenings in Algeria. The Bonn correspondents covered not only West Germany but the cold war in central Europe and the Czech uprising. The Rome correspondent in addition to covering Italian politics, the papacy, and the Rome film industry might be asked to back up the two Middle East correspondents. Meanwhile the *Daily Telegraph* and *Sunday Telegraph* together had four correspondents in Washington and five in New York.[2]

New York had traditionally been the main location for British correspondents, but the focus gradually switched to Washington. New York remained the prime location for showbiz, and 'Americana' coverage, which, combined with the United Nations, made an exotic mix. But since John Kennedy won the 1960 Presidential Election, Washington had increasingly become the main centre for other upmarket papers. I was in both cities in 1965. Typical of some highly experienced correspondents of that era was Stephen Barber, then the *Sunday Telegraph* man in Washington (and later *Daily Telegraph* bureau chief there). Barber was then aged 43 and had been a foreign correspondent since the age of 19 in wartime (1941) Cairo. He followed the allied forces across North Africa and Italy and was first with the British news of Mussolini's death. He covered wars, civil wars, and wars of independence in Greece, Palestine, Korea, Lebanon, Iraq, Algeria, and Cyprus. He interviewed Nasser and Khruschev and in 1959 rode an elephant over Hannibal's alpine route from France to Italy. He was in New Delhi before moving to Washington; he was the *Daily Telegraph*'s man in Dallas on the day of the Kennedy assassination.

Another outstanding British correspondent was Louis Heren of *The Times*. In 1965 he was aged 46. He had served in the Second World War in the Far East. He also covered the Palestine and Korean wars. In the late 1950s he was *The Times* man in Bonn, where he kept a close, critical, and controversial watch on Konrad Adenauer and the new German democracy. In Washington from 1960 he was highly critical of John Kennedy. When I met Heren in 1965 he was probably the most vocal foreign media critic of Secre-

---

[2] Oliver Boyd-Barrett, interview with Eric Marsh, *Daily Telegraph*, foreign editor, 2 May 1968.

tary of Defense MacNamara and his systems science approach to the Vietnam war. But following the common Washington pattern, the enemy of Defense was friendly with the State Department. He told me that he had a private drink with Secretary of State Dean Rusk at least once a month.

Most Washington correspondents loved Washington and the (mainly popular paper) New York correspondents liked New York so much that they did not want to go home. The 1960s were altogether a wonderful time to be a British foreign correspondent. Boring Brussels could be largely ignored; British journalists were taken seriously in Washington; the end of the British Empire generated lots of dramatic stories of interest to British readers. The popular dailies also had correspondents—the *Express*, *Mail*, and the downmarket *Daily Mirror* in 1965 had respectively thirteen, thirteen, and eleven staff foreign correspondents. They also had staff correspondents in Paris as well as in Bonn and Rome. Their US correspondents gave much coverage to the drama and melodrama of the Kennedy brothers, Johnson, and Nixon; the popular paper correspondents prided themselves on their aggressive on-the-spot coverage of civil rights stories in Alabama, Mississippi, and Georgia. While the world had its numerous inviting trouble spots, Britain was free of its empire, not yet wedded to Europe; and whatever the political realities might be, these journalists felt that there was a special relationship between American and British journalism. The world was an adventure playground and it was bully to be a Brit in the foreign news business.

II

The power of the newspapers and television was demonstrated in 1975 by the result of the British referendum on the Common Market. The referendum took place on 5 June 1975 and resulted in a Yes vote of 67 per cent for Britain remaining in the EEC. Only six months earlier—in December 1975—the polls indicated a majority in favour of leaving the EEC. What had swung opinion in favour of the EEC between December and June? The bulk of the leadership of all three main political parties were in favour of the EEC; so was the bulk of industry and big business. But so also, as Table 20.2 shows, was the press. Every single daily newspaper (except the Communist *Morning Star* with its tiny UK sale) carried more

Table 20.2. 1975 British referendum on whether to remain in the European Economic Community (EEC): percentages of content for and against in national daily newspapers

Daily newspapers	Percentage of all space			Total space column cms	Number of items
	For EEC (%)	Against EEC (%)	Mixed neutral, other (%)		
Upmarket (*The Times, Guardian, Telegraph, FT*)	38	20	42	3,912	94
Midmarket (*Mail, Express*)	45	14	41	1,492	26
Downmarket (*Mirror, Sun*)	52	16	32	2,230	48

Note: These figures include advertising, but McQuail states that the exclusion of paid advertising 'does not greatly change the overall position'.

Source: Denis McQuail, *Analysis of Newspaper Content* (London: HMSO for Royal Commission on the Press, 1977), 320–1.

positive than negative EEC stories. The party leaders were able to convey their opinions via television and radio; but the very small amount of anti-EEC material in the press must have been significant. In the popular dailies—mid and downmarket—accounting for four-fifths of the daily sale, only 15 per cent of all EEC coverage was hostile. Had this figure been much higher the 'hostility of the press' would have received more TV and radio coverage and the result might have been very different.

Incidentally, the strength of voter support for the EEC correlated with the strength of the national press in different regions of Britain. Voter support for the EEC was strongest in England (where the national newspapers were strongest), then in Wales, then in Scotland, and weakest in Northern Ireland (where the national press was weakest).[3]

Although 1975 was a year in which the newspapers demonstrated their foreign policy potency, it was also a bad year for foreign correspondence. As Table 20.1 shows, there was a sharp

[3] David Butler and Gareth Butler, *British Political Facts, 1900–1994* (London: Macmillan, 1994), 220.

drop in the number of staff correspondents at this time. 1975 was a financially disastrous year for Fleet Street, with rocketing news-print costs and falling advertising. But the general point to note here is that it is not just the work of foreign correspondents which is relevant. Equally or more important was the editorial policy of the newspaper on a foreign issue of major domestic political significance.

By the 1990s none of the tabloids (except the *Daily Mail*) had a foreign desk. Some of these tabloids did, however, have a 'foreign editor', assisted—in some cases—by one other journalist. This type of 'foreign news team' writes stories based on the agencies, covers 'diplomatic' stories (Foreign Office and London embassies) and goes on occasional foreign trips. An example was Nicholas Davies, foreign editor at the *Daily Mirror* in the Robert Maxwell era. Davies at one stage was a Maxwell favourite and went on various world trips with him. As his then editor wrote: 'He was well-informed enough about international affairs to have held his own on any broadsheet foreign desk but his advantage over the serious journalist was that he could write about complex events in a tabloid style.'[4]

In the 1990s there were small, but more genuine, foreign news operations at the *Daily Mail*, *Evening Standard*, and the broadsheet Sundays. Here there would be a few foreign staff correspondents, some stringers, and an active foreign desk. This type of foreign operation focused mainly on feature and background coverage; at the more popular end of the feature spectrum such a foreign desk can organize 'life-style phone-arounds'. Such a foreign operation relies on the international agencies for basic coverage, while using its few staff people for high-profile on-the-spot accounts of current foreign crises and disasters. This foreign desk makes huge efforts to get its staff correspondent rapidly to disasters and into the crisis areas across closed frontiers; circuitous routes are followed to obtain visas and the only flight still operating. On arriving in the crisis country, these correspondents use colourful and expensive methods such as the 200-mile taxi-ride and the chartered plane. One such foreign editor described it as 'a global game of chasing fire-engines'.

The only British newspapers to run a substantial foreign news

---

[4] Roy Greenslade, *Maxwell's Fall* (London: Simon and Schuster, 1992), 133–6, 326–38.

effort are the five broadsheet dailies. The *Financial Times* is a special case (Chapter 21). A 1990s foreign operation typical of *The Times, Guardian, Daily Telegraph,* and *Independent* is shown in Table 20.3. This Table lists, as well as staff correspondents, 'stringer' journalists. The assumption made here is that there are three categories of these non-staff journalists. 'Super-stringers' may be full-time or nearly full-time people who are often paid for a minimum of say 150 days a year; another stringer category has been assumed here to be 30 per cent of a full-timer—such a stringer may write once or twice a week for each of several publications; finally, there are more occasional stringers, often in very small countries. In addition to the staff correspondents and stringers, the foreign editor also controls three other categories of people. First, there are the desk personnel who run this foreign news operation; secondly, attached to the desk are typically at least two diplomatic correspondents who cover the diplomatic circuit in London but who also go on fireman trips and may write foreign leaders. Finally, there is a team of foreign sub-editors. A foreign desk with seventeen staff correspondents would probably be employing forty staff journalists in total, plus the part-time stringers.

Table 20.3. Upmarket national daily newspaper: deployment of staff foreign correspondents and stringers, early 1990s

Region	Staff correspondents		Number of stringers	Full-time equivalent correspondents[a]
	Numbers	Locations		
Western Europe	5	Bonn, Paris, Brussels, Rome	23	10.7
Eastern Europe	2	Moscow, Warsaw	7	4.1
Asia	2	Delhi, Tokyo	17	6.6
North America	4	Washington, New York	5	5.3
Middle East	2	Cairo, Jerusalem	9	4.6
Africa	1	Johannesburg	10	3.4
Latin America	—	—	14	3.2
Australasia	1	Sydney	5	1.9
TOTAL	17		90	40

Note: This table describes a daily paper like the *Daily Telegraph, Guardian, Independent,* or *The Times*. It does not describe the *Financial Times*.
[a] Based on three separate categories of 'stringers'—weighted as 0.8, 0.3, and 0.1 of a full-time correspondent.

The foreign desk has its own pages, which are often some way into the paper and carry advertising. Thus the normal ration of space may be described in column terms—such as 18 columns per day. On the broadsheet dailies the foreign desk is running the most expensive of the editorial departments. Foreign correspondents are well-paid senior journalists; the cost of running a foreign correspondent is typically about twice the basic salary level in a cheap location like India, two to three times in most places, and four or five times in Tokyo, New York, and Moscow.

Despite its uniquely intricate subject matter and the logistical complexity, the foreign desk is in some respects less autonomous than the sports desk. Although the foreign desk has its own pages, the newspaper's editor also wants some foreign stories on the front page, where they move out of the direct control of the foreign desk. The foreign editor also wants to place some longer pieces with the features editor or onto specialized life-style, travel, and arts pages or sections.

Whereas Reuters correspondents are moved around the world on a regular basis, the newspaper foreign editors have a much less clear policy. Correspondents put down roots, marry, and have children in the foreign location; they do not then necessarily want to shift countries and continents every three years. Foreign editors talk about the unusual management problems and the foreign correspondent's peculiar mix of extreme independence and dependence:

As a foreign correspondent you are required to exercise a very high level of independent judgement in how you operate and what you say, but you are also required to be extremely obedient and responsive to the machine in London; these are much-prized jobs, which also have a high price—the re-entry problems, when you've been on the road for 20 years after 4 or 5 postings.

Another foreign editor said that smoothing down ruffled correspondent egos was a major requirement. He added that the worst foreign correspondent problem was 'coming in from the cold'.

The recent strengthening of market forces and stardom in British journalism has affected foreign correspondents. The arrival of the *Independent* in 1986 and its decision to emphasize foreign news added to these tendencies. Robert Fisk, the celebrated Middle East specialist, was persuaded to leave *The Times* and join the *Independent*. One foreign editor discussed how this more active market had reduced his ability to move correspondents between postings; in several cases if he tried to make such a move, the correspondent would simply stay in the same location but switch employers.

The foreign editor tends to suffer the frustration of not being out in the field either abroad or even at home; one such pointed out that as a 'deskbound editor' he relied on his diplomatic correspondent to go the London diplomatic rounds. The foreign editor may also miss the opportunity to write; although one did write a weekly column and others write occasional anonymous editorial leaders on foreign topics. Nevertheless, the foreign desk still does have a lot of freedom and autonomy. For these journalists with a strong interest in international affairs the foreign desk constitutes a splendid seat at the theatre. On some days the desk tells the correspondent to follow his or her choice of story. But the foreign desk personnel feel that they have a better understanding of how the international news agenda fits with that day's British news agenda. Thus the desk will on many days tell the correspondent which story to cover, or which agency item to follow up.

One general change from the late 1980s onwards was the rise in status of Moscow and Eastern Europe as foreign correspondent postings. In some London newspapers Moscow took over from Washington as the number one posting. These and other changes also lead to new day-to-day demarcation problems. For example, when a senior Russian politician visits Germany, should it be the Moscow or Brussels correspondent or the London-based diplomatic correspondent who goes to Bonn to assist the staff correspondent based there? The London desk must decide.

The foreign desk is typically also in charge of the foreign sub-editors and is thus in broad control of how its stories appear in the paper. In recent years there has been an increased focus on layout and page design, and a strategic emphasis on good foreign pictures to attract the reader. A variety of other factors also support foreign desk autonomy. The possibility of making mistakes in simple things—such as politicians' names or place-names—means that foreign desk (and sub-editor) expertise must be respected. There is also the dimension of foreign language ability—a qualification for foreign sub-editors as for correspondents. There is the factor of time-zones—how to co-ordinate the work of correspondents who are so far apart in terms of time of day. But the factor which most argues for autonomy is the prestige of the foreign operation. You can do this much more cheaply, either by having no foreign news or by using the various agency and feature syndication services. If a newspaper invests in an expensive foreign operation it seems illogical not to grant the foreign desk a high degree of autonomy.

IV

Although the upmarket British dailies devote more correspondents and more space to Europe (west and east), there are still unique features to the coverage of the United States. At both ends of the British newspaper market, the USA receives much more coverage than any other single country. In Denis McQuail's study of 1975, for example, the USA received 17.5 per cent of all foreign coverage, against 3.9 per cent for the USSR and 10.7 per cent for the whole of Asia.

Since 1975, there has been a further polarization between upmarket and tabloid newspaper coverage of the USA. The tabloid coverage has become more tabloid, showbiz, and fantasy-oriented; the upmarket coverage has become more serious. Recent Presidents have seemed to lack the hero/villain potential of the Kennedy–Johnson–Nixon sequence and, without a dominant presidential figure as a personality peg, it is difficult to make US domestic politics interesting even to upmarket British readers. Increasing proportions of the total upmarket coverage now deal with American business; this is partly because the financial pages are now more salient in London, but also because American business provides more clashes of companies and personalities than does European business. The latter is seen as difficult to popularize and it lacks contested company take-overs; US business, on the contrary, has offered numerous take-over battles, colourful novelties such as junk-bond billionaires, and plenty of plain old vulgar, ostentatious tycoonery. Much of the latter is New York related. How to make the main upmarket location, Washington DC, seem interesting? The ideal would be a combination of political skulduggery and hero/villain personality—such as Watergate and Nixon. However, the President-in-trouble always makes a story, if there's nothing better available. Consequently with both George Bush and Bill Clinton the British upmarket newspapers focused on the President-in-trouble, rather than, for example, upon the details of Health Insurance reform.

While the British tabloids have ceased to employ staff correspondents even in New York, they still carry a lot of American material. This is overwhelmingly about showbiz—films, TV, and music; despite focusing on stars who mostly live in Los Angeles, much of this material in fact originates in New York—from publicity people, from the New York tabloids, the TV stations, and the trade press. The London tabloids obtain their showbiz stories from New York-based stringers, freelances, and publicists; often the stories are rewritten in London to look as if they come direct from Hollywood. But some of this showbiz material does come from the British tabloids' Los Angeles stringers. At least one British-based agency—The Write Stuff—specializes in supplying freelance material from American journalists working on Los Angeles local media, such as radio and TV stations. This material is, of course, heavily keyed to the British release dates of Hollywood films, and to the handful of Hollywood TV shows which are current successes on British television. Much of this material carries an 'exclusive' label. Some of it has been acquired from a New York tabloid or a Florida-based supermarket shock magazine. Some of it is simply an exclusive rewrite of American material. Some of it is 'exclusive' because no domestic American publication will touch it. Thus it was Baz Bamigboye, the *Daily Mail* showbiz journalist, who first told the world that Rock Hudson was gay and had Aids.

Although the London upmarkets focus on Washington and Wall Street, while the tabloids focus on Los Angeles and showbiz, the two are not kept entirely apart. The upmarket dailies also have their Los Angeles stringers and the upmarket Sundays like to carry Americana, often long pieces on golden-oldie entertainment stories, exotic multiple murders, or eccentric billionaires.

Another upmarket tabloid meeting ground is Washington stories involving sex. The US Senator as sexual predator is one such story type. Consequently President Bill Clinton's personal life and financial problems—while Governor of Arkansas—were irresistible to the British tabloids and the upmarkets alike.[5] The *Telegraph* Washington correspondent Ambrose Evans-Pritchard took a particularly strong interest in the death of Vincent Foster, the White

---

[3] Howard Kurtz 'Barbed wires across the sea', originally in the *Washington Post*, reprinted in the *Guardian*, 8 May 1994.

House Deputy Counsel.[6] Part of the argument here was that the liberal East Coast US press was not interested in doing anti-Clinton investigative journalism. The same point was also made to me by another senior *Telegraph* journalist: 'American journalists are so anal retentive. . . . Clinton is a gangster—a mixture of money, sex and drugs. Arkansas is a banana republic. . . . People do keep dying in peculiar circumstances; it's a world of fear and intimidation.' One linked argument is that London has become a new laundering location for politically sensitive Washington stories. If the liberal, respectable (and anal retentive) US newspapers won't run the story, always remember that British journalists have a passion for raw meat; throw your raw meat to one of them and the story will then appear in a respectable London newspaper like the *Sunday Telegraph, Sunday Times*, or *Mail on Sunday*. Then once it's in the foreign press, it can be quoted in the usual moral-division-of-labour manner. We wouldn't have run it ourselves; but this is what they're saying in London.

V

With the end of the cold war, issues of foreign trade and international economic relationships have achieved great importance. These big international issues also impinge centrally on domestic politics; and for Britain (as for other countries) relationships with Brussels and with Europe are at the core of domestic politics. In the 1990s the old saga of the British press and Brussels took on new forms. Much of the newspaper press, especially from 1992 onwards, became increasingly hostile to Brussels. This was true of upmarket papers, which had staff correspondents in European capitals; but it was also true of midmarket dailies (such as the *Daily Mail*) and downmarket dailies (such as the *Sun*) which contained very little European news.

The *Daily Mail* in 1975 (edited by David English) still had a significant foreign news effort and supported Britain's continued membership in the EEC referendum. But in the next two decades that news coverage gradually declined. No effective way was found to make Brussels interesting and readable. It was difficult to personalize (except for negative coverage of Jacques Delors). The

[6] e.g. Ambrose Evans-Pritchard, 'Suicide is hard to sell', *Daily Telegraph*, 2 Feb. 1995.

issues seemed too complex, and the negotiations too drawn out; ideologically it was awkward. But after 1993 a new editor, Paul Dacre, moved the *Daily Mail* into a fully Euro-sceptical position. There was still very little European news coverage, but the negative editorial leaders were highly readable; equally readable was the *Daily Mail* 'Red Tape Alert'—which reported on 'bizarre red tape nightmares' emanating from Brussels, and the disastrous consequences for British business and British consumers.

This *Daily Mail* approach—lively criticism of Brussels, with very little boring news coverage—was another example of how newspapers (in parallel with politicians) can define, negatively in this case, a central foreign and domestic issue.

21 Financial News Take-over

'**F**INANCIAL news has moved centre stage.' 'The financial pages have become part of the newspaper's engine room.' The metaphors vary and clash, but journalists, and not only financial journalists, broadly agree that financial news has become a more salient part of newspapers.

Finance has long been a significant news area for upmarket newspapers; but it now is increasingly important also for midmarket papers like the *Daily Mail*. Moreover, this is a news area where neither television nor radio can make much impact. The newspaper strengths of depth, detail, and numbers are especially relevant in financial news. As finance and economics seem to dominate everything from the individual's livelihood to the future of planet earth, so also financial news has tended to take over from political news and foreign news as the premier serious news field. An alternative formulation of the same point: financial news now increasingly drives both domestic political and foreign news. This increased salience of financial news has occurred in many countries. In Britain the trend may have gone somewhat further, because financial services and the 'City' of London loom so large in the imagery and the actuality of the British economy. Newspapers everywhere select, and identify themselves with, particular areas of national success. The British newspaper press sees Britain as Good at Finance and, identifying itself with this national success, also Good at Financial News.

Financial journalism tends to offer polarized images of financial strength and weakness; it also offers images polarized between on the one hand the world level—hundreds of billions of dollars worth of foreign exchange transactions flickering each day across the foreign exchange dealers' screens—and, on the other hand, Bill

Smith struggling with his flexible interest mortgage payments. One financial journalist told me that the Westminster Parliament was complaining about European interference with British sovereignty only after the horse had already bolted. 'The European Union has already done a take-over on the British Parliament.' But this same journalist also stated that 'Financial journalism is still 90 per cent British, and little of the other 10 per cent is European.'

Within British newspapers the financial pages have been increased, partly because the coverage fits well with the industrial and competitive changes of recent years. Financial news attracts prestige and upmarket, high-income readers; secondly, it sells copies also to midmarket readers—several papers sell more copies on their special personal finance day of the week; and thirdly, the financial pages attract advertisers who are willing to pay high rates. In line with this uniquely attractive commercial appeal, financial news has broadened out to include several distinctive sub-fields. There is economic policy, business and industry coverage, traditional City coverage of the stock market and other financial markets (such as commodities), and finally personal finance. The last of these has seen the biggest growth. People increasingly look towards London's City, 'because they know that their pensions and their mortgages are down there' and thus they read 'Your Money' and 'Personal Finance' sections to keep track.

The financial press—like the press in other fields—is partly a message-carrier, but partly also the compiler of the message. Just as political journalism defines political crises, so financial journalism defines and frames financial crises and suggests solutions. At national level the newspapers play a big part in defining whether a downward movement in the exchange rate is a 'devaluation crisis' or merely a minor structural readjustment. Similarly at key moments in the life of public companies—such as a contested take-over battle—the participants are typically deeply concerned about the support or opposition of the financial press.

Rather as *The Times* during 1850–1950 was seen around the world as the semi-official voice of the British government, so the *Financial Times* is now printed and read each day in Tokyo, Frankfurt, and New York and regarded as the semi-official voice of the City of London. The London financial press in general and the *Financial Times* in particular also ensure that the performance of the British economy is particularly well documented and known around the world. This is another case of strength combined with weakness; one of the great strengths of British financial journalism lies in its power to convey to the world images of British financial weakness.

A side-effect is the elevation of the *Financial Times* to its new status as the leading élite British newspaper. In two of three heavy-weight news fields—finance and foreign—the *FT* is clearly in the lead; its domestic political coverage would probably be voted about second equal among the upmarkets. This is a winning serious news combination. Yet the paper's success involves problems, some of them reminiscent of *The Times*'s problems of 1850–1950.

I

Sixteen senior financial journalists interviewed in 1968 included some one-man financial bands as well as the *Financial Times* editor, Sir Gordon Newton, who presided over 140 journalists.[1] The general impression was remarkably low key and consensual. There was—among these financial editors—little of the contempt for Harold Wilson and his government evident in interviews with political (lobby) correspondents also in 1968. This was a time of rapid growth in financial journalism. During the decade 1958–68 the *Financial Times* circulation increased by 88 per cent. After Thomson's purchase of *The Times* its number of financial journalists was doubled for the launch of its expanded business news in April 1967.

Financial journalists during the first three years of Labour government after 1964 were keenly aware of the weakness of the pound at its $2.80 fixed exchange rate. The pound was eventually (over the 18–19 November 1967 weekend) devalued to $2.40. There was what amounted to a conspiracy of silence by British financial journalists in the months before November 1967. Extremely little discussion of the possibility of devaluation was printed in the press. This was partly a simple patriotic instinct and partly fear of being accused of causing sterling devaluation. It was certainly based on experience of the potential damaging consequences of negative press comment. Perhaps more than anything else, this reluctance to predict devaluation reflected journalists'

---

[1] Of these interviews some were conducted by Oliver Boyd-Barrett, some by the author, and some by the two of us together.

adherence to a City code of things which 'were not done'. The 'professional' standards of financial journalism—as developed up to 1967—required the journalist to be independent, neutral, and detached; loudly to predict sterling devaluation would be partisan interference. Behind this devaluation episode of the financial journalist dogs failing to bark, there also lay the embarrassment of concentrated newspaper power which seemed too great to be used. Throughout the three years of Labour government from October 1964, Harold Wilson's government had been fighting to defend the $2.80 level. By subsequent standards the 14 per cent devaluation of 1967 may seem quite modest; but it was a severe blow to the reputation of both Britain and the Labour government.

The BBC had appointed its first economics specialist, Graham Turner, in 1964. Although he had written an excellent book, *The Car Makers*, he had no background in finance or economics. He moved from the *Sunday Times* to the BBC as a general reporter in 1964. A year later (August 1965) he told me of the nervousness with which the financial establishment had reacted to the introduction of a BBC 'economics reporter'. He was attending Treasury briefings (with the heavier newspapers). Graham Turner's big stories tended to be the monthly trade figures. In reporting the July trade figures (on 12 August 1985) he had commented that the good results might be a 'freak'. Within an hour the Prime Minister, Harold Wilson, was on the telephone denying that the good trade figures were a freak. The monthly trade figures were published at noon and available to Graham Turner at 11.30 a.m. He then would do up to ten separate television and radio reports and interviews on the figures. But the interviews would normally be with government Ministers; the City financial analysts of later years did not yet exist—at least on radio and TV.

The *Financial Times* in the late 1960s was in a period of growth and success. Having decided not to merge with *The Times*, the *FT* successfully resisted *The Times*'s business news onslaught of April 1967. The *Financial Times* sales continued to grow and its editor, Sir Gordon Newton, when interviewed in 1968, exuded cautious confidence. He was then in his twentieth year of *FT* editorship. He was proud of his record of recruiting able young graduates—nearly all young men with good degrees from Oxford (and a few from Cambridge). Then when they moved into a specialist area they were left very free. Newton believed that on such a specialist publication it was necessary to shift correspondents around. In the case of journalists assigned to commenting on company performance in the 'Lex' column, it was inevitable that they would soon receive enticing outside job offers. 'Promotion to Lex confers a capital bonus on the journalist', said Gordon Newton (who was famously sparing with humour). Newton's main emphasis was on objectivity, absolute accuracy with market prices and other facts, and general excellence. 'Financial dishonesty', he said was rare and resulted in instant dismissal. The aim clearly was to avoid the malpractices, as well as the insecurities, of 1930s financial journalism.

Outside the *Financial Times* the bulk of financial journalists in 1968 were located on the other three upmarket dailies. Much the largest team were the business news journalists on *The Times*. The smallest of these three teams was at the *Guardian*, whose ebullient and (cautiously) outspoken[2] City editor, William Davis, was 'close to' the Labour government and appeared frequently on television and radio; when we interviewed him in 1968 he was about to take up a new job as editor of *Punch*. More representative of the heavier dailies was the City office of the *Daily Telegraph*. Like most other dailies, the *Telegraph* had a separate City office located less than a mile from the main building in Fleet Street; this office also housed the financial advertising sales force and it meant that financial journalists 'lived' in the City, just as lobby journalists 'lived' at Westminster. Kenneth Fleet was the *Daily Telegraph* City editor. He presided over sixteen 'writing' journalists, mostly involved in traditional stock market journalism, with an (increasing) few covering industry. Also under Kenneth Fleet's control were another thirty or so people—including sub-editors in London and Manchester and people who handled market prices. The interview took place on the day the August (1968) trade figures were announced. Fleet talked on the office intercom to a *Daily Telegraph* leader writer assigned to write an editorial leader on the trade figures; 'he's trying to find out what I'm going to say' said Kenneth Fleet, making clear that he liked to keep the editor's team of leader writers at a distance.

The midmarket dailies had carried small amounts of financial news before 1939. But the development of a distinctive midmarket pattern of financial journalism only really took place in the 1950s. A key figure in this was Patrick Sergeant of the *Daily Mail*. After

---

[2] See, for example, William Davis, 'The Press and the £', *UK Press Gazette*, 25 July 1966.

service in the Royal Navy, Sergeant worked in the Stock Exchange, switching to the city pages of the *News Chronicle* in 1948. During his twenty years of newspaper experience Sergeant had, he said, developed a new style of popular financial journalism. He avoided the Frederick Ellis (*Daily Express*) style of attacking company bosses; Sergeant focused his negative coverage on companies, while seeking to cultivate close connections with their bosses. Certainly this seemed to have paid off in financial advertising, and Sergeant had a distinctly entrepreneurial streak (which he demonstrated more fully in subsequent years). We saw him on three separate occasions, and each time Patrick Sergeant and his crew seemed to be at action stations. He had recruited a number of bright young men (seven out of ten were Oxbridge graduates) whom he presided over in a somewhat captain-on-the-bridge style. On one occasion the Treasury press office phoned to announce a briefing (on sanctions against Rhodesia) to start in fifteen minutes' time; Patrick Sergeant dispatched his chosen journalist with generous arm waving and advice to 'get moving'. Sergeant was clearly on lunching terms with many of the big names of the City and British industry, and was also seeing the current Chancellor of the Exchequer (Roy Jenkins) once or twice a month (collective briefings and individual meetings). He used to see a previous Conservative Chancellor of the Exchequer (Reginald Maudling, 1962–4) a little more frequently, because he was a 'personal friend'.

Even the tabloid circulation leader, the *Daily Mirror*, had its own financial office in the City. According to the IPC/Mirror orthodoxy of the time the *Mirror* City editor, Robert Head, ran an operation of extreme probity. One of Head's four journalists was solely engaged in answering readers' letters; the *Daily Mirror* had received 17,000 finance letters in 1967—about house purchase and insurance as well as investment—and was heading for 25,000 letters in 1968. Among the Sundays was Hamish Conochie; running a one man City operation in the (pre-Murdoch) *News of the World*, off Fleet Street, Conochie divided his time between some simple share-tipping and answering readers' letters.

At the opposite end of the Sunday spectrum was Peter Wilsher at the *Sunday Times* where business news was an immediate success from its launch in 1964; the flow of advertising exceeded even Roy Thomson's expectations. The section, initially of 12 pages, was by 1968 normally running to 24 pages. The dominant group of readers (again contrary to expectation) had become the '750,000 or so people who call themselves "businessmen"'. The *Sunday Times* business section had twelve journalists focusing primarily on business and industry. During the week the journalists mostly worked on features. Friday was the big news day—'on the phone from 10 to 6, and then writing their news stories from 6 to 10 p.m.'. Peter Wilsher emphasized that access to the highest levels of British industry was excellent. 'Senior business journalists have access to the strategic thinking of a wide range of major companies; most senior businessmen don't have that access, which is one reason why they want to talk to the journalists.'

These City editors of 1968 were—like the top lobby correspondents—an able group of individualists. The typical City editor admitted to being the highest paid journalist on his paper apart from the editor; he lunched with sources in the City two or three times a week; he travelled abroad several times a year, usually covering the Chancellor of Exchequer but often staying behind in Washington or Switzerland (for skiing). The City editor was more entrepreneurial than most journalists; he had his own personal strategy for combining comment and criticism with a certain advertiser-friendliness. There was a high degree of camaraderie amongst City editors—they met frequently at briefings, lunches, and also dinners. These editors also combined a sense of professional responsibility with a high degree of tactical freedom. The typical upmarket City editor said that he was left remarkably free of interference from the editor and the main newspaper; he controlled his own pages and his own sub-editors. (The popular paper financial material was subbed by general news sub-editors.) The only occasion when the City editor lost control over his own material was when it appeared on the front page under back-bench control; this could lead to what the City editor regarded as exaggerated headlines and presentation.

Through the 1960s and 1970s the financial journalists carried on a relatively non-confrontational relationship with both the Treasury and the government of the day, including the Wilson and Callaghan Labour government. Denis Healey, for example, who was Chancellor of the Exchequer (1974–9) comments on his relationship with senior journalists:

I regularly invited the top editorial staff of the leading newspapers to dinner, and accepted their invitations in return. I would discuss my problems frankly with them, and never had a confidence betrayed. As a result, at least they understood what I was trying to do, even if they did not approve of it. However much I deplored their criticisms, I rarely felt it was unfair. This was true at least of the so-called 'quality press', including newspapers which supported the Conservatives.

Healey goes on to deride the 'knee jerk interpretations' of the popular newspapers, but even here he specifically refers to 'editorials', not financial news columns.[3]

Financial journalists in the 1960s (and 1970s) already played a prominent part in the newspaper coverage of government. There was considerable competition between government departments each wishing to tell its story; and there was also significant competition between different groups of specialist correspondents to present major economic policy stories. There were certainly some established pairings of a particular journalist specialist group with a particular Ministry. The City editors were close to the Treasury and its Ministers, whereas the Department of Economic Affairs was close to the Labour correspondents; but the latter were also close to the Department of Labour (later Employment).[4] There were various other overlaps; the Ministry of Defence talked to both defence and aviation specialists; but the aviation specialists also covered civil aviation and were close to the Ministry of Technology. The Department of Transport talked to both motoring and transport correspondents, but preferred the latter. All of this competition—between Ministers and journalists—meant that a conscientious newspaper reader could discover a great deal about the contending positions of different Departments in Whitehall.

Many journalists in the late 1960s complained about the lack of coverage of government departments. Although not fully valid, this criticism came about partly because the newspaper City offices were so socially separate from the main offices in Fleet Street. Most journalists did not fully appreciate how much information was available on the financial pages. They did not recognize that City editors were in such frequent contact with Treasury Ministers (and civil servants). The financial journalists already in 1968 had a particularly broad overview of government activity and

---

[3] Denis Healey, *The Time of My Life* (Harmondsworth Penguin, 1990), 442–3.

[4] Based in part on interviews in 1967–8 with senior press relations people at the Department of Economic Affairs, and the Departments of Labour and Transport. Also an interview in 1976 with the head of information at the Treasury. See also Jeremy Tunstall, *Journalists at Work* (London: Constable, 1971).

expenditure. Many Treasury briefings were devoted to countering the complaints of other Departments which generated stories by 'their' journalists—complaints that the Treasury was making dangerous cuts in Defence, Transport, Health, Education, and so on, expenditure plans.

Another reason why many journalists failed to 'notice' what appeared in their own newspapers was that the general tone of financial coverage in the 1960s and 1970s was broadly so bland, consensual, and non-ideological. All of this changed subsequently.

II

Financial journalism after 1970 increasingly moved away from the cautious consensualism of the 1960s. Financial journalism and journalists broadly welcomed the Thatcher–Lawson revolution of the mid-1980s. This revolution included the deregulation and internationalization (or globalization) of financial services, which in Britain involved the deregulation of the City of London. In Britain over forty state businesses were sold off or 'privatized' during 1982–92. Keynesian economics was succeeded by various versions of monetarist economics, especially during 1975–85.

In addition to broadly welcoming these changes, London financial journalism also benefited from them—as financial advertising, news, and public relations all expanded. But a few British financial journalists—mainly at the *Financial Times* and *The Times*—played a leading role in bringing Chicago monetarism to Britain. They also advised and promoted the ideas of Sir Keith Joseph, the prophet who went before (and indeed converted) Mrs Thatcher.

The leading journalist introducers of monetarism to Britain were Samuel Brittan of the *Financial Times* and Peter Jay and William Rees-Mogg of *The Times*. Also important here was Nigel Lawson, Chancellor of the Exchequer 1983–9, who was a *Financial Times* journalist from 1956 onwards. All four of these men had similar backgrounds before they became young financial journalists, or what Lawson himself later described as 'teenage scribblers'. All four came from affluent middle-class backgrounds, and all attended Oxford or Cambridge; three of the four went straight from university via Gordon Newton's recruitment scheme into the *Financial Times*. One of the four went from Oxford into the Treasury and from there to *The Times* business news. All four experienced the close proximity of economic policy, City finance, and élite journalism which characterizes London. Sam Brittan and Peter Jay both had remarkable family connections in the political world. Sam Brittan's brother, Leon Brittan, was a Treasury Minister (Chief Secretary) during part of the first Thatcher administration (1981–3) and then held other Cabinet posts before going to Brussels as a Commissioner. Peter Jay had the most remarkable family connections; his father was Douglas Jay, a financial journalist and Labour Cabinet Minister who in his own day propagated the Keynesian cause. Peter Jay's father-in-law was James Callaghan, Labour Chancellor of the Exchequer (1964–7) and Prime Minister (1976–9).

It was around 1967–9 that both Samuel Brittan and Peter Jay became converts to monetarism. Samuel Brittan arrived at the *Financial Times* in 1955 and later moved to the *Observer*; he then worked at the Department of Economic Affairs, which Harold Wilson created in 1964. As a Treasury civil servant Peter Jay also saw government economic policy from the inside. Both men looked westward to Chicago for new ideas. Sam Brittan says that he was converted by Milton Friedman's 1968 presidential address to the American Economic Association.[5] Peter Jay's conversion occurred around the same time; in 1968 as the youthful economics editor of *The Times* he began to focus on monetary statistics and in 1969 went to Washington for a year. His editor William Rees-Mogg later wrote: 'Asking Peter Jay to go to Washington turned out to be the most influential decision I took as editor of *The Times*. There is no force changes history as much as the contagion of ideas.'[6] Rees-Mogg himself became a monetarist convert. Wayne Parsons in his *The Power of the Financial Press* argues that *The Times* and the *Financial Times* introduced monetarism to Britain, and were ahead of the Treasury civil servants, the Bank of England, and the academic economists in this. Certainly by the mid-1970s monetarism was well known in the Treasury and to Denis Healey,[7] who was Chancellor of the Exchequer, 1974–9.

The most dramatic and politically influential recantation of Keynes and conversion to monetarism was that expressed by Keith

[5] David Kynaston, *The Financial Times: A Centenary History* (London: Viking, 1988), 368.
[6] William Rees-Mogg, *Picnics on Vesuvius* (London: Sidgwick and Jackson, 1992), 21.
[7] Healey, *The Time of My Life*.

Joseph in his September 1974 speech in Preston; Samuel Brittan, Peter Jay, Margaret Thatcher, and Geoffrey Howe all commented on this speech when it was in preparation.[8] *The Times* published the full text of Keith Joseph's speech and encouraged a continuing debate on its ideas. The initial front-page headline said: 'Sir Keith blames full employment for inflation.'[9] *The Times* was increasingly adopting a more proactive, partisan, and ideological approach to financial journalism.

In parallel with this move to monetarism was another London financial thrust towards internationalism. The *Financial Times* began its first foreign printing (in Frankfurt) in 1979, the year of Mrs Thatcher's first election win. It continued to follow the *Wall Street Journal* pattern of multi-centre printing; new printings were added in New York, Paris, and Tokyo. By the mid-1990s the *FT* was obtaining 40 per cent of its circulation and over half of its advertising revenue from outside Britain. The Pearson managers also had a second international strategy—full ownership of the Paris financial daily *Les Echos* and minority ownership stakes in *Recoletos* (Spain) and the *Financial Post* (Canada). The overall *Financial Times* strategy was to be the leading press voice of European finance in the world.

Meanwhile the British international news agency, Reuters, had since the 1960s been converting itself into a new kind of global financial data-and-news agency. Reuters' total revenue reached £1 billion for the first time in 1988 and reached $2 billion in 1990. Reuters by 1992 was supplying financial data on 200,000 computer screens in banks and offices around the world. Reuters was directly operating as a market through which large-scale currency trades (and other financial transactions) are made in seconds. Reuters also continued after 1980 to widen its wholesaling of news; it expanded from its previous newspaper and radio-oriented news into a world-wide news photograph service and, in taking full control of Visnews (in 1991), it also became the leading world supplier of video news.

The main weekly voice of London finance—*The Economist*—also followed its own international pattern of expansion. Its sale passed 100,000 in 1973, 200,000 in 1980, and 500,000 in 1992. During the 1980s *The Economist* transformed itself from being a

---

[8] Hugo Young, *One of us: A Biography of Margaret Thatcher* (London: Pan, 1993), 88.
[9] Wayne Parsons, *The Power of Financial Journalism* (London: Edward Elgar, 1989), 189–92.

domestic British weekly with sizeable foreign sales into an international publication whose United States sales alone easily outweighed its British sales. The bulk of its advertising revenue also comes from outside Britain. The change is symbolized by the fact that dollar figures are used in all editions including the British edition.

The development of these three financial news entities meant that London had Europe's leading financial voice in weekly financial journalism, in daily financial journalism, and also in comprehensive on-screen fast news and data. The international expansion and success of *The Economist*, the *Financial Times*, and Reuters raised the profile and prestige of financial journalism in London; it also raised salary levels and improved career prospects. London financial journalism was no longer the small thing it had been in the 1930s, nor the growing but consensual entity of the 1960s. By the 1990s London financial journalists felt that they were an élite group within journalism, close to the centre of both finance and policy. London financial journalism had a voice in the world; it had long since left behind any inhibitions over criticizing the incumbent British government.

III

The British national newspapers in 1994 employed about 200 financial journalists and sub-editors; this excluded a similar number on the *Financial Times*, who tend to be so specialized (into particular markets, commodities, or countries) that many of them disclaimed the label of 'financial' journalist. Other newspapers also had their peculiarities and their own definitions, but there were four main categories of financial journalism:

Traditional 'City' journalism continued to focus on the stock market and share tipping; related to this are the lists of prices, not only for shares but for government bonds, Unit Trusts, and so on; the stronger papers charge for the inclusion of prices which become 'half reader service, half advertising medium'. Senior financial journalists glance enviously at these numerous columns of small figures, in much the same way that sports editors barely tolerate the horse-racing cards. Most papers acquire the market prices in pre-baked form, provided electronically by one of several outside agencies.

Economics and economic policy is another key field; this is the newspaper giving its advice and criticism on Treasury and Bank of England policies for the economy, interest rates, and so on. On the upmarket papers this is a prestigious field. The economic advice is typically offered by some combination of an economics editor, an economics columnist, and the editor in charge of the financial pages (variously called City, business, or financial editor).

Industry and business coverage is aimed at people in business, especially senior and middle managers, but also at anyone else who may be interested in business. In some publications there is a deliberate focus on smaller businesses and the tone can become quite populist and opposed to big banks and big government.

Personal finance is the final main sub-field and the one which has expanded the most in recent years. Often it is a completely separate weekend section, or a midweek pull-out section. The personal finance section tends to operate along the lines of other separate sections; typically it is run by only two or three full-time journalists who farm out much of the work to freelance specialists in particular subjects (real estate, pensions, Unit Trusts, mortgages). A high proportion of personal finance journalists are women. The orientation is overwhelmingly towards the reader-as-consumer.

Financial journalism is, of course, primarily an upmarket and midmarket phenomenon. *Financial Times* journalists regard the *Daily Telegraph* as their strongest competitor. The *Daily Telegraph* operation has maintained its traditional closeness to the City as well as retaining its separate office there. In 1994 there were twenty-five writing financial journalists in this office, separated from ten financial sub-editors in the main office at Canary Wharf.

The Times business news has been through many changes of direction in recent decades; in 1994 its new business editor represented two revolutions—she was a woman and moreover from personal finance journalism. The *Independent*'s 1994 financial operation still reflected the fact that the paper had been established by a *Daily Telegraph* financial journalist. The *Guardian*'s financial news differed from the other daily upmarkets in several respects. Uniquely the *Guardian* contained almost no advertising specifically on its financial pages; however, this left it free to provide a range of British, European, and American financial coverage not found in the other eight upmarket papers. The upmarket Sundays all carry substantial amounts of business news; the *Sunday Times* has maintained its industry/management focus (with some additional 'City' coverage) to remain the clear leader.

Among the midmarket papers the three Associated titles have been outstandingly successful. The *Evening Standard* has developed an influential pull-out financial section. The *Daily Mail* has maintained its midmarket daily leadership; Andrew Alexander has adopted the idiosyncratic columnist approach to finance, greatly helped by his previous success as a Parliamentary sketch writer. The *Mail on Sunday*'s financial pages blossomed in 1994 and were then generating £300,000 of advertising each Sunday.

The downmarket papers have also maintained modest financial news efforts. In 1994–5 Isabelle Murray was single-handedly running the *Sun*'s daily Money page. 'We like companies being profitable, but we temper it with how they treat their workers and customers,' she said.

'I lunch for a living' said one City editor, describing the previous day's lunch with the four top people in one of Britain's largest companies. There are many industrial companies, and many senior people in business and finance who want to influence senior financial journalists. One Sunday financial editor said:

I have three business lunches—Tuesday, Wednesday and Thursday each week; and two business dinners. And I'm booked out for the next three months. One day recently began with 7.30 breakfast at Simpson's; then 1.00 p.m. lunch at the Savoy, and dinner at the Ritz. I stayed on and won £1,000 in the Casino, arriving home at 3 a.m. My wife said: 'You do this for a living?'

A common upmarket Sunday practice is to invite about four senior people to lunch—including a banker, a stockbroker, and a businessman. One Sunday does this each fortnight, another Sunday does it each week.

Many meetings are routine—'we lunch about twice a year'. But other meetings are focused onto take-overs or other special happenings. There are the usual big differences between daily and Sunday journalism. The daily financial journalists are confronted by pre-arranged events—company results, government financial numbers, product announcements. The Sunday financial journalists are hunting for stories which will still be fresh at the end of the week.

'Teenage scribblers' are quite numerous in financial journalism. A common career path is for a graduate to start work with a financial weekly, like the *Investors Chronicle*, or a trade publication with a financial emphasis. By age 28 the journalist can already have reached the middle levels of financial journalism and the higher levels of journalism salaries. By now the personal phone book is bulging with the phone numbers of very senior people in business.

The more senior financial journalists have been lunching, dining, breakfasting, and gossiping with and writing about senior business people for twenty or thirty years. Their knowledge of business people is now very extensive: 'I know personally at least one director of each of the top one hundred companies'. They not only know numerous present directors, but they know scores of ex-directors and former employees: 'Recent ex-employees are often very talkative.' Such senior financial journalists have lunched and dined not just with the present Chancellor of the Exchequer, but with his half-dozen predecessors as well; they not only remember Nigel Lawson as Chancellor in 1983–9, they had known him since before 1974, when he was first elected to Parliament.

V

The power of financial journalism can be illustrated with three examples—the financial public relations business, exchange rate movements, and exchange rate policy. Financial public relations has been one of the City of London's fast-growing specialist services in recent years. Public relations companies, employed in major contested take-over battles, can be paid up to one million pounds for ten weeks' work.[10] This, of course, is a small sum compared with the size of a major take-over bid; but since there are only about ten individual journalists who 'vote' on the bid on behalf of the ten main publications read in the City, this seems to put a high value on trying to persuade each one of these ten journalists.

A more dramatic example of financial journalism's power is its potential ability to influence or upset the delicate balance between exchange rates and interest rates. Nigel Lawson blames a big 1985 increase in UK interest rates on stories which appeared in the financial press in general and especially in the *Sunday Times* which,

[10] Jeff Randall, 'PR Power: myth or reality'. *Sunday Times* Business News, 18 Sept. 1994.

says Lawson (the former *FT* and *Sunday Telegraph* financial journalist), is 'a paper to which the business world tends to pay exaggerated attention'. Lawson calls this episode 'The Ingham run on the pound'; he claims that Bernard Ingham unwisely gave a Downing Street press briefing in which he said that the British government would not seek to support the pound sterling even if it fell below a one pound/one dollar parity. As a direct result of this briefing and a *Sunday Times* story on 6 January 1985, UK base rates were raised five days later by 1 per cent; and partly as a result of continuing fall-out from the *Sunday Times* comment, base rates were raised twice more, on 14 and 28 January. Within twenty-two days of the original *Sunday Times* story UK bases rates rose from $9\frac{1}{2}$ per cent to 14 per cent.[11]

This latter example is an extreme case. But it does indicate the spectacular impact of newspaper comment in the short run. It seems highly probable also that newspaper comment influences longer-term, and more carefully considered, exchange rate and interest rate policy-making. We have noted earlier in this chapter that, before the 1967 Wilson–Callaghan devaluation, the press was a dog which did not bark. In the late 1980s and early 1990s the reverse was the case; the financial press barked vigorously on the subjects of British membership of the European Exchange Rate Mechanism (ERM) and a Single European Currency. This press coverage is a complex story which might repay detailed and comprehensive analysis; alongside and linked to this ERM story went the fall of Mrs Thatcher (in 1990) and also the poll decline of John Major (1992–3). Nigel Lawson says that as Chancellor he convened his first serious meeting on joining the ERM in January 1985; from this first Treasury meeting to Norman Lamont's sacking as Chancellor of the Exchequer in 1993 was a period of over eight years. During these years much advice was given to the government by financial journalists and editors. There was certainly extensive support for the policy up to the point of ERM entry in October 1990. Two years later there was fierce criticism of the forced departure from the ERM (September 1992). Then a continuing wave of press criticism was directed against Norman Lamont for the entire eight months between the UK exit from the ERM and Lamont's own exit from the government in May 1993.

The newspapers named the ERM exit day (16 September 1992)

[11] Nigel Lawson, *The View from No. 11* (London: Corgi, 1993), 468–71.

'Black Wednesday'. Financial editors, interviewed by me in summer 1994, were still denouncing the Major–Lamont ERM exit of nearly two years ago. The financial editor of a normally Conservative upmarket newspaper said, 'Nailing their colours to this particular mast has sunk the ship really. . . . They had no other policy than the ERM membership, and then that policy collapsed. This was the single biggest economic policy disaster of the last five, perhaps the last ten, years. . . . The thing to do is to quit on the day . . . but Lamont hung on . . . and he's now a joke figure.' It could be said that the financial journalists—speaking on behalf of the financial community—eventually forced John Major to change his mind and to sack Norman Lamont. Close examination of what the newspapers said over the entire 1985–93 period might indicate that the very newspapers which derided the ERM policy of Major and Lamont had in the late 1980s advocated that same policy. The newspaper financial editors would probably reply that the fatal government error occurred in entering the ERM at too high a rate against the mark and the franc in 1990.

What seems undeniable is that during long years of debating the ERM, as well as the single European currency and related interest rate issues, the newspapers have not only changed their own minds, but they have played an active part in changing the minds of the politicians and the great British public.

VI

Financial journalism has become the senior specialist field within British journalism; and the *Financial Times* has taken over from *The Times* as the leading prestige paper in Britain. No other newspaper can match the *Financial Times*'s overall output in foreign, financial, and political news and comment. But the *FT* has also inherited some negative characteristics which previously belonged to *The Times*. It is still weak in British sales outside the South-East of England. Strong competition from four other upmarket dailies has meant that the *FT*'s British sale expanded very little between 1965 and 1995; nearly all of the increased sale came from the Frankfurt, New York, Tokyo, and subsequent foreign printings. As a financial daily it is a semi-monopoly; and despite its international concerns, the *Financial Times* is rather inward-looking and a trifle smug.

As finance has become more central in British journalism, financial journalists have become editors and also chief executives. One financial journalist became deputy governor of the Bank of England. Sarah Hogg was an experienced financial journalist and editor who became head of John Major's Downing Street policy unit and was described as 'deputy Prime Minister in all but name' by journalists and politicians. Like Samuel Brittan and Peter Jay, Sarah Hogg came from a political family background. Prime Ministers find in such people an unusual combination of financial expertise, political insight, and loyalty, along with the ability to think and write quickly.

Of all these financial journalists who have had an influence on British government policy, the most striking example has been Nigel Lawson. His political career had some unique elements. Having worked on the *Financial Times*, he became the first City editor of the *Sunday Telegraph* when still aged only 29. He told a small lie about his age, claiming to be 30, because he thought Lord Hartwell might find his real age too young.[12] He then became editor of the *Spectator* during 1965–70. Lawson acquired a most unusual view of national politics because he worked as a speech-writer and ideas man for three different Prime Ministers—Harold Macmillan, Alec Douglas-Home, and Edward Heath—before he himself finally became an MP in 1974. Indeed it could be said that Lawson specialized still further in Prime Ministerial communication because when he did become an MP (aged 42) he persisted in asking Parliamentary Questions to Harold Wilson during 1974–6. He also helped Margaret Thatcher with her Questions to Wilson when she was first Conservative leader.[13]

When the Conservatives won the 1979 Election Lawson became part of Sir Geoffrey Howe's Treasury team. Howe subsequently acknowledged that Nigel Lawson was the 'chief draftsman' of 'The Medium Term Financial Strategy'.[14] This was a key 1980 policy document with strong monetarist overtones. With his financial journalism background and his experience in working with no less than four Prime Ministers on their spoken output and as a 'chief draftsman', Nigel Lawson had become a specialist in

[12] Duff Hart-Davis, *The House the Berrys Built: Inside the Telegraph 1928–1986* (London: Coronet, 1991), 278.

[13] Young, *One of Us*, 112.

[14] Lawson, *The View from No. 11*, 66.

political communication in general and in brief statements of economic strategy in particular.

Like most other financial journalists, Lawson was not an economist by academic training (he studied mainly philosophy at Oxford), but he became a journalist who specialized in finance and economics. He nevertheless retained some academic connections (with Nuffield College, Oxford). He also had a highly individual personality. As a young man he wore yellow waistcoats; when editor of the *Spectator* he was still relatively slim and handsome, while his level of self-confidence (or arrogance) was exceptional even by the standards of journalism. During a 1966 interview Lawson emphasized to me the general ignorance of most politicians. When Mrs Thatcher appointed him Chancellor of the Exchequer in 1983 she gave him one piece of advice—to get his hair cut.

Nigel Lawson's book *The View from No. 11* is surely the outstanding British political autobiography of recent years. He was clearly quite right to see himself as possessing abilities, expertise, and writing skills which most Cabinet Ministers lacked. These qualities which Lawson so transparently possessed are quite widespread—if perhaps in slightly smaller doses—among many other financial journalists. These journalists tend to share the Lawson belief in the lowish quality of most politicians. They see themselves as having the normal journalist ability to produce rapidly against a deadline; but they see this ability as being combined with a depth of specialist knowledge and a respect for hard facts, which other journalists do not possess.

Specialization has been one of the key developments of twentieth-century journalism. These financial journalists have become the leading group of British specialist journalists. Several underlying trends have aided the rise of financial journalism—especially the growth of pages and the expansion and deregulation of the City of London. Financial journalism is also well in tune with the trend towards a sharper commercial realism.

But whether or not financial journalism has really overtaken political journalism is perhaps beside the point. Of the four specialist fields we have just looked at three have grown—political, financial, and royal—while foreign correspondence has both grown (upmarket) and shrunk (tabloids). These are all fields in which television is secondary, and in which the newspapers take the lead. While growing in scale, in expertise, and in self-confidence, these specialist fields have all tended to bypass Parliament and to focus on the executive branch of government. Like sports journalism, so also financial, foreign, political, and royal journalism have become bigger; the legislature has become smaller.

Part V
PRIME MINISTER, PRESS, AND MEDIA POLICY

22 Press Monopoly (Press Preservation) Policy

IN recent decades the British Prime Minister has set national media policy and has agreed most media policy initiatives with the national press in advance. This includes policy not only for the press itself, but also for television, radio and the various 'new media'. Media and communications policy is increasingly close to the core of politics, of government, and of the modern economy. Both political scientists and political journalists have largely failed to recognize this important area of Prime Ministerial and press power.

The British tradition has been of No Special Law for the press and only a fairly minimal amount of law for radio and television. That tradition included having media policy scattered around a number of government departments; media policy issues were consequently left to be settled within the Cabinet committee system. This in turn allowed Prime Ministers to control media policy.

The birth and growth of television caused rising anxiety among the powerful owners of the press. Prime Ministers increasingly negotiated with the newspaper owners over all significant television and other media policy issues. Prime Ministers bargained with newspaper owners in anticipation of electoral support; the newspaper owners bargained with the Prime Minister in order to control—or to participate in—the commercial success of television. Two decades of Macmillan–Home–Wilson–Heath–Callaghan (1957–79) saw a gradual evolution of this control of media development by Prime Minister and press. After 1979, in the Thatcher–Major era, this control of media policy acquired greater salience—as the present chapter and the two following chapters will describe.

The present chapter looks at the special monopoly law which applies to the press and which allows the government huge leeway to waive the law and to wave through newspaper mergers of which the Prime Minister approves. The Waive and Wave powers as exercised by Mrs Thatcher allowed for massive press ownership changes in the 1980s. In practice a monopoly law, intended to restrain concentration, was manipulated into a Newspaper Preservation Policy under which preservation in practice meant, not less, but more, concentration of ownership.

The next chapter (23) deals with the British system of 'Self-Regulation' by the Press Council (PC) and its successor the Press Complaints Commission (PCC). In contrast to the elaborate regulation of television and radio output, the self-regulatory arrangements for the press amount to a fig-leaf system which covers only a tiny fraction of the whole body of newspaper output. This delightfully muddled voluntary system also conceals the underlying reality that both the Prime Minister and the newspapers prefer it this way. The press can always make a small tactical retreat but remains entirely free of any formal press regulation. The Prime Minister avoids the press animosity which any formal regulation would generate, and meanwhile retains some residual press goodwill and leeway for tacit bargains with the newspapers over politically and electorally more salient issues.

Chapter 24 describes how broadcasting policy is made by the Prime Minister in consultation with the newspapers. In a long-drawn-out transformation of public service broadcasting into a more market-driven broadcasting system, legislative and regulatory decisions are crucial to the success or failure of companies, channels, and technologies. Such decisions are also extremely important to newspapers. The newspapers deploy key powers in these policy areas. The technical details are complex and boring, and it is in the newspapers that the broadcasting policy debate takes place. The newspapers are 'close to' politicians and are also able to ensure that their own commercial interests are not forgotten.

Newspapers also have another power—the power of personal and corporate vilification. Newspapers can easily focus negative attention on the current Director-General of the BBC, or upon the high command of the Independent Television Commission, or upon particular Members of Parliament who criticize the press. An individual editor may merely run the occasional editorial critique, and encourage a 'good story' about a high-profile broadcasting personality. Once a news story is running, an individual editor cannot stop it; competition ensures that several papers continue to follow the story. But this is little consolation to the targeted individual who within one week may be attacked in scores of separate hostile newspaper stories, editorials, letters, and follow-up gossip, columnist, and feature items. Most people who experience this kind of massive vilification do not easily forget it. Moreover, it is not merely the vilified public figure who is reminded that the teeth of the press are sharp; such attacks are a warning to other broadcast executives, and other politicians.

Media policy in Britain has a peculiar Through The Looking Glass quality. A newspaper monopoly policy, supposedly intended to limit concentration, actually works to increase concentration. A self-regulation policy, supposedly intended to protect the public, in fact protects the press. A broadcasting policy, supposedly intended to maintain British broadcasting as politically neutral and commercially independent, effectively gives newspaper interests a policy veto.

While the informal power realities are so different from the supposed policy intentions, there are some consequences unintended at either level. One unintended consequence of prevailing policies has been to encourage sensational-journalism 'excesses' as well as the 'excesses' of negative political coverage. This happens because a 'monopoly' policy which is in reality a 'preservation policy' effectively increases the number of surviving titles, heightens competition, and thus preserves the editorial excess which goes with excessive commercial competition.

I

During the thirty-four post-war years up to the beginning of Mrs Thatcher's premiership (1945–79), formal British policy towards the press took two main forms—a series of committees (grandly called Royal Commissions) on the press and some special press provisions in the anti-monopoly law. Although Conservative Prime Ministers were also involved, it was Harold Wilson during 1964–70 who first saw the possibility of using newspaper anti-monopoly policy as a potential means of gaining newspaper electoral support.

None of the three Royal Commissions on the Press (1949, 1962,

1977) had a lot to say in terms of policy. The main consequences were the minimalist system of self-regulation, initially the Press Council (next chapter), and a minimalist system of anti-monopoly provisions. All three Royal Commissions were used by the incumbent Prime Minister as a neutral mechanism for dealing with a politically delicate issue. In each case the Prime Minister also undoubtedly saw the setting up of a Royal Commission on the Press as a convenient way of warning the newspapers to be on their best (or better) behaviour. Clement Attlee established the Ross Royal Commission on the Press, which concluded in 1949 that there was no undue concentration of newspaper ownership.[1]

Newspaper monopoly or concentration was the central focus which Harold Macmillan had in mind when he set up the Shawcross Royal Commission in 1961. But he only set up this Commission after two major concentrations had already taken place—the *News Chronicle* and the *Star* (London evening) had been closed down and Daily Mirror Newspapers had acquired the *Daily Herald*, the *People*, and the rest of Odham's. Macmillan had done nothing about these events; he argued that he had no powers to intervene, but of course he could have threatened legislation to unscramble the Mirror-Herald merger. He may have anticipated political danger in 'interfering' in the affairs of the two main pro-Labour dailies. He also ignored the Shawcross Royal Commission's 1962 report which called for some anti-monopoly measures.

It was thus left to Harold Wilson to enact in 1965 the first legislation to modify the lengthy British tradition of No Special Law for the press in peacetime. The special press provision was a small part of a general piece of monopoly legislation; the 1965 law was passed at a time of high political excitement—between the two General Elections of 1964 and 1966.

The special press provisions in the Monopolies and Mergers Act 1965 were broadly consensual in that they accepted the general approach of the Macmillan-appointed (Shawcross) Royal Commission on the Press of 1961–2. That Commission had wanted a special Press Amalgamations Court, whereas the 1965 Act did not establish any such special procedure. However, the Act did require that

---

[1] Sir William Ross (chairman), *Royal Commission on the Press 1947–1949 Report* (London: HMSO, 1949).

substantial proposed purchases of one press group by another should be referred to the Monopolies Commission. The law also broadly accepted the Royal Commission's size threshold; if after the merger the resulting group would have a circulation above 500,000 copies per day then the reference should take place. However, the Wilson government chose to ignore the Royal Commission's expressed wish to immunize press merger decisions from party political concerns. The Shawcross Commission had said:

> The question whether a specific transaction should or should not be allowed to take place is, in our opinion, essentially a matter which should not be under the direct control of Parliament or the subject of party political considerations; it should be kept entirely free of Government responsibility or political association.[2]

Harold Wilson as Prime Minister and the former journalist Douglas Jay, as the relevant senior (Trade) Minister, chose to ignore this last piece of advice. The 1965 Act stated that if the Board of Trade was satisfied that the newspaper to be acquired was 'not economic as a going concern' and as a separate newspaper, then the Trade Minister could give immediate approval to the merger, without a report from the Monopolies Commission. This deliberately vague wording was obviously designed to allow Harold Wilson to interfere in newspaper merger cases in the interest of preserving Labour Party support and discouraging enemies of the Labour Party.

In practice, during some eleven years of Labour government between 1964 and 1979, the incumbent Labour Prime Minister could not rely on a steady supply of Labour supporters eager to purchase newspapers. Instead Wilson seems usually to have broadly encouraged the leading contender—in the hope of implanting some residual sense of gratitude during the next General Election. A broad consensus over British press policy and newspaper mergers was evident in the first big merger case after the passage of the 1965 Act. This was the 1966–7 acquisition by Lord (Roy) Thomson of *The Times*. The case was referred to the Monopolies Commission because Thomson was already a substantial newspaper owner (although without, as yet, a national daily).

[2] Lord Shawcross (chairman), *Royal Commission on the Press, 1961–1962 Report* (London: HMSO, 1962), 107.

The Monopolies Commission duly reported in favour of *The Times* going to Thomson. A broad consensus of support for Thomson was manifest in the House of Commons Debate (7 February 1967);[3] Douglas Jay for Labour and Edward Heath for the Conservatives agreed with each other in almost all respects. There was an even more consensual tone to the relevant House of Lords Debate (25 January 1967). Lord Thomson himself spoke in that debate and there was a strong element of Thomson being fêted by the establishment and accepted as a new member of the club of national daily newspaper owners.[4] Harold Wilson was deeply involved in all of this; before they gave evidence to the Monopolies Commission, Lord Thomson and Denis Hamilton spent a weekend with Harold Wilson at Chequers.[5] But only one year later, Harold Wilson was complaining to Denis Hamilton, as Cecil King records:

Denis Hamilton came to lunch today. Apparently Wilson thought that having given some small assistance to get *The Times–Sunday Times* merger through the Monopolies Commission, he would have the paper in his pocket. Anyway, soon after the merger he had Denis to lunch and specified by name four members of *The Times* staff who were to be dismissed. . . . He didn't apparently realize that no newspaper director could possibly accede to such demands.[6]

Although Harold Wilson seems to have gained little through the Monopolies Commission mechanism in the case of *The Times*, he was more successful in maintaining political support in decisions shortly before the General Election of June 1970.

The *News of the World*, as Rupert Murdoch's first British newspaper purchase (in 1969), required no Monopolies Commission approval, but from Harold Wilson's point of view almost any new owner would have been preferable to the previous owner and his far-right political views. Rupert Murdoch's second British newspaper acquisition—of the *Sun*—also occurred in 1969 and it was a much more politically sensitive case. The International Publishing Corporation (IPC) had relaunched the old *Daily Herald* as the *Sun* (1964) but had honoured the *Herald*'s loyalty to Labour Party and Trades Union Congress policy. By 1969 IPC itself was encountering severe financial and management problems and was keen to be

---

[3] House of Commons, *Official Report*, 8 Feb. 1967.
[4] House of Lords, *Official Report*, 25 Jan. 1967.
[5] Denis Hamilton, *Editor-in-Chief* (London: Hamish Hamilton, 1989), 135.
[6] *The Cecil King Diary, 1965–1970* (London: Jonathan Cape, 1972), 145.

rid of the *Sun* and its losses. With the 1970 General Election looming, the Labour Party and Harold Wilson were keen to retain the *Sun*'s support and thus initially favoured the Labour MP Robert Maxwell as the new owner. However, the Maxwell solution—despite the support of Wilson and Cudlipp—itself ran into severe difficulties. After four months of delay during summer 1969, the printing union SOGAT lost patience with Maxwell and withdrew its support. Ten weeks later Rupert Murdoch printed the *Sun* for the first time on his *News of the World* presses. While he had given undertakings to IPC and to the trade unions, he had not been submitted to investigation by the Monopolies Commission. Harold Wilson had decided to use the get-out clause, which said that a commercially failing paper did not need to be referred to the Commission. The Labour Party in the long run deeply regretted allowing Murdoch to acquire the *Sun*; but in the short run it was not a political mistake, because the *Sun* supported Labour at the 1970 election.

Just before the 1970 election, Harold Wilson was involved in yet another newspaper purchase which did not go to the Monopolies Commission. This was the acquisition in early 1970 by Reed of the whole of IPC, including the Labour Party's main press supporters, the *Daily Mirror*, *Sunday Mirror* and the *People*. In this case Harold Wilson—as Labour Prime Minister facing an election—was again dealing with a seller (Hugh Cudlipp) whom he knew well as a long-term pro-Labour propagandist. Wilson also seems to have trusted Don Ryder, the chief executive of Reed, under whom the *Daily Mirror* and the two Sundays did indeed continue to support Labour.

II

When Harold Wilson resigned as Prime Minister in 1976 he had effectively changed the Press Monopoly law into a policy of newspaper preservation; this change had broad consensual support. During the first eleven years of the new law (1965–76) some larger mergers were discouraged; numerous mergers of weekly papers were allowed to take place. *The Times* was preserved in Thomson ownership; both the *Sun* and the *Daily Mirror* were also preserved with—at least initially—their Labour support still intact. There had been some minor tightening up of the monopoly arrangements

Table 22.1. The Monopolies and Mergers Commission and examples of proposed newspaper mergers and acquisitions

Date	Publications	Seller	Buyer	Decision of Monopolies Commission	Report number	Final outcome
1966–7	*The Times*	Astor	Thomson	Approved	(36)	Took place
1969	*Sun*	IPC	Murdoch	Not referred		Took place
1970	*Daily Mirror Sunday Mirror People*	IPC	Reed	Not referred		Took place
1976	*Observer*	David Astor	Arco	Not referred		Took place
1977	*Daily Express Sunday Express*	Beaverbrook	Trafalgar House	Not referred		Took place
1981	*The Times Sunday Times*	Thomson	Murdoch	Not referred		Took place
1981	*Observer*	Arco	Lonrho	Approved	(139)	Took place
1984	*Daily Mirror Sunday Mirror People*	Reed	Maxwell	Not referred		Took place
1985	*Daily Express Sunday Express*	Trafalgar/Fleet	United	Approved	(190)	Took place
1986	*Daily Telegraph Sunday Telegraph*	Hartwell	Black	Not referred		Took place
1987	*Today*	Lonrho	Murdoch	Not referred		Took place
1990	*Bristol Evening News Western Daily Press*	Lonrho	Sullivan	Refused	(274)	Did not take place
1993	*Observer*	Lonrho	Guardian	Not referred		Took place
1994	*Independent, Independent on Sunday*	Newspaper Publishing	Mirror & Irish Independent	Not referred		Took place
1994	*Nottingham Evening Post*	B. Forman	Mail	Refused	(358)	Took place; govt. rejected report

in the Fair Trading Act of 1973 and the McGregor Royal Commission on the Press in 1977 asked for some additional minor tightening up.[7] The Royal Commission Report of 1977 serves as a summary of a consensual period; the fudging of an anti-monopoly policy into a preservation policy had broad consensual support.

The 1979 election marked a switch into a much more activist and politically partisan newspaper preservation policy. Margaret Thatcher rejected Harold Wilson's low-profile style of personal Prime Ministerial intervention in newspaper merger and monopoly issues. In 1981 she supported Rupert Murdoch's purchase of Times Newspapers and accepted his transparent fiction that both *The Times* and *Sunday Times* were loss-making newspapers in danger of dying which therefore should not be referred to the Monopolies Commission. The most unusual feature of this event was the use of misleading figures to suggest that the highly profitable *Sunday Times* was close to death. Gordon Brunton, chief executive of Thomson British Holdings, announced on 12 October 1980 that Thomson was selling *The Times* and *Sunday Times*. On 22 January 1981 (three months after the initial announcement) Thomson and Murdoch jointly announced that Murdoch was the purchaser. There still remained the issue of a reference to the Monopolies Commission. Murdoch was determined to resist such a reference—because the Monopolies Commission might well have found several grounds on which to oppose the purchase.

Rupert Murdoch had from 1969 onwards had social contact with current British Prime Ministers, including both Harold Wilson and Edward Heath. Mrs Thatcher had met Murdoch before she received the support of the *Sun* during her winning election campaign of 1979.[8] Soon after the 22 January 1981 announcement it became clear that Mrs Thatcher was not going to refer the merger to the Monopolies Commission. The first Thatcher argument was that the Thomson 'absolute deadline' of mid-March left only seven weeks, less than the time required for a Monopolies Commission investigation. The second argument was that neither *The Times* nor the *Sunday Times* was a 'going concern'; both were losing money and in danger of imminent closure. The Thatcher argument that the *Sunday Times* was losing money rested entirely on its financial performance during the one year of 1980. This year of 1980 had

[7] O. R. McGregor (chairman), *Royal Commission on the Press: Final Report* (London: HMSO, 1977), 127–40.
[8] Larry Lamb, *Sunrise* (London: Macmillan, 1989), 154–8.

been a unique year because it followed the fifty-week shutdown of Times Newspapers—caused by the industrial dispute about new technology—a shutdown which had ended on 17 November 1979. During 1980 the Thomson management had successfully rebuilt the circulation of both *The Times* and *Sunday Times*; but naturally the initial shortfall in revenue and the heavy expenditure on promotion made for substantial losses by Times Newspapers in the one unique year of 1980.

This 1981 use of the get-out clause to deny a reference to the Monopolies Commission is the most remarkable single example of how the government of the day was able to use the vague wording of the monopoly law for its own political purposes. Important in this Thatcher–Murdoch collusion was the general acquiescence of much of the rest of the press and of the trade unions. Even the journalists on the two newspapers failed to follow through on their intention to take the issue to court.[9]

This case was important in itself. But it was also the first of a series of 1980s newspaper ownership changes, which redrew British newspaper ownership and showed how determined newspaper buyers and a determined Prime Minister could combine together. In this *Times–Sunday Times* case we can see the interaction of several timetables. The first timetable was that of the Thomson executives who, through Gordon Brunton, laid down an arbitrary sale period of six months. A second timetable was that of Mrs Thatcher and her government; the two newspapers changed ownership in early 1981 at a time of government unpopularity, with an election likely to occur in 1983. Naturally it would help to have *The Times* and *Sunday Times* in politically friendly hands. While the Thomson clock began running, Rupert Murdoch initially held back. This deliberate delay enabled Murdoch then to argue that the Thomson deadline did not leave time for a three-month Monopolies Commission investigation.

By now there was a media consensus that preservation of the two titles was essential. The other major newspaper groups all (publicly at least) favoured preservation, although none of the groups had the financial confidence during the bad economic times of 1980–1 itself to launch a determined bid. In the absence of other determined bidders Rupert Murdoch quickly had not only the active support of

---

[9] Harold Evans, who was editor of the *Sunday Times*, subsequently argued that already by the end of 1980 his paper was returning to its normal profitable ways. See Harold Evans, *Good Times, Bad Times* (London: Coronet, 1984), 185–99.

the government, the Thomson management, and the printing unions, but also the passive support of the other newspaper owners. The Labour Opposition in Parliament were torn between supporting the unions and worrying over the political and electoral consequences of *The Times* and *Sunday Times* moving from a pattern of group neutrality and editorial autonomy into the Conservative fold. The only group whose antagonism seriously worried Murdoch were the journalists. The notion of some kind of journalists' co-operative ownership, or journalist-supported management buyout, was popular amongst the journalists on both newspapers. But Rupert Murdoch had by 1980–1 very extensive previous experience of these take-over situations and separate initiatives by the two editors meant that he scarcely needed to adopt divide and rule tactics against the journalists. Murdoch 'reluctantly' made some fresh undertakings and concessions to the journalists, knowing from extensive experience that such undertakings had little or no long-term significance.

In 1987 *Today* became (News International's and) Rupert Murdoch's third British national daily newspaper, and again there was no reference to the Monopolies Commission. Mrs Thatcher's Ministers again quoted the familiar get-out clause to the effect that *Today* was not a 'going concern'. In the ensuing Commons debate the Conservative MP, Jonathan Aitken, pointed out that each of three contenders had in fact been bidding around £38 million for *Today*:

I think that the activities of these three dinosaurs of iron whim show only too clearly that a paper that was worth £38 million to three tycoons is a going concern. . . . Mr Murdoch is well experienced in setting menacing artificial deadlines in stand-and-deliver Ned Kelly fashion. . . . I think that had his bluff been called . . . there would have been a delay of several weeks—perhaps three months—which would have knocked £3 million or £4 million off the price of *Today*.[10]

This 1987 use of the get-out clause was the most blatant to date. Murdoch was, after all, acquiring—without any monopoly scrutiny—his third national daily newspaper. The seller, Tiny Rowland (of Lonrho), and the buyer, Rupert Murdoch (of News), had given the British government just one day in which to accept the decision without a Monopolies Commission reference. The *Independent* described this ultimatum as 'effrontery', while the

---

[10] House of Commons, *Parliamentary Debates*, 6 July 1987, col. 37.

Financial Times called for a Monopolies Commission reference which 'almost certainly' would not have led to the closure of *Today*. The chairman and the director of the Press Council together concluded that the government's failure to refer the issue 'signals that newspaper buyers and sellers need not have a Monopolies Commission inquiry if they do not want one'.

III

A new Department of National Heritage was created by John Major after his 1992 General Election victory. The new department was given a number of strands of media policy, but cynical journalists were soon saying that DNH stood for Department of Nothing Happening.

John Major's government continued to agree media policy decisions with its friends in the press. An exceptionally transparent example of this occurred when in 1994 the government overruled a Monopolies Commission decision against the Daily Mail group's purchase of the evening newspaper in Nottingham. The Monopolies Commission unanimously disapproved of the proposed purchase, because the family-owned *Nottingham Evening Post* would link up two other groups of Daily Mail/Northcliffe evening papers to create an overall grouping of eight contiguous evening newspapers. The purchase of the Nottingham paper would complete a grouping of eight local monopoly daily newspapers together covering 8,000 square miles and inhabited by 4.75 million people.

The Daily Mail and General Trust already owned the big Northcliffe group of regional dailies, as well as the London *Evening Standard* and 54 per cent of Bristol United Press. After the proposed merger the Daily Mail company would control 25 per cent of all non-national daily newspaper sales in Britain—in addition to the national newspapers. The Monopolies Commission could find no reasons for making an exception to the normal monopoly prohibitions; the Commission was worried about the lack of separate editorial voices, the threat to competing local weeklies, and the high profit targets which would result from the very high price being paid.[11]

---

[11] Monopolies and Mergers Commission, *Daily Mail and General Trust plc and T. Bailey Forman Limited* (London: HMSO, 1994).

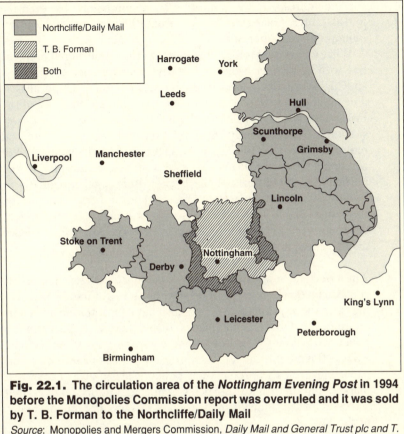

Fig. 22.1. The circulation area of the *Nottingham Evening Post* in 1994 before the Monopolies Commission report was overruled and it was sold by T. B. Forman to the Northcliffe/Daily Mail

Source: Monopolies and Mergers Commission, *Daily Mail and General Trust plc and T. Bailey Forman Limited* (London: HMSO, 1994), 7.

In the history of Monopolies Commission reports on proposed newspaper mergers this report was unusual in opposing the merger, and doubly unusual in rejecting the merger proposal so emphatically. Why then did the Major government overrule the unanimous 'Against the Public Interest' finding of the Monopolies Commission? The inescapable reason was that the Daily Mail executives made a very persuasive argument at a time when the Mail national titles were being editorially critical of the Major government.

The other national newspapers did not, of course, ignore this press policy saga, but they did give it fairly low-profile news coverage. The other national newspaper groups had their own rather specific interests in the application of the monopoly law; even the left-of-centre Guardian Media Group had its profitable local monopoly press interests.

What we see here is a combination of Prime Ministerial prerogative with newspaper owner prerogative which has led to special—and highly flexible—legal rules for major newspaper purchases. The chief executive of a selling company will be well aware of the Prime Minister's key informal powers in newspaper take-over situations. Consequently the chief executive will make informal inquiries with relevant Trade Ministers and/or Downing Street personnel as to the Prime Minister's probable attitude. In the normal run of political life the Prime Minister talks regularly to friendly newspaper owners and editors both in person and on the telephone. Given that they already know each other, not a great deal may need to be said. In some cases Prime Ministerial silence may be enough.

The effective newspaper preservation policy has two important consequences which have not been widely noted. First, by preserving titles the *de facto* policy heightens both concentration and competition. It led to larger companies (than a strict anti-concentration policy would allow), including one company with three national dailies. But by putting such emphasis on the avoidance of newspaper closures, the preservation policy leads to an overcrowded market. This in turn leads to belligerent competition and its related 'excesses' of sensationalism, invasion of privacy, and the royal hunt of the *Sun*.

A second unintended consequence of the effective newspaper preservation policy is to favour a certain type of management, namely the mogul or owner-operator. The newspaper preservation dance—high-tempo negotiations with government, unions, and seller, while making tactical concessions—is a dance best attuned to a single surefooted entrepreneur, and not by a top-heavy conventional public company. The preservation policy in practice is a policy for preserving not just existing newspapers but also for preserving and encouraging the newspaper mogul.

23 Token Self-regulation

THAT Something Must Be Done about the editorial excesses of British national newspapers has been widely perceived as a truism. The main something that has been done about newspaper sensationalism and editorial excess has been a system of voluntary 'self-regulation'—a Press Complaints Commission (previously a Press Council) which looks at specific complaints and issues adjudications on them. This system of self-regulation, however, is of no more than token proportions because the politicians cannot get the newspapers to agree to more than a minimal or token system of voluntary self-restraint. Why do the politicians in power not insist on a stronger compulsory system? Because the politicians in power fear antagonizing the newspapers.

Each nation has its own idiosyncratic approach to newspaper regulation and the full complexities are often hard for the native citizens—let alone foreigners—fully to grasp. But one reliable generalization is that most daily newspapers in Europe, North America, and elsewhere are regional and local dailies which enjoy monopoly or semi-monopoly situations; these favourable market conditions encourage the newspaper to appeal across a broad range of local interests. The very facts of localism and monopoly favour constraint. The other main type of newspaper is the élite or prestige newspaper, usually based in the national capital or a regional or state capital. This type of newspaper exercises self-constraint as part of its élite/prestige character. But Britain's national newspapers belong to neither of these two categories; they are subject to the constraints neither of local monopoly nor of being unique élite national publications.

Britain is unusual in the extent to which its audio-visual media are regulated and its press is unregulated. At least five separate legally constituted bodies regulate British TV, radio, and films; but only one voluntary body operates in the press. Britain is of course also unusual or unique in the degree of polarization between its upmarket and its downmarket national newspapers; any comprehensive system of content regulation has to encompass both the *News of the World* and the *Financial Times*.

Self-regulation can be effective especially if its voluntary character is supported by elements of compulsion; the Advertising Standards Authority (ASA) is a self-censorship body for print advertising which has impact because all publications agree in advance to accept all ASA decisions. But pre-publication censorship of news is not acceptable. Nevertheless self-regulation of British editorial content did operate with some success in the 1960s; it worked effectively then for the same reason that the ASA works now, because the Press Council in the 1960s had the full and effective support of the newspaper owners. But in the more competitive subsequent decades, that support was no longer there. Also relevant were broad changes in society, in sexual behaviour, and so on, from the 1960s onwards. It could be said that the British public became less socially deferential and less sexually inhibited, while it retained elements of puritanism and voyeurism.

The voluntary self-regulation approach has, of course, operated against the background Anglo-Saxon preference for 'No Special Press Law'. But the Press Council represented a quasi-legal approach, which has drawn on what looked like relevant legal parallels, in this case the law of libel and defamation. Consequently self-regulation shares with the libel law the fallacy that a simple adjudication—Smith is right, the *Daily Excess* is wrong—can be satisfactory. Self-regulation has also shared with libel law the added disadvantage that the complainant has to undergo a complex procedure before (perhaps) 'winning' an adjudication.

The voluntary self-regulation system seems to make further false assumptions. It assumes that a few scores of adjudications each year can exercise a significant influence over the millions (probably about 15 millions) of separate stories which appear in British newspapers and magazines each year. The self-regulation system also assumes that the sins of the press are sins of commission—there are no reprimands for events, persons, and countries which are not reported. The focus is always on single stories—on the legal analogy—not on the whole output of a newspaper or of a particular journalist.

Many politicians have observed British press self-regulation in action and have found it to be inadequate. Something More Needs To Be Done has been a common view among politicians. A 1994 survey of 216 MPs found that a majority favoured a statutory press regulatory body (55 per cent) and an ombudsman with statutory powers (68 per cent) while 71 per cent rated the existing Press Complaints Commission as either 'poor' or 'very poor'.[1] Between 1961 and 1989 Private Members' Bills on Privacy were introduced on six separate occasions. One of these Bills, introduced by John Browne (MP for Winchester, 1979–92) helped to trigger the renewed debate on press performance after 1989. Browne himself pointed out that the top politicians were less enthusiastic about privacy legislation than were back-bench MPs and other Ministers:

> The privacy Bill I introduced in the House of Commons in 1988 received overwhelming support from MPs of all parties and was discussed in detail for three days in committee. It was then killed by the Government although the cabinet committee on the Bill had previously voted 9 to 2 in its favour. The two dissenting votes of those ministers, ultimately responsible for enactment and operation, reflected a certain fear of being 'picked off' individually by the press.
>
> The fact is that our ministers are afraid to introduce a privacy Bill to protect the basic human rights of the individual to privacy. Looking at the parliamentary demise of those MPs who have introduced such Bills and to the ministerial resignation of David Mellor, who threatened a Bill, may illustrate a justifiable fear by ministers of a press that can bring about the political downfall of anyone who annoys it or threatens its vast earnings. . . .
>
> We have a government afraid of the media, so afraid that it refuses to offer the public the legal protection it seeks.[2]

Personal fear of the press by top politicians is clearly of crucial importance. But there are other problems about privacy legislation. One argument is that existing legislation already protects most relevant forms of privacy; and most complaints from the general public are about accuracy, not privacy. Moreover, the state and the intelligence services—not the newspapers—are responsible for most bugging and phone-tapping. As William Rees-Mogg observes, the state engages in bugging on an industrial scale; and it appears to have been the intelligence services that bugged the phones of various members of the royal family.[3] This embarrassing issue would arise for discussion in the legislative passage of any general legislation on privacy.

[1] 'MPs support control of the press', *UK Press Gazette*, 10 Oct. 1994
[2] Letter from John Browne published in the *Independent*, 16 Jan. 1993.
[3] William Rees-Mogg, 'The Paparazzi are preferable', *The Times*, 11 Jan. 1993.

Perhaps the key political reality here is that a normally divided newspapers press is united in saying 'No Press Law'; meanwhile the politicians are divided—many politicians favour punitive measures whereas the incumbent Prime Minister and key senior colleagues are wary of enraging the press dogs.

I

While Lord Devlin was its chairman, during 1964–9, the Press Council was seen by everyone—including editors and politicians—as a success. These years in the mid and late 1960s were the Press Council's golden era. It was three decades earlier, in 1938, that Political and Economic Planning's report, *The British Press* had said: 'much of the Press intrusion on private grief, of which there are periodic complaints in Parliament and elsewhere, is due to the idea of news values insisted on by certain editorial executives, who drive their staff to perform tasks which must be repellent.' In 1937 the Home Secretary consulted the press industry on this issue; all of the main organizations of newspaper owners, of editors, and of journalists at their annual meetings that year passed resolutions decrying press intrusion into privacy and grief.

The PEP Report had called for a Press Tribunal with a lay chairman (an eminent lawyer or public person), which would consider cases of intrusion and other complaints against the press; its case decisions would lead to a working code. PEP also called for a Press Institute to conduct research; and PEP was very concerned about the low levels of education and training in journalism.[4] The 1947–9 Royal Commission on the Press was familiar with the PEP recommendations. The Royal Commission, in collecting evidence, was aware of a confusing multiplicity of organizations of owners, editors, journalists, printers, and other employees. The Commission saw the General Council of the Press as the future focal point of a fragmented industry:

It is remarkable that although a number of organisations exist to represent sectional interests within the Press there is none representing the Press as a whole. . . . Indeed, the Press has taken fewer steps to safeguard

---

[4] Political and Economic Planning, *The British Press* (London: PEP, 1938), 113, 161–2, 171–2.

its standards of performance than perhaps any other institution of comparable importance. . . .

There are two problems of outstanding importance to the quality of the Press which we consider that a General Council could usefully study: the problem of recruitment and training and the problem of formulating and making effective high standards of professional conduct.[5]

The response of the press to this ringing call was reluctant, footdragging, and minimalist. Eventually, for fear of something worse (legislation), the press adopted the Press Council idea but in a watered-down form without any lay, non-press, membership. While claiming to represent the public interest, the Press Council was fairly transparently a defender of the press interest. Press reluctance and footdragging meant that four full years elapsed between the June 1949 Royal Commission proposals and the July 1953 birth of the Press Council. Press representatives filled all the membership positions; the first three chairmen (1953–64) were all press representatives. Even this press-only Press Council was adopted after complaints from Parliament; a Labour MP's private member's bill finally persuaded the press to adopt a version of self-regulation.

In its very first case the Press Council sided with royalty against the tabloid press—the Council sided with Princess Margaret and reprimanded the *Daily Mirror* for asking its readers to vote for or against the Princess marrying Group Captain Peter Townsend. The early Press Council handled remarkably few cases; in the politically explosive years of 1956–7 the annual report detailed only ten adjudications. One of the ten cases concerned a freelance journalist who tried to attend the Duke of Kent's 21st birthday party without an invitation. In another case the *Daily Telegraph* was condemned for breaking an embargo. In the glorious annals of press history, this was small-time stuff.

The second Royal Commission (chaired in 1961–2 by Lord Shawcross) criticized the Press Council for failing to engage in the wide range of activities envisaged by the previous Royal Commission; the Press Council had not looked at monopoly, it had not scrutinized ownership, it had ignored advertising and journalist training. The Council still had no lay members, and concentrated almost entirely on hearing specific complaints. The Shawcross

---

[5] *Royal Commission on the Press, 1947–1949 Report* (London. HMSO, 1949), 165.

Commission concluded that the Council should be given a limited time to improve itself; if it failed to improve, legislation and compulsory regulation should follow.

It was against this recent background that Lord Devlin became Press Council chairman in 1964. The first chairman from outside the press industry, Devlin was a distinguished judge; he was still relatively youthful and energetic. His intellectual ability, his modest personal style, and his diplomatic skills were widely admired. Devlin was also lucky in the time of his arrival. After a decade, the press now broadly welcomed the Press Council and its attempts to eliminate some indefensible forms of press behaviour. The Council accepted its first group of five lay members (in addition to the chairman). Crucially it had the active support of Cecil King and Lord Thomson, the two leading employers in the press industry. The 1964–9 period was one of relatively mild competition, which meant that good behaviour and profitability seemed to be compatible.

The Devlin Press Council made a number of 'Declarations of Principle'. One of these denounced 'cheque-book journalism' (September 1965) defined as paying 'for the discreditable memoirs of a notorious person'. Although Devlin preferred to stick to the Common Law tradition and not to have a basic code, a 500-page volume, *The Press Council*, was published in 1967.[6] The Devlin Press Council had the support of both national and regional daily newspaper editors. But national newspaper editors were much less enthusiastic than their provincial brethren at the lay representation, which then constituted 20 per cent of Press Council membership.[7]

This surge of relative success in the Devlin years of 1964–9 was misleading, because the Press Council was still a fragile thing, very dependent upon press goodwill. Lord Devlin himself was well aware of this. He openly acknowledged that the active support of Cecil King (and the *Daily Mirror*, then circulation leader) was crucial. The Press Council was dependent on the press for its finances (which had expanded in the 1960s). It needed the active support of the editors especially of the popular papers. The Press Council was also—like everyone else—acutely dependent on the press for publicity (for publishing its adjudications). The key weak-

    [6] P. H. Phillip Levy, *The Press Council* (London: Macmillan, 1967).
    [7] Paul B. Snider, 'The British Press Council: A Study of its Role and Performance, 1953–1965', University of Iowa, Ph.D. dissertation, 1968, 194–5.

ness, however, was the overall goal and purpose of the Press Council. Lord Devlin, as chairman for five years, managed to project a public service image for the Press Council. But the real long-term purpose of the Press Council (as seen by the industry) was to act as a public buffer, protecting the press from formal legislation and allowing it to carry on in much the same old undisciplined way.

II

Towards the end of the 1980s the Press Council had largely exhausted its goodwill within the press and also amongst politicians. There was the increased competition of the mid-1980s, the Murdoch/News move to Wapping, and the arrival of macho management; probably all of these contributed to increased aggressiveness in newspaper reporting, fiercer competition generally, and more of the various abuses which the Press Council had long tried to eliminate. As disquiet was increasingly expressed by politicians in 1987–8, the main offenders were the same as they had always been. The Press Council chairman, Sir Zelman Cowen, in his preface to the annual report covering 1986, singled out the *Sun* for criticism.

The first Royal Commission's 1949 conception of a 'General Council of the Press' was that its activities would indeed be 'general' and varied. Although it continued to list a number of activities, the Press Council in fact adopted an extremely narrow focus. It proclaimed itself willing and eager to hear complaints from across the British population and to pursue complaints made by ordinary readers of the press; however, in practice the Press Council mainly adjudicated complaints from members of a few professionally articulate occupations. A large majority of adjudicated complaints involved an elevated level of organizations and articulate occupations—namely individual Members of Parliament and local councillors; ministers of religion, senior trade union officials; commercial companies; Chief Constables and other senior policemen; major charities, pressure groups, and voluntary organizations; and last, but not least, academics, teachers, and journalists. A large majority of adjudicated complaints came from people who were professionally articulate in that they were complaining as part of their work or their political and public life.

The complainant required significant forensic skills in order to assemble and document the case and to argue it against the shadowy criteria and uncodified rules of the Press Council. Even some successful complainants were embittered by the process and became more critical of the Press Council and its procedures than they were critical of the original press story.[8] A substantial number even of successful complainants stated that the procedures of the Press Council amounted to systematic and in-built bias in favour of the press defendant and against the complainant. Newspapers were allowed to demand a personal hearing and to bring along their high-priced specialist newspaper lawyers. Complainants could not bring a lawyer and had no right to a personal hearing. When a hearing did take place before the complaints committee, an adversarial approach was followed; the lone complainant was confronted by an experienced senior journalist and a senior lawyer. The procedure was slow, taking in some cases as much as a year from original story to final adjudication. The Press Council showed its draft adjudication to the relevant editor—supposedly in order to confirm factual details; in some cases this allowed the editor to exert informal pressure on the adjudication. The Press Council was always dependent on press goodwill in order to achieve widespread and reasonably prominent publication of the adjudications. There was no similar need to maintain the goodwill of a particular complainant.

In most of these ways, and for most ordinary citizens, a letter to the editor was probably a better, cheaper, quicker, and more effective way of seeking some redress. A key point is that British daily papers, if they do publish the letter, normally publish it within three days of receipt—thus providing the chance for a quick reply, which is what many complainants most want. A continuing dilemma for the Press Council was that it was a small organization (with a small staff and minuscule finance) which could in practice only handle a few hundred complaints and adjudicate on perhaps a hundred per year. In 1976 only 21 per cent of the total British population had both heard of the Press Council and knew what it did. The Press Council might have wanted more publicity, but this would have led to a complaints deluge which it was not staffed to handle. Even with one-fifth of the population being aware of it, the Press Council staff were over-stretched.

[8] Geoffrey Robertson, *People against the Press* (London: Quartet, 1983), 38–53.

One indication of the passivity of the Press Council was the remarkable energy and success of a single complainant in the 1980s; this was Bob Borzello—an American citizen who became the Press Council's most determined, most frequent, and most successful complainant. Bob Borzello instigated many complaints against irrelevant newspaper references to a person's ethnicity. He won a succession of adjudications on this issue, but there continued to be much newspaper backsliding into previous racist patterns. By 1990 a remarkably active and determined Bob Borzello, with the help of a remarkably passive and half-hearted Press Council, had largely eliminated irrelevant ethnic descriptions from the British press. But by 1990 the Press Council itself was on its deathbed. It was first abandoned and starved by the press and only then killed by the politicians.

The issue of compulsory press regulation versus voluntary self-regulation became part of Britain's national policy agenda from 1989 to the end of the royal *Annus Horribilis* of 1992. In early 1993, the government's chosen investigator—Sir David Calcutt—produced a report, *Review of Press Self-Regulation*, which called for a compulsory system of press controls operated by an official Press Tribunal. Nearly all the national newspapers denounced Calcutt's conclusion. The *Sun*'s news coverage, for example, was headlined:

CHEAT'S CHARTER: Rich and famous will hide behind Press gag.

Faced with this burst of semi-automatic gunfire from almost the entire press, the Major government quickly announced that it rejected the bulk of the proposals; and later the government withdrew still further. Compulsory regulation was again repulsed; meanwhile self-regulation was confirmed.

This 1989–93 saga began with two Private Members' bills. John Browne, a Conservative MP, introduced a Privacy Bill under which disclosure of private information would have become a statutory civil offence. A Labour MP, Tony Worthington, introduced a Right of Reply Bill which would have required the correction of inaccuracies automatically to be carried by the offending publication with the same prominence. Both Bills failed. But the government was impressed by the strength of anti-newspaper feeling amongst both Labour and Conservative MPs. A junior Minister (Timothy Renton) warned that the press was on 'probation'. In July 1989 the Home Secretary (Douglas Hurd) appointed Sir

David Calcutt to report on privacy and the press. While waiting for this report, the national newspaper editors held a series of meetings resulting in two moves, both intended to pre-empt Calcutt. First, the national editors agreed a brief Code of Practice, largely based on previous Press Council adjudications. Secondly, the editors decided that a system of in-house ombudsmen should be adopted; by spring 1990 nearly all the national editors had appointed ombudsmen to consider readers' complaints.

David Calcutt and his committee were not impressed by these two moves. Most committee members apparently wanted to go for a policy of statutory controls. However, two journalist members of the committee—Sheila Black and Simon Jenkins, persuaded the committee to give the press 'one last chance'. If the former system of self-regulation was not radically and quickly improved, statutory regulation should be introduced:

Should the press fail to set up and support the Press Complaints Commission, or should it at any time become clear that the reformed non-statutory mechanism is failing to perform adequately, this should be replaced by a statutory tribunal with statutory powers and implementing a statutory code of practice.[9]

The committee denounced the Press Council as inadequate. A new more effective body was needed which must be (unlike the Press Council) 'authoritative, independent and impartial'.

Calcutt's June advice to kill off the Press Council was quickly accepted; the newspapers had only tolerated the Press Council as a fairly benign body which quietened criticism and avoided significant change. Within six months of the Calcutt Report, the Press Council was dead. It had indeed been starved of funds by the press industry which financed and created it. Other previous trends continued through the terminal year of 1990. The number of complaints was still increasing. In the Press Council's last year 42 complaints were upheld against national newspapers; 13 of these 42 adjudications were against the *Sun*.

In January 1991 the successor body, the Press Complaints Commission, began work. There were several differences from the Press Council. The Press Complaints Commission was given more money; it focused almost entirely on quick responses to complaints; it was a much smaller and more streamlined body. The PCC also

---

[9] David Calcutt (chairman), *Report of the Committee on Privacy and Related Matters* (London: HMSO for Home Office, 1990).

had the active participation of several national editors, and it also operated the Code drawn up by the national editors. In returning to a press majority the PCC was reverting back to the position before 1980.

The similarities between the new Press Complaints Commission and the old Press Council greatly outweighed the differences. Both bodies were overtly deferential to Parliament, and the royal family; both bodies were extremely anxious to keep editors and press owners on board. Both bodies regarded the national tabloids as their main problem, but were anxious not to be seen as persecuting the tabloids or martyring their editors. The Press Complaints Commission—like the Press Council—had been set up following parliamentary criticism and a 'one last chance' offer by the government of the day. These bodies were neither independent nor 'captured' regulators; both were part of the press industry, financed, established, and tolerated by the press.

Nevertheless the new Press Complaints Commission had a busy existence during 1991—its first year of life. The PCC could and did claim that it was having a big impact; complaints were being handled much more quickly, and the press was behaving better. The PCC handled two high-profile cases in 1991. In May the PCC found that the *News of the World* had invaded the privacy of the Labour MP, Clare Short, and had also broken the accuracy clause in the Code;[10] Clare Short claimed that she had been targeted by the *News of the World* after attempting to outlaw the tabloid practice of publishing nude photographs. The PCC's other high-profile case of 1991 involved another Sunday tabloid. This time it was the *People*, which had published photographs of a naked baby Princess Eugenie, daughter of the Duke of York; the photographs of the small child in a high-walled garden had been taken 'surreptitiously'.[11]

However, this relatively serene first year of the PCC was followed by the turbulence of the *Annus Horribilis*. 1992 was a horrible year for several national politicians too, and also for the Press Complaints Commission, which was made to look ineffectual, if not somewhat ridiculous, as it failed to get a handle on a succession of sensational press stories; two political stories involved the private lives of the Liberal Democrat leader (Paddy Ashdown) and the

[10] Press Complaints Commission, *Report Number 1 January–June 1991*, 9–11.
[11] Press Complaints Commission, *Report Number 2 July–September 1991*, 18–19.

Chancellor of the Exchequer (Norman Lamont). The most bizarre political 'scandal' of 1992 concerned David Mellor, who at the time had very recently become the Cabinet Minister in charge of the new National Heritage Department, and thus responsible for national policy (if any) on the press. David Mellor had referred to his Arts and Media responsibilities as amounting to a 'Ministry of Fun'. He also described the newspapers as drinking in the 'Last Chance Saloon', and in July 1992 David Mellor asked Sir David Calcutt to conduct a second investigation, this time specifically into 'press self-regulation'. But also in July the *People* newspaper revealed that Mr Mellor was having an extra-marital affair with an actress, Antonia de Sancha. Through nine weeks of the news-thin summer silly season the Mellor–de Sancha affair received massive press publicity. It became clear that the couple's meeting-place had been bugged for sound. Fresh (PR enhanced) details emerged—for example of the (somewhat overweight) young Minister clad only in a Chelsea football shirt. After many protestations from Mr Mellor (and some from the Prime Minister) that there would be No Resignation, Mr Mellor did finally resign—partly because of another 'scandal' about his allegedly accepting a free foreign holiday from a Palestinian.

The Press Complaints Commission had almost nothing to say about these three political 'scandals' because it received no complaints from any of the politicians. This problem of lacking a complaint to adjudicate also affected the PCC's handling of Andrew Morton's book *Diana: Her True Story*, which the *Sunday Times* serialized in June 1992. According to its initial procedure, the PCC could only act on a complaint if it came from one of the people directly involved; but neither Diana nor Charles complained. The PCC did, however, receive many complaints from members of the public about the press coverage surrounding the *Diana* book. This quickly led to a public statement from the PCC about the royal press coverage in general. The words from Lord McGregor's statement which were quoted and requoted were his description of the press coverage as 'an odious exhibition of journalists dabbling their fingers in the stuff of other people's souls'. McGregor and the PCC were in a difficult position. They could hardly denounce the *Sunday Times* for publishing extracts from a book. But nor could they remain silent at the frenzied press coverage, during a period when both the press and the PCC were trying to impress the government with the virtues of 'self-regulation'.

It was the Diana–Charles sensations of June 1992 which triggered David Mellor's setting up of the second Calcutt inquiry. It was also the press sensations and 'scandals' of 1992 upon which David Calcutt focused in his second report, published in January 1993. Calcutt's analysis of the Press Complaints Commission was sweeping and devastating: 'As constituted, it is, in essence, a body set up by the industry, financed by the industry, dominated by the industry, and operating a code of practice devised by the industry and which is over-favourable to the industry.'[12] Calcutt's basic analysis of the PCC as a press industry body was valid. But his collection of evidence had been rather superficial and his blunt recommendations were politically naïve. The second Calcutt Report called for legislation to set up a powerful statutory Press Tribunal; these proposals were certain to worry senior politicians and to unite the press in condemnation along such lines as state control, political muzzle on the press, and Fascism.

Central to Calcutt's proposals was his Press Complaints Tribunal, which would have extensive powers to compel publications to print apologies and corrections. The Tribunal would also have the power to award legal costs and to impose large fines. Further measures would clamp down on physical intrusion, the bugging of phone calls, and so on. Within a few confused days in January 1993 Calcutt's proposals were published, savagely denounced by the press, and quickly rejected by the Major government. The entire episode was another illustration of an old rule of politics: no government wants to fight against a united press.

With the sympathy and support of nearly all newspapers and their editors, the PCC and its chairman, Lord McGregor, were able to upstage the publication of the Calcutt Report with an adroit leaking operation. When the publication of the Calcutt Report was imminent, a leaked McGregor letter appeared in the *Guardian* on Tuesday 12 January 1993. This letter made it clear that back in June 1992 Lord McGregor had unwisely believed a Buckingham Palace assertion that Princess Diana had not co-operated with the Andrew Morton book. After his 'dabbling their fingers in the stuff

---

[12] Sir David Calcutt, QC, *Review of Press Self-Regulation* (London: HMSO for Department of National Heritage, 1993), p. xi.

of other people's souls' outburst, Lord McGregor had been informed by several editors and senior press persons that the Palace assurances were untrue. Diana had indeed co-operated with Andrew Morton—and other journalists—in spreading her 'true story' of the royal marital conflict. The leaked letter made Lord McGregor look somewhat naïve. Many or most leaks always have come from the horse's mouth; leaks from the Palace (and the PCC) were probably no exception.

The Calcutt Report made David Calcutt appear to be wilfully ignoring the obvious plain truth. The second Calcutt Report revolved around the assumption that invasion of privacy was the most urgent press problem. David Calcutt was aware of the argument that Princess Diana had in practice been invading her own privacy, but he still believed that privacy was the problem.[13] He did not seem to recognize that press, politicians, and public might not agree.

III

The *Sun* is widely believed to be the single newspaper which has most damaged the reputation of national newspapers with the British public and politicians alike. Certainly it was the Press Council's most difficult single customer in the 1970s and 1980s. But the Council also found the *Daily Mail* to be another loose cannon. For example, of 55 Press Council adjudications against national dailies in 1987 and 1988 the *Sun* accounted for 21, but the *Daily Mail* was the second most frequent transgressor with 13 complaints upheld. Thus two dailies, out of eleven, accounted for 62 per cent of transgressions.

The 1977 Royal Commission on the Press directed exceptionally severe criticism at the *Daily Mail* for its coverage of two stories. One was the British Leyland 'Slush Fund' story, a corruption exposé which was based on fabricated evidence. The second case concerned a *Daily Mail* story about the Labour MP Maureen Colquhoun, which she had referred to the Press Council. The Royal Commission criticized the *Daily Mail* 'which had been censured in an adjudication, trying to turn that adjudication to its own

---

[13] '8.7 My recommendations . . . are designed principally to ensure that privacy, which all agree should be respected, is protected from unjustifiable intrusion . . .' Sir David Calcutt, *Review of Press Self-Regulation*, 63.

advantage'. The Commission also criticized the Press Council for responding to *Daily Mail* pressure to rewrite the relevant press release in such a way as to soften its criticism.[14]

A somewhat similar response by the *Daily Mail* in 1980 to censure by the Press Council played a key role in the decline and fall of the Council. The case concerned a Mac cartoon published in the *Daily Mail*. This case led to a polarization between the right-wing views of the *Daily Mail* and the left-wing views of the National Union of Journalists' members of the Press Council; following this case the NUJ withdrew from the Press Council, leaving it adrift in the heightened partisanship of the 1980s.

The Mac cartoon was published in the *Daily Mail* during the 1979 General Election campaign and the day after a confrontation in London between National Front members and an Anti-Nazi League counter-demonstration. This was the event in which an ANL demonstrator, Blair Peach, was killed and a sizeable number of police injured. The Press Council adjudication

upheld a complaint by the National Union of Teachers' branch at Beaufroy School, Lollard Street, London SE11 that the *Daily Mail* published a tasteless and offensive cartoon which was a gross distortion of the Southall demonstration in that it suggested Anti-Nazi League demonstrators were killers of policemen . . .

On the day it gave eye-witness accounts of the demonstration at Southall in which teacher Blair Peach died, the *Daily Mail* carried a Mac cartoon on its diary page showing Anti-Nazi League members in a car decorated along its side with eight silhouette heads of helmeted policemen. There was no caption. . . . The cartoon grossly misrepresented the truth of the Southall demonstration.

The *Daily Mail* next day attacked the adjudication and reprinted the offending Mac cartoon alongside some controversial cartoon classics of the past including a 1791 cartoon by Gillray.

There were several additional aftershocks. The Press Council Director, Ken Morgan, claimed that David English and the *Daily Mail* did not know the difference between 'censure' and 'censor'.[15] The schoolteacher who had initiated the successful complaint was editorially attacked by the *Daily Mail*, which subsequently refused to publish his letter to the editor. The *Daily Mail* was thus again

---

[14] O. R. McGregor (chairman), *Royal Commission on the Press: Final Report* (London: HMSO, 1977), 105–8, 211–12.
[15] *UK Press Gazette*, 25 Feb. 1980.

snubbing the Press Council, which had long asked newspapers to publish a letter in such circumstances. The *Mail* was also severely censured for breaking the 'cheque-book journalism' rules of the Press Council during the Sutcliffe 'Yorkshire Ripper' multiple murder trial of 1981: 'In the Press Council's view the explanation offered by the newspaper amounts to a confession that the *Daily Mail* was guilty of gross misconduct'.[16]

Yet another example of *Daily Mail* attitudes towards Press Council decisions was provided by Robert Borzello. After a Borzello complaint against the *Daily Mail* was upheld by the Press Council, the *Daily Mail* attacked Borzello by name and printed his address. Borzello, who told a Commons Committee that he already received hate mail and death threats ('race obviously excites some people') described this as 'invasion of privacy by vindictiveness'.[17]

The *Daily Mail*, like the *Sun*, has a reputation for treating its enemies severely. In the 1980s one of its enemies seemed to be the Press Council. With a supposedly respectable middle-class newspaper behaving in this manner, it is not difficult to see that in the 1980s newspaper self-regulation had severe limitations.

IV

Since it was first suggested by the PEP Report in 1938, British press self-regulation has frequently faced the 'last chance', the new broom chairman, and the reshuffling of self-regulatory personnel. This happened once more in January 1995 when the senior Conservative politician, and former Chief Whip, Lord Wakeham took office as the new chairman of the Press Complaints Committee.

But it was very much business as usual. The 'Code of Practice' continued to be a two-page marvel of concision and ambiguity. The Press Complaints Commission still seemed to be one group of rather upscale people handling complaints from some other rather upscale people. All but one of the fourteen Commission members in 1995 was a Lord, a Lady, a Sir, a Professor, or an Editor.

[16] The Press Council, *Press Conduct in the Sutcliffe Case* (London: Press Council, 1983), 138–54.

[17] House of Commons, National Heritage Committee, Fourth Report, *Privacy and Media Intrusion*, ii: *Evidence* (London: HMSO, 1993), 191.

The PCC Report for March–April 1995 details the thirteen complaints which were adjudicated during that time (346 complaints were rejected as 'Outside Remit' or 'No Case Under Code'). Of the thirteen cases considered, four were from the Earl Spencer and three were on behalf of a nephew of Peter Lilley; both groups of cases concerned very serious issues of invasion of privacy—one involving bulimia and one involving Aids. Nevertheless seven out of thirteen cases adjudicated concerned either the brother of the Princess of Wales or the nephew of a Cabinet Minister. Of the remaining six cases, four complaints came from sizeable commercial companies and their senior executives; one complainant had successfully sued the *Daily Express* for defamation; the final complaint was from a man in prison as the result of a major fraud case. All thirteen adjudicated complaints seemed to come from people at the extreme top end of society.

One could argue that the Press Complaints Commission now faces a much more aggressive and competitive press. Consequently the PCC should perhaps be congratulated if it is still trying to do much the same as the Press Council was trying to do (with a bit more success) in the 1960s. When Lord Wakeham had been chairman of the PCC for a few months he made some speeches which contained this repeated sentence: 'The PCC will not survive if it ever becomes common currency among public and politicians alike that it is merely a public relations exercise by the press to stave off statutory regulation.' But a slightly different—and appropriately more cynical—view was expressed by the journalism trade paper: 'Wakeham's presence at the PCC will subdue the wilder forces of reaction on the Conservative backbenches while his belief in self-regulation will pacify anxious editors and journalists.'[18]

After six months of Lord Wakeham's chairmanship of the PCC, the Major government at last published its proposals for press regulation; there would be no new press law. Once more a government put its faith in self-regulation, with some suggestions for minor improvements. Once more the press rejected the minor improvements, but welcomed the continuation of self-regulation. Once more the press had won.[19]

---

[18] 'Our best chance to fight for self-regulation'. *UK Press Gazette*, 28 November 1994.
[19] *Privacy and Media Intrusion: The Government's Response* (London: HMSO, 1995).

24 Prime Minister, Press, and Broadcasting Policy

THE leading few newspaper ownerships have shared with the Prime Minister (and the government) of the day the main direction of British broadcasting policy. This was true of the birth of the BBC in the 1920s. It was still so in the 1980s and 1990s, as the newspapers had an active say in the transformation towards a more market-driven, and multi-channel, system. Had he not first controlled newspapers, Rupert Murdoch would not have been allowed by Mrs Thatcher to dominate BSkyB's provision of new satellite and cable channels. In 1995 a newspaper lobbying group (British Media Industry Group) were able to persuade the Major government to allow radically bigger newspaper participation across the range of audio-visual media.

Britain adopted a system of independent regulators—initially BBC Governors, then in 1954 the Independent Television Authority. These regulators made important decisions and were interposed between government and television editorial decisions. But these regulators carried out broad policies laid down by government. Under British conditions broadcasting policy follows a well-worn sequence of Broadcasting Committees, White Papers, Bills debated in Parliament, and Broadcasting Acts which decide strategic questions such as the creation of new channels.

During this policy process the government of the day typically negotiates with the press on an agreed and acceptable solution. In some cases the press is divided, and in other cases the newspaper executives have not been adequately aware of the technical issues; they have always been (and still are) weakly informed on satellite and cable. But more often the press has been well aware of its commercial interests; and, especially when the newspapers have been united, the government has been unwilling to confront them. Typically, then, the government seeks to divide and rule, or to reach at least tacit agreement with some of the leading press ownerships.

Since the appearance of advertising-funded television in the 1950s there have been at least five distinct ways in which senior newspaper people have influenced broadcasting policy and decisions. First, newspaper owners and editors have always had direct access to the Prime Minister and other senior Ministers; and they have used this access to influence TV and radio policy. Secondly, it is in the newspapers that long-drawn-out broadcast policy debates take place. Thirdly, the commercial interests of the press—especially in relation to both TV and radio advertising—have always had salience. Fourthly, newspapers have been able to define broadcasting 'crises' and, on occasion, to mount attacks on prominent individuals, such as the current BBC Director-General.

Fifthly, Prime Ministers tend to promote suitably friendly people from the newspaper world into the House of Lords and/or onto the various Committees, Commissions, and regulatory bodies which operate in the media policy world in general and within broadcasting policy in particular. These Great and Good newspaper persons play a leading—or even dominating—part in broadcast policy debates via their location on the relevant committees and bodies, from their public platform in the House of Lords, and in some cases via their newspaper columns. The House of Lords connection in particular has become even more important than in the past; as newspapers became ever more interested in audio-visual diversification, Press Lords such as Blakenham (Pearson), Rothermere (Mail) and Stevens (Express) had an ideal platform from which both to observe and to influence broadcasting policy.

The broadcast policy connection has been especially noticeable in the case of *The Times*. Lord William Rees-Mogg, a former *Times* editor, was deputy chairman of the BBC Governors (and subsequently chairman of the Broadcasting Standards Council). Charles Douglas-Home as editor of *The Times* was responsible for what was seen in the BBC as an anti-BBC campaign, which eventually led to the sacking of Alasdair Milne as BBC Director-General. If two *Times* editors prepared the way, it was a former general manager of *The Times*, Marmaduke Hussey, who actually fired

Alasdair Milne; Hussey was chairman of the BBC Governors from 1986. Lord Woodrow Wyatt was a columnist on *The Times* and close to Mrs Thatcher on broadcasting policy issues. Another former journalist at *The Times*, Lord Chalfont (defence correspondent, 1961–4), was also close to Mrs Thatcher and he became chairman of the Radio Authority.

Such connections were not confined to *The Times*. Two of the key people on the Peacock Committee which set the agenda for late Thatcher broadcasting policy were Alastair Hetherington (former editor, *Guardian*) and Samuel Brittan (*Financial Times*). One final example is Jocelyn Stevens, a former general manager of Express newspapers who was deputy chairman at the IBA/ITC.

I

Mrs Thatcher adopted in broadcasting the twin-track approach which she also used in some other policy-making fields. She had a traditional set of policies and she also had a radical set of new media competitive policies.

The traditional policy strand emphasized a loosely defined (and redefined) public service broadcasting. This latter policy tradition since 1954–5 had incorporated, alongside the BBC, a carefully regulated ITV, funded by advertising. Part of this consensual policy approach was the inclusion of newspaper interests in the ownership of ITV companies. In 1954–5 the Independent Television Authority wanted both newspaper capital investment and newspaper editorial support. At the very beginning the Daily Mail group and the Kemsley group did invest in ITV and then withdrew. The Mirror group blew hot and cold but made a major (and highly profitable) investment in 1957.[1]

This liking of British TV regulators for newspaper investment played a key role in helping two other newspaper groups to international success—these were the Thomson and Murdoch companies. Roy Thomson, mainly on the basis of owning *The Scotsman* newspaper, was allowed to acquire 80 per cent of Scottish Television. The second tier of five ITV regional companies was about 50 per cent press owned in 1961, when the 'licence to print money' levels of profit were being earned. The official policy increasingly

---

[1] Bernard Sendall, *Independent Television in Britain*, i: *Origin and Foundation 1946–62* (London: Macmillan, 1982).

became to confine press owners to only minority slices of ITV companies and this policy prevented Rupert Murdoch from acquiring control of London Weekend Television in 1970–1. But from 1971 onwards the Murdoch investment in LWT was profitable and in 1977, for example, Murdoch's News International still held 39.75 per cent of the non-voting and 11.8 per cent of the LWT voting shares.[2] Thus Rupert Murdoch's expansion in the United States was partly financed by the entry into ITV which Murdoch had been allowed as the owner of the *Sun* and the *News of the World*.

Mrs Thatcher's broadcasting policy divides into four pieces— conventional and radical, as well as early and late. In the early Thatcher years the traditional public service broadcasting policy continued under the direction of Willy Whitelaw as Home Secretary; the main event here was the launch of Channel Four in 1982 as an advertising-financed version of BBC2. This traditional policy continued to take into account the wishes of the newspapers, because Channel Four was always planned to attract only a minority audience and therefore not to take much advertising away from newspapers.

There was a second track of early Thatcher policy and this was evidenced in enormous enthusiasm for 'direct broadcasting by satellite' and also cable television. Both were conceived of in high-technology, high-cost formats. Despite a series of ecstatic government documents about satellite and cable, the insistence on high technology was a mistake and in practice prevented any significant development of either.[3]

Mrs Thatcher encouraged plenty of creative tension between the Home Office (traditional public service broadcasting) and Trade and Industry (high-technology industrial policy). She herself only occasionally focused her attention on these issues. She knew precisely what she disliked (union feather-bedding and BBC arrogance); what she wanted—more competition, more market forces, more channels—was frustratingly difficult to achieve.

The Peacock Committee—initially aimed at punishing the BBC

[2] David Docherty, *Running the Show: 21 Years of London Weekend Television* (London: Boxtree, 1990), 69–75. *News International Limited, Annual Report and Accounts 1971*, 3. *The Press and the People: 24th Annual Report of The Press Council 1977*, 158.

[3] Michael Palmer and Jeremy Tunstall, *Liberating Communications: Policy-making in France and Britain* (Oxford: Blackwell, 1990), 282–300.

by making it carry advertising—was a turning-point[4] for both policy tracks. Down the conventional policy track the Peacock Committee led to a tougher regime for ITV and its trade unions. Four years after the 1986 publication of the Peacock Report, this policy phase was culminating in the parliamentary passage of a Broadcasting Act which required ITV franchises to be renewed on an auction (plus quality) basis.

The second policy track was also during 1990 moving towards a decisive outcome. At last, no less than nine years after the Home Office's first *Direct Broadcasting by Satellite* document, British households in 1990 were finally being offered—in addition to cable—two separate and competing satellite-to-home antenna services. One of these was British Satellite Broadcasting (BSB), the official, high-cost, high-technology, high-powered-satellite, British offering. However, Rupert Murdoch had in 1989 pre-empted BSB by launching on a Luxembourg-regulated (medium power) satellite a low-cost, low-technology service called Sky.

1990 quite accidentally happened to be a make-or-break year for a number of players in this British multi-channel game—for BSB, for Sky, for the Broadcasting Bill, for Rupert Murdoch himself, and for Margaret Thatcher herself. The Broadcasting Bill had just received the royal assent when BSB and Sky (both losing money at spectacular speed) announced a merger. Also in late 1990 Murdoch's News Corporation was near to collapse, under its massive load of bank debt. Also in late 1990 Mrs Thatcher was near her political end. She was forced to resign on 28 November 1990.

One month before this (29 October), Mrs Thatcher had been visited by Rupert Murdoch, who told her of the forthcoming merger of the two satellite services. This merger not only made a nonsense of the carefully considered Broadcasting Bill, but it did actually contravene the law. However, Mrs Thatcher agreed to what Rupert Murdoch told her; at least she apparently made no objection, and also did not hand on the information. The BSB/Sky merger was agreed on 2 November and announced on 3 November—six days after Mrs Thatcher was first informed.

Mrs Thatcher did not know that she had already entered her last month as Prime Minister. She did know in early November 1990

---

[4] Alan Peacock (Chairman), *Report of the Committee on Financing the BBC* (London: HMSO, 1986).

that another election must occur within eighteen months. Consequently when she again offered Rupert Murdoch a fresh variant of the Wave and Waive treatment, Mrs Thatcher was doubtless quite happy at the thought of upsetting the BBC and the rest of the established broadcasting world. But her main reflex was almost certainly the traditional reflex of a British Prime Minister in offering a favour to an important and friendly newspaper owner not long before an election.

II

The latest lunacy of the BBC has been a standard newspaper headline since the 1920s. A stream of such stories can be experienced by an individual broadcast executive as a personal vendetta and a warning against further transgressions. Jeremy Isaacs has recorded how in its early days Channel Four was repeatedly attacked by the *Daily Mail*—'Storm over TV Language', 'Storm over IRA Film', and 'Storm over Gay Film'. Isaacs points out that the 'Storm' is generated by the reporter asking a Mr Rentaquote politician to condemn whatever it is that the reporter happens to be cooking up a storm about. Typically the politician has not seen the programme in question: 'A stormover is a conversation between a journalist and a Member of Parliament in which the journalist tells the MP something he does not know, and the MP calls for the banning of something he has not seen.'[5] This journalist–politician combination can on occasions escalate into what is widely perceived as a full-blown 'crisis'—a broadcasting sub-species of the political crisis.

Alasdair Milne, as BBC Director-General, experienced several such crises. The first was at the height of the Falklands War in April and May 1982. Milne in his autobiography portrays the attack on the BBC as coming from a loose alliance of Conservative MPs and Conservative newspapers. The BBC was accused of being at best inappropriately even-handed between the British and the Argentine military; at worst they were engaged in treason.

During most of 1984 and 1985 the BBC was portrayed by the newspapers as being in a state of crisis. According to the newspaper criticism the BBC was too big, too bureaucratic, and too accident-

---

[5] Jeremy Isaacs, *Storm over 4* (London: Weidenfeld and Nicolson, 1989), 57–60.

prone; most painful of all for the BBC was the newspaper argument that the BBC's claim for a big licence fee increase was not justified. As seen by the BBC's Director-General, this anti-BBC campaign was led by *The Times*, the *Sun*, and the *Sunday Times*—all Murdoch-owned newspapers; but it was also supported by other Conservative-supporting dailies, especially the *Daily Mail*: 'January 1984 was the month the press began to turn on us, in a campaign sustained for eighteen months or more and, I believe, unprecedented in the history of the BBC.'[6]

As seen by the chief executive of the BBC, Alasdair Milne, this newspaper attack had three linked strands of motivation. First, there was a motive of political partisanship—resentment at the BBC's political independence during the early Thatcher years. Secondly, there was commercial rivalry; the Murdoch/News company was already involved in a satellite television channel called Sky (aimed at cable systems across Europe) and was resentful of the BBC's prominent place in the British government's plans, from 1981 onwards, for 'direct broadcasting by satellite'. Thirdly, Milne also detected resentment from the press in general and *The Times* in particular at the BBC's reputation for quality news coverage. Meanwhile, the newspapers repeatedly portrayed Alasdair Milne as remote, arrogant, abrasive, and incapable of controlling the BBC.

While 1984 had been a year of crisis for the BBC, 1985 was another crisis year. In January and February *The Times* devoted no less than five separate anonymous leading articles to denouncing the BBC. Next month—March 1985—the government announced the setting up of the Peacock Committee to report on the BBC's finances; there was a remarkably close fit between the government's approach and *The Times*'s five-barrelled denunciation. In view of its own transparent self-interest, *The Times*'s editorials were unusual in several ways. The tone was fierce and the proposals radical. The first editorial said that 'The BBC should not survive this Parliament at its present size, in its present form and with its present terms of reference intact'. *The Times* also argued that, despite rapid recent price inflation, there should be no licence fee increase, until a Committee had looked into the BBC's finances.

Sunday newspapers—hungry for exclusive stories—precipi

---

[6] Alasdair Milne, *DG: The Memoirs of a British Broadcaster* (London: Coronet, 1989), 160.

tated at least two other significant BBC 'crises'. One concerned a 1985 programme called *Real Lives*, which according to the current *Radio Times* would feature an interview with the IRA/Sinn Fein leader, Martin McGuinness. The *Sunday Times* precipitated this story by obtaining a quote from Mrs Thatcher who (in true Stormover style) knew nothing about the programme but condemned the notion of the BBC interviewing terrorists. This led to perhaps the biggest single public conflict between Mrs Thatcher and the BBC.

The *Independent on Sunday* initiated another press-driven BBC crisis in 1993. This focused on the current BBC Director-General, John Birt, and his mildly unusual salary and tax arrangements. Had this salary story concerned the chief executive of a large industrial company, it would have been of little interest. But some minor unorthodoxies in John Birt's conditions of employment were built up by the press into a major sensational story. John Birt certainly believed that he came near to having to resign; like Alasdair Milne, he was made to feel that whether or not he could continue in his job would be determined by what the newspapers chose to write about him.

Another press campaign probably played a part in the London ITV weekday company, Thames, losing its franchise in 1991. Thames's *Death on the Rock* was a 1988 programme about the killing in Gibraltar of three unarmed IRA members by British SAS personnel. The programme generated huge quantities of both praise and condemnation. Several newspapers engaged in an open campaign of vilification against Thames Television and the programme's executive producer, Roger Bolton.[7] The *Sunday Times* was perhaps the most belligerent participant in the newspaper campaign. In the new bidding process set up by the 1990 Broadcasting Act, Thames was outbid by Carlton. Thames could still have been awarded the franchise on exceptional quality grounds. But the newspaper campaign had somewhat tarnished Thames's image; had the Independent Television Commission chosen Thames over Carlton, the ITC itself might well have faced a renewed newspaper campaign. The ITC had recently been subjected to what was seen at a senior level as 'a campaign of deliberate newspaper vilification'. The ITC did not come to the rescue of Thames.

[7] Roger Bolton, *Death on the Rock* (London: W. H. Allen, 1990).

III

British national newspaper companies are used to having their advice on broadcasting policy taken seriously by Prime Ministers and governments. But most newspaper groups have been hesitant about accepting the investment opportunities available to them. Only three press companies made significant investments in satellite broadcasting—Pearson and Reed initially in BSB and Murdoch/News International in Sky. Nevertheless, after the merger, the new company BSkyB was about 70 per cent owned by companies with major press involvement.

The Broadcasting Act of 1990 continued the recent pattern by confining press interests to a maximum of 20 per cent of an ITV company; after the 1991 ITC decisions four additional press companies—the Guardian, Telegraph, and Mail groups, as well as EMAP—had small slices of ITV companies. This somewhat uneven level of participation still meant that both satellite and ITV systems were well protected from major press criticism. BSkyB had all the Murdoch papers plus the *Financial Times* on board; BSkyB plus ITV involved seven major press companies including the publishers of four of the five upmarket dailies.

In retrospect some of the newspaper groups recognized that they had allowed the Thatcher–Murdoch combination to pull an extraordinary *fait accompli* in the BSkyB merger at the end of 1990. Those British companies which wanted to risk their money had put it into the dubious enterprise of BSB. Others held back and relished the Fleet Street gains of 1986. There was after 1986 a considerable period during which several newspaper managements either felt gratitude towards Murdoch, or at least did not feel ready to campaign against him. BSB ran a modest anti-Murdoch media and lobbying campaign in early 1990, but it was well mannered and rather feeble.

After 1991 this mood changed. Four newspaper companies—Mail, Telegraph, Guardian, and Pearson—formed themselves into the British Media Industry Group. The word 'British' was significant and BMIG very deliberately did not include Murdoch and News International. The leader of BMIG was Sir David English of the Mail/Associated group. BMIG wanted the entire media industry—newspapers, magazines, TV, radio, cable, and satellite—to be seen as one. Newspaper groups should be allowed to become diversified media groups spread across several media. In May 1995 the

Major government accepted this general notion.[8] BMIG was pleased, and Rupert Murdoch was displeased. British broadcasting policy was again being radically reshaped to meet the requirements of a united group of newspaper companies.

[8] Department of National Heritage, *Media Ownership: The Government's Proposals* (London: HMSO, 1995).

Part VI
CONCLUSIONS

25 Powerful Newspapers

THE 200 senior journalists and newspaper executives interviewed for this book are the core of a newly potent élite within British national newspapers. The book has first looked at the top end of the internal hierarchy within newspapers; secondly, it has looked through the eyes of this journalism élite at the political world beyond. That still leaves the political side of the politics–press relationship; the book also says little directly about the even bigger topic of the societal side of the society–press relationship.

Although there are studies of the formal press relations structure within government, there has been little systematic study of the ways in which politicians, or civil servants, relate to and are affected by the press and the media. Certainly many politicians are reluctant to reveal much about their media-directed activities or publicly to acknowledge the importance of the press in building and in destroying their careers. Peter Riddell of *The Times* comments:

Margaret Thatcher received a more consistently favourable, and at times fanatically loyal, press than any recent Prime Minister, and certainly than her successor. Yet she almost entirely ignores these supporters in the 914 pages of her *Downing Street Years*. *The Sun* never rises on these pages, nor does the *Daily Telegraph*. Sir David English, Kelvin MacKenzie, Sir Nicholas Lloyd and even Rupert Murdoch might never have existed. That is curiously ungrateful given what they did to sustain her in power.[1]

One main explanation for such reticence lies in the previously quoted observation of the politician-journalist, Julian Critchley: 'Vanity . . . is the fuel of public life. . . . When praised we blush with a maiden's pleasure: when abused we first sulk then shout.'

[1] Peter Riddell, 'Not a word of thanks from Lady Thatcher', *British Journalism Review*, 5/1 (1994), 6–8.

Conclusions

The emotional impact of press criticism shocks the public person's ego into private anger and obscenity, while shocking the same person's public persona into tight-lipped silence.

This tight-lipped British silence is also required in order to match the secretive way in which the press–politics relationship is conducted. These relationships are not secret in any absolute sense but secretive in the whispered senses of 'off the record', 'use with discretion', 'attribute to "my friends"', 'cannot reveal my source'. Accompanying these phrases are the poker rituals of interviews and the subtle (unusually implicit, but unspoken) terms of trade involved in maintaining trust and relationships with key friends on the other side of the press–politics divide.

Artists, authors, actors—and many others through the alphabet—are also known calmly to accept press praise while bitterly resenting press criticism. Successful politicians receive massive amounts of coverage. The British national newspapers each year carry over 10,000 separate mentions of the current Prime Minister. It would be positively inhuman not to harbour some strong resentments about the sizeable fraction of these press references which are negative.

Most successful politicians were assisted in their rise by certain key friendly journalists and by steadily increasing waves of 'rising star' publicity. Although such a relationship could be noted by the truly zealous newspaper reader, neither journalist nor politician wants to draw attention to it. Eventually all political careers turn downwards and the career descent is typically accompanied by negative coverage. Many politicians who have suffered this experience seem to believe that they were politically assassinated by formerly friendly colleagues and formerly friendly journalists. This very public experience of political rejection and media assault may account for the bitterness with which many retired politicians seem to look back on their later careers.

Although senior journalists seem willing to talk at length about these matters, most (but not all) are reluctant to say much about their few key working relationships either with other journalists or with public figures. More specialist journalists are willing to specify details of competing working partnerships than are willing to reveal details of their own partnerships.

Political scientists belong to another occupational sub-species which seems oddly reluctant to pry into politics and the press. Colin Seymour-Ure is one honourable exception. Many political scientists may wish not to draw too much attention to their own dependence on the press; but surely there is no dishonour in being—like everyone else including politicians—dependent on the press for a broad range of political and governmental information? Whatever the reasons for this reluctance, the existing political science literature on the Prime Ministership is somewhat unreal or two dimensional, because it lacks the press and media dimension which is so central to the political rise, reign, and fall of Prime Ministers. In particular there is no study of the destabilizing impact of contemporary political reporting on the entire relationship between Parliament, the Prime Minister, and the Cabinet committee structure. With the present wolf-pack of political journalists stationed between the Westminster Electoral College and the Cabinet, is the doctrine of Cabinet Collective Responsibility still viable?

The media coverage of Britain's month-long General Election campaigns has been studied; in particular the national network television side of these campaigns make for a neat and economical research design. But most of the media impact on politics occurs during the other fifty months when there is no General Election. The British national newspapers provide a continuing drip-and-drizzle of words day-after-day. Each week the national newspaper industry sells about 100 million copies of a book-length product. Each year trillions of newspaper words drizzle down on the great British public; presumably at least a few billion of these words sink into the sub-soil of the public's collective consciousness.

Individual journalists also have an impact. A revealing study could be conducted on the relationship between David English, during two decades as *Daily Mail* editor, and the five Prime Ministers who spanned the same years. Much could be discovered about the modern Labour party by studying the relationship over nearly four decades between two editors of the *Guardian* (Alastair Hetherington and Peter Preston) and the seven men who led the Labour party during those decades.

Rivalry between government departments for funding and policy success spills over into the media and this could easily be studied. Ralph Negrine, for example, has shown how the Commons Select Committees constitute one useful research site for such studies; civil servants, politicians, and journalists can all be seen at play in a single playpen.

A freshly important élite has emerged at the top level of British

Conclusions

national newspapers. This élite of a few hundred senior journalists and newspaper executives as a group is many times larger than the handful of editors and a few others who constituted the journalism élite of the early twentieth century. This study has not systematically collected data on these people's educational qualifications. But a fair proportion of them certainly do have the kind of educational qualifications which earlier in the century might have led them to enter the Foreign Office or the Indian Civil Service. Paradoxically while journalism at large has a low reputation, the ideal career for many fresh university graduates is to be a national newspaper journalist or a BBC TV producer.

Well educated, well paid, and envied by their own children, these senior print journalists now constitute not merely an occupational élite within their own industry. They see themselves—and are increasingly widely seen by others—as a key occupational élite in the society at large. Few of these people want to become professional politicians. In contrast with the past, there now seem to be more politicians who want to become journalists than vice versa.

The British national newspapers have an especially turbulent relationship with certain aspects of national life. There is a distinct lack of fit between the royal reporting in the tabloid newspapers and the goals and statements of the British monarchy. There is a further lack of fit between the national press and the political parties. Not only does one party—the Conservatives—attract most of the love, and a good deal of the hate, of the national press; a paper like the *Sun* supports both Scottish Nationalism and English jingoism.

There is also a remarkable lack of fit between the way in which Europe (and the European Union) is portrayed in different sections of the same newspaper. In the financial pages the British economy is portrayed as being located in Europe. In the news pages, and in the editorials, Europe is portrayed as too boring to report, but also too threatening to trust. Meanwhile in the travel, leisure, food, and sports pages Europe appears warm, welcoming, photogenic, and even positively exciting.

The national newspapers seem to operate in neat parallel with some other large-scale features of the surrounding society. The meltdown of local government in England and Wales parallels the meltdown of local newspapers in these countries. The prominence of financial services in the British economy is paralleled by the

424

prominence of financial journalism in the newspapers. The upmarket, midmarket, and downmarket split-level character of the British press is paralleled by similar splits in the social class and educational systems. The *Sun* and the *Daily Mirror* throw light on and mirror Britain's schools.

The strength of national (as opposed to local) media has become self-perpetuating. The power of the press in relation to the entire media landscape seems likely to continue. Deregulation takes the audio-visual media away from consensus and into more political and more turbulent waters. The press uses its political strength both directly to enter the audio-visual fields and to have a big say over the public service areas. Whether the BBC survives depends heavily upon what the newspapers will say editorially and will do commercially over the next two decades. The BBC will have little say in the survival of the *Daily Mail*; but the *Daily Mail* will have a significant say in the survival of the BBC.

Continuing turbulence within the newspaper and broader media industries was ensured by a series of partly linked decisions in 1994–5. The Major government, having already allowed convergence to occur between cable and telephone services, acknowledged (in its 1995 *Media Ownership* document) the need for a converged policy to include all print as well as electronic mass media. Print media competition received a further twist from a combination of rising newsprint prices and Murdoch-led cuts in cover prices. Also in 1994–5 a number of large media companies decided to redefine their core activity, to focus on higher profit activities, and to sell off their 'lower margin' businesses. British press companies were thus tending to redefine themselves as either international, or national, or mainly regional press enterprises.

All of the companies focusing on *international* media were looking for market leadership in high profit markets. In 1994–5 Thomson, Reed-Elsevier, and Pearson were all losing interest in regional newspapers. All three were increasingly interested in what might be called international 'multi-window' publishing—selling information in linked formats, especially printed periodicals, electronic on-line services, and reference book formats. The Murdoch/News company had a different kind of international approach; its pursuit of UK dominance focused on market leadership in each level of the national newspaper business.

At the opposite end of the British newspaper industry, the regional press was being reshaped. In 1994 eleven companies controlled two-thirds of the sales of non-national newspapers in Britain. With the reduced interest of the international companies, the regional lead was increasingly being taken by 100 per cent regional companies such as Trinity (of Liverpool) and Midland Independent (of Birmingham). These companies are aiming at local versions of multi-window delivery. Such companies will stick to their chosen knitting by delivering to local households a range of newspaper products (daily and weekly, paid and free); also as many local electronic services (radio, cable, digital TV and data) as the law will allow; and in addition they will focus on databasing, smart cards, and the like, in order to tailor specialized offerings both for advertisers and for households.

Piggy-in-the-middle between these internationally and regionally focused companies, there will continue to exist some mainly *nationally* focused newspaper companies, such as the Mail/ Associated, Mirror, and Guardian groups. The dilemma for such national specialists will be the continuing severity of national competition and the relative scarcity of national newspaper advertising. One solution is likely to be the 'partial merger'. The simplest form of this—the shared printing plant—became common practice after 1986. A more advanced version—the merging of advertising, circulation, marketing, and all other services, as well as printing—was pioneered in Britain by the management integration of the Independent papers into the Mirror Group. The established consensual policy of newspaper preservation will tend to favour such 'partial mergers', which will in turn pose difficult questions about editorial independence and monopoly law.

British press policy developments will be strongly influenced by at least three different competition policy regimes; not only will the British and European monopoly and competition rules apply, but United States monopoly rules (especially on cable and telecommunications) will have an impact on British newspapers.

Media regulation will increasingly be contested and in such contests the political strength of newspapers will be in evidence. There are also likely to be more newspaper versus newspaper regulatory battles as different groups pursue their different strategies. Already during the early 1990s there was the emergence of significant opposition to Murdoch/News from some other newspaper groups. With the increased salience of digital technology and policy, we can anticipate a *de facto* alliance of British 'national' media (the BBC and ITV as well as some newspaper companies) in opposition to some of the 'international' media companies.

The leading newspapers in Britain (and probably in most comparable countries) will continue to be extremely powerful both within the media and across the broad range of public policy and public life. On some measures the newspapers will continue their industrial decline. But the newspapers are likely to remain the most politically interested, most policy focused, most partisan, and most potent of the mass media.

Bibliography

ALDRIDGE, MERYL, *Making Social Work News* (London: Routledge, 1994).

ANDREWS, LINTON, and TAYLOR, H. A., *Lords and Laborers of the Press* (Carbondale, Ill.: Southern Illinois University Press, 1970).

BAINBRIDGE, CYRIL, and STOCKDILL, ROY, *The News of the World Story* (London: Harper Collins, 1993).

BOLTON, ROGER, *Death on the Rock* (London: W. H. Allen, 1990).

BOWER, TOM, *Maxwell: The Outsider* (London: Mandarin, 1991).

BOYD-BARRETT, OLIVER, 'The Collection of Foreign News in the National Press', in Oliver Boyd-Barrett, Colin Seymour-Ure, and Jeremy Tunstall, *Studies on the Press* (London: HMSO for Royal Commission on the Press, 1977).

BUCKINGHAM, DAVID, *Public Secrets: EastEnders and its Audience* (London: British Film Institute, 1987).

BUTLER, DAVID, and KAVANAGH, DENNIS, *The British General Election of 1992* (London: Macmillan, 1992).

——ADONIS, ANDREW, and TRAVERS, TONY, *Failure in British Government* (Oxford: Oxford University Press, 1994).

——and BUTLER, GARETH, *British Political Facts 1900–1994* (London: Macmillan, 1994).

CALCUTT, DAVID (chairman), *Report of the Committee on Privacy and Related Matters* (London: HMSO for Home Office, 1990).

——*Review of Press Self-Regulation* (London: HMSO for Department of National Heritage, 1993).

CANNADINE, DAVID, 'The Context, Performance and Meaning of Ritual: The British Monarchy and the 'Invention of Tradition' c.1820–1977', in Eric Hobsbawm and Terence Ranger (eds.), *The Invention of Tradition* (Cambridge: Cambridge University Press, 1983).

CHESTER, LEWIS, and FENBY, JONATHAN, *The Fall of the House of Beaverbrook* (London: Andre Deutsch, 1979).

CHIPPINDALE, PETER, and HORRIE, CHRIS, *Stick it up your Punter! The Rise and Fall of the Sun* (London: William Heinemann, 1990).

CHISHOLM ANNE, and DAVIE, MICHAEL, *Beaverbrook: A Life* (London: Hutchinson, 1992).

CHRISTIANSEN, ARTHUR, *Headlines All my Life* (London: Heinemann, 1961).

CLARK, ALAN, *Diaries* (London: Weidenfeld and Nicolson, 1993).

CLEVERLEY, GRAHAM, *The Fleet Street Disaster: British National Newspapers as a Case Study in Mismanagement* (London: Constable, and Beverly Hills, Calif.: Sage, 1976).

COCKBURN, CYNTHIA, *Brothers* (London: Pluto, 1983).

COCKERELL, MICHAEL, HENNESSY, PETER, and WALKER, DAVID, *Sources Close to the Prime Minister* (London: Macmillan, 1984).

COCKETT, RICHARD, *Twilight of Truth: Chamberlain, Appeasement and the Manipulation of the Press* (London: Weidenfeld and Nicolson, 1989).

——*David Astor and the Observer* (London: Andre Deutsch, 1991).

COHEN, YOEL, *Media Diplomacy: The Foreign Office in the Mass Communications Age* (London: Frank Cass, 1986).

CONNOR, ROBERT, *Cassandra: Reflections in a Mirror* (London: Cassell, 1969).

CROSSMAN, RICHARD, *The Diaries of a Cabinet Minister*, ii (London: Hamish Hamilton and Jonathan Cape, 1976).

CURRAN, JAMES, and SEATON, JEAN, *Power without Responsibility* (London: Routledge, 1991).

DALYELL, TOM, *Dick Crossman: A Portrait* (London: Weidenfeld and Nicolson, 1989).

DEMPSTER, NIGEL, *Nigel Dempster's Address Book: The Social Gazetteer* (London: Pan, 1992).

DIMBLEBY, JONATHAN, *The Prince of Wales: A Biography* (London: Little, Brown, 1994).

DOIG, ALAN, *Westminster Babylon: Sex, Money and Scandal in British Politics* (London: Allison and Busby, 1990).

DOUGARY, GINNY, *The Executive Tart and Other Myths: Media Women Talk Back* (London: Virago, 1994).

Economist Intelligence Unit, *The National Newspaper Industry* (London: EIU, 1966).

EDELMAN, MAURICE, *The Mirror: A Political History* (London: Hamish Hamilton, 1966).

EDWARDS, ARTHUR, *I'll Tell The Jokes, Arthur* (London: Blake, 1993).

EDWARDS, ROBERT, *Goodbye, Fleet Street* (London: Coronet, 1989).

EVANS, HAROLD, *Good Times, Bad Times* (London: Coronet, 1984).

FERRIS, PAUL, *Sir Huge: The Life of Huw Wheldon* (London: Michael Joseph, 1990).

FREIBERG, J. W., *The French Press: Class, State and Ideology* (New York: Praeger, 1981).

GARLAND, NICHOLAS, *Not Many Dead* (London: Hutchinson, 1990).

GERALD, J. EDWARD, *The British Press under Government Economic Controls* (Minneapolis: University of Minnesota Press, 1956).

GILBERT, MARTIN, *Churchill: A Life* (London: Minerva, 1992).

Glasgow University Media Group, *Bad News* (London: Routledge, 1976).

GLOVER, STEPHEN, *Paper Dreams* (Harmondsworth: Penguin, 1994).

GOURLAY, LOGAN (ed.), *The Beaverbrook I Knew* (London: Quartet Books, 1984).

GRAY, TONY (ed.), *Fleet Street Remembered* (London: Heinemann, 1990).

GREENSLADE, ROY, *Maxwell's Fall* (London: Simon and Schuster, 1992).

Bibliography

HALL, PHILIP, *Royal Fortune: Tax, Money and the Monarchy* (London: Bloomsbury, 1992).

HAMILTON, DENIS, *Editor-in-chief* (London: Hamish Hamilton, 1989).

HAMMOND, ERIC, *Maverick* (London: Weidenfeld and Nicolson, 1992).

HARRIS, ROBERT, *Good and Faithful Servant* (London: Faber and Faber, 1990).

HART-DAVIS, DUFF, *The House the Berrys Built: Inside the Telegraph 1928–1986* (London: Coronet, 1991).

HARTWELL, LORD, *William Camrose: Giant of Fleet Street* (London: Weidenfeld and Nicolson, 1992).

HEALEY, DENIS, *The Time of My Life* (Harmondsworth: Penguin, 1990).

HENRY, HARRY, 'Thirty Three Years of Colour Supplements', *ADMAP* (Sept. 1994), 58–61.

HETHERINGTON, ALASTAIR, *Newspapers, News and TV* (London: Macmillan, 1985).

HILL, CHARLES, *Both Sides of the Hill* (London: Heinemann, 1964).

HOLDEN, ANTHONY, *Charles, Prince of Wales* (London: Weidenfeld and Nicolson, 1979).

——*Charles: A Biography* (London: Weidenfeld and Nicolson, 1988).

——*The Tarnished Crown* (London: Viking, 1993).

HOLLINGSWORTH, MARK, *The Press and Radical Dissent* (London: Pluto, 1986).

HOWARD, ANTHONY, *Crossman: The Pursuit of Power* (London: Jonathan Cape, 1990).

ILLSLEY, PAULINE, *The Drama of Cleveland* (London: Campaign for Press and Broadcasting Freedom, 1989).

INGHAM, BERNARD, *Kill the Messenger* (London: Harper Collins, 1991).

ISAACS, JEREMY, *Storm over 4* (London: Weidenfeld and Nicolson, 1989).

JACOBS, ERIC, *Stop Press: The Inside Story of The Times Dispute* (London: Andre Deutsch, 1980).

JAMES, ROBERT RHODES, *Bob Boothby: A Portrait* (London: Hodder and Stoughton, 1991).

JENKINS, SIMON, *Newspapers: The Power and the Money* (London: Faber and Faber, 1979).

JUNOR, JOHN, *Memoirs: Listening for a Midnight Tram* (London: Chapmans, 1990).

KAVANAGH, DENNIS, *Thatcherism and British Politics* (Oxford: Oxford University Press, 1990).

——and SELDON, ANTHONY (eds.), *The Thatcher Effect* (Oxford: Oxford University Press, 1989).

The Kemsley Manual of Journalism (London: Cassell, 1950).

KING, ANTHONY (ed.), *The British Prime Minister* (London: Macmillan, 1985).

KING, CECIL, *The Cecil King Diary: 1965–1970* (London: Jonathan Cape, 1972).

KURTZ, HOWARD, *Media Circus: The Trouble with America's Newspapers* (New York: Times Books, 1993).

KYNASTON, DAVID, *The Financial Times: A Centenary History* (London: Viking, 1988).

LACEY, ROBERT, *Majesty: Elizabeth II and the House of Windsor* (London: Hutchinson, 1977).

LAMB, LARRY, *Sunrise* (London: Macmillan, 1989).

LAWSON, NIGEL, *The View from No. 11* (London: Corgi, 1993).

LEVY, P. H. PHILLIP, *The Press Council* (London: Macmillan, 1967).

LINKLATER, MAGNUS, and LEIGH, DAVID, *Not with Honour: The Inside Story of the Westland Scandal* (London: Sphere, 1986).

LINTON, MARTIN, *Money and Votes* (London: Institute for Public Policy Research, 1994).

LITTLETON, SUELLEN, *The Wapping Dispute* (Aldershot: Avebury, 1992).

MACARTHUR, BRIAN, *Deadline Sunday: A Life in the Week of the Sunday Times* (London: Hodder and Stoughton, 1991).

MCDONALD, IVERACH, *The History of The Times,* v: *Struggles in War and Peace 1939–1966* (London: Times Books, 1984).

MACMILLAN, HAROLD, *At the End of the Day* (London: Macmillan, 1973).

MCQUAIL, DENIS, *Analysis of Newspaper Content* (London: HMSO for Royal Commission on the Press, 1977).

MELVERN, LINDA, *The End of the Street* (London: Methuen, 1986).

MILNE, ALASDAIR, *DG: The Memoirs of a British Broadcaster* (London: Coronet, 1989).

Monopolies Commission, *The Times Newspaper and the Sunday Times Newspaper* (London: HMSO, 1966).

Monopolies and Mergers Commission, *EMAP PLC, Reed International PLC and Trinity International Holdings PLC* (London: HMSO, 1991).

——*The Supply of National Newspapers* (London: HMSO, 1993).

——*Daily Mail and General Trust plc and T. Bailey Forman Limited* (London: HMSO, 1994).

MORTON, ANDREW, *Diana: Her True Story* (London: Michael O'Hara, 1993).

MURPHY, DAVID, *The Silent Watchdog* (London: Constable, 1976).

——*The Stalker Affair and the Press* (London: Unwin Hyman, 1991).

National Board for Prices and Incomes, *Costs and Revenues of National Newspapers* (London: HMSO, 1967).

——*Journalists' Pay* (London: HMSO, 1969).

National Heritage Committee, House of Commons, Session 1992–3, *Privacy and Media Intrusion*, 2 vols. (London: HMSO, 1993).

NEGRINE, RALPH, 'The Organisation of British Journalism and Specialist Correspondents', University of Leicester, discussion paper, 1993.

PALMER, MICHAEL, and TUNSTALL, JEREMY, *Liberating Communications: Policy-Making in France and Britain* (Oxford: Blackwell, 1990).

Bibliography

PARSONS, WAYNE, *The Power of Financial Journalism* (London: Edward Elgar, 1989).

PATMORE, ANGELA, *Marje: The Guilt and the Gingerbread* (London: Little, Brown, 1993).

Political and Economic Planning, *The British Press* (London: PEP, 1938).

PRESS COUNCIL, *Press Conduct in the Sutcliffe Case* (London: Press Council, 1983).

REES-MOGG, WILLIAM, *Picnics on Vesuvius: Steps towards the Millennium* (London: Sidgwick and Jackson, 1992).

Report of the Committee of Privy Counsellors Appointed to Inquire into 'D' Notice Matters (London: HMSO, 1967).

Report of the Tribunal Appointed to Inquire into the Vassall Case and Related Matters (London: HMSO, 1963).

RIDDELL, PETER, *Honest Opportunism: The Rise of the Professional Politician* (London: Hamish Hamilton, 1993).

RITCHIE, HARVEY, *Success Stories: Literature and the Media in England, 1950–1959* (London: Faber and Faber, 1988).

ROBERTSON, GEOFFREY, *People against the Press* (London: Quartet, 1983).

Royal Commission on the Press, 1947–1949 Report (Chairman: Sir William Ross) (London: HMSO, 1949).

Royal Commission on the Press, 1961–1962 Report (Chairman: Lord Shawcross) (London: HMSO, 1962).

Royal Commission on the Press: Interim Report: The National Newspaper Industry (London: HMSO, 1976).

Royal Commission on the Press: Final Report (Chairman: O. R. McGregor) (London: HMSO, 1977).

SCHLESINGER, PHILIP, and TUMBER, HOWARD, *Reporting Crime* (Oxford: Clarendon Press, 1994).

SEYMOUR-URE, COLIN, *The Press, Politics and the Public* (London: Methuen, 1968).

—— *The Political Impact of Mass Media* (London: Constable, and Beverly Hills, Calif.: Sage, 1974).

—— *The British Press and Broadcasting since 1945* (Oxford: Blackwell, 1991).

SHAWCROSS, WILLIAM, *Rupert Murdoch* (London: Chatto and Windus, 1992).

SMITH, A. C. H., *Paper Voices* (London: Chatto and Windus, 1975).

SNIDER, PAUL B., 'The British Press Council: A Study of its Role and Performance 1953–1965', University of Iowa Ph.D. dissertation, 1968.

SNODDY, RAYMOND, *The Good, the Bad and the Unacceptable* (London: Faber and Faber, 1992).

SOMERFIELD, STAFFORD, *Banner Headlines* (London: Scan Books, 1979).

TAYLOR, S. J., *Shock! Horror! The Tabloids in Action* (London: Bantam Press, 1991).

THOMAS, HARFORD, *Newspaper Crisis: A Study of Developments in the National Press in Britain, 1966–67* (Zurich: International Press Institute, 1967).

TUNSTALL, JEREMY, *The Westminster Lobby Correspondents* (London: Routledge, 1970).

—— *Journalists at Work* (London: Constable, and Beverly Hills, Calif.: Sage, 1971).

—— *The Media Are American* (London: Constable, and New York: Columbia University Press, 1977).

—— 'Letters to the Editor', 'Editorial Sovereignty in the British Press', 'The Problem of Industrial Relations News in the Press', in Oliver Boyd-Barrett, Colin Seymour-Ure, and Jeremy Tunstall, *Studies on the Press* (London: HMSO for Royal Commission on the Press, 1977), 203–397.

—— 'Will Fleet Street Survive until 1984?' Evidence to the Royal Commission on the Press, 1977.

—— *The Media in Britain* (London: Constable; and New York: Columbia University Press, 1983).

—— *Television Producers* (London: Routledge, 1993).

—— and PALMER, MICHAEL, *Media Moguls* (London: Routledge, 1991).

WATERHOUSE, KEITH, *Waterhouse: On Newspaper Style* (London: Penguin, 1993).

WATKINS, ALAN, *A Conservative Coup: The Fall of Margaret Thatcher* (London: Duckworth, 1991).

WAUGH, AUBERON, *Will This Do?* (London: Century, 1991).

WILLIAMS, FRANCIS, *Nothing So Strange* (London: Cassell, 1970).

WINSBURY, REX, *New Technology and the Press: A Study of Experience in the United States* (London: HMSO for Royal Commission on the Press, 1975).

WINTOUR, CHARLES, *Pressures on the Press* (London: Andre Deutsch, 1972).

WORSTHORNE, PEREGRINE, *Peregrinations* (London: Weidenfeld and Nicolson, 1980).

WYATT, WOODROW, *The Confessions of an Optimist* (London: Collins, 1985).

YOUNG, HUGO, *One of Us: A Biography of Margaret Thatcher* (London: Pan, 1993).

ZIEGLER, PHILIP, *King Edward VIII* (London: Fontana, 1990).

—— *Wilson* (London: Weidenfeld and Nicolson, 1993).

Index

Index

Index

Index

rape news 209–10
readership 213, 215–25
    reader telephone votes 222–3
    readers, heavy to nil 223
    readership research 215–16
Rees-Mogg, Lord W. 100–3, 173, 180,
        244, 282–3, 292–5, 362–3, 393, 409
Referendum on EC (1975) 344–5
regulation of the press, self-
        regulation 391–407
    statutory regulation 393
Renton, T. 399
Repetitive Strain Injury (RSI) 137
retailers 219–20
Reuters 19, 20, 22, 340, 364
reviewers 170
Riddell, P. 283–5, 421
Robertson, F. 342
Robertson, G. 398
Rothermere, Lord 83, 114, 409
Rothwell, B. 116
Royal Commissions on the Press 379–80
    Ross (1947–9) 394–5, 397
    Shawcross (1961–2) 380–1, 395–6
    McGregor (1964–7) 385
royal family:
    Anne, Princess Royal 318, 323–4
    charities 319–20
    Duke and Duchess of York 314–15,
        326–8
    Prince of Wales problem 316–17
    as soap opera 336–8
    television 320–2, 324, 335–8
royal journalism 313–38
    gossip origins 330–1
    journalists 315, 330–4
    royal PR 327, 333–5
Rumbold, J. 327
Rusbridger, A. 132–3
Ryder, R. 277

'sale or return' 219–20
satellite broadcasting 416
Saturday sales 164–5
Scotland 62–4, 424
Scott, L. 111
Scott, R. 111
Scottish TV 410
secrecy 236–7
sectionalization 119, 155–6, 163–7, 167–71
'self-regulation' 391–407
Sendall, W. 267
Sergeant, P. 358–9
sex as news 193–4, 210, 213
Seymour-Ure, C. 100, 101 n., 114 n., 422

Shah, E. 20, 24, 26
Shields, M. 83
Short, C. 401
Snowdon, Lord 334
Soames, N. 337
'sound bites' 236
Spectator 150–1
sports columnists 172, 211 n.
    sports editor 162, 211–12
    sports news 194, 211–14
stars:
    film and TV 188–9, 195–6
    royal 322
Steven, S. 15, 122
Stevens, J. 410
Stevens, Lord 90, 409
Stothard, P. 133–5
Stott, R. 122–4, 129–30
sub-editing 161–3
Summerscales, R. 265
Sun 13–14, 41, 43, 45–6, 124–7, 159–60,
        207, 329–30
    news values 201–3
    politics 240–1, 251–3, 290
    in Scotland 64
Sunday Citizen 39
Sunday Express 57, 99, 175
Sunday Mirror 100
Sunday Telegraph 49–51, 160
    politics 288
Sunday Times 16, 47–51, 82, 103–4,
        109–10, 124–7, 164, 179–80, 359–60,
        368–9
    politics 244–5, 253, 265, 300
    versus BBC 414–15
*Sunday Times/Sun/*BSkyB joint news
        activities 185, 204
Sutcliffe, P. 210

tabloids 59
    and news agenda 200
    partisanship 246–8
television and newspapers 184–98,
        213–14, 218–25
    reviews and reviewers 187–8
    TV listings 188
    TV news 151, 191–2
    TV soaps 185, 188, 201
Telegraph newspapers 21, 37, 86, 106–9,
        341–2
Thames TV 415
Thatcher, M. 22, 29, 109, 272–6, 286,
        364, 408–10, 421
    broadcasting policy 410–15
    press adulation of 247–50, 252, 421

440